Good Governance and Development

Also by B. C. Smith

Field Administration: An Aspect of Decentralization

Advising Ministers

Administering Britain
  (with J. Stanyer)

Policy-Making in British Government

Government Departments: An Organizational Perspective
  (with D. C. Pitt)

The Computer Revolution in Public Administration
  (with D. C. Pitt)

Decentralization: The Territorial Dimension of the State

Bureaucracy and Political Power

Progress in Development Administration (edited)

British Aid and International Trade
  (with O. Morrissey and E. Horesh)

*Understanding Third World Politics: Theories of Political Change
  and Development*

Good Governance and Development

B. C. Smith

palgrave
macmillan

First published 2007 by
PALGRAVE MACMILLAN
Houndmills, Basingstoke, Hampshire RG21 6XS and
175 Fifth Avenue, New York, N.Y. 10010
Companies and representatives throughout the world

PALGRAVE MACMILLAN is the global academic imprint of the Palgrave
Macmillan division of St. Martin's Press, LLC and of Palgrave Macmillan Ltd.
Macmillan® is a registered trademark in the United States, United Kingdom
and other countries. Palgrave is a registered trademark in the European
Union and other countries.

ISBN-13: 978–0–230–52565–8   hardback
ISBN-10: 0–230–52565–2   hardback
ISBN-13: 978–0–230–52566–5   paperback
ISBN-10: 0–230–52566–0   paperback

This book is printed on paper suitable for recycling and made from
fully managed and sustained forest sources. Logging, pulping and
manufacturing processes are expected to conform to the
environmental regulations of the country of origin.

A catalogue record for this book is available from the British Library.

A catalog record for this book is available from the Library of Congress.

10 9 8 7 6 5 4 3 2 1
16 15 14 13 12 11 10 09 08 07

Printed and bound in China

Contents

List of Tables

Preface

Concerns about 'governance' have come to occupy a prominent place in the interventions and expenditure of aid agencies, both international (multilateral) and national (bilateral). Governance is variously seen as an end in its own right (when, for example, it is about the protection and advancement of human rights), as a means to development (when, for example, the rule of law is seen as necessary for economic growth) and as a means to the reduction of poverty (when, for example, reducing corruption is regarded as a strategy for increasing the assets and therefore wealth of the poor). This book explores the constitutional, political, administrative and public policy implications of various 'good governance' agendas for the governance of developing and newly democratizing countries, especially those in transition from authoritarian rule in one or other of its forms, and for whom aid in areas other than governance may be dependent upon satisfying 'political conditionalities'.

The book has three main aims. First, each item on the 'good governance' agenda is assessed for its contribution to development and the cost to society of bad governance. Second, it is asked how international development agencies view each dimension of governance, and what reforms they are backing in order to improve its quality. What aid agencies do in pursuit of governance objectives is described before conceptual and empirical questions are raised which need to be considered by those intending to engage in political engineering of this kind.

Third, the contribution political science can make to an understanding of each dimension of governance is specified, in respect both of the actions being undertaken by aid agencies and recipient governments, and of aspects of political reform which fall beyond the scope of foreign intervention. A particular aim here is to expose the controversies which surround some of the assumptions on which the presuppositions and interventions of aid agencies are based. It is assumed here that it is as important to know what foreign aid in support of governance cannot do as to know what is susceptible to external guidance and assistance. For

x

example, some reforms may require changes in political culture which take decades to complete, whereas aid agencies usually have to respond to short-term imperatives.

The ways in which donors attempt to bring about good governance in aid-dependent states fall into two broad categories: coercion and cooperation. These 'political conditionalities' required by donors and lenders are a response to political developments in the second half of the twentieth century. This book is mainly concerned with cooperative forms of aid for good governance, whereby donors and lenders seek to support reforms rather than punish shortcomings.

The common elements of good governance, as defined by political leaders and international agencies, fall into four sets of attributes requiring reforms to corresponding parts of the polity: constitutional, political, administrative, and the content of public policy. At the *constitutional* level good governance is perceived as requiring changes to the fundamental principles and rules by which government is carried on. Economic and political development is believed to be dependent upon four sets of constitutional reforms designed to strengthen the accountability of political leaders to the people, ensure respect for human rights, strengthen the rule of law and guarantee the decentralization of political authority. Chapters 2–5 expose the controversies surrounding these concepts in order to clarify the problems posed for countries under pressure to improve the quality of governance through these means.

The three *political* attributes of good governance that occur in the governance agendas of international aid agencies require changes in political action and organization. What is sought here are pluralism, participation and an end to corruption. These are the subjects of Chapters 6–8. First, aid is provided to support political *pluralism*, in the belief that a plurality of autonomous political associations contributes to good governance in a number of important ways. Freedom of association is more than a fundamental right. It is also a means of supporting democracy. Pluralism implies formal political equality, protected by the fundamental political rights to vote, to free speech and to association for political ends; a two-party or multi-party system, offering electoral choice; and functional representation. Political associations are the most important organizations in pluralist democracy, whether for interest aggregation (political parties) or interest articulation (civil society organized for political ends).

Participation is understood within the donor community either as an end in itself (for example, an objective of a policy of political decentralization) or as a means to other political and administrative objectives, such as increasing the effectiveness of development projects and programmes, or empowering the beneficiaries. Participation affects the people who participate, making them more effective both politically and, when they take responsibilities for service delivery, administratively. The concept of articipation has different meanings in different settings and among different advocates. Hence the need to distinguish between different forms of participation and their effects on development projects and service recipients.

There can be no doubt as to the seriousness with which the aid community views the task of increasing probity and incorruptibility in the use of public powers and offices by servants of the state. Every facet of development is found to be harmed by *corruption*. It is regarded as a particularly significant adversary in the fight against poverty. All leading multilateral agencies have formulated detailed assessments of corruption on which they have built strategies for reform. But knowing how to eradicate corruption from governance is made difficult by the multitude of definitions used in its analysis.

In the following two chapters (9 and 10) the *administrative requisites* of good governance are discussed. Administratively, good governance requires accountable and transparent public administration and effective public management, including a capacity to design, as well as implement, good policies.

Administrative accountability is not always clearly distinguished from political accountability in aid programmes supporting administrative reform, and is usually included among the aims and objectives of reforms designed to enhance the efficiency of public services. Unfortunately for those who wish to use international development assistance to improve accountability in new democracies, the concept is plagued by ambiguities. But in essence administrative accountability poses the question of whether policies are being implemented as intended, and resources are being used for the purposes specified by the law-makers.

The essential components of *administrative efficiency* and a capable public sector are a strong central capacity for formulating and coordinating policy, efficient and effective delivery systems, and motivated and competent staff. The most favoured solutions to problems of administrative inefficiency currently are: contracting out service delivery to private firms or NGOs; performance-based agencies with managerial autonomy but accountable for outputs and outcomes; and a 'customer orientation' involving user participation, client surveys, and published benchmarks (commitments to minimum standards), all leading, it is hoped, to stronger citizens' 'voice'. In order to produce motivated and capable staff in public services, developing and transitional countries need to institutionalize meritocratic recruitment and promotion (that is, a neutral, professional and depoliticized civil service), adequate compensation, improved *esprit de corps,* and stronger incentives (bonuses, performance allowances and so on).

The policy dimension of good governance (Chapter 11) has responded to the disappointing outcomes of state economic planning and public ownership, growing doubts about the subsequent confidence in the ability of free markets to increase welfare, especially that of the poor, and a renewed acceptance of the importance of the state, particularly in the campaign to reduce poverty which now dominates official approaches to aid. The World Bank and other agencies recognize that expenditure on social services not only in the short run protects the vulnerable against the effects of economic reforms, but also in the longer term contributes to economic growth and human development.

The concluding chapter takes a synoptic look at concerns about good governance by examining its relationship to development, reviewing the prospects for success in externally inducing good governance, and asking whether the example set by developed countries in respect of human rights, the rule of law, corruption and the other notions of good governance in their own countries is good enough to convince poor and newly democratizing regimes that they have an obligation to reform along the lines prescribed by Western donors.

The work represented by this book owes a debt of gratitude to many with whom I have had the pleasure of discussing problems of governance over recent years, especially Edward Horesh, formerly of the University of Bath, and Jeffrey Stanyer, formerly of the University of Exeter. The Politics Department of the University of Exeter provided a congenial working environment, and I am grateful for the visiting professorship which enabled me to present early drafts to postgraduate students. The librarians of the university were, as ever, remarkably efficient in responding to my requests for help. At Palgrave Macmillan, Steven Kennedy's cogent insights and usual enthusiasm were much appreciated, as were the positive criticisms of an anonymous reader. Finally, I thank my wife, Jean, for her unfailing tolerance and support, and for bearing the burden of reading the whole manuscript and correcting numerous mistakes. But responsibility for the final result rests with me alone.

Exeter   B. C. Smith

1

Governance Agendas

Political conditionalities

Much official development assistance comes with conditions attached, whether the aid be in the form of grants, soft loans, mixed credits or technical assistance, and whether the donors be bilateral (nation-states such as the USA and the UK) or multilateral (international agencies such as the World Bank or the European Development Fund). Conditionalities have included requirements to target the aid at specified social groups (such as the poor), the tying of aid to the purchase of goods and services from the donor country, and structural adjustments to the recipient economy (notably public sector reform and trade liberalization). Even before the introduction of specifically political conditionalities, government in the recipient country has always been heavily influenced by the presence of aid if only through its effects on public policy.

Ever since the Second World War there have been occasions when aid has been linked to political objectives, such as democratization or respect for human rights. Postwar reconstruction in Germany and Japan was in part aimed at the establishment of democracy, as were the unsuccessful efforts of the USA's Alliance for Progress in Latin America. Donors such as Canada, the USA, the Netherlands and Sweden have linked their aid programmes to governance reforms since the 1960s, even though in most cases 'the policy rhetoric did not translate into much practical substance' (Burnell, 2000: 37). Such concerns have usually been far outweighed by bilateral and multilateral support for states with bad records of government under authoritarian regimes because this has served the economic and security interests of Western governments (Leftwich, 2000: 109). But from the end of the 1980s the quality of 'governance' in recipient countries became an increasingly common and explicit aid objective as the first generation of

1

aid conditionalities, related to structural adjustment, gave way to second-generation conditionalities related to democracy, human rights and good government.

A number of political developments came together to prompt donors to adopt 'political conditionalities' (Moore, 1993; Robinson, 1993). First, the collapse of the Soviet bloc made it no longer necessary for the West to support authoritarian regimes because they were anti-communist. It also encouraged the view that political liberalization was a necessary condition for economic liberalization and growth. However, the promotion of democracy as a theme of Western policy predates the end of the cold war (though not always reflected in practice), with aid expressing 'some quite deep-rooted political and even cultural characteristics of the established liberal democracies' (Hawthorne, 1993: 249). In addition, there have been deliberate acts of imposition by intervention from outside, unrelated to aid conditionality.

Second, democratization was already underway in other parts of the world by 1990 (for example, in Latin America and parts of East and South-East Asia such as Taiwan, South Korea and the Philippines), and the indigenous pro-democracy movements provided the West with legitimacy for its pro-democracy aid policies. Donors could claim that the political conditionalities being laid down reflected and supported popular demands within aid-recipient countries. Indeed, indigenous non-governmental organizations had been among those that criticized international development strategies for not being concerned with the quality of government and politics.

Third, domestic political pressures in donor countries encouraged a demand for good governance as a condition of aid being given. Governments believed that public support for aid expenditure could be strengthened by making aid conditional upon democratization and respect for human rights. In the USA this response to public opinion was made easier by a lessening of the security problem in the early 1990s (as aid became less important in ensuring the protection of US interests abroad) and by the widely acknowledged ineffectiveness of much aid when measured by the economic development achieved (Lancaster, 1993). Some donors also needed to find a justification for reductions in overseas aid, and bad governance provided a reason. Legitimacy for the interventions of Western donors could also be secured by being presented as measures to improve the quality of governance, even when such assistance was in reality mainly designed to secure the donors' strategic foreign policy objectives, as in South Africa (Hearn, 2000).

Fourth, in the 1990s blame for the failure of structural adjustment and economic liberalization to achieve the intended beneficial results was directed at poor-quality governance, notably weak governmental structures, administrative incompetence, corruption, a lack of accountability and openness in policy-making, and an absence of the rule of law. There has been a growing recognition that development cannot occur unless the political conditions are right. For example, economic reforms are unlikely to be effective when political leaders act arbitrarily, corruptly and to the exclusion of all interests other than their own. The quality of political life was also seen as significant when trying to alleviate the social costs, especially for the poor, of economic reforms. The state was recognized as a necessary condition of development, and not, as it had been earlier, an obstacle to it.

Finally, it was recognized that governance has itself been affected by aid. Aid can actually undermine good governance. As aid increased, so the quality of governance was observed to decline as political accountability for the use of aid money could be evaded, as corruption became easier and intragovernmental conflict over access to bribes increased, as scarce talent was 'poached' from civil services, and as pressure to reform inefficiency and defective policy-making was eased. Hence a growing belief that aid programmes had to be designed so that they would sustain good governance by, for example, targeting weak institutions such as the civil service and judiciary so that administrative capacity and accountability are strengthened (Knack, 2000).

Meanings of 'good governance'

It will have become clear by now that it is 'governance', and not just 'government', that is crucial to the language of political conditionalities and developmental objectives. However, when the representatives of donor agencies speak of governance they do not necessarily refer to the same thing (Doornbos, 2001). Sometimes 'governance' and 'government' are used interchangeably, possibly because the former is regarded as a useful buzz-word, or because it is difficult under its articles of agreement for the World Bank to take non-economic considerations (that is, politics) into account, which limits it to a technocratic and managerialist approach to government reforms. But usually governance means government plus something else: public policies, institutions, a system of economic relationships, or a role for the non-governmental sector in the business of the state. 'Good governance' thus expresses approval not only for a type of government (usually democracy) and its related political values (for example respect for human rights) but also for certain kinds of additional components.

Equating governance with *government* focuses on technical problems of administrative and legal capacity and the improvement of public sector management, the legal framework for development, accountability through better auditing, decentralization, the policing of corruption, civil service reform, and improved information on policy issues for both decision-makers and the public. This approach has been criticized for its 'managerialist fixes', 'detached from the turbulent world of social forces, politics and the structure and purpose of the state' (Leftwich, 2000: 108). Consequently, donors have come to recognize the importance of support for civil society in order to encourage political accountability, legitimacy, transparency and participation (Williams and Young, 1994: 87–8).

In another usage 'good governance' implies government that is democratically organized within a democratic political culture and with efficient administrative organizations, plus the right *policies*, particularly in the economic sphere. These have generally included trade liberalization, the deregulation of economic activities, the privatization of state enterprises, and 'pro-poor' policies such as reductions in military expenditure in favour of public spending on education and health care. The Netherlands led the way in 1990 when it decided to take excessive military expenditure into account in the distribution of its foreign aid (Hoebink, 1999: 204). Good governance thus requires policy reform as well as the reform of governmental organizations (for example for tax collection) and institutions (such as the rule of law). For example, the UN defines good governance as *policies* for sustainable human development (including enabling the private sector to create employment); and *government* that is democratic, decentralized, empowering, and accountable (with properly functioning legislatures, legal and judicial systems to protect the rule of law and human rights, and electoral processes).

Aid agencies sometimes extend the range of organizations and institutions which they perceive as involved in governance to include most aspects of social, economic and political life. Governance is equated with *managing a country's resources*. Both the World Bank and United Nations Development Programme (UNDP) see governance as the 'manner' in which a country's economic and social resources are managed and power is distributed. For the UNDP, 'governance encompasses every institution and organization in society from the family to the state' (UNDP, 1997b: 10; World Bank, 1992). This view of governance recognizes the importance for development of institutions, particularly private property and the rule of law. Good governance then entails organizations and policies which protect property rights and sustain an independent judiciary (Lancaster, 1993).

Governance can be extended further to denote a whole *ideology*, wherein political and economic principles, relationships and rules governing economic production and distribution are combined. Good governance thus entails liberal democracy, free enterprise, free trade, a minimalist state and free markets – that is, capitalism – a view expressed frequently by Western political leaders during the 1990s (Leftwich, 2000: 118–19).

Finally, 'governance' has been defined as a *network* (or patchwork) of private non-governmental bodies that have a role to play in the formulation and implementation of public policy and the delivery of public services. Governance is government plus the private and 'third' (not-for-profit) sectors. Non-governmental bodies may be private firms (contracted by a government agency to provide some part of a public service, for example building maintenance, hospital catering, refuse collection and disposal); foreign and domestic NGOs involved in emergency relief, service provision, or advocacy; voluntary bodies and community organizations (whether based on territorial or social divisions, for example village water associations or women's groups); and trade unions and employers' organizations entrusted with the implementation of some aspect of industrial policy. Governance thus implies a degree of interdependence between governments and non-state actors. This understanding of governance is adopted in the *World Development Report 1997*, meaning 'encouraging wider participation in the design and delivery of these goods and services through partnerships among government, business and civic organizations' (World Bank, 1997: 110). This view has also been adopted by the UN – see for example its *Human Development Report* for 1993.

Governance' thus combines ideas about political authority, the management of economic and social resources, and the capacity of governments to formulate sound policies and then perform their functions effectively, efficiently and equitably (Blunt, 1995). If the various conceptualizations of 'governance' found in the international development discourse are not synonymous with 'government', they are with 'politics': the way power and authority are exercised; the management of a country's affairs; the relationships between rulers and ruled; how conflict is resolved; how interests are articulated and rights exercised; and so on (Weiss, 2000).

The assistance which represents the governmental concerns of aid donors and lenders is grouped by the Development Assistance Committee of the OECD into support for democracy (elections, legislatures, political parties, civic education, advocacy groups and the media); human rights (rule of law, civil and political rights, legal, penal and judicial reform, and human rights advocacy); and good governance (civil service reform, public sector management, decentralization, accountability and participation) (Robinson, 1999: 410–11). However, when the statements of government ministers and international agencies are examined more closely it is possible to identify four sets of attributes requiring reforms if good governance is to be brought about: constitutional, political, administrative and the content of public policy.

At the constitutional level good governance requires changes that will strengthen the accountability of political leaders to the people, ensure respect for human rights, strengthen the rule of law, and decentralize political authority. At the level of political action and organization, three attributes of good governance are common to the governance agendas of most aid agencies: political pluralism, opportunities for extensive participation in politics, and probity and incorruptibility in the use of public powers and offices by servants of the state. Administratively, good governance requires accountable and transparent public administration; and effective public management, including a capacity to design good policies as well as to implement them.

Finally there is the policy dimension of good governance. Policy prescriptions for developing and transitional countries have moved through different phases. But the good governance agendas of Western agencies throughout have been driven by the neo-liberal economics and politics that have dominated the official theoretical and ideological profile since the 1980s (Leftwich, 2000).

The enforcement of political conditionalities

The major aid donors have frequently attempted to force good governance on aid-dependent states. Sometimes this has been through negative or punitive measures, suspending or terminating aid because of the denial of basic civil and political rights. Examples include the British government's suspension of capital aid to Burma, Somalia and the Sudan, the withdrawal of American aid from Haiti, the suspension of aid from Denmark and the Netherlands to Indonesia, the withdrawal of Belgian aid to Zaire in 1990 and the reductions or withdrawals of German aid in 1991 to the 'repressive' regimes of Haiti, Malawi, Togo and Zaire, and the 'authoritarian' regimes of China, Indonesia and Kenya (Ashoff, 1999).

More recently, political torture and other human rights abuses in Uzbekistan led the USA to withdraw its US\$100 million aid package, despite cooperation in the so-called 'war against terrorism'. In 2004 the European Union banned all European companies from investing in Burmese firms controlled by or linked to the military, and failure of the authorities to respond to EU demands for reforms on democracy and human rights, including lifting the house arrest of opposition leader Aung Sang Suu Kyi, led to the imposition of sanctions. However, aid for health and education was increased after consultation with democratic groups including the National League for Democracy. In 2005 the USA made continuation of military aid to Nepal conditional upon the restoration of human rights. The World Bank suspended loans to India, Bangladesh and Ethiopia in 2005, as well as debt relief to the Republic of Congo, because of concerns about corruption.

Human rights have become part of conditionality in that good governance has been made a condition of membership of international political and economic organizations such as NATO, the Commonwealth and the Council of Europe. In 2003 Zimbabwe was expelled from the Commonwealth because of the Mugabe government's human rights abuses, interference with the media and judiciary, and electoral malpractices. In 2004 the European Commission warned Turkey that entry negotiations would be ended if EU ministers found a 'serious and persistent' breach of democratic and human rights in the country.

Other benefits (such as aid, trade concessions, and loans) may be conditional upon the achievement of a satisfactory level of performance in the sphere of human rights. For example, the European Bank for Reconstruction and Development will limit loans to the private sectors in Belarus and Turkmenistan until progress is made on human rights, and has reduced lending to Uzbekistan because of human rights violations and the lack of progress on economic reforms. In 2002 the US administration announced it would not consider increasing economic and military aid to Egypt because of the state's persecution of pro-democracy activists. In Africa, the Western partners in the New Partnership for Africa's

Development, designed to secure foreign aid, investment and debt relief, have declared that support is conditional upon governance reform, including human rights, in the African member states.

However, a preferred option is to give positive support for measures specifically designed to improve individual aspects of governance (such as civil service reform, decentralization, the funding and training of electoral commissions, election monitoring, or the reform of financial management in government) or the transition to democracy generally (Robinson, 1999: 410–11; Burnell, 2000b: 26–9). This move from coercive to cooperative conditionality is part of a wider recognition that aid generally is likely to be more effective if done in partnership and dialogue with recipient governments, NGOs and the private sector, and in support of what the recipients themselves want to do. However, this is always conditional upon the recipients' plans being broadly in line with the donor's objectives (Pender, 2001). Aid may also be induced by regional initiatives to improve the quality of governance, as when in 2001 the European Union and other industrial nations promised support in the form of aid for infrastructure and education, increased foreign investment, and the lifting of trade barriers, to the New African Initiative, launched by leaders of African states and designed to reduce conflict, end human rights abuses, and establish open and accountable government.

Another explanation for support to good governance projects is the damaging effect for the most vulnerable members of society of terminating aid to countries with repressive governments. Suspending aid is not guaranteed to change regimes for the better, as the cases of Zaire and Sudan show. Cuts in aid are too often accommodated by reductions in public expenditure on services of importance to the livelihoods of the poor, such as health and education, as in the case of Malawi in 1992, when aid was suspended until civil and political rights were respected. Furthermore, threats to suspend aid have often proved empty when trade and foreign policy considerations have outweighed the West's concerns for human rights. This was shown to be the case in 1991 when donors threatened to suspend their aid programmes to Indonesia after the army's massacre of peaceful protesters against the occupation of East Timor. Only the Netherlands eventually took action, but as Dutch aid to Indonesia accounted for only 2 per cent of development assistance received by the country, this did little to reduce internal repression, though it had disastrous consequences for local NGOs and those who depended on them (Robinson, 1995).

Governance assistance grew rapidly in scale during the first half of the

1990s, with most of the leading Western donors initiating projects. All the dimensions of good governance have their associated aid projects: support for human rights activists, capacity-building in local authorities, training for the judiciary and so on. Governance aid takes the form of grants, loans and technical assistance to provide policy advisers (for example to ministries responsible for decentralization), consultants (for example on financial and human resources management), equipment (for example for information and communications technology), supplies (for example of law books and documents), information (for example for the public on law reforms), research (for example assessing the need for electoral assistance), logistical support (for example staff for new election commissions), and training (for example for civil servants and elected representatives). Donor government support is also channelled via Western NGOs, such as the National Endowment for Democracy set up in the United States in 1984, the Westminster Foundation for Democracy created by the UK parliament in 1992, and the Swedish International Institute for Democracy and Electoral Assistance. The political party foundations in Germany give extensive support to trade unions, cooperatives, self-help organizations, human rights groups and political education programmes, as well as political parties. The German aid ministry allocates substantial funds to human rights and democratization projects through political foundations and churches (Pinto-Duschinsky, 1991; Lee, 1995; P. Waller, 1995).

An intermediate position which donors can adopt, between withdrawing or freezing aid disbursements and supporting good government policies, is to switch aid from governments to civil society organizations. Donors have often bypassed governments, especially when authoritarian, to support NGOs working in the fields of human rights, legal aid, advocacy, civic education, electoral monitoring and other spheres relating to good governance. Examples include Denmark, which in 1991 withheld US$8 million of bilateral aid to the Kenyan government, channelling the funds instead to NGOs and grassroots organizations. The foreign funding of Chilean pro-democracy NGOs amounted in 1989 to US$50 million. British aid to South African NGOs and church-based organizations during the 1980s and early 1990s amounted to £8 million in 1990–1. In 1995 USAID decided to support a coalition of churches, NGOs and community groups seeking constitutional reform in Kenya, and opposing the government of President Daniel arap Moi. This was in response to Moi's authoritarian tendencies. Success by the end of the 1990s in extracting reforms by this method enabled USAID to consider redirecting its governance assistance back to state institutions such as parliament, the judiciary and local government (Robinson, 1995; Carothers, 2002). In 2006 the UK redirected aid through humanitarian agencies in Ethiopia, having frozen aid to the government because of electoral irregularities and repression of opposition. Rather than fund a Hamas government in Palestine in 2006, the EU distributed the bulk of emergency aid, worth US$140 million, through utility companies, health care providers, and the UN Relief and Works Agency.

Support for governance reforms

It is difficult to estimate the scale of financial assistance to governance reforms, partly because of the different definitions of good governance employed by donors, but also because aid to social sectors such as education and health may contain governance-related projects and requirements, for example to increase levels of user participation in the delivery of services.

The OECD's breakdown of aid by major purposes shows that volumes have been increasing, with the proportion of bilateral aid destined to support 'government and civil society' at 6.8 per cent in 2001, and the share of multilateral aid at over 17 per cent (see Table 1.1). Expenditure on government and civil society support was less than 2 per cent of total aid commitments in 1994. Some donors made allocations well above the bilateral average, such as Portugal with 25.3 per cent of its overseas aid devoted to governance, Australia with 18.5 per cent, and Finland with 14.9 per cent. In 2001 the UK allocated 5.5 per cent of its aid to governance (up from 0.8 per cent in 1994), and the USA 13.3 per cent. The share of official development assistance going to support good governance has not always reflected the policy commitments made by donor governments.

By 1999 the World Bank was providing over US $5 billion for governance reforms in some 24 countries, including anti-corruption programmes. Spending on the European Union's Initiative for Democracy and Human Rights rose from 39.2 million ecus in 1993 to 129.7 million in 1997. Generally, however, aid donors spend far less on governance than on economic transformation. Only 0.56 of the EU's total assistance to Eastern Europe in the mid 1990s was devoted to governance and democratization. The USA made grants to Central and Eastern European countries of US $234 million between 1990 and 1996 for building democracy, compared with US $1.67 billion for economic

Table 1.1 *Aid by major purpose, 2001 (%)*

Purpose	Bilateral	Multilateral
Education	8.6	3.1
Health	4.1	2.7
Population[1]	2.7	1.3
Water supply and sanitation	4.8	4.2
Government and civil society	6.8	17.4
Other social infrastructure	5.4	9.6
Economic infrastructure[2]	14.9	31.3
Production[3]	8.7	10.1
Multisector	7.2	9.4
Programme assistance	6.8	3.6
Debt relief	9.8	–
Emergency aid	7.1	1.4
Administrative expenses	6.5	0.3
Unspecified	6.6	5.6

SOURCE: data from Organisation for Economic Co-operation and Development (2003), Table 19.

NOTES: 1. Includes reproductive health.
  2. Mainly transport, communications and energy.
  3. Agriculture, industry, mining, construction, trade and tourism.

restructuring, plus US $576 million to improve the 'quality of life'. From the point of view of the recipient, however, assistance with governance reforms can be very significant. In South Africa, for example, it constitutes an exceptionally large proportion of foreign aid (Burnell, 2000).

The aims of good governance

At first glance it might seem that good governance is self-evidently an end in itself, or at least a direct means to an improvement in human well-being. It must surely be better for people to have their civil and political rights respected rather than denied and abused, to receive entitlements without having to bribe officials, and to have those officials answerable to the law. However, standards of living have sometimes been dramatically improved without all of the components of good governance being present, as in Singapore for example. This is why it is necessary to reflect on the orthodoxy behind the advocacy of good governance – that it is compatible with economic and social development. This relationship will be further examined in the final chapter.

Since it is clearly an assumption of aid donors that good governance will improve the chances of development taking place in countries less favourably placed than the industrialized democracies, it is important to know how 'development' is conceived in this context. As is so often the case in the social sciences, we are dealing here with a contested concept. It is possible to distinguish between economic and human development, or growth-centred development, and people-centred development, the former represented by the World Bank's approach to aid and its objectives, the latter by the UN's concern with people's well-being (Clarke, 2002). However, this is by no means a clear-cut distinction as there is a good deal of common ground in the two approaches.

Development in the economic sense refers to growth in the wealth of countries as measured by indicators such as gross national product (GNP) and gross domestic product (GDP). Countries and regions can then be compared in terms of average annual growth rates and their relative levels of development assessed (see Table 1.2). However, it would be quite wrong to think that a growth-centred approach to development is unconcerned with the social causes and effects of growth. Much is revealed about social well-being by the per capita levels of GNP in different countries and the distribution of national income between households. The

Table 1.2 *Annual average economic growth rates*

Countries	Average annual % growth of GDP 1980–90	1990–99	Per capita % growth of GDP 1998–99
Low income	4.7	3.2	2.1
Middle income	3.3	3.5	1.9
Lower middle income	4.2	3.4	2.5
Upper middle income	2.6	3.6	1.2
Low and middle income	3.5	3.5	1.7
East Asia and Pacific	8.0	7.5	5.6
Europe and Central Asia	..	-2.3	0.9
Latin America and Caribbean	1.7	3.4	-1.5
Middle East and North Africa	2.0	3.0	0.6
South Asia	5.6	5.6	4.0
Sub-Saharan Africa	1.7	2.2	-0.5
High income	3.4	2.3	1.7

SOURCE: data from World Bank (2001a), Tables 1.1 and 4.1, pp. 14 and 196.

World Bank recognizes the importance of investing in social development, and of comparing countries in terms of their levels of education and
health. Its development indicators regularly include access to health care,
safe water, and sanitation, as well as infant mortality rates, school enrolments and the percentage of people living on less than US$1 a day. It also
sees the alleviation of poverty as the most important goal of development
(though its actual policy decisions have not always been consistent with
this).

Comparisons of human, or people-centred, development are usually
made by reference to life expectancy, literacy levels, gender inequalities
and human deprivation. Human development has been defined as

> creating an environment in which people can develop their full poten-
> tial and lead productive, creative lives in accord with their needs and
> interests . . . expanding the choices people have to lead lives that they
> value . . . building human capabilities. (UNDP, 2003b: 1)

People-centred development is represented by the UN's Millennium
Development Goals (MDGs) and targets for poverty, education, gender
equality, health and the environment. Official development policy has
here been informed by the burgeoning literature attempting to define
human development in terms of 'ingredients' of the quality of life, basic
human needs, 'aspects', 'domains' and 'dimensions' of well-being,
universal human values, central human 'capabilities' and the 'features' of
a full life (Alkire, 2002).

While human development is seen to some extent as an end in itself,
and not as a means to economic growth, the concept is in part expressed
through economic variables. For example, the United Nations
Development Programme's Human Development Index (HDI) combines
life expectancy at birth, the adult literacy rate, educational enrolment and
GDP per capita, indicators representing longevity, knowledge and standard of living. This index shows how far human development in some
regions of the world, and some countries, lags behind levels in high
income-countries (see Table 1.3). The HDI is based on the conviction that
people and their capabilities, not economic growth, are the ultimate criteria for assessing development. The concept of human development also
recognizes that economic achievements are dependent on social factors.
For example, labour productivity is affected by levels of primary and
secondary education. Equally, however, economic growth is needed to
achieve human development objectives such as poverty reduction and

Table 1.3   *Human development by region, 2001*

Region	HDI Values
Developing countries	0.655
Least developed countries	0.448
Arab States	0.662
East Asia and Pacific	0.722
Latin America and Caribbean	0.777
South Asia	0.582
Sub-Saharan Africa	0.468
Central & Eastern Europe & CIS	0.787
OECD countries	0.905
High-income OECD	0.929

SOURCE: data from United Nations Development
Programme (2003c), Table 1, p. 240.

public investment in health and education. There is in effect a virtuous circle of human and economic development, each enhancing the other.

Nevertheless, comparisons of levels of human and economic development show that much can be achieved even without high levels of economic growth. Some countries have much better levels of human development than their economic status would lead one to expect. For example, though Vietnam and Pakistan have similar levels of income per person, their life expectancy and literacy levels differ greatly: for example, Vietnam ranks 109th in the world by human development, Pakistan 144th. Cuba, a lower-middle-income economy, has an HDI (0.806), higher than the average for all upper- and lower-middle-income countries combined (0.744), and higher than some upper-middle-income countries such as Brazil, Malaysia, Mexico and Saudi Arabia (UNDP, 2003a).

Interdependencies

The first group of items on the governance agenda calls for constitutional reform. Good governance here requires certain fundamental rules of the political game to be in place. They may also have to be accompanied by changes in political attitudes and behaviour (for example recognition of the right to vote for all citizens) which might not have occurred were reform being enforced by way of aid conditionalities but which may be necessary if political accountability, human rights, the rule of law and decentralization are to be built into the structure of governance and become effective.

Wherever constitutional reform is needed to improve the quality of governance, it will have to be accommodated by often very different histories and contexts, raising important questions about the viability of universal models, especially those constructed by Western aid donors with their own ethnocentric views on governance. There is also a high level of interdependence between all types of reform. For example, political accountability depends on freedom to form political associations, as well as legislation which stipulates how and when elections should be held. Freedom of association needs to be buttressed by respect for human rights. People then have to be mobilized to form and sustain political movements. For legislation to be effective there have to be efficient and honest administrative arrangements, and impartial adjudication of disputes. Political accountability is dependent upon the rule of law, the entrenchment of civil and political rights, a pluralistic articulation of political interests, and opportunities for high levels of participation, especially voting. Accountability can also be supported by public policies which aim to empower marginalized sections of society such as the poor, women or ethnic minorities. Such dependencies make the business of promoting good governance in different cultural settings extremely complex.

Conclusion

The concept of 'governance' is contested. Different meanings have been attached to the concept when used in debates about development in poor and post-communist countries. Political developments in the second half of the twentieth century encouraged the adoption of 'political conditionalities' to bring governance into the mainstream of international development assistance. The ways in which donors attempt to bring about good governance in aid-dependent states can be distinguished as coercion and cooperation.

The common elements in the definitions of good governance implicit in the statements of political leaders and international agencies can be grouped into four sets of attributes requiring reforms to corresponding parts of the polity: constitutional, political, administrative, and policy content. At the *constitutional* level good governance is perceived as requiring changes to the fundamental principles and rules by which government is carried on. Economic and political development is dependent upon four sets of constitutional reforms designed to strengthen the accountability of political leaders to the people, ensure respect for human rights, strengthen the rule of law, and guarantee the decentralization of political authority. The following four chapters explore the controversies surrounding these principles and their related institutions.

2

Political Accountability

Good governance and democratic accountability

Most aid donors are convinced that the achievement of development objectives is likely to be assisted by stronger forms of political accountability. Political accountability is linked to human development because it is a necessary condition for democracy. However, leading aid agencies have also linked accountability to more precise objectives, especially the reduction of corruption and poverty.

For example, the United Nations Development Programme makes poverty alleviation the primary aim of political accountability. Properly functioning electoral processes and legislatures composed of freely and fairly elected members representing different parties are seen as essential for accountability, which then becomes part of an 'enabling environment' for the eradication of poverty. Consequently the Programme has provided technical assistance to a number of countries to strengthen electoral and legislative systems, including Cambodia, Mozambique, the Philippines and Vietnam. Since the establishment of an Electoral Assistance Division in 1992, the UN has provided assistance to over 70 member states. UNDP support for legislatures has included strengthening the capacity of political parties and civil society, empowering women by helping them reach positions of political leadership, strengthening the internal organizations of legislatures, especially for oversight and audit, and training MPs and parliamentary staff.

United States' aid policy also places electoral accountability at the centre of good governance because it enables bad leaders to be removed and prevents corruption. If elections are not fully free, fair and competitive, and administered by a politically neutral agency, corruption becomes endemic and human rights are abused. Political accountability also

17

requires that the public have the freedom and institutional means to scrutinize the conduct and policy choices of office-holders between elections. So in addition to free, fair and competitive elections there has to be an 'elected parliament that is autonomous and capable of checking the power of the executive branch' (USAID, 2003).

For the World Bank the main function of political accountability is to act as an anti-corruption strategy. The stronger the accountability, the greater the costs to political leaders of acting selfishly and corruptly. The strength of accountability depends upon the effectiveness of the sanctions and of the institutions for monitoring decision-making. Effective sanctions require meaningful political competition through the electoral process, though the Bank warns against excessive competition which can fragment the political system and undermine the legitimacy and the capacity of state institutions, thus creating conditions conducive to administrative corruption and 'state capture' (World Bank, 2000: 40).

The World Bank has to avoid overtly political interventions, but the World Bank Institute engages in a number of activities in support of national parliaments in governmental matters currently given priority by the Bank itself: financial oversight, poverty reduction, and public participation. The Institute's programme of work on Government Accountability and Parliamentary Oversight (GAPO) aims to strengthen the capacity of parliaments to oversee the allocation and use of public funds, while the programme on Parliaments, Governance and Poverty Reduction is designed to assist legislatures to represent the interests of the poor in the policy process. GAPO focuses on public accounts, finance committees, budget cycles, and audit, for example in Bangladesh, Cambodia, Ghana, Indonesia, Kenya and Uganda. The programme on parliaments and poverty reduction is to help elected representatives, their staff and key civil associations to play a more effective role in designing and monitoring their countries' poverty reduction strategies when these are required under World Bank and IMF conditionalities. Since 2001, and in collaboration with UNDP, the Institute has provided assistance to Cambodia, Ethiopia, Ghana, Kenya, Malawi, Niger and Nigeria.

Support for parliamentary development also comes from the European Union. In 1991 the European parliament started to budget for training courses and fact-finding missions for officials of the new parliaments of Central and Eastern Europe. Subjects covered included library, research and documentation services for MPs, committee work, relations with the press and public, and the management of parliamentary administrations (both staff and finances). The following year the European Parliament voted to establish a European Democracy Initiative for the same regions, whose projects have included training in parliamentary processes, aid in drafting and implementing human rights legislation, and the development of democratic structures for political parties (Blackman, 1995). Together donors provided some US $200 million in loans and grants for legislative development projects in the 1990s.

The costs of bad governance

When political accountability is absent, or malfunctioning, human rights are at risk. Limitations on freedom of speech (for example Zimbabwe), freedom of association (in most one-party states, for example Uganda from 1986 to 2005), freedom to stand as a candidate (as in Iran), and freedom to campaign (for example Belarus in 2001) are all restrictions on fundamental human rights. Other abuses which undermine democracy include the extension of terms of office by incumbents (for example the Sri Lankan president in 2004), the mismanagement of polling (Guinea in 2003), and inflated electoral rolls (Kosovo in 1997). They also include a lack of transparency during the counting and tabulation of votes, as in Belarus in 2001, where the provisions of the electoral code for the tabulation of results at district, oblast and national levels did not allow an independent audit by the representatives of voters, candidates or observers, and the central electoral commission was obliged to publish only national totals and not the details of results in districts and oblasts.

Restrictions on the mass media also indirectly undermine democratic rights. The early years of the twenty-first century witnessed a worrying change in government–media relations, reversing a movement towards greater press freedom during the late 1990s. In 2003 10 countries – all bar one, Italy, in the Third World or post-communist Europe – registered a loss of press freedom, while two – Kenya and Sierra Leone – managed to climb from the 'not free' category to 'partly free'. A minority of countries in the Asia-Pacific region, Latin America and sub-Saharan Africa enjoy press freedom. In the Middle East and North Africa only one country has a free press, and 90 per cent are classified as 'not free' by Freedom House, the independent organization which monitors trends in liberty throughout the world. Despite democratization in post-communist Europe only 8 countries out of 27 have a free press. In no region of the world do the majority of people enjoy freedom of the press (see Table 2.1). The proportion of the world's population living in countries with free media declined by 5 per cent from 2001 to 2003.

Table 2.1   *Press freedom by region, 2003 – number and percentage of countries in different categories*

Status	Sub-Saharan Africa		Americas		Asia Pacific		Middle East/N. Africa		Post-communist Europe		Western Europe		World	
	No.	%	No.	%	No.	%	No.	%	No.	%	No.	%	No.	%
Free	7	15	17	49	17	44	1	5	8	30	23	92	73	38
Partly Free	17	35	13	37	8	20	1	5	8	30	2	8	49	25
Not Free	24	50	5	14	14	36	17	90	11	40	0	0	71	37
Totals	48		35		39		19		27		25		193	

SOURCE: data from the regional tables in Freedom House (2004).

When the rules providing free and fair elections are violated, both economic and political development are further compromised by the political violence that is likely to ensue unless severely repressed. For example, electoral fraud during the 1983 national presidential and state gubernatorial elections in Nigeria, including large-scale falsification of the electoral register and the count, and the bribery of election officials, not only led voters to boycott elections for the national assembly. It also led to violent protests resulting in the loss of life, the destruction of property and, within three months, a military coup (Diamond, 1988).

Another major violation of the principles of political accountability occurs when the government refuses to accept the result of a properly conducted election. Cases include Burma in 1990, when the ruling military junta refused to hand over power after multi-party elections were won decisively by the main opposition party; and Nigeria in 1993 when the military annulled the results of the presidential election won by Moshood Abiola, who was arrested a year later after declaring himself the country's rightful president. A similar rejection by the military of what appeared to be properly held elections occurred in Algeria in 1991 when the Islamic Salvation Front won twice as many votes as its nearest rival in the first of two ballots. The military cancelled the second round, appointed a High State Council, and embarked on repression of the fundamentalist movement.

Deviations from the norms of freedom and fairness as applied to elections have led to 'electoral authoritarianism' in a number of countries that are supposed to be in transition to democracy. A comparison of regimes in developing and post-communist countries conducted in 2002 revealed that over 38 per cent of regimes were 'electoral autocracies', with another 16.5 per cent classified as 'closed authoritarian', lacking all democratic credentials. The region with the highest proportion of regimes in the electoral authoritarian category – 87.5 – was Central Asia and the Caucasus. Of the 58 regimes of this type the largest number – 26, or 44.8 per cent – were found in sub-Saharan Africa (Schedler, 2002).

Both social and economic development suffer if political accountability is weak. By making corruption more difficult, political accountability contributes to economic development. If accountability empowers the poor, pro-poor policies may be introduced, with their attendant social and economic benefits.

Components of political accountability

The emphasis in aid initiatives on elections and legislatures reflects the two theoretical requirements of political accountability: electoral choice to enforce sanctions on badly performing leadership; and public scrutiny of the executive which makes such choice meaningful. Unfortunately, however, detailed consideration of accountability is sometimes complicated by conceptual ambiguity and confusion with other aspects of the political process which also require decision-makers to answer for their actions or omissions.

For example, the World Bank fails to separate out political accountability from the need to make wrong-doers (public or private) answerable to the courts by identifying the judiciary as the main mechanism for holding public officials accountable (World Bank, 1997: 99–100). Such fusion of accountability with the rule of law loses sight of the political and electoral dimensions of accountability and the mechanisms needed for decision-makers to be replaced in an orderly and legitimate fashion when they perform badly. The essential political connotation of accountability should not be lost. While the rule of law is certainly important for good governance, the concept of political accountability does not mean keeping public officials within the rule of law. It means 'punishing' those of them who are elected for making the wrong decisions, even when made within the law. It means voting elected representatives out of office at the earliest opportunity because of their policy errors, failures to act, or broken promises. Political accountability should not be expanded into the realm of legal violations. Protecting governance against these requires its own specific concepts and remedies, and not conceptual confusion. Accountability should be focused on power rather than legality. While the legal system can prevent the abuse of power, other institutions are required to enforce political accountability.

Accountability under representative democracy combines enforcement with answerability (the latter presuming the requisite information, plus opportunities for the justification of action). *Enforcement* assumes free and fair elections, or occasions when voters can punish leaders or reward the opposition, having reflected on the performance of those to whom they entrusted office at the previous election. The prospect of having soon to go before the voters in competition with other effective parties forces responsiveness and ultimately accountability to the electorate. *Answerability* assumes supporting institutions and practices that provide electorates with information and explanations through the medium of legislative oversight and investigation of executive action.

Political accountability thus raises two fundamental questions in a democracy: are elections effective in holding political leaders accountable? (the enforcement dimension); and is the legislature effective in holding the executive accountable? (the information and justification, or answerability, dimension).

Enforcement

The first dimension of political accountability requires free and fair elections for all rule-making bodies authorized by the constitution. The conditions for free and fair elections extend well beyond what happens on polling days. Other democratic prerequisites have to be present to ensure that 'fairness' means the impartial administration of electoral laws, and 'free' means equal opportunities for the exercise of essential freedoms (Elklit and Svensson, 1997).

Free elections

First, for elections to be free the right to freedom of speech has to be respected. Whether during elections or the intervening periods, citizens should not be harassed and intimidated by those in power when speaking out in favour of the opposition or in criticism of the incumbent govern-ment. Freedom of speech is vital to democracy at all times, and not just during election campaigns, but it is then that it acquires the sadded signif-icance of complementing freedom of association, on which political competition and full accountability depend.

Second, free elections entail freedom of association to form or join a political party without the risk of prosecution because opposition to the government is regarded as treason, or because only one party is licensed under the law, all others being proscribed. The enforcement of political accountability requires electoral choice between competing sets of leaders and policies, implying a two-party or multi-party system offering choice to voters and providing opposition in the legislature. Free elections were thus not possible under the one-party states of the Soviet bloc and many Third World countries in the post-independence period. While some one-party states, for example Tanzania, could with some justification claim that intra-party democracy, and vigorously contested elections by candi-dates from the sole party, could provide a degree of real electoral choice, such instances were rare exceptions to the rule.

The third requirement for free elections is freedom to participate: to register as a voter or a candidate and to campaign on behalf of others. Restrictions must be based on rational grounds, such as age or mental status. They cannot be based on ideological distinctions which discrimi-nate against legitimate opposition. Nor should restrictions on campaign-ing be imposed by the incumbent government.

The universality of the suffrage now usually extends to gender, though there are still some countries that extend the suffrage to women differently from that to men. For example, in Lebanon proof of education is required before women can register as voters. In Kuwait, where only 10 per cent of the population is eligible to vote, the discrimination faced by women in legal and social matters includes being denied the right to vote or run for office. It is also likely that the Shia majority in Iraq will use its power to reduce women's voting rights. A woman's right to vote is also restricted in Brunei, Saudi Arabia, Qatar and the United Arab Emirates .

Free elections also need to be direct, with directly elected legislatures, meaning law-makers are chosen by the people, rather than intermediaries who break the direct line of accountability between voter and elected representative. The indirect system of election, where representatives at one level choose some of their number to serve at another level or on the governing bodies of other organizations, is usually found in either local government (as, for example, in India) or the upper houses of bicameral legislatures (though *appointment* to national legislative positions has frequently been used in the past and is still found in some countries, for example Saudi Arabia).

Deciding between direct or indirect elections is particularly important when it applies to the relationship between the executive branch of government and the electorate. Here the question is whether political accountability is best served by a directly elected president or by a parliamentary form of executive. A strong case can be made for an executive recruited from among parliamentarians, though quantitative comparative analysis is inconclusive (Smith, 2003). A preference for the parliamentary model raises the question of whether all particularistic interests are equally represented in systems where parliamentarians are required to sustain governments. This is highly unlikely within capitalistic states. Nevertheless a parliamentary system, especially if not too fragmented and dependent on difficult coalition-building, may be preferable if hitherto under-represented and marginalized groups, including the poor, are to benefit from public policy-making. But this in turn will depend upon the party system and the presence of pro-poor parties or alliances.

Fair elections

For elections to be fair requires a combination of equally difficult rules and procedures. First, elections should be held at regular intervals so that those currently in office cannot postpone them indefinitely, or choose to hold them only when it suits them politically. There must be constitutional rules preventing incumbents from extending their own terms of office. Second, the media should be given the opportunity to advocate and criticize, and not be overwhelmed by government monopolies of election coverage, as in Russia. Third, elections need to be organized by a professional administration free from partisan manipulation.

Impartiality entails a secret ballot. It must not be possible for the authorities to discover how individuals have voted. Voters should not have to fear the consequences of voting in a particular way, and especially against the incumbents. Providing for absolute secrecy can be difficult, especially in rural areas where officials and voters are closely acquainted, but it should always be possible for sealed ballot boxes to be removed from polling stations, including the smallest, without their contents having been seen by administrative staff. It is thus unusual and very controversial to find a government proposing to move from secret to open voting as happened in India in 2003 when the parliamentary affairs minister announced the government's intention to amend the Representation of the People Act to provide for open polling instead of a ballot in Rajya Sabha elections.

It is equally obvious that the administration of elections must be in the hands of people who are politically impartial. Too often the impartiality of electoral commissions is compromised. Alternatively, election officials come under intolerable pressure to mismanage the process in favour of the incumbents. Electoral officials must be free from the intimidation by the police that occurred in some districts of Albania during the 2001 parliamentary elections, and in Azerbaijan in 1992. Constitutional rules are required to prevent the executive branch abusing its powers to change the management of elections arbitrarily, as happened during the 2001 presidential elections in Belarus. Here the electoral code also failed to ensure a fair representation of political interests on the local electoral commissions, so that 81 per cent of members were closely associated with or dependent on different parts of the state's executive hierarchy.

It should not be possible for ineligible votes to be cast, as they were in Kosovo in 1997 when in some districts voting rolls were inflated with the names of deceased residents and people living abroad. The potential for fraudulent voting was increased throughout Serbia by a failure to number ballot papers and stamp them individually before handing them to voters. All instances of suspected electoral mismanagement and fraud should be subject to appeal before the courts.

Counting the votes is a particularly important stage in the management of elections. The process needs to be open to scrutiny by representatives of those competing for office to ensure that only properly completed and recorded ballot papers are included in the count. Fair elections also require the prompt declaration of results, with laws preventing the incumbent government from delaying or nullifying the results (though democracy is faced with a dilemma when elections are won by movements which reject democratic principles and promise a reversion to some sort of authoritarianism).

Finally, it is necessary to have rules which prevent the gerrymandering of electoral districts, so that electoral boundaries make it impossible for minorities to obtain a fair share of legislative seats. Electoral constituencies must be kept under review in order to take account of population movement, and reorganization should not be delayed to favour a government's party base. Avoiding the appearance of gerrymandering is particularly difficult in local government reorganization involving the merger of local districts. Populations supporting opposition parties fear being merged with larger populations supporting the party of government or ruling coalition, as in the government of Estonia's proposal in 2001 to cut the number of local governments from 247 to 82 (Huang, 2001).

Voters and representatives

Even when the conditions for holding free and fair elections are present there may be aspects of political life and the rules of the game which break the link between the performance of elected representatives, or other political office-holders, and voters. The process of political account-ability can thereby become weakened.

This may happen if elections are perceived as doing no more than conferring legitimacy on political elites. While it is a fundamental tenet of democratic theory that the prospect of having to compete for the elec-torate's support makes rulers accountable to the electorate, it is also evident that elections often serve the interests of elites and the state, rather than the electorate, by legitimizing decision-makers who will never be fully accountable. Rather than holding parties and leaders to account, elections 'incorporate' dissent safely into the system and call the validity of alternative forms of political action into question. Popular participation becomes an infrequent and fleeting engagement, the main aim of which is to educate voters in the concerns of elites. Elections, according to this view, are essentially a top-down process designed to strengthen the power of elites, not their accountability to voters.

Yet legitimizing the power of elites can be part of an exchange between voters and leaders which makes elections a combination of top-down and bottom-up influences. Elite power is exchanged for a degree of respon-siveness. A measure of voter influence is forgone in exchange for dele-gated decision-making authority. And elite power is expanded on the understanding that it will not be abused. Elections also legitimize other aspects of good governance, such as political communities, political equality, freedom of speech and association, and the rights of opposition (Harrop and Miller, 1987).

There is nevertheless evidence of the importance of elections for legit-imizing elites when opposition groups organize boycotts, fearing that participation in elections will confer underserved legitimacy on the antic-ipated winners, the results being the outcome of procedures which are believed to be deeply flawed. Low turnouts, even without an opposition boycott, may reduce the authority of the subsequent government. Boycotts are thus one way of denying winners legitimacy. If the legitimacy of the process is lost, so is the legitimacy of the outcome. For example, in 1997 opposition parties in Jordan boycotted the elections for the House of Representatives because of government restrictions on public assembly and freedom of speech, especially through restraints on the press, 'throwing into question the credibility of the electoral process as well as that of the new parliament itself' (Ryan, 1998: 183). The violent protests which so often follow elections that have been rigged and during which the opposition has been obstructed and repressed similarly reveal a loss of legitimacy.

The liberal principle of representation is further undermined for many people, especially the poor, by social and economic dependency that leads to clientelism. Here dependencies based on traditional forms of reciprocity and economic vulnerability are mixed with modern forms of political behaviour to present the poor with opportunities and constraints in political as well as other transactions. But during elections choice of party and candidate is severely constrained by clientelism, and the link between voter and elected representative is a distant one, with intermediaries determining electoral choices.

Accountability is also diminished if the link between voting and policies is lost. In so far as political accountability is dependent upon the assessment by voters of the policy performance of incumbents and the policy intentions of opponents, there are numerous factors which minimize the significance of policies in the choices made by voters. First, the voter faces formidable problems when trying to evaluate policy options. He or she tends to be interested in ends rather than means and in outcomes rather than policies, and probably does not understand the complex relationships between policy instruments and desired goals.

Electorates may also respond to the images which parties have for them (perhaps comprising the reputation of its leadership and a historical association with their class or ethnic interests) rather than to policies. Many voters are ill-informed about policy issues, finding difficulty in differentiating between parties in terms of policies, and often have policy preferences different from those of the parties they support. They also have to register preferences on a range of policy issues with a single vote, unless referendums can be held on specific policy proposals. This may pass the initiative from elites to the mass of voters, but does not operate as a mechanism for holding office-holders accountable for their stewardship.

Nor can it be assumed that political parties will present full manifestos when contesting elections. For example, despite a strong and stable two-party system, 'published manifestos outlining a coherent set of medium-term policies are not a strong feature of Jamaica's electoral process', creating difficulties for voters when trying to compare party promises with outcomes (Harrigan, 1995: 71). Similarly in Botswana, where there has been little ideological variation between the parties in a one-party-dominant form of government, clear manifestos are rarely presented to the electorate (Healey, 1995a).

New circumstances arising between elections may make it difficult for voters to know whether their initial preferences still reflect their interests. Circumstances beyond the control of government may force it to take decisions that could not be predicted when its party's manifesto was drawn up. A policy on which a party stands for election may prove impossible to carry out after forming a government. This may be because the promises were rash, or because of administrative problems at implementation. A government's policy intentions may be overtaken by events, so that office is lost before they can be carried out. Elected representatives may develop interests of their own, especially, in developing countries, or respond to special interests in exchange for contributions to party funds (Manin *et al.*, 1999).

Not only do the public generally lack time and expertise to monitor the developments of public policies, but also much public business is not on public view. Furthermore, many decisions are made by collectivities, notably legislatures, making it difficult to assign responsibility to individuals or party groups (though the stronger the party discipline and cohesion, the easier such identification becomes, not least because 'defectors' from the party line usually gain publicity). Nor can it be assumed that electorates will always be assisted in their evaluation of politicians' policy choices by effective pressure groups specializing in policy areas, and monitoring government performance on behalf of sectional interests or altruistic causes, even when there is freedom to associate for political purposes and electoral competition between political parties, as in Botswana, Jamaica, Sri Lanka and Zambia (Healey, 1995b).

Consequently voters need to be able to evaluate politicians' behaviour on procedural matters as well as on substantive policy decisions. Their honesty, respect for parliamentary procedure and constitutional rules, and personal conduct all become important aspects of accountability. When it is difficult for voters to monitor and evaluate the policy decisions of office-holders, they may adopt the strategy of trying to select 'good types' rather than sanction poor performance, that is, candidates who are thought to have integrity, competence, and values that coincide with those of the voter (Fearon, 1999). Thus elections have been said to give leaders a mandate to govern rather than a mandate to implement specific policies. A policy mandate requires four conditions that rarely exist simultaneously: clear policy alternatives offered by parties; greater concern among voters with policies than party loyalty or personalities; election results which make the policy preferences of the majority of voters clear; and leaders who keep their campaign promises. In the absence of these conditions elections should be seen as allowing voters 'to influence who shall govern rather than exactly what they should do' (Harrop and Miller, 1987: 256).

In addition, voters may have no say in the choice of candidates, party leaders, or issues for decision, unless they become activists within party organizations, or can participate in primaries or nominating conventions. While politicians may be inclined to implement policies desired by the public if there is a high probability that failure will be exposed, such exposure is difficult to achieve. Furthermore if politicians judge voters to be adopting a 'mandate' view of elections rather than an 'accountability' view (that is, are more interested in what is being promised for the future than in how governments have used their power since the previous election), they have little incentive to ensure policy choices match manifesto promises. This is why the 'answerability' enforced by parliaments is such an important element of political accountability. So if it is difficult for voters to understand complex policy issues, it is equally difficult for them to monitor politicians, including their propensity to implement the promises made in their manifestos (Manin *et al.*, 1999).

The electorate's choices and verdicts may be overridden by external forces, especially in countries dependent upon external financial assistance. For example, in Jamaica structural adjustment and stabilization programmes have been externally imposed. The country has been under pressure to comply with IMF macroeconomic targets since 1978, especially for the reduction of budget deficits. This has led to a convergence of party policies, despite contrasting ideological rhetoric. Consequently,

> political accountability in the wider sense of democratic participation in a transparent process has been sacrificed to a narrower concept of target-based accountability to an external agency ... Both PNP and JLP Governments have found it difficult to reflect election promises in public expenditure allocations. (Harrigan, 1995: 96–7)

As well as enforcing external priorities on reluctant governments and publics, international developmental agencies can also undermine accountability by motivating governments to conceal expenditure, negotiating with governments in secrecy, and upsetting budgetary procedures (for example, by not including aid projects in departmental estimates: Healey, 1995b).

Unequal votes also damage accountability. When designing institutions for political accountability it is important to remember that not all votes count equally. Political practice may assign more power to some groups than to others. Political accountability thus becomes distorted, leaving some groups feeling that parties and governments can afford to be less responsive to their interests.

First, the voting system may be designed to ensure a succession of pro-regime majorities. For example, in Jordan since 1993, of the 80 seats in the House of Representatives 6 are reserved for the rural Bedouin, 9 for the Christian community, and 3 for the Circassian community, in order to bolster support for the ruling elite (Ryan, 1998).

Second, levels of voting (turnout) frequently vary between income groups, educational levels, and age groups, as well as being influenced by marital status, membership of organizations and access to information. However, there is no correlation between a country's wealth and the propensity of its citizens to vote (see Table 2.2). Furthermore, there is evidence to show that distinctions between individual voters (such as their knowledge, wealth, and membership of organizations) have less effect on turnout in legislative elections than do differences between electoral context. 'Context' here refers to the number of elections held during a given period, the proportionality of the electoral system (reducing the number of contests with foregone conclusions and thus wasted votes), whether voting is compulsory, whether elections are held on days of the week that make it easier to find time to vote, and, most importantly, the significance of elections for policy choices. The effect of 'high salience' elections on turnout shows that 'going to the polls is an activity motivated primarily by the desire to affect the course of public policy' (Franklin, 1996: 231), a finding that carries implications for both the design of electoral systems and the relationship between legislative authority and policy outputs which need to be recognized by those providing support for good governance.

Third, the choice of electoral system is important in this context. The first-past-the-post system means that some votes are more valuable than others. Parties accumulate 'unnecessary' votes because of the simple-majority rule. Therefore the party with the smallest number of votes on average needed to win constituencies has a greater proportion of 'effec-

Table 2.2   *Average turnout in free elections to the lower house, 1960–1995 (%)*

Venezuela	85	Netherlands	83
Bulgaria	80	Portugal	79
Brazil	83	Norway	81
Costa Rica	81	United Kingdom	75
Hungary	66	Canada	76
Russia	61	Japan	71
India	58	Switzerland	54
		USA	54

SOURCE: data from Franklin, 1996, Table 8.1, p. 218.

tive' votes. The majority of post-communist countries in Central and Eastern Europe and the former Soviet Union eventually adopted PR for the lower houses, or single chambers, of their legislatures, and the rest have included PR in a mixed system – for example Russia, where half of the deputies in the Duma are chosen by simple majority in single-member districts, and the other half from party lists under PR (Birch *et al.*, 2002). But a surprising number of developing countries use the first-past-the-post system, including Bangladesh, Malawi, Nepal, Pakistan, the Philippines, South Korea, Thailand and Zambia. Fears about wasted votes do not necessarily produce higher levels of turnout under PR than under the simple-majority, or single-member-plurality, system (see Table 2.3), perhaps reflecting the salience of particular elections in the minds of voters.

Table 2.3   *Turnout in legislative elections and electoral systems (%), 1997–2002 – selected countries*

Proportionality	Year	Turnout	Simple majority	Year	Turnout
Colombia	2002	42.4	Bangladesh	2001	74.8
Costa Rica	2002	68.8	Malawi	1999	41.8
Czech Republic	2002	58.0	Pakistan	2002	92.0
Nicaragua	2001	71.1	Philippines	2001	85.0
Slovakia	2002	70.0	South Korea	2000	57.2
Sri Lanka	2000	75.6	Thailand	2000	71.9
Ukraine	2002	69.3	Zambia	2001	70.0

SOURCE: data from www.psephos.adam-carr.net.

Another disadvantage of the simple-majority system and single-member constituencies is that the distribution of legislative seats among the parties is unlikely to reflect the percentage of votes won. The simple-majority system makes it difficult for small parties to gain a representative proportion of seats, allowing a party to become dominant without the support of a majority of the voters. For example, from 1952 to 1971 India's Congress Party won between 54 and 73 per cent of Lok Sabha (lower house) seats with less than a majority of votes – between 40.7 and 47.8 per cent. Depending on the turnout, this could mean that two-thirds of the legislative seats could be won with the support of a quarter of eligible voters, which was not always conducive to stable government or peaceful political life (Rubinoff, 1988). However, the scale of disproportionality in simple-majority systems can vary greatly, as Table 2.4 shows – compare Bangladesh with Pakistan and Malawi, for example.

Among the other consequences of differences in electoral systems of which good governance advocates need to be aware is the likelihood of the number of political parties represented in legislatures increasing as the proportionality of the electoral system is strengthened. One concern is that PR makes it easier for extremist parties to gain legislative seats. Another is that it is not certain that the policy choices of governments will reflect the policy choices of the electorate if legislative seats are won in proportion to the percentages of votes won by political parties, especially since proportional representation might lead to coalition governments that have to produce compromises which no group of voters supports. Another concern is the stability of the party system. In the transitions to democracy of 1985 to 2002 in post-communist Europe the fragmentation of parties encouraged by PR, especially when open lists are used to give voters the option of voting for individual candidates, was a threat to accountability: 'voters cannot "throw the rascals out" if the rascals no longer exist as a unified group' (Birch, 2003: 120).

However, there appears to be no significant difference in the stability of governments formed under PR compared with the simple-plurality system (Farrell, 2001). Indeed, under some circumstances stability may depend upon the inclusive representation of interests in national legislatures, even if this is at the expense of coherent policy programmes. In multi-ethnic societies there is evidence that PR, and especially the alternative-vote and single-transferable-vote varieties, contributes to political stability by encouraging parties to aggregate interests rather than appeal to exclusive ethnic identities, a trend graphically reversed in Papua New Guinea by the replacement of the alternative-vote (AV) system by the simple-plurality

Table 2.4 *Share of votes and legislative seats under the simple majority system, selected countries, 1998–2002*

Country	Party	Votes (%)[1]	Seats (no)	Seats (%)
Malawi	Alliance for Democracy	10.6	29	15.1
1998	Congress	33.8	66	34.4
	United Democratic Front	47.3	93	48.4
	Others	8.3	4	2.1
Bangladesh	Awami League	40.1	63	21.0
2001	Jatiyatabadi Dal	42.7	198	66.0
	Jamaat-e-Islami	4.3	17	5.6
	Jatiya Dal	7.2	14	4.7
	Others	5.6	8	2.7
Nepal	Congress	37.2	111	54.2
1999	National Democratic	10.4	11	5.4
	Communist	31.6	71	34.6
	Goodwill Party	3.2	5	2.4
	National People's Party	1.4	5	2.4
	Others	1.5	2	1.0
Pakistan	People's Party	25.8	71	26.1
2002	Muslim League (Q-e-A)	25.7	69	25.4
	Independents	14.1	21	7.7
	Muttahida M-e-A	11.3	53	19.5
	National Alliance	4.6	12	4.4
	Mohajir Quami	3.1	13	4.8
	Muslim League (Nawaz)	9.4	19	7.0
	Others	5.7	14	5.2
South Korea	Grand National	39.0	133	48.7
2000	Millennium Democratic	35.9	115	42.1
	United Liberal Democratic	9.8	17	6.2
	Independents/Others	15.4	8	3.0
Thailand[2]	Thais Love Thais	40.6	248	49.6
2001	Democratic Party	26.6	128	25.6
	New Aspiration Party	7.0	36	7.2
	National Development Party	6.1	29	5.8
	Thai National Party	5.3	41	8.2
	Others	14.3	18	3.6
Zambia	MMD	27.5	69	46.0
2001	UPND	23.3	49	32.6
	Forum for Dem. And Dev.	15.3	12	8.0
	UNIP	10.4	13	8.7
	Heritage Party	7.4	4	2.7
	Others	14.3	3	2.0

SOURCE: data from www.psephos.adam-carr.net.

NOTES: 1 Excludes invalid votes.

2 The House of Representatives consists of 500 members elected from single-member constituencies and 100 members elected from national party lists on a proportional basis.

system in 1975. There are of course other necessary conditions which must be satisfied before conflict management in plural societies becomes effective and of which electoral engineers should be aware: moderation on the part of a 'core' of leaders and voters; continuity of election rules; and a match between electoral rules and the degree of ethnic fragmentation in electoral districts (Reilly, 2002). A balanced electoral system is arguably the best. Election rules that group legislative seats into 3- or 5-seat constituencies, with candidates selected by open-list PR or the single transferable vote, combine the advantages of single-member constituencies and simple-majority voting with those of PR: few parties, stable cabinets rather than unstable coalitions, links between MPs and their constituents, and fair representation rather than the under-representation of minorities and political interests (Taagepera, 1998).

A further benefit from PR is that it appears to increase the number of women in elected legislatures. For example, India and Malawi, both with plurality systems, have only 8 per cent of MPs who are women, whereas Ecuador and Lithuania have 17 per cent. However, the average representation of women under PR systems is still only 17 per cent, falling to 13.5 per cent on average in non-PR countries, suggesting the need for additional ways to guarantee the representation of designated groups, such as quota rules (Farrell, 2001). For example, it is proposed that 25 per cent of seats in a new Iraqi parliament should be set aside for women.

Even if the accountability function of elections is weak, elections which give meaningful choices to voters and place an opposition group in the legislature serve other important purposes in transitional societies. We have already seen how properly conducted elections can strengthen the legitimacy of governments and regimes. Free and fair elections may also strengthen confidence among foreign investors. It may also be important for people to have opportunities simply to affirm their support for leaders, parties or movements, without reflecting too much on how well power or the rights of opposition have been used. But the non-policy functions of elections, such as the political education of citizens, political stability, and the smooth transition from one government to another, are by no means irrelevant for political accountability. Even if we accept that policy is less the result of electoral choice and more the result of bargaining between governments and organized interests, especially the powerful producer groups of business and labour, this does not preclude voters making a judgement about the intentions of political parties towards the incorporation of such functional representation into the policy-making process.

Answerability

The second dimension of political accountability is answerability. For voters to be able to evaluate the behaviour of politicians, including the wisdom of their policy choices, they need information about the policy process. There must be openness and transparency in the way governments go about their business. Parliamentary democracies in particular proceed on the assumption that the accountability of governments is mediated by the legislatures from which members of the government, including its prime minister, are drawn (Dunn, 1999).

The mass media

This presupposes investigative capacity on the part of the mass media so that individuals and groups can monitor policy choices and their outcomes. Thus the media have an importance that extends well beyond election campaigns. Voters and activists rely on the mass media for much of their information about politics, including not only the decisions of politicians but also the opinions of counter-forces found within civil society, such as trade unions, professional associations, research institutes, pressure groups and community organizations. The public can then expect full accounts and justifications to be given by politicians via the media. A free press is also essential for exposing corruption, the purchase of favours, unwarranted secrecy, abuse of office, and violations of human rights. Answerability depends upon an informed public that can use its voting power when the time comes to punish or reward politicians for their handling of the nation's affairs or the effectiveness of their opposition.

A free press also enables groups of citizens to communicate with each other, enabling political consciousness to be raised and opposition to be organized. It is further recognized as a necessary condition of good policy-making, assisting the free expression of ideas, stimulating proposals for reform, exposing flawed thinking, revealing problems before they reach crisis point, remedying errors, and articulating all sides of a question. A free press is founded on the belief that the possibility of refutation is necessary before the truth of any matter can be known. When subject to rules preventing harm (for example, to national security), press freedom 'is justified by its beneficial effects on the quality of collective decisions' (Holmes, 1990: 33).

Where, as in Botswana, growth in the effectiveness of an independent press in exposing the deficiencies of governments is found, this is regarded as one of the most important political developments in a country's democratic evolution (Healey, 1995a). But press freedom in transitional states is too often restricted by both undemocratic practices and resource constraints. The legal context may contain limits on freedom of expression and information. There are rarely effective pressure groups or professional associations campaigning in support of independent mass media. Resources for the development of the media may be in short supply, leaving this during the consolidation of democracy either in government hands or under the control of economic oligarchs who can be equally intolerant of political opposition (USAID, 1999).

Legislative scrutiny

Answerability also requires legislative institutions which can force members of the executive to explain and justify the use made of the powers entrusted to them by statute. To perform this function of oversight and scrutiny legislatures need to be constituted on the basis of three principles.

The first is that the rights of opposition groups within the legislature are fully respected. In the Czech Republic this has been enshrined in the constitution, art. 6 of which says that 'Minorities shall be protected by the majority in decision-making'. This is not just a question of ensuring that opposition MPs are not terrorized with the violence and intimidation that has come to disfigure Zimbabwean government. (In 2004 a survey by the Zimbabwe Institute, an NGO based in South Africa, found that 90 per cent of opposition MPs had experienced imprisonment, violence or the threat of it. A quarter had survived murder attempts, 42 per cent had been physically assaulted, and 16 per cent had been tortured. Almost half had had their cars or homes vandalized. Three MPs had had members of their staff murdered by the authorities or party militias; see *The Guardian*, 9 March 2004.) It is also a matter of putting in place rules and procedures which recognize the legitimate role of opposition in all legislative business, including holding parliamentary offices, submitting bills and amendments, and questioning ministers.

The importance for accountability of effective opposition within legislatures cannot be exaggerated. To maintain credibility the opposition should not oppose regardless of the merits of the case, nor collude with the government: 'the opposition plays a role in informing voters only when it neither always colludes with nor always contradicts the government' (Manin *et al.*, 1999: 49). However, such a balance is very difficult to achieve, especially if opposition parties feel compelled to put 'clear water' between themselves and the governing parties. In developing countries the opposition in parliament is too often regarded by the government as lacking legitimacy, a view frequently reciprocated in the opposition's attitude towards the government, as in Bangladesh at many points in its post-independence history and especially during 1991–5 when proceedings in parliament were frequently disrupted by opposition boycotts and infringements of the chamber's rules of procedure (Ahmed, 1997).

Second, parliamentary scrutiny of both policy formation and implementation must be effective. This presupposes freedom of information (FOI) to ensure that the actions and decisions of law-makers, especially those relevant to their mandates, are in the open. Accountability is denied by 'state furtiveness' (Dunn, 1999: 239). Many transitional states have FOI laws, such as the Philippines Code of Conduct for State Employees, Thailand's Official Information Act 1997, and South Korea's Act on Disclosure of Information by Public Agencies 1996. At least 12 countries in Asia and 13 in Central and East European have adopted FOI laws, sometimes after significant agitation by NGOs, as in Bulgaria, Romania and Slovakia. In Latin America legislation has been passed in 6 countries and is under consideration in 12 more. South Africa enacted its legislation in 2001 and Ghana, Kenya and Nigeria are likely to follow suit soon (Baniser, 2003).

Third, oversight of the executive branch in support of accountability also requires effective parliamentary scrutiny committees specializing in policy areas (such as trade and industry), government agencies (such as ministries and departments) and processes of accountability (such as audit and budgeting). Such committees need to be supported by professional staff, research capacity, libraries, information technology, and links with policy research institutes. India's Lok Sabha, for example, has a set of specialist committees to monitor the departments of agriculture, communications, defence, energy, external affairs, finance, food, civil supplies, labour and welfare, petroleum and chemicals, railways, and urban and rural development. These collect data, hear testimony, examine legislative proposals, scrutinize budgets and monitor administration (Rubinoff, 1998). In Ghana select committees monitor the expenditure of ministries, departments and agencies to ensure that spending conforms to government plans as approved by parliament (Obimpeh, 2001).

These conditions are easy to specify as norms of political accountability. It is more difficult for them to be applied in practice. Developments in executive–legislative relations have tended to undermine the capacity of assemblies to provide the *answerability* dimension of accountability. Technical assistance in support of good governance needs to be based on an awareness of the impediments to legislative oversight needed for transparency.

Constraints on legislative oversight

First among these are the many sources of executive power which create an imbalance between the powers of executive and legislature. Parliamentary majorities may willingly support the party's leaders in government, even when groups within it disagree with particular policy stances. Dissent may exert little influence. In Nepal, for example, highly centralized party control of the parliamentary candidate selection process enables the executive to manipulate parliament in the interests of the government, weakening parliament's role in the policy process (Subedi, 1998). Elected representatives may even be willing to defect from the opposition to join the majority party in order to further their careers, as in India's Lok Sabha (Rubinoff, 1998).

In parliamentary systems party discipline may extend beyond appeals to party loyalty to the threat of dissolution which could see elected representatives losing their seats. In Kenya, according to one MP, a 'no confidence' motion is in effect a 'suicide motion' (Kombo, 2001: 19). When re-election is more dependent upon constituency concerns than effective engagement with the executive, parliaments are likely to fail to use their formal powers effectively. Support from the opposition against 'extremist' rebellions among its own back-benchers has also been known to help a government in its management of its parliamentary party group. Party discipline within legislatures is also strengthened by the fact that many elected representatives hope for government office rather than a career on the back benches.

Modern executives also tend to control the legislative timetable, including the important power of initiative, whereby policies are formulated by the cabinet with the support of the administration, often after consultation with outside interests of different kinds. In Botswana, for example, national economic planning entails consultation with a number of interest groups such as the business community, trade unions and agriculture, but secrecy surrounds decision-making when the consultations have been completed, and the role of the national assembly is limited to 'rubber stamping' the government's spending proposals (Healey, 1995a: 33).The executive's business tends to dominate the work of legislatures, rather than the questions, motions and proposals of government and opposition back-benchers. The number of policy areas excluded from parliamentary oversight, such as loans negotiated with bilateral and multilateral donors in Kenya, is worrying and may, as in Bulgaria, lead to a loss of confidence among voters in the capabilities of their elected representatives (Centre for the Study of Democracy, 2001). Such shifts towards executive power and away from parliamentary back-benchers and the official opposition have been noted in countries as diverse as Jamaica, Sri Lanka and Zambia, where 'elected representatives have tended increasingly to surrender their power to a centralized political executive which was not reluctant to take it' (Healey, 1995b: 241).

The problem appears to grow under presidential executives. Accountability fails to develop under what has been called 'delegative' democracy. Presidentialism then means largely that presidents govern as they think fit. They claim to be the embodiment of the nation, and custodian and definer of its interests. There is practically no 'vertical' accountability in the sense of answerability and electoral sanctions (O' Donnell, 1994: 60). Many Latin American countries fall into the category of delegative democracies, notably Peru under President Fujimori. But if presidentialism is viewed more widely there may be more scope for scrutiny and accountability when legislatures and executives are separately elected. For example, empirical studies of legislatures in the new democracies of Central and Eastern Europe suggest that 'the independent political activity and influence of legislatures is greater in presidential systems than parliamentary systems' (Olson and Norton, 1996: 7).

The political culture may also inhibit legislative oversight of the executive branch, as in South Korea where the national assembly is constrained by a culture that favours conformity, hierarchy and compliance with leadership, and is not conducive to consensus-building, consent, bargaining and compromise. So despite a good formal structure, there remains strong executive dominance. Furthermore, legislators are members of unstable parties lacking ideological coherence, and pursue constituency representation in an 'excessively particularised and personalistic manner ... They behave as district voters' private guardians rather than as public officials working to fulfill their proper obligation' (Park, 1998: 80).

When it comes to the scrutiny of government business, legislatures find it difficult to perform an effective watchdog role, even when formal procedures are in place. Scrutiny of expenditure to ensure that the budgets approved by parliament are achieving their objectives efficiently and effectively, and that there has been no misappropriation of funds, is central to transparent and accountable government. A number of devices are used to enable government to evade scrutiny. Funds may be established outside the estimates voted by parliament, as in Sri Lanka. Arbitrary political interventions in expenditure decisions following parliamentary approval can occur (as in Jamaica). Limited time may be available for parliamentarians to digest and debate financial and other types of information problems, as in Botswana. Sometimes estimates are not fully presented to parliament, as in Zambia, making it impossible to tell whether there has been effective and legal expenditure. Auditor generals have been hampered by inadequate staffing and information problems. Sometimes precise expenditure priorities are not articulated, and when they are they can have little influence on actual spending decisions. Responses from departments to the reports of auditors and public accounts committees are often inadequate. The formal mechanisms of accountability may be available, but the political will to follow up with sanctions and reforms is often weak, leading to cynicism and alienation (Healey, 1995b).

Efforts are being made to strengthen parliamentary scrutiny committees, but again success is constrained by the maldistribution of power between legislatures and executives. Parliamentary committees have little impact because, as in Bangaldesh, reports and recommendations are not seen as important by the government, parliament itself does not give serious consideration to reports, and committees lack power to enforce their recommendations (Ahmed, 1998). Committee work may be carried out in a partisan atmosphere, rather than on the basis of expertise and independence, thus favouring the majority party and executive, as in South Korea (Park, 1998). In Bulgaria, while parliamentary committees can order ministers and senior civil servants to attend sittings and answer questions, their effectiveness is limited by the government party's majority on each of them (Centre for the Study of Democracy, 2001: 36). Officials supporting committee work, and especially Comptroller and Auditor Generals, need to be independent and not, as in Kenya, an official of the Ministry of Finance.

Elsewhere the emphasis can be on policy-making rather than ensuring the executive branch has used its powers and resources properly. Parliaments in the newly democratized Central and Eastern European states have tended to establish permanent committees to consider the drafts of bills, giving elected representatives an important role in preparing legislation rather than just rubber-stamping government proposals. Accountability is less in evidence as an aim of parliamentary work. However, legislative committees in Bulgaria are empowered to investigate 'legal breaches and abuse in the work of administrative agencies', and some permanent committees in Poland's Sejm hold administrative agencies accountable. Under the constitution of the Slovak Republic the national legislature can establish committees 'for purposes of supervision' and with powers to summon ministers and senior civil servants. Legislative committees can also inquire into the work of administrative agencies and state-owned enterprises (Karasimeonov, 1996; Malova and Sivakova, 1996; Simon, 1996).

The reform of legislatures also has to confront the poor calibre of elected representatives in many new democracies. There are clearly obstacles to stronger accountability when elected representatives can be described as lacking 'knowledge, interest, training, competence, discipline and decorum' (Hardgrave and Kochanek, 1993: 81), or have poor educational qualifications and criminal connections, as in the case of India's Lok Sabha (Rubinoff, 1998: 29). In Nepal, parliamentarians are described as entering politics 'after failing elsewhere or becoming incapable of doing well in education, professional life or business'; as demonstrating 'an appalling lack of understanding of how democracy and state machinery should work'; and as lacking 'high ethical and moral standards' (Subedi, 1998: 175). Legislators in Bangladesh are reportedly more concerned with patronage than accountability, and with using their committee positions to secure personal and financial benefits (Ahmed, 1998). However, 'calibre' can easily become a subjective and highly politicized concept, reflecting biases on the part of the critic in favour of certain types of person with certain ideological leanings.

One dimension of 'calibre' which is considered objectively to be important in the development of legislatures is experience. A low retention rate of MPs is damaging to the viability of legislatures, as in Central and Eastern Europe where the rapid turnover of members 'has significantly disturbed the activities of the new ECE parliaments and has decreased their efficiency' (Agh, 2000: 25).

Impeded access to information about the implementation of government policy is a further obstacle to accountability and transparency. Even where freedom of information legislation has been enacted it has not necessarily had broad coverage and is often easily circumvented by determined officials. For example, India's Freedom of Information Act contains seven broad categories of exemptions and gives civil servants extensive discretion to decide what can be made public. In Pakistan, government officials can decide whether an applicant seeking information is a 'fit' person, and there are no penalties for refusal. Some governments have adopted rules about access which contradict the intentions of the FOI law. In much of the legislation passed in developing countries, exemption clauses and administrative discretion make it relatively simple for officials to withhold information and engage in delaying tactics such as refusing to accept applications, ignoring requests, interpreting the law in perverse ways, seeking court orders to prevent release of documents, or claiming that the papers being sought are needed for other purposes such as audits or committees of inquiry. Internal appeal mechanisms are often used as a delaying tactic. Fees may be set high to deter applications. In some countries, such as Zimbabwe and Serbia, freedom of information laws are designed to restrict the flow of public information. The concept of 'national security' is often extended to prevent access to information which has nothing to do with protecting the state. As globalization shifts more decisions to international bodies, more become subject to the secrecy of the diplomatic system (Krishnan, 2001; Baniser, 2003).

The context of reform

The reform of processes for political accountability is deeply vulnerable to political setbacks. Many countries that have managed to escape from complete authoritarianism are stuck in a 'grey zone' of façade, pseudo- or virtual democracy, with political elites that are corrupt, self-serving and ineffective. The distinction between the state and ruling party is blurred (Carothers, 2002). This makes an understanding of the political context vitally important if governance programmes and projects initiated by the international development community are to be effective.

The political setting of governance reforms includes political cultures of deference and hierarchy which, as we have seen, militate against freedom of speech, freedom of association, and the autonomy of parliamentarians. Autocratic and personalistic political traditions provide infertile ground for the growth of accountability. Religious persuasion may contradict Western concepts of equality as embodied in the principle of universal suffrage. Ethnic or religious hostilities and rivalries may undermine the fairness of electoral systems through gerrymandering by dominant political elites. Such antipathies can affect the way voters and activists align themselves with leaders and parties so that there is no room for compromise, and politics is seen as a zero-sum game with some particularly vicious consequences for losers. This is the case in societies where the most effective political appeals are to primordial distinctions such as ethnicity, or where cross-cutting identities such as class are weak.

Economic dependency and clientelism may undermine freedom of political association, indicating that governance reforms not only encounter widely differing economic circumstances, but also face long time periods during which the political and economic setting is hostile to them. The development of the campaigning dimension of civil society, also important for securing the foundations for political accountability, may also have to await economic developments that take time to materialize.

The variability of such contexts makes it doubly complex when attempting to choose between political institutions for accountability whose outcomes are less predictable, such as parliamentary and presidential executives, or alternative electoral systems. It also prompts the conclusion that political environments are unique, making it fallacious to assume that there are universal solutions that can be applied with the support of the donor community.

Conclusion

The essential components of political accountability are electoral choice and public scrutiny of the executive. Elections must be effective in holding political leaders accountable, and legislatures must be effective in holding the executive accountable. The enforcement dimension of political accountability requires free and fair elections. The answerability dimension requires voters to be able to evaluate the behaviour of politicians. For this they need information about the policy process. Government must be open and transparent. Parliamentary democracies assume that accountability is mediated by legislatures.

Reviews of donor programmes and projects to strengthen accountability have provided some clear lessons. First, donors need to be well informed about the social and political context in which reforms are being proposed. For example, the incentives which parliamentarians have to scrutinize the executive will be affected by the party system. If the party organization has a strong role in the selection (and deselection) of candidates, members of parties elected to the legislature might find it very costly to subject the leadership to scrutiny. Levels of control by the party leadership over the careers of congressmen and MPs will also affect backbench behaviour. Another influence is whether the government is single-party or coalition, the latter providing more opportunities for independent action.

Second, stand-alone reforms, especially of legislatures, are less likely to be successful than ones which are integrated into attempts to strengthen other institutions and processes, particularly the legal system, political participation, political parties, civil society and poverty reduction. There are clearly institutional changes that are needed wherever political accountability is sought within a context of democratization. Constitutions should not confer overwhelming powers on the political executive, including empowering presidents to make policy by decree or extend the terms of their office unilaterally. A competitive party system is needed to give voters a meaningful choice. An independent electoral commission is an indispensable means of ensuring free and fair elections. Universal suffrage is the only way to provide all sections of the community with equal rights to hold governments to account. The media need to be free from state control. Effective freedom of information laws are required if the executive branch is not to conceal wrongdoings, whether they be corruption, incompetence, waste, or maladministration, by secrecy or mendacity. Legislatures everywhere require effective committee systems to give specialized and expert attention to individual areas of public policy.

The spread of sustainable institutions for political accountability requires improvements in other spheres of governance, especially human rights and the rule of law, vital constitutional conditions supportive of political accountability through representative government. Free and fair elections together with legislative oversight of the executive need above all a criminal law and its agents to ensure that violations of legal rules by politicians and public officials are detected, prosecuted and punished, even though this will not be enough to constrain behaviour which, though legal, is stupid, cowardly and mendacious (Dunn, 1999). If citizens are to engage effectively in political activities, the state must recognize their political rights. These are among the essential human rights which are the subject of the following chapter.

3

Human Rights

Rights and claims

Human rights are claims to entitlements that are held to be morally defensible regardless of the law in any particular sovereign state. They are often thought to be universal – that is, defensible for all people everywhere, regardless of local cultural and historical circumstances. Rights are claims for action or inaction against institutions capable of meeting such claims. They are extensively claims against the state which has the power to prevent violations of human rights by its own agencies or other powerful social and economic institutions, such as organized religion or industrial corporations. Rights claim that others should act in a particular way, or refrain from acting in ways which restrict the enjoyment of what is claimed, such as freedom of speech. Rights logically imply duties, again normally on the part of states or their governments. They are part of a relationship governed by moral rules (Plamenatz, 1968). Historically human rights have always constituted a challenge to the prevailing political order, nationally or (increasingly today) globally.

Rights can be broadly classified as negative and positive. Negative rights are the civil and political rights which imply a duty of restraint on the part of others (rights to life, liberty, freedom of speech and association, freedom from slavery and torture, equality before the law, freedom of thought and religion, or to a fair trial). It is somewhat misleading to refer to such rights as negative when in fact they empower people to participate in politics (the right to vote) or free them to enjoy fundamental aspects of their lives without restraint (such as religious observance). But they might be thought to be negative in that they restrain others, and particularly the state, from restricting actions in morally unjustifiable ways. Civil and political rights create negative obligations (a duty to leave alone).

Identifying such rights as 'negative' enables them to be distinguished from *positive* economic, social and cultural rights, and even a right to development, which imply a duty to act (for example, to provide work, fair pay, a minimum wage, or social security). Cultural rights are the collective claims of national and ethnic minorities, or indigenous peoples, to self-determination; or of sections of society seeking protection from discrimination to ensure equal citizenship (for example, women, gays, the disabled, or, again, ethnic minorities). The latter groups *should* in theory be protected by the enjoyment of individual human rights, but the former present special problems arising from cultural and political distinctiveness.

This gives a flavour of the sorts of claims which are made when people claim their rights, or act politically to protect the rights of those too vulnerable to provide adequate self-protection. According to a number of writers, whatever their philosophical status, universal human rights are now uncontroversial, a 'fact of the world', hegemonic, 'global by fiat', and the express will of the international community, so that theoretical debate is pointless, unhelpful, redundant and even disruptive (for instances see Chandler, 2002: 12). This aggressive optimism is admirable, but ignores the fact that theoretical problems, such as the extension of the language of rights to economic, social and cultural policies, have serious implications for the way human rights flourish or perish in contemporary societies.

Rights and development

Since the international development community bases its support for human rights on the belief that rights are fundamental to development, both human and economic, international concern for rights is not difficult to understand. Despite every nation-state in the world having ratified at least one of the many human rights declarations, conventions and charters, widespread acceptance of human rights principles has been characterized more by their violation than their observance. For example, it has been estimated that since the UN Declaration, governments have murdered over 45 million of their citizens. According to Amnesty International, 123 of the 185 sovereign states were found to be *routinely* practising torture at the end of the twentieth century (Dunne and Wheeler, 1999; Freeman, 2002).

In 1999 a global opinion poll of 57,000 people in 60 different countries found widespread concern that human rights were not being respected as much as they should be. In many countries people reported extreme abuse and discrimination as commonplace. The protection of human rights was seen as the most important role for the United Nations in the new millennium (Gallup International, 2004).

Daily violations of civil and political liberties are found across sub-Saharan Africa. Human rights groups are often at risk, with advocacy restricted or banned. Of particular concern is systemic discrimination and violence against women, including rape and harmful traditional practices. In Asia the so-called 'war against terrorism' has provided excuses for governments to reverse some of the gains made in respect for human rights during the 1990s. Civil liberties have been limited, including freedom of expression and association. Governments have taken increased powers of surveillance, have modified trial procedures, and have extended preventive detention. Human rights activists have been increasingly marginalized and harassed, especially in Indonesia, Malaysia, Pakistan and the Philippines. Departures from agreed human rights principles are extensive within the Middle East and North Africa. Freedom of speech and association are commonly restricted. The judicial process is often deeply flawed. Women face systematic discrimination in personal status, freedom of movement, family law and criminal law, under which little legal redress is available for victims of domestic violence, including so-called 'honour' crimes.

The human rights situation in Latin America is generally less worrying. The commonest problems occur in the field of employment, including frequent violations of labour rights, the use of child labour, discrimination, and restrictions on freedom to associate in trade unions. Serious human rights problems persist in some of the post-communist states of Eastern Europe and Central Asia. Arbitrary arrest, illegal detentions and deportations disfigure Georgia's transition to democracy. In Kazakhstan, Belarus and Kyrgyzstan political freedoms are curtailed by the harassment and detention, often without fair trial, of opposition leaders, journalists and human rights activists. Uzbekistan violates human rights on a massive scale.

Regrettably there is considerable confusion within the international community about the relationship between rights and development, with at least three distinct views on offer: that development, and especially human development, *includes* the enjoyment of one's human rights; that development will *enable* rights to be enjoyed; and that recognition of rights is a *means* of bringing about development. In its desire to link human rights to human development the United Nations Development

Programme has adopted all three positions. It defines human development as the enjoyment of rights. Human development means improving human well-being, which 'includes living with substantial freedoms' including the right to participate in political decision-making. At the same time human rights enable people to improve their well-being because 'those who hold power have political incentives to respond to acute deprivations when the deprived can make use of their political freedom to protest, criticize and oppose'. In addition, the realization of human rights, especially economic and social ones, depends on appropriate conditions: 'When a country is very poor, it may not be capable of achieving the fulfilment of every right that is judged important' (UNDP, 2000a: 19–21).

The relationship between human rights and economic development is also ambiguous. For some, violations of human rights prevent sustainable development, a view expressed by the 1989 International Conference on the Relationship between Disarmament and Development which reported that: 'Gross and systematic violations of human rights retard genuine socio-economic development.' However, for others, including the World Bank, human rights are the *consequence* of economic development: 'creating the conditions for the attainment of human rights is a central and irreducible goal of development' (World Bank, 1998: 2). This is an understandable point of view, given that the Bank's articles of agreement allow only economic considerations to inform its decisions. While a proper human rights regime needs enlightened legislation and a vigorous civil society (that is, political rather than economic factors), it also requires the right economic conditions and institutional development. For example, laws designed to end child labour will be more effective in economic conditions that provide families with decent incomes. Thus all the things the World Bank can promote – primary education, health care, sanitation, housing, accountable and transparent governance, and effective judiciaries – are part of an environment 'in which people are better able to pursue a broader range of human rights' (World Bank, 1998: 3). The advancement of human rights is seen as particularly important for the world's poorest people, for without rights they are unlikely to escape poverty.

International support for human rights

Support takes two main forms: the enforcement of international agreements, and aid. International relations have become populated with many institutions which seek in varying ways to enforce the agreements into which states have entered. If it is true that there is in some sense a realm of international governance, then human rights are a very important part of the international policy agenda. State sovereignty is expected to concede priority to international human rights standards, and sovereign states have, since the Second World War, created numerous institutions, in the form of rules and organizations, to monitor their own actions and adjudicate on accusations of human rights violations. There is now an international law of human rights to which states formally subscribe, formulated by the UN and regional groupings. It offers human rights activists a foundation for their claims against nation-states (Donnelly, 1989; Baehr, 1999; Forsythe, 2000).

The main global institutions function under the auspices of the UN, and include the Human Rights Commission, the International Labour Organization, and the Office of the High Commissioner for Refugees. Committees have also been set up by specific treaties, such as the Human Rights Committee and the Committee on Economic, Social and Cultural Rights. Regional organizations include the African Human Rights Commission set up by the 1981 Charter on Human and Peoples' Rights.

The global and regional institutions for protecting and enforcing human rights fall into two broad categories. 'Soft' forms of implementation operate through inquiry, monitoring, fact-finding and exposure. Various UN agencies have power under human rights treaties to monitor reports by governments on how far they have complied with the requirements of those treaties (Story, 1995). The Office of the High Commissioner for Human Rights monitors human rights and provides technical assistance and advisory services to member states. Its formal responsibility is to promote universal human rights and ensure the coordination of all UN efforts. This way of protecting human rights has been dubbed the 'mobilization of shame'.

Examples of monitoring include the documentation by the UN High Commission for Human Rights of abuses by all involved in the civil war in Colombia. The Council of Europe's Committee for the Prevention of Torture has helped identify what progress Turkey needs to make if it is to be admitted to the European Union. The Inter-American Commission on Human Rights issues recommendations to Latin American governments regarding specific human rights cases, including the problems faced by AIDS victims. The United Nations maintains human rights offices in a number of countries, including Guatemala and Colombia. The EU, through its association agreements with Israel, Jordan, Morocco and Tunisia, has opportunities to raise human rights problems within individual states.

'Hard', or coercive, measures include non-recognition, aid conditionalities, economic sanctions, conflict resolution, prosecutions, peace-keeping missions, and military intervention in defence of human rights under the UN Charter (Hurrell, 1999: 282–4). 'Safe havens' for Kurds and Marsh Arabs were created by military intervention in Iraq. International military action was undertaken against Serbia for its repression of Kosovo. UN protectorates have been established in Kosovo and East Timor, and an international administration has been placed in Bosnia (Chandler, 2002).

Stronger forms of enforcement have developed in response to humanitarian crises and crimes against humanity. War crimes tribunals have been set up in The Hague and Arusha, Tanzania, to prosecute those accused of crimes against humanity in the former Yugoslavia and Rwanda respectively. Regional institutions include the European Court on Human Rights, the African Human Rights Court set up in 1998, and the Inter-American Court of Human Rights which in 2002 ordered Venezuela to pay compensation of over US$1.5 million to relatives of 37 people killed by security forces during a revolt in 1989.

Material support for human rights, and sanctions against violations, are part of many aid programmes. Canada, Denmark, the Netherlands and Norway have made improvements in human rights an explicit aim of their aid policies. Since 1990 the European Union has linked human rights to development aid policies. The UK government links human rights to poverty reduction within its aid programme. The Nordic and Dutch donors have tended to support economic and social rights, whereas the USA has consistently opposed the idea of social and economic rights, emphasizing civil and political rights in its aid programme. Since 1990 aid donors have tended generally to give priority to civil and political rights rather than to welfare-related rights (Stokke, 1995). All of this, however, still leaves human rights 'at the margins of development aid', the bulk of which is devoted to economic and social projects and programmes (Tomasevski, 1993: 3).

The scope of human rights

The concept of a human right is highly complex and controversial. The two most serious controversies are examined in this chapter: the *scope* of human rights, and the controversy over whether it is helpful or damaging to human rights claims to extend them from civil and political rights to the economic, social, collective and developmental spheres; and the *univer-*

sality of human rights, and the controversy over whether certain cultural imperatives override human rights in the political life of citizens.

Social and economic rights

The presence of social, economic and cultural rights within the 1948 Universal Declaration of Human Rights and many of the conventions that have followed it now appears to be regarded as uncontroversial. In addition to political and civil rights the Universal Declaration asserts the right of everyone to economic, social and cultural rights including social security, work, equal pay, 'just and favourable' remuneration, periodic holidays with pay, education, and a standard of living providing health and well-being. Other documents emphasizing that economic, social and cultural rights are no less important than civil and political rights include the International Covenant on Economic, Social and Cultural Rights of 1966. The 1986 Declaration on the Right to Development refers to rights to development, self-determination (including full sovereignty over natural resources), a fair distribution of income, and 'equality of opportunity' in access to basic resources, education, health services, food, housing, and employment. The Vienna Declaration and Programme of Action of 1993 includes the rights to self-determination, the benefits of scientific progress and its applications, medical care, housing and social services. This declaration emphasized social, economic and cultural rights, paying limited attention to civil and political rights, arguably representing a victory for authoritarian regimes, as well as making it more difficult to build a global consensus on human rights and respect for international law (Amstutz, 1999).

As the things we claim a right to increase in number, the risk of the concept losing its distinctive content grows. Social and economic rights represent a process of turning every want, need, desire or demand into a 'right'. They shift rights from being protection against the incursions of others (sometimes referred to as 'rights of forbearance') towards being policies for the provision of goods claimed as necessary for people to achieve some desired end. Social and economic demands and aims, however justifiable and desirable, are inevitably in competition with demands from other sections of society with conflicting interests. In democracies, the outcomes of such conflicts require negotiations and compromises. Rights, on the other hand, are non-negotiable and inalienable. An ideal is something to aim at; a right is something that can and must be respected now.

Other objections to social and economic 'rights' arise from the moral implications of practicability. Something that is impossible to achieve, such as holidays with pay for everyone in the world, or social security, which requires more wealth than most countries have, cannot reasonably be claimed as a right or duty (Cranston, 1967). Civil and political rights, on the other hand, incur no costs and require no particular level of economic development. A responsible agency may not have the capacity to fulfil its obligations, yet in ethics 'ought' entails 'can'. Many countries have used financial constraints to excuse human rights deficiencies, for example being unable to afford full access to free primary education. It is difficult to know how the necessary resources for universal access to health care, for example, can be afforded by many countries. If governments are expected to acknowledge their responsibilities to take on the burden, this can amount to turning themselves into violators if they do not have the necessary resources, or the freedom to balance such demands with others. Equally, states should not be allowed to defer rights until resources are available.

The view that practicability excludes social and economic claims from the status of 'rights' has been challenged by questioning whether it is true that poor countries are totally unable to provide assistance to the needy. Governments can be said to have a duty to do what they can (especially when art. 22 of the UN Declaration refers to rights being provided 'in accordance with the organisation and resources of each state'). It has even been argued that there are sufficient resources and technical knowledge in the world to provide everyone with basic rights (Beetham, 1995). Alternatively, economic and social rights could be classed as 'weaker' universal rights, and held against a specific group, such as members of one's own state (just as political participation refers to the governance of one's own state). This is like the French distinction between the 'rights of man' and the 'rights of the citizen' (Raphael, 1967).

It has further been pointed out that political and civil rights are not without their costs. Like social and economic rights, they too need *positive* actions on the part of the state to secure them. For example, the right to vote needs extensive provision by governments, as do the rights to equality and a fair trial (Evans, 1997). Similarly, before any international obligations under human rights treaties, covenants and declarations can be honoured there have to be sufficient lawyers to draft laws and provide legal assistance to the population. 'Negative' rights require more than forbearance on the part of others, including arrangements and interventions by the state to protect rights to life and liberty, for example (Shue,

1996). So a positive right to health, for example, is no different from negative rights, combining as it does freedoms (from actions likely to harm
health, such as industrial pollution) and entitlements such as 'a set of
social arrangements – norms, institutions, laws, an enabling economic
environment' which it is the obligation of governments to provide, including access to health services (UNDP, 1998: 73; Evans, 2002). As regards
affordability, 'a right to health does not require granting universal access
to the latest technological and scientific resources for health, but rather a
minimum that provides the basis for leading a dignified life' (Evans,
2002: 216).

However, while it may be true that political and civil rights also need
resources to sustain them, and therefore the expenditure of public funds,
it is not as difficult to raise revenues for these as it is for social and
economic rights. Compare the cost of protecting freedom of association
(practically zero) with the cost of even primary education for all. In fact
'negative' rights, or rights of forbearance, are where democracies make
savings compared with autocracies which spend hugely on organs of
repression. There are also political difficulties with many social and
economic rights: 'the correlative duties lie with governments and through
them with the rich and powerful' (Barry, 2000: 15).

References to the minimum intervention needed for a dignified life
leave open the question of what this dignified condition is and thus what
scale and type of intervention is required from governments. Also to be
queried is the assumption that all governments in low- or even middle-
income countries, even when the political will is present, are in a position
to prevent the harm caused to health and other social conditions by powerful external forces. These include structural adjustment programmes
enforced by the IMF and requiring budget cuts which regularly fall
disproportionately on social service expenditure; and multi-national
corporations whose investments are desperately needed and must be
attracted, often with low levels of taxation, further undermining the state's
capacity to provide for economic and social rights.

It is also unsatisfactory to defend economic and social rights by allowing states to avoid their obligations (see for example Hausermann, 1998:
63–4), though this is indeed provided for in some international agreements. For example, even in the Covenant on Economic, Social and
Cultural Rights, the only obligations on states are to 'take measures
towards the progressive achievement' of such rights and to provide for
them 'to the maximum of available resources', both of which allow
governments maximum scope for non-action. Nor is it convincing to

defend 'positive' rights against concerns about their cost by arguing that delays in implementing them are acceptable for developing countries because developed countries had to wait a long time before rights were recognized. This begs the question under debate of whether there are such rights, and ignores the fact that civil and political rights are not dependent on levels of development, economic growth or state budgetary capacity.

Doubts can further be raised about economic rights because they are inevitably culturally distinct (such as a claim to a certain standard of living). Since no universal standard can be achieved, economic rights cannot be fundamental and universal (Evans, 1997). Against this it might be argued that without an economic right to at least subsistence, no other rights can be enjoyed (though it could be said that this is covered by the right to life). Beetham argues that everyone ought to be guaranteed the basic means of sustaining life, that those denied these are the victims of a fundamental injustice, and that human rights claims are the best way of approaching the problem. The most general preconditions for exercising 'a reflective moral and purposive human agency' (a capacity for reflective moral judgement; being able to determine the 'good' for one's life, individually and in association with others; and choosing goals and seeking to realize them) include physical integrity or security, the material means of existence, the development of capacities, and also the enjoyment of basic liberties (Beetham, 1995).

Since rights imply correlative duties, it is necessary to be able to identify the duty-holder. Duties are more obvious in the case of 'negative' rights where the duty is not to take actions that infringe the rights of other citizens. But who are the duty holders of economic and social rights? Can anyone (especially states) be said to have a 'positive' duty to provide for those in need as well as a negative duty to refrain from harming them?

One answer is that the wealthy have a duty to ensure the subsistence of the poor (Evans, 1997). Unfortunately there is little evidence of the acceptance of this duty. It will be very difficult politically to bring about the redistribution that would be required to realize rights to basic health care, free education, and food security, for example, especially when developments in the international community since 1980 have redistributed wealth from the poor to the wealthy within and between countries.

It might be thought that the state has a duty to recognize economic and social rights because communities have a duty to meet needs (for example, of children) when those with whom the duty normally resides (the parents) cannot perform it (such as in the case of orphans). This does not run into the problem of assigning a potentially *limitless* duty to the community (only to children in need) or of *non-assignability* because it is possible to specify who should take responsibility (the child's community). After all, 'a publicly acknowledged duty so to aid those in need, with whom we stand in no special relationship, forms one of the principles of the modern welfare state' (Beetham, 1995: 53). And it is widely accepted that states have a duty to support international actions and organizations in support of those in need where national resources prove insufficient (for example through aid).

Beetham admits that politically such an assignment of responsibility looks doubtful, given both domestic and global distributions of power. But it may be that those with power can be persuaded that it is in their interests to help those in need, or that duty and self-interest converge. This might be the 'insurance principle', when the insecurity that is commonplace for the poor penetrates other social strata or classes. Or a 'boomerang effect' might be felt – that is, fear that the ills of the poor will rebound on the wealthy (for example, when unemployment leads to crime, or neglect of education retards economic development and therefore general welfare).

Finally, there is the question of justiciability, or the capability of rights to trigger legal redress. A criticism of the concept of economic and social rights is that they are not justiciable, whereas civil and political rights are. It is very difficult to specify the level below which a right is denied and a case for redress could be made. Can statistics on infant mortality, life expectancy, school enrolments, and other 'basic needs' with which development planners often work, provide evidence of rights denials?

Collective rights

Including claims to cultural rights raises the question of whether such collectivities as ethnic and national minorities, religions and indigenous peoples have rights which are held by the group rather than the individuals who comprise them. The Declaration on the Rights of Persons Belonging to National or Ethnic, Religious and Linguistic Minorities, adopted by the UN General Assembly in 1992, makes it the responsibility of states to protect the existence and identity of such minorities within their territories. Persons belonging to minorities are held to have the right to enjoy their own culture, to profess and practice their own religion, and to use their own language, in private and in public, freely and without interference or any form of discrimination. They also have the right to participate effectively in cultural, religious, social, economic and public life, including decision-making at the national level as well as in their minority regions. Other rights conferred on minorities include the right to establish and maintain their own associations and contacts with other members of their group and with persons belonging to other minorities, as well as contacts across frontiers with citizens of other states to whom they are related by national or ethnic, religious or linguistic ties. States are obliged to ensure that persons belonging to minorities can exercise their human rights and fundamental freedoms without any discrimination and in full equality before the law, as well as create favourable conditions, for example through education programmes, for a minority to develop its culture, language, religion, traditions and customs. These rights are not supposed to prejudice the enjoyment by all persons of universally recognized human rights and fundamental freedoms, or the principle of equality contained in the Universal Declaration of Human Rights.

A great deal of effort has been put into attempts to demonstrate that collective rights are different from individual civil and political rights, and that the enforcement of individual rights still leaves minorities vulnerable to unjust discrimination. Ethnic communities have been described as 'right-and-duty-bearing units', and as corporate bodies to which moral rights should be accorded. Some of the rights of members of such groups are the familiar individual rights of liberal democracies, but others are 'aboriginal' or 'intrinsic' to the group. It is claimed that group rights can be distinguished from group interests, such as those of occupations or socio-economic classes (van Dyke, 1995). Collective rights (for example, of a minority to enjoy its distinctive culture, use its own language or practise its own religion) extend the concept of rights from individuals, implying the equality of all citizens, to collectivities, implying a differential treatment of groups (Freeman, 2002).

In attempting to justify the claim that collectivites have rights it has been argued that, if human rights are based on human interests (for example in life, liberty and security), and some human interests are interests in collective goods (such as self-determination rather than colonial status), then collectivities and only collectivities can be the holders of rights to collective goods. Furthermore, collective rights may be the precondition of individual human rights (for example, by removing external oppression). And the fact that some collectivities have their rights recognized in practice is also offered as further proof of the existence of collective rights. Examples include proportional ethnic representation in some ethnically divided societies, constitutional provisions of devolution to regions in which national minorities are regional majorities, the emergence of new states (such as those created by the break-up of the former Soviet Union and Yugoslavia), separate educational systems and property rights, affirmative action policies, and quotas in legislative assemblies (van Dyke, 1995).

Yet collective rights are far from being as uncontroversial as they seem. One objection is that 'the logical and practical relations between these collective claims and individual human rights is uncertain ... the conceptual character of these rights is unclear' (Freeman, 1995: 25, 28). One reason for this is that reference is sometimes made when asserting the existence of collective rights to the rights of 'persons' belonging to groups and minorities. For example, when the right to self-determination is claimed in the abstract as a universal right, the 'peoples' to whom the right is supposed to attach are not defined. Another example is the right to freedom from genocide. It has not been demonstrated in what respect a violation of a collective right would take a form different to that of a violation of an individual human right. So, for example, it is not clear what aspect of religious or linguistic discrimination is not covered by individual civil rights.

As with social and economic rights, collective rights look like demands to enjoy advantages that other citizens do not enjoy (such as subsidies for education or devolved political institutions), or to be exempt from laws by which other groups have to abide, such as laws governing the use of land. Collective rights are reducible either to individual rights or to public policies sought by groups of people defined by ethnicity rather than by characteristics that give rise to sectional interests, such as income, age or occupation. Group *interests* in such things as language policies, quotas and affirmative action provide a better explanation of them than group *rights*. This then allows cultural attributes to be judged on their merits rather than being assumed to have moral worth simply because of their existence.

It is also important to recognize that some communities have cultures that restrict and violate individual human rights. If judgement is disallowed, one community is required to stand silently by as another discriminates against women, forces young people into marriages against their will, withholds children from education, discriminates against non-members of the group who have historically strayed across its borders, mutilates young girls, or performs 'honour' killings on members of the group and people from other cultural communities deemed to have violated crucial parts of the cultural code. If individual rights are suspended in favour of group or cultural rights, a false inequality is introduced which favours the rights of some individuals over others (Freeman, 1995; Hartney, 1995).

The histories of post-colonial and post-communist states warn us that self-determination is far from being a guarantee that people's rights will be respected. It is true that minorities frequently suffer discrimination. This can lead to a demand for secession which is then met by state repression. Human rights violations then worsen. But there can be no confidence that the disintegration of ethnically plural societies will protect the rights of people in the constituent parts, especially minorities. Nationalism is by no means necessarily supportive of human rights. This can be seen among the republics of the former USSR that have seceded in the name of self-determination. For example, 'Ossetians in Moldova and Georgia have simply seen new ethnic oppressors replace the old' (Donnelly, 1993: 153). There is discrimination against Serbs in the new Croatia and against Hungarians in the new Slovakia (Buchanan, 1995).

Attempts to solve such problems with a 'right' to self-determination risks fragmentation, instability and harm to the majority community. It is highly destabilizing for states to be confronted with demands affecting territory and boundaries which they are not free to manage themselves (Anaya, 1995). The needs of minority groups for self-determination are better satisfied by political processes through which solutions can be negotiated between all sections of society. Again, universal civil and political rights guarantee equal representation of interests in this process. It is where individual human rights are most respected that minority demands for a measure of self-determination are most likely to be managed politically in ways acceptable to both majority and minority communities, even when compromises have to be made.

It is thus likely that the interests of minority groups are better served by the vigorous enforcement of individual human rights that empower people to benefit equally from economic opportunities and to participate equally in political processes. This is especially pertinent if the idea of the ethnic group as homogenous in all respects is abandoned. Founding a notion of group rights on concepts such as the consent of the group to self-determination or the preservation of a distinctive identity runs up against the obvious diversity of such 'corporate' communities, not only in terms of gender, age and occupation, but also in terms of characteristics which are relevant to political power, such as wealth, income, social status, class, kinship connections and educational status. Even self-determination, or 'national liberation', may be viewed with different levels of enthusiasm by different sub-sectors of the community assumed to be giving its support.

The fact that minority *areas* are hardly ever totally homogenous ethnically raises another problem: to whom are collective rights attached – all those living within the special historically and culturally defined area, or only members of the major ethnic group? And if the right pertains to all within the area of the minority group, on what grounds are those living beyond the area excluded? The theory of collective rights fails to make clear what it is that entitles a minority to some exclusive benefit, as in the case of the 'right' to natural resources found within the territory of a culturally distinct group.

Minority interests are protected indirectly through individual rights, such as the right to freedom of worship in the case of religious minorities. Distinctive cultural attributes can be enjoyed privately (such as wedding ceremonies) or used as a basis for political mobilization (for better housing, bilingual education, or land reform, for example). All the state is obliged to recognize are individual human rights. Even the right to self-preservation, claimed for some indigenous groups such as Native Canadians, is reducible to the individual's right to life and liberty (Johnston, 1995; Waltzer, 1995).

A further objection to collective rights is that their value is reducible to the value of what they contribute to the lives of their individual members. If a collectivity is given the right to be different, its choices can only be judged by their effect on the interests of individuals. So-called collective rights to human well-being are thus contingent on what use is made of the powers they bestow. Consequently 'there are no unconditional rights, in other words no universal collective rights' (Barry, 2000: 18).

The question of whether people's interests are best served by universal human rights or specific collective rights is raised again by the claim that particular non-culturally related social groups have rights, such as children, disabled people, refugees, migrant workers, and women. Upon closer examination it appears that the concerns of such treaties as the Convention on the Rights of the Child are that governments should adopt policies which protect vulnerable groups – in the case of children by reducing infant mortality, raising literacy and nutritional levels, expanding access to safe water and education, and outlawing child labour. Discrimination against women would similarly be ended by their full and equal enjoyment of all individual human rights. 'Women's rights' turn out to be the duty of governments to ensure that the conditions for such equality exists – by legislating effectively against sexual harassment, violence against women, political exclusion, and discrimination in the workplace and the legal system, for example. Such legislation, where needed, makes it possible for women to enjoy their human rights as humans rather than as women.

A right to development

The extension of rights to include a right to development virtually reduces the rights discourse to empty rhetoric. The idea was promoted by less-developed countries in the early 1970s, and was eventually adopted by the UN in 1986 with the Declaration on the Right to Development, which claims that development itself is a right, whose realization 'involves the full observance of economic, social, cultural, civil and political rights'. This was reaffirmed by the Second UN World Conference on Human Rights held in Vienna in 1993. The right to development was claimed as 'a universal and inalienable right and an integral part of fundamental human rights'.

Lumping all rights together and calling it 'development' helps little when trying to identify who has the obligation to perform the corresponding duty. The problem is certainly not solved by asserting that the right 'specifies a norm of action for the people, the institutions or the state and international community on which the claim for that right is made'; or that 'all human beings, individually and collectively have a responsibility for securing the right to development' (Sengupta, 2002: 845, 853), especially since such loose hyperbole simply burdens those claiming the right to development with the duty of fulfilling it.

The right to development is reducible either to individual human rights or to policy prescriptions for national and international agencies. It is the former when the right is referred to as 'a process of development which leads to the realization of each human right and all of them together'. It is reducible to the latter when it is stated that economic growth, industrialization and other types of economic development must be accompanied by the provision of equal opportunities and social development; or that states have the duty to formulate appropriate national development policies; or that states must provide equitable redistribution, food, education, sanitation, literacy, nutrition, primary health care, housing, and 'appropriate national development policies' such as poverty programmes and the growth of GDP; or that the international community must continue with development assistance to promote a new economic order, transfer resources from rich to poor countries, stabilize commodity prices, give preferential access to markets, respect human rights, achieve a higher standard of living, and alleviate the external debt burden.

When the right to development is defined in terms of morally acceptable development – development with equity and justice, development with poverty alleviation, participatory development, social and human development, the expansion of capabilities and substantive freedoms and so on – it soon loses whatever distinctive content might justify referring to development as a 'right'. The distinctive moral claim associated with the concept of rights is lost. When it is defined as development in which all human rights are respected, but at the same time as dependent upon the observation of individual rights, it soon becomes tautological, as in the observation that 'the implementation, promotion and protection of those rights would be essential for realizing the right to development' (Sengupta, 2002: 853); in other words, the protection of rights is needed for the realization of rights.

Simply rewording the debate about development policy in the language of rights provides no assistance in the choice of policies that best support different concepts of development, nor how they can best be afforded. The only way to get round the problem is to accept that it is good enough for a state to promise to do its best 'depending upon the objective conditions in the states', or to make progress, or 'to move as expeditiously as possible', or 'to begin to take steps', or to make 'the best endeavour' (Sengupta, 2002: 864) – weasel words that allow it enormous scope to justify failure to promote real rights.

Universalism vs. relativism

A universalistic view of human rights is based on a belief in a common humanity, regardless of society or culture. Such common humanity is capable of recognizing a *natural law* that endows it with human rights. Knowledge of the morality prescribed by natural law is possible because of human reason, a faculty that transcends culture. Thus human rights are predicated on assumptions about the nature (physical and moral) of human beings.

The problem for some political philosophers has been to know how the exercise of reason should provide a *particular* content to natural law. They question whether 'humanity' can be meaningful other than in a particular community with its own values and traditions. Rights have no separate ontological status (or independent existence). Rather they are a by-product of a particular kind of society in which the state operates constitutionally under the rule of law; where the state is separate from civil society; and where the public and private realms are capable of demarcation. Human rights are thus symptoms of a certain kind of civilization, not a cause, and so cannot be isolated from their social context.

Thus efforts to promote rights (for example by the international community) are efforts to promote a particular kind of society. On what moral authority can this be attempted? (See Brown, 1999.)

This sceptical approach to universal human rights is reflected in Ernest Gellner's view that 'preaching across cultural boundaries seems to me in most circumstances a fairly pointless exercise' (quoted in Brown, 1999: 123). However, in the same paragraph Gellner also says 'the existence of a culture-transcending truth seems to me the most important single fact about the human condition'. If there is a truth that transcends culture, surely it must be 'preached'. In fact Brown and others often seem desperate to reconcile their cultural relativism with a belief in a universal principle of human rights, just as many international declarations and treaties are.

For example, the United Nations tries to square the circle in its Vienna Declaration, in which human rights are held to be universal, indivisible and interdependent, but national and regional 'particularities' and historical, cultural and religious 'backgrounds' have to be 'borne in mind'. Other human rights institutions concede that standards should be differentially applied in different cultural context (Freeman, 2002: 104). This does little to help resolve the controversy since 'bearing in mind' these backgrounds may simply remind the universalist just how dreadful some cultural and religious practices are.

The controversy about the universalism or relativism of human rights is exemplified in the debate about 'Asian values', which confronts the question, prompted by some influential Asian political leaders, of whether 'human rights' are appropriate for non-Western cultures such as those in East Asia. In 1993 a number of East and South-East Asian states, including China, Indonesia, Malaysia and Singapore, issued the Bangkok Declaration setting out a distinctive Asian view on human rights. The universal validity of human rights was questioned for a number of reasons.

First, some authoritarian regimes, such as Singapore's, have produced economic 'miracles' by giving priority to family and community rather than the individual, and to strong government, stability, harmony and consensus. Duties and obligations, not rights (and demands), are emphasized, promoting harmony and stability (as well as economic benefits). Second, government leaders are expected to be protective of society, with a duty to do what is right. So the cultural emphasis is on collective, not individual human, rights, such as freedom from hunger, a right to development, and a right to social order. For example, in 1992 Singapore's Prime Minister Lee Kuan Yew said that his first task had been 'to lift my country out of the degradation that poverty, ignorance and disease had wrought. Since it was dire poverty that made for such a low priority given to human life, all other things become secondary' (quoted in Bauer and Bell, 1999: 7). Third, leaders in non-Western countries have deemed the discourse on universal human rights to be just another form of imperialism, using concepts which support the hegemony of Western states.

Cultural relativism as a response to claims about the universality of human rights deserves severe scrutiny. In some circumstances it is clearly no more than an ideological device. For example, the claim that 'Asian values', not Western ones, should determine human rights regimes in South-East Asia has been used by authoritarian regimes to shore up their own legitimacy and justify their violations of civil liberties and political rights. Claims to cultural uniqueness have been deployed to insulate regimes from political and social change, particularly democratization. Relativist human rights sentiments have frequently been expressed by self-serving political leaders who themselves rarely match the Asian credentials of benevolence, wisdom, protectiveness, consensuality and so on. The appeal to Asian values is less a convincing description of cultural distinctiveness and more a critique (some of it justified) of Western trends that suits the interests of authoritarian leaders by linking democracy to decadence. Asian values also serve as a populist ideology designed to depoliticize class conflicts by an appeal to the virtues of consensus and discipline (Christie, 1995; Foot, 1997; Thompson, 2001).

The presence of relevant universalistic features in societies and regimes that reject universal conceptions of human rights are also significant. In the case of Asia, for example, political leaders have claimed that full human rights *are* a desired objective, though dependent on economic and social development. Also, since Asia is enormously diverse economically, politically and culturally, it is doubtful if there can be an 'Asian' case against the universality of human rights. India's democracy shows just how lacking in uniformity the idea of Asian values is (Brzezinski, 1997). Furthermore, some of the values said to be specifically Asian – such as respect for tradition, family, education and authority – are not unknown in Western societies, where human rights are looked to in order to protect groups of equal concern to Asians, such as the elderly, married women, or children (Chan, 1997).

The political leaders who reject universal human rights as a Western imposition nevertheless use equally Western concepts to defend their own stances: state sovereignty, for example. When it comes to economic principles, it is noteworthy that the emphasis on market mechanisms in so many Asian economies and official ideologies stresses an individualism that is readily recognizable in the West, rather than collective interests (Foot, 1997). Conversely, while Asian cultural traditions uphold individualism, Western political thought has been known to include communitarian values (Tatsuo, 1999). Indeed, individual rights contribute to vibrant communities, while curtailing rights can harm traditional cultural preferences, as in the case of China's policy of only allowing one child per family. There is also nothing culturally specific and non-Western about cherry-picking rights that suit a regime (usually social and economic) while discarding those – notably civil and political – that do not. This is something that communist states in Europe engaged in for decades.

Then there is the fact that political activists from the same region advocate support for fundamental human rights when confronted by state repression. It is notable that opposition leaders in Asia (and elsewhere) see no contradiction between human rights and Asian culture (for example, Burma's Aung San Suu Kyi). Members of pro-democracy movements and human rights organizations in the region believe governments to have an obligation to protect human rights. A particular example is the democratic movement in Hong Kong (Ng, 1997: 20). Following the Bangkok Declaration of 1993 Asian non-governmental organizations issued a statement saying categorically that 'cultural practices which derogate from universally accepted human rights including women's rights, must not be tolerated' (quoted in Baehr, 1999: 11). A middle-class protest movement in Malaysia also finds democratization compatible with Asian society and culture. In Singapore 'those with the strongest "Asian" identities are often the most adamant in calling for democratic reforms' (Thompson, 2001: 162). Thus activists in the regions where cultural peculiarities are supposed to take precedence over universal rights do not support relativism.

Public opinion also confirms the acceptability of universal human rights to Asians. For example, 'Singaporeans' hierarchies of rights are not very different from those of their Western counterparts, save in some areas such as respect for authority and freedom of speech' (Tan, 1999).

Anti-Western and culturally relativist arguments are also deployed in Islamic states, where violations of universal rights are justified by appeal to religious doctrines. However, the incompatibility between Islam and human rights has been seriously questioned by both Islamic and non-Islamic scholars. According to some interpretations, the Islamic stance is characterized by 'assimilation' (creating no problem of reconciling Islam and universal human rights) and 'appropriation' (where human rights are realizable only under Islam), rather than confrontation or incompatibility between Islam and human rights. Islamic scholars have argued that while some Islamic *regimes* often violate human rights, Islam as a set of religious beliefs can be interpreted so as to be compatible with universal human rights, even to the extent of providing a foundation for international human rights law (Freeman, 2004). Some Muslim societies have built states on secular principles, and the political opposition in repressive Islamic states frequently appeals to international, universalistic principles, including human rights. The Islamic world is also highly differentiated and factional, making it difficult to confront universal human rights with a coherent alternative (Halliday, 1995).

Relativism further suffers from being both ahistorical and culturalist. It assumes erroneously that because culture dictates certain values today, it always has and always will. Writing about cultural relativism exudes a 'tyranny of presentism', whereas societies and cultures change and are open-ended, in that there is a freedom inherent in human consciousness. Humans have the capacity to make history, including doctrines of human rights, so that today's truths are a future generation's historical curiosities (Mendus, 1995; Booth, 1999). The increasing fluidity of political boundaries and identities also challenges the argument that rights cannot be universalized. Rights can develop into universal moral prescriptions in non-Western societies just as they did, in the face of religious and political opposition, in Western societies. Cultures and societies whose governments once proclaimed their uniqueness, resisting the imposition of universal human rights by the West, are not only undergoing change but are changing in the direction of universal human rights. For example, democratization in Taiwan and Korea shows that 'Asian values' are neither static nor incompatible with universal human rights (Brzezinski, 1997: 5).

We also find congruencies between Western liberal values and other major epistemological traditions which show that convergence upon universal human rights is far from impossible. For example, there is the respect for the dignity of human beings found within Sharia and support for gender equality found in the Koran (Othman, 1999). Freedom of speech within Confucianism, as in Western liberalism, is seen as a way of avoiding errors in ethical reasoning. And there are many in the West who would agree that freedom of speech is abused when appealed to in defence of pornography (Chan, 1999).

Relativism is 'culturalist' because it emphasizes the uniqueness and exclusivity of cultures, each with its own particular values, beliefs and rationalities. This exaggerates the self-contained quality of societies, and the level of consensus on cultural values found in them: if they are disputed internally (as they always are), to whose version are human rights supposed to be 'relative'? In which 'ethical community' (cultural, class, gender, nation, generation) are human rights meant to be embedded, according to this anti-universalistic slant? Cultures are a descriptive matter, and provide no basis for moral judgements about the worth of values that claim universality (Amstutz, 1999: 75–6). 'Culturalism' and its attendant traditionalism merely perpetuate certain values and power structures. If non-Western cultural values put more emphasis on community, society or nation than on the individual of supposedly Western concepts of universal human rights, the question arises as to who represents and interprets the 'rights' of such collectivities. The common response – the current government – offers little reassurance to those concerned about the rights of individuals in vulnerable groups, such as minorities, women, employees or indigenous peoples.

One factor which may appear to undermine the universalist argument is that some victims of rights violations support the cultures or religions which deny them equal consideration and treatment. The obvious example is women in some Islamic societies. One response is that such people are not in a position to choose between real alternatives. Rather they experience false consciousness and give 'false consent'. Nor can there be certainty about the values and beliefs said to make up a culture if large sectors of society are silenced. Respect for human rights allows everyone a voice. Respect for diverse cultures is actually dependent upon the universalization of human rights.

Since Western liberal universalism does not assert the supremacy of individual rights over every other value, there is no inevitable incompatibility with the culturalist view that sometimes a right (such as freedom of expression) might have to give way to other values, such as society's morals or public safety. The problem for liberals is to know whose view of such morals and safety should prevail. To answer this, the universalist would ask about the effects of an exercise of freedom on the rights of others. For example, an appeal to the right of free expression to justify pornography might be subordinated to the rights of women and children put at risk. The universalist asks whether harm is done by respecting a right. If no harm is done, then it is not justifiable to reject a right. This would be the response to the Malaysian law which prohibits Moslems from marrying non-Moslems.

A culturally relativist stance also places an obligation on non-Western societies to recognize the right of Western universalists to condemn practices they believe to be inhuman and unjust. It is not as if the universalist argument condemns all that is non-Western. It retains respect for cultural diversities that do not inflict harm on people. But it is not obliged to respect cultural attributes which deny to others the moral worth extended to them by universal human rights. This particularly applies to religions which reject the right of people to hold alternative religious beliefs.

There is clearly an urgent need among scholars and activists to find common ground on which a regime of universal human rights can be based. There is a very broad global consensus on the specification of human rights, even though states do not always uphold these standards (Donnelly, 1999). There is also much human solidarity with the pain and suffering experienced by people from other cultures, even by those who reject moral universalism and – perhaps reluctantly – adopt a relativist position. There are frequent assertions of moral duty to come to the aid of 'distant humans' (Midgley, 1999: 161). There is much advocacy of 'non-ethnocentric' universal values, or 'minimum universalism' established by cross-cultural argument and debate, in order to find a consensus on values that are the rationally most defensible. Few critics of universalism from a relativist perspective condemn all universal principles, such as anti-racism (Freeman, 2002: 104). Such a consensus is *more* than some lowest common denominator of different cultural traditions (Parekh, 1999).

Processes of globalization are also producing a single cosmopolitan culture, and demands for universal human rights are in part a response to some of the economic, social and political consequences. So despite scepticism in both Western and non-Western contexts about the universality of human rights, the concept has 'a strong intuitive appeal to many people in many different cultures insofar as it is designed to protect the most fundamental human interests, honour human dignity and provide the basis of peace and mutual respect among peoples' (Freeman, 2004: 400).

Attempts to reconcile universalism with relativism sometimes become quite desperate. For example, Donnelly argues that internationally recognized human rights are a good starting-point for guaranteeing human dignity, something threatened by both states and markets. Universalism is an 'initial assumption'. It is not possible reasonably to deny rights to life, liberty, security, protection against slavery, arbitrary arrest, torture and racial discrimination. But deviations from the 'initial assumption', demanded by different cultures, may be acceptable in some cases. Human rights can thus be specified at three levels: *concepts*, for example the right to political participation where 'very little cultural variability is justifiable'; *interpretations* of a right where some variability is justifiable (for example free and fair elections); and the *form* in which interpretations are implemented when 'considerable variation ... may be justifiable' (for example between simple majority or proportional representation as electoral systems – Donnelly, 1989: 37).

The problem with this, and other, attempts to reconcile universalism and relativism is that the flexibility advocated for 'lower-level' rights seems always to have the potential to threaten rights which are held to be inviolable. For example, the acceptability of arranged marriages as a deviation from the right of spouses to give their free and full consent to marriage depends on the rights of the sons and daughters involved to give their consent to the principle of parents choosing spouses for them. Similarly, the choice between electoral systems can only be made by reference to the consequences for fundamental human rights. It is not an area of rights that can be cut off from the 'initial assumption'.

When critics of universal rights fall back on the argument that the actual application of rights principles has to be sensitive to specific cultural contexts, it is usually without explanation of how the two – universal rights and local context – can be made compatible when the context itself supports violations of the rights it is somehow supposed to accommodate. So it is by no means clear why 'The struggle to promote human rights is more likely to be won if it is fought in ways that speak to local cultural traditions' (Bauer and Bell, 1999: 12). If universal rights are acceptable under local conditions, there is no rejection of their universality. If they are not, how can the problem be overcome by 'speaking' to inhospitable social norms and values?

Enforcing human rights

Enforcement of an international human rights regime confronts a number of problems of particular interest to aid agencies. First, the continuing strength of state sovereignty as a principle in international relations affects every type of activity designed to enforce international human rights standards. Human rights remain an area where states are least prepared to compromise their sovereignty. States do not define their national interests to include strong and impartial international monitoring and enforcement of human rights. They prefer to retain the power to decide how human rights will be affected by their own public policies.

Challenging the human rights record of a country involves criticism of both political rules and cultural practices, unacceptable within a world of sovereign states. The far-reaching reforms which may be needed can readily be presented as unwarranted external interference in a state's domestic jurisdiction. Externally imposed human rights are thus perceived as 'subversive'. National sovereignty blocks the intervention of international bodies, major powers, or neighbouring states (Amstutz, 1999: 84). The principle of state sovereignty forces the UN, the main international guardian of human rights, to respond to the demands of states (as represented by their current political leadership) and not to the human rights of their citizens (Evans, 2001: 629).

Sovereign states also decide which pieces of international 'law' they will accept, in a way not possible for a citizen under domestic law. The protection of rights is made more complex when states are allowed to designate some rights as 'derogable', that is, able to be detracted from. In addition, though most states sign most of the international agreements on human rights, many weaken their obligations by adopting reservations and exceptions. For example, 35 of the 127 signatories to the International Covenant on Civil and Political Rights have between them entered 150 reservations. None of the major international covenants and agreements has been ratified unanimously. Socio-economic rights attract reservations among Western countries, while in non-Western societies it is likely to be the area of civil and political rights from which governments claim exemption (Baehr, 1999: 5; Montgomery, 1999).

Second, international law rests largely not on coercion and enforcement but on reciprocity, and one state may have little interest in how another treats its citizens, except when this gives rise to large movements of refugees. In the post-communist era the rationale for much support by the West for regimes which violated human rights in order to contain left-wing forces may have disappeared. But this does not mean that positive support for human rights abusers has been replaced by positive intervention on behalf of human rights and those who suffer from their violation, especially if human rights concerns conflict with other foreign policy objectives of the major powers (Donnelly, 1993). States can remain 'disengaged' from the requirements of the treaties they have ratified, escaping criticism because the system is based on consent and because those that comply with their obligations to report and provide for redress run a greater risk of exposure, so that a high level of engagement seems to be rewarded by international condemnation. Neither the 'engaged' nor the 'disengaged' states are likely to press for more effective international enforcement, the latter because of the exposure they might face, the former because they have learnt that while they are identified as violators, countries with worse records 'get away virtually without punishment' (Heyns and Viljoen, 2001: 489).

International bodies such as the UN have few resources and weak authority when it comes to enforcement. Recommendations in reports of inquiries into human rights abuses are not enforced, though they may mobilize NGOs and opposition movements. Processes of investigation are very slow and restricted to 'situations' (systematic violations, not individual cases). International bodies are dependent on the perpetrators for information. For example, the human rights work of the Council of Europe in Chechnya is dependent on information provided by the 'host' country, Russia.

The supervision of national laws and practices by international organizations may have become more extensive, but shaming a government by publicizing its human rights record is unlikely to produce change when governments are so shameless when justifying their behaviour. So while the UN's Human Rights Commission can review and investigate human rights abuses, member states frequently refuse to take remedial action, despite the condemnation this generates. In fact, most international bodies have no sanctions at their disposal, only diplomatic pressure. And the publicizing of violations is limited to the 66 countries (mainly democracies) that have signed up to the Human Rights Commission's optional protocol allowing publicity of violations. So with the commonest types of human rights violations, state sovereignty has meant that international declarations and covenants are only 'laws' up to a point, lacking as they do enforcement mechanisms (Brown, 1999: 115; Forsythe, 2000).

Real enforcement against the will of individual states is likely only in exceptional circumstances and crises, such as famine resulting from political disorder (as in the case of Somalia in 1992 and southern Sudan in 2004), crimes against humanity (such as in the former Yugoslavia from 1992 to 1995), genocide (as in Rwanda in 1994), and war crimes (as in Iraq in 1991). The UN is then dependent upon member states to enforce their resolutions. But even then member states need to find some support within their own sphere of domestic interests before taking on such heavy responsibilities. For example, in 2004 the Security Council passed a resolution demanding that Sudan disarm the ethnic Arab militias currently committing atrocities against ethnic Africans in the Darfur region. However, most Western countries were reluctant to support military intervention, other than to help refugees in neighbouring Chad.

Consequently international organizations are reluctant to use their powers against human rights violations. The UN Security Council can act only if its members agree that international peace and security are threatened, an extremely difficult agreement to secure, and little comfort to migrant workers in Saudi Arabia, indigenous people in the Amazon rainforest, women in Iran and Afghanistan, the inhabitants of the oil-rich Niger Delta, bonded labourers in India, victims of torture in Turkey, the parents of Argentina's 'disappeared', Brazil's street children, or garmentworkers in Honduras.

Underpinning these and other weaknesses is the UN's tendency to pass ambiguous resolutions unrelated to the legal systems of member states, and the unwillingness of its political organs to put pressure on states to secure compliance in even such modest obligations as reporting to relevant treaty organs in a timely manner (Alston, 1992). Politics rather than legality determine whether violations are even considered by international agencies, exposing the UN to charges of double standards, for example when in the past it has debated human rights violations in South Africa and Israel while ignoring Uganda under Amin and Cambodia under Pol Pot until too late (Baehr, 1999: 70).

When international enforcement on behalf of human rights has taken place, as in the case of military intervention in countries experiencing acute crisis, or arrests and prosecutions before international courts, it has usually been extremely controversial. Critics of those initiating such international interventions have accused them of overriding state constitutional law (as in the abduction of President Milosovic from Belgrade), unilaterally rescinding provisions of international treaties (for example, that those accused on genocide should, under the Convention on the Prevention and Punishment of Genocide, be prosecuted in their own courts), double standards (for example bombing Yugoslavia in the name of human rights but tolerating Russia's campaigns in Chechnya), modifying humanitarian law while insisting it to be universal (for example, dropping the principle that the violation of state sovereignty by force is a crime against peace and outlawed by the UN Charter, as in the unprovoked Anglo-American invasion of Iraq), and of lacking accountability and legitimacy (for example, the International Criminal Court for the former Yugoslavia which 'has broken almost every rule in the book': Laughland, 2002: 53). Furthermore, the emergence since 1990 of international actions undermining state sovereignty, previously believed by Western governments to be unlawful, appears more a consequence of Western, and especially US, hegemony following the end of the cold war, than of humanitarian concerns (Holbrook 2002).

Third, foreign policy considerations override concern for rights, even when there are international mechanisms for indicting political leaders for crimes against humanity, and for seeking redress through international courts. In the USA the Bush Administration has tried to undermine support in the Americas for the proposed International Criminal Court by threatening to cut off military aid to countries that support its creation. The Western powers have frequently turned a blind eye to human rights violations when it suits them. Diplomacy has highly variable results which depend upon the target country's perceptions of its own national interest. So, for example, in 2002 US diplomacy helped ease the human rights crisis in southern Sudan, but made little impact on the Mugabe regime in Zimbabwe. And the situation in the Sudan soon deteriorated again, especially in the western region of Darfur.

Fourth, there is no retaliation against a state found to be abusing human rights that can be exclusively targeted on human rights. So if a country resorts to economic sanctions against a state which abuses human rights (such as South Africa under apartheid) it exposes itself to the charge that it is doing additional harm to an already distressed population. This dilemma is illustrated by the European Union's decision in 2004 to continue to make development aid available to the Sudan, at the same time as calling for UN sanctions to end the violence in Darfur, because cutting off aid would harm the most vulnerable members of the community.

Finally, there are numerous cultural obstacles to the creation of a satisfactory human rights regime, only some of which are gradually being removed. There is often ignorance of the treaty system within political elites (such as Supreme Court judges in Jamaica) and civil society (especially when treaties are not available in local languages). Weak human rights cultures and inactive civil society (in Brazil, Iran and Zambia, for example) have meant that states have been under little political pressure when found to be defaulting on their obligations. There has been a shortage of journalists with human rights training (for example, in the Czech Republic and Senegal). Socio-economic factors such as illiteracy, poverty, corruption and marketization have impeded human rights reforms, as have customs, tradition and religion, such as the Indian caste system and Sharia law in Iran. Political instability (as in Colombia) and the association of rights with unpopular political movements (as with secessionist movements in India) have further undermined human rights. Reporting obligations under human rights treaties are seen by governments as periodic tests rather than a continuous monitoring exercise, allowing one administration to shift blame on to a predecessor. The international community needs to be aware of such local circumstances when targeting development assistance at the human rights dimension of good governance.

There is probably no blueprint which will suit all circumstances when human rights are violated. So the injunction to concentrate on 'quiet diplomacy', more easily accommodated in a world of sovereign states than public condemnation and isolation of defaulting regimes (Amstutz, 1999), may not work in cases such as Iraq before the Anglo-American invasion, where 'isolation' did little to help support the human rights of those most repressed by the regime. The idea that human rights programmes should be limited in scope so that they are less easily accused of imperialism, ethnocentrism and hypocrisy might play similarly into the hands of some authoritarian regimes which are liable to resist any support for human rights in their countries. A combination of soft diplomacy and minimal strong intervention makes little impact on the human rights situation in most countries in the Third World and post-communist regions, leaving victims with little redress and perpetrators enjoying impunity.

Conclusion

There are three facets of human rights regimes that the international development community can hope to influence for the better. The first concerns the *scope* of human rights, and the controversy over whether it is helpful or damaging to human rights claims to extend them from civil and political rights to the economic, social and collective spheres. On balance, extending human rights to cover an ever-expanding list of political demands does more harm than good, despite many of those demands being desirable policy objectives. The second feature of human rights concerns their *universality*. Here the controversy is over whether certain cultural imperatives override human rights in the political life of citizens, enabling governments to reject fundamental rights on the grounds that they are incompatible with other cultural and religious norms. The argument in favour of universality far outweighs those derived from a culturally relativistic position.

The third question is more frequently addressed by the aid community. It concerns the *enforceability* of human rights, in a world where violations are so commonplace, despite most states being signatories to numerous international declarations, charters and conventions. On balance, the effects of the international human rights regime have been far less than the elaborate institutional structure might lead one to expect. Foreign policy considerations (often reflecting economic interests within the donor state) too often overwhelm international concerns about human rights under a particular national regime.

One of the ways donors try to protect civil rights is support for the rule of law, so that the law serves all citizens equally, both in their private dealings and especially in their encounters with the state. The next chapter seeks to clarify the scope of this concept, and assess its contribution to development.

4

The Rule of Law

International support for the rule of law

Technical assistance to establish the rule of law is an important part of multilateral and bilateral aid in support of good governance, though bilateral donors have greater freedom to impose political conditions which acknowledge the significance of the rule of law for democratic politics and human rights (Faundez, 1997). The World Bank has taken the lead since 1980, though under restrictions imposed by its articles of agreement, limiting its formal role to capacity-building and the development of laws needed for the establishment of a market economy. The Bank regards a 'foundation of law' as essential for the development of markets, the protection of property rights and economic development generally. Its first priority in poor countries is 'to lay the initial building blocks of lawfulness: protection of life and property from criminal acts, restraints on arbitrary action by government officials, and a judicial system that is fair and predictable'. When the rule of law is weakened by 'arbitrary and capricious state action', state officials can place themselves above the law, and development 'hits a brick wall' (World Bank, 1997: 45, 99). The rule of law is also seen as contributing to social stability, a necessary condition for economic development. The legal framework of a borrowing country is thus brought within the Bank's mandate, as in the case of the Judicial Infrastructure Project in Venezuela.

The UN's Development Programme links the rule of law to poverty eradication, human rights and human development. The Inter-American Development Bank also sees the financing of judicial reforms as contributing to the protection of human rights and thus social stability (Messick, 1999; UNDP 2004).

Considerable sums of money have been allocated by leading multilateral and bilateral donors for programmes of assistance designed to strengthen the rule of law. Between 1994 and 1998 the World Bank, Inter-American Development Bank and Asian Development Bank contributed over US $500 million in loans for judicial reform in 26 countries. In the 1990s USAID devoted US $200 million to projects related to the rule of law. Between 1990 and 2001 the World Bank allocated US $10.8 billion to 95 projects in 21 countries in Eastern Europe and Central Asia, including US $58 million to Russia in 1996 to support the drafting of legislation, legal education, public awareness, judicial training and alternative dispute mechanisms. Between 1992 and 2000 the new independent states of the former Soviet Union received US $216 million, the main recipients being Russia and the Ukraine. Russia is the largest single recipient of aid in support of the rule of law, with assistance from the World Bank, the European Bank for Reconstruction and Development, Denmark, Germany, the EU, the Netherlands, the UK and the USA (Carothers, 1998; USGAO, 2001).

International assistance falls into three broad categories. First there are programmes of law reform consisting of projects designed to modernize the body of legislation in particular fields, such as commercial, civil and banking law. For example, the European Union provides grants to Rwanda for the reform of its administrative, criminal and commercial codes. Second, there are projects for capacity-building in the judicial sector, modernizing institutions such as courts, ombudsmen, police forces, prisons and ministries of justice, and training judicial personnel such as judges, court officials and public prosecutors. For example, in Cambodia the UN has promoted the independence of the judiciary by placing consultants in the courts to train and assist judges. Advisory services are also provided on judicial structures, the rehabilitation of court houses, the remuneration of judges, and the organization of defence in criminal cases.

The third type of support for the rule of law consists of reforms which complement changes to the judicial system by improving its accessibility, especially to the poor. For example, the World Bank provides loans and grants to fund public awareness campaigns in Russia, and legal aid for women and children in Cambodia. The UNDP's justice sector programme includes legal aid, public participation in legal and judicial reforms, and support for informal extrajudicial methods of dispute resolution accessible to the poor such as Jueces de Paz in parts of Latin America and Lok Adalats in South Asia.

Defining the rule of law

Before it is possible to establish the significance of the rule of law for development, it is necessary to identify precisely what it means. The rule of law is a complex constitutional principle. It has multiple facets comprising different conceptions of justice – as regularity, as equality, as ubiquity and as natural. Some commentators add that the rule of law implies the existence of 'good' law. This is problematic, seeing the rule of law as sufficient, rather than just a necessary condition, for the good society.

Even after having supported many projects relating to the rule of law the World Bank was forced to admit that 'overlooked in much of the dialogue about the rule of law is that the term has no fixed meaning', being 'open-ended' and contested. The difficulty in arriving at an agreed meaning is partly the fault of those who, like the World Bank, tend to confuse formal and substantive definitions in their anxiety to recommend a particular choice of public policy in terms of the intrinsic nature of law itself. This conceptualization of the rule of law as substantive *policy* will be returned to.

Justice as *regularity* requires the rule of law to provide a 'regular and impartial administration of public rules' (Rawls, 1972: 235). The rule of law is observed when laws are administered consistently under relevant circumstances. Arbitrary power gives way to the supremacy of regular law. According to the American philosopher John Rawls, 'one legal order is more justly administered than another if it more perfectly fulfils the precepts of the rule of law' (1972: 236). Justice under the rule of law recognizes that 'ought' implies 'can'. Rules should not impose a duty to do what cannot be done, and legislators and judges should in good faith believe that the laws can be obeyed and orders carried out. The legal system should recognize the impossibility of performance as a defence (or at least a mitigating circumstance).

The rule of law also entails *equality* before the law in the sense that like cases are treated alike, which significantly limits the discretion of judges and others in authority. Reasoned arguments for discriminatory judgements must be given by reference to the relevant legal rules and principles. Equity may sometimes require discretion when the specific circumstances of a unique case require it. The rule of law requires that this must not constitute an arbitrary departure from the rules, reviving Aristotle's conception of the rule of law as the rule of reason. When a sovereign parliament endows administrative discretion with legality, the rule of law requires governmental actions to be circumscribed by rules which limit the scope of official discretion (Allen, 1985; Shklar, 1998). Limiting the discretion available to public officials makes the law predictable. But the rule of law may have to accommodate the value of discretion in providing flexibility and responsiveness to need, rather than condemn discretion for leading to arbitrary decision-making. Justice requires that like cases be treated alike, but the spirit of public policy may require officials to exercise discretion in judging whether cases really are alike.

Another form of equality is crucial to the rule of law, namely the equality before the law of all persons and classes, *including government officials*. This is essential if the rule of law is not to be replaced by the rule of man. Government officials, whether elected or appointed, should not be above the ordinary law. The legality of their decisions should be subject to review by independent courts. Citizens need only fear 'the office of the law, not its administrators' (Shklar, 1998: 23, quoting Montesquieu). Thus the rule of law conveys Aristotle's precept that judges should act fairly and lawfully, following wherever the law leads and not deviating because of personal bias. This applies to both judicial and administrative officials (Frischtak, 1997; Shklar (1998).

However, the practice of judicial review is one way in which the rule of law is found to be a contentious concept. For if judges rule on political and administrative decisions taken under existing statutes they run the risk of imposing their own interpretation of the law's intentions over those of the legislature. This is especially problematic when judicial review extends to constitutional issues such as whether a legislature is entitled to make law in a particular area, or seek particular objectives through statutory enactments. This power is often given to the judiciary, either through a constitutional court (in the civil law tradition) or through the ordinary courts (in the common law tradition). The practice also varies according to whether the courts can adjudicate only if a dispute is brought before them, or can express a view on proposed legislation, or can investigate any matter which they believe constitutes a violation of human rights, as in India, for example. In all cases the courts are inevitably brought into the policy-making process, raising fears about the power of an unelected body overriding that of a democratically composed legislature.

The rule of law also requires the *ubiquity* of law in the sense that there can be no offence without a law. Laws should be known, general, expressly promulgated, clearly formulated and not retroactive. Without these precepts rules cannot provide a basis for 'legitimate expectations' on the part of citizens. The rule of law thus guarantees that citizens know what obligations are imposed by the law, and can expect these obligations to remain unchanged until the law is changed. Under the rule of law there is no uncertainty as to who is required to act, or refrain from acting, under different sets of circumstances.

Finally, the law should be imbued with the rules of *natural justice*, that is, rules to be followed in the administration of the law. These rules are: that trials and hearing should be held in an orderly manner; that rules of evidence guarantee rational procedures of inquiry; that judges be independent and impartial; that no one may be 'judge in his own cause'; and that trials must be fair and open. Natural justice helps allay fears (expressed for example by the World Bank) that emphasis on the 'law in the books' may distract attention from 'the law in action', when official rules do not appear to 'map onto' the actual operation of the legal system. Judgements about the rule of law are dependent on observations of the law *in operation*.

The idea of the rule of law becomes much more controversial when, as was noted above, it becomes in part a substantive conception referring to the quality of the law's content and purpose, that is, to public policy. Definitions of the rule of law in terms of the rule of *good* law need to be approached with great caution. It is quite clear that some who have reflected on the rule of law cannot bear to acknowledge that an unjust and repressive regime might function according to the rule of law. For example, in 1959 the International Commission of Jurists resolved that the rule of law should be employed not only to safeguard and advance the civil and political rights of the individual in a free society, but also to establish social, economic, cultural and even educational conditions under which 'legitimate aspirations and dignity may be realised' (quoted in Allen, 1985: 114). Much more recently the rule of law has been defined as a system of laws which guarantees private property rights.

The problem with turning the rule of law into a social philosophy or programme of public policy is that, no matter how admirable the social goals, to do so detracts from its role of securing protection against arbitrary political power. Since it is not claimed that the rule of law is a sufficient, rather than just a necessary, condition of a just society, it is quite possible for it to coexist with public policies to which there are strong moral objections or the absence of policies necessary to secure social justice. However, it may be comforting to reflect that the potential for such coincidence is reduced by the fact that repressive regimes place at least some of their officials beyond the reach of the law (for example, parts of the security apparatus in South Africa under apartheid), thus violating one of the most vital principles of the rule of law. Nevertheless, what constitutes 'bad' public policy depends on one's interests and values, and it will always be possible for critics of a public policy to recognize that the rule of law has not been violated.

Using the rule of law to distinguish between good and bad laws also risks such a substantive definition being co-opted by highly ideological arguments, such as those used by neo-liberals when defining the rule of law as an economic system based on minimal state intervention and the sanctity of private property. Even here, however, it is notable that in its discussion of the role of the rule of law in economic development the World Bank contrasts private property rights and free markets not with a managed economy based on well-known and consistently applied rules, but with 'arbitrary government actions – ranging from unpredictable, ad hoc regulations and taxes to outright corruption' (World Bank, 1997: 41). In other words, a formal rather than a substantive conception of the rule of law is a requirement of economic development.

The rule of law and political development

It can readily be demonstrated that the rule of law is necessary for political and economic development, including the alleviation of poverty. The rule of law is a foundation of democratic political development, first because it is an indispensable protection against arbitrary government. The rule of law is essential for liberty, minimizing the potential hazards from collective action (public policy) backed by sanctions. It helps prevent such sanctions from wrongly interfering with the freedom of the citizen. It enhances the people's capacity to exercise their rights and preserve their freedoms. It guarantees independent and neutral electoral processes, judicial protection of dissent, open and pluralistic politics, confidence in multi-party democracy, and participation that is 'unrestrained – and most importantly fearless' (Sen, 2000: 22).

Second, the rule of law helps establish an ordered society in which the principles of democracy can take hold. The 1948 Declaration of Human Rights requires rights to be protected by the rule of law 'if man [sic] is not to have recourse as a last resort to rebellion against tyranny and oppression' (Solum, 1994). More recently the World Bank has drawn attention to the social as well as economic damage done when state officials 'place themselves above the law *and tempt the rest of society to do the same'*

(World Bank, 2001b: 99, emphasis added). Defects in the judicial systems of many developing and transitional states undermine confidence in the law and the institutions responsible for it. Such defects include judicial corruption, political interference, and long delays in bringing litigation to a conclusion (up to 15 years in Bangladesh). This last factor has worsened in some Latin American countries, with adverse consequences for the consolidation of democracy (Messick, 2000).

Third, the rule of law contributes to democratic consolidation by holding state officials accountable for their decisions and personal behaviour. An independent judiciary is the most important institution for resolving disputes between citizens and their governments, as well as for clarifying ambiguities in the law and ensuring compliance with it. The judiciary is the only institution that can rule on the legality of administrative decisions and the constitutionality of legislative acts. Judicial review is a vital component of accountability in a democracy. The rule of law is especially important in transitional regimes because it helps establish a clear break with the past, and a new political culture in which all participants respect the law (Larkins, 1996; Feld and Voight, 2003).

The rule of law and economic development

The relationship of the rule of law to economic development reflects the assumption in economic theory that economic growth is dependent on non-interference by governments in private property rights. Less controversial is the view that the abuse of state power is particularly damaging in economic terms when economic policies are changed without changes in the law (by manipulating or ignoring courts), when there is uncertainty about property rights, when entrepreneurial minorities suffer harassment by the state, and when there are frequent and arbitrary changes in taxation, regulation and other economic and fiscal policies.

Such weaknesses in the legal foundation of economic policy lead to uncertainty for domestic and foreign investors (especially in infrastructure and new technology). Firms and citizens have to find other ways to monitor contracts and enforce dispute resolution, such as personal relationships, family networks, and traditional lineages such as clans. Levels of productivity are also reduced. Without the rule of law, workers and investors cannot be confident that they will be able to retain a substantial portion of the wealth they create, and not see it distributed to politicians and their supporters (as distinct from seeing it taxed for public purposes).

Economic development requires institutional arrangements to resolve disputes among firms, citizens and government, and the clarification of ambiguities in laws and regulations. Adequate resources need to be devoted to the enforcement of compliance with the law. For example, in Poland enforcement is constrained by reluctance on the part of the authorities to provide adequate resources to serve court documents, or seize and dispose of assets. Markets cannot function without social order underpinned by institutions, in particular a judiciary with the independent, efficient and effective authority to rule on the legality of actions by the executive branch of government. The rule of law is required to ensure that debts are repaid, contracts enforced, licences withheld on legal grounds (and not because bribes have not been paid), and compensation paid when property is appropriated. A fair and effective judiciary thus offers some prospect of recourse in disputes, which is why the efficiency of the judicial system, which varies enormously (in Brazil it takes an average of 1500 days to clear a case, in France 100), is so important for development (World Bank, 1997; Messick, 2000).

Furthermore, where there is violation of legal norms and disregard for the rule of law by public officials, the wider society and economy become infected, as manifested in black markets, tax evasion, financial irregularities within the private sector, and an increase in crime generally (as in the case of Argentina, for example), leading to further losses of productivity and investment (Stotzky and Nino, 1993).

If the rule of law secures and enforces contracts and property rights, it constitutes one of the 'significant determinants of the speed with which countries grow'. Using data from the *International Country Risk Guide*, Knack and Keefer found that 'institutions that protect property rights are crucial to economic growth and to investment', as well as to 'the efficiency with which inputs are allocated' (Knack and Keefer, 1995: 207 and 223). There is also strong empirical evidence that the predictability of the law is positively associated with economic growth (Brunetti *et al.*, 1998)

When the rule of law provides a secure context in which agreements and exchanges between private interests can be made, and long-lasting contracts enforced, the costs of such transactions are lower than alternative arrangements (such as trusted intermediaries), and lowering the risk of unenforced contracts encourages investment. Governmental, rather than private, enforcement and protection is also needed because of the number of non-simultaneous transactions between lenders and borrowers, customers and suppliers, insurers and the insured, shareholders and management, and management and labour. Without the guarantees which such exchanges receive from the rule of law, investment in production, innovation and new technology remains low, holding back the rate of economic growth. The differences in the behaviour of governments towards contracts and property rights thus affect levels of productivity, investment, growth, capital stock, per capita incomes, and development in the financial sector (Clague *et al.*, 1999).

A problem facing many developing countries is that the absence of the rule of law encourages opportunistic breaches of contract, such as delayed supplies and payments, or lower-quality goods and services, which raise the cost of commercial transactions. A lack of commercial discipline, where the threat of court action carries little credibility, necessitates recourse to expensive alternatives such as long-term personalized relationships with suppliers or customers, harassment as a debt collection strategy, and the use of intermediaries between contractors and contractees to compensate for the lack of information about previous contractual performance. Informal mechanisms to enforce legal obligations may be necessary when the inflexible requirements of formal legal rules collide with the many unpredictable economic events in developing countries, such as drought. So it may be wise for judicial reform projects to build on informal enforcement mechanisms such as credit bureaux, business reputations, business associations, and savings and credit associations, which can share information on credit worthiness or exert pressure to ensure loans are repaid. However, economic and technological development is likely to increase such transaction costs when compared with the formal courts (Fafchamps, 1996; Messick, 1999).

An independent judiciary is thus generally thought to ensure that governments behave in ways supportive of economic growth. But the relationship between economic development and judicial independence turns out to be quite complex. A survey which distinguished between *de facto* and *de jure* independence in 56 countries found the former to be more important for economic growth. The countries investigated were all at different levels of development, ranging from Switzerland to Ghana, and Japan to Pakistan, and included 11 countries from Central and Eastern Europe (East Asia and Africa were under-represented). The foundations of *de jure* judicial independence as found in legal documents, such as appointment procedures for judges, rules of judicial tenure, and the constitutional status of the high court, were found to have no impact on economic growth, when the influence of economic, legal and political variables (such as measures of economic freedom, legal traditions and political stability) was controlled. In contrast, *de facto* independence, as measured by such variables as the average length of terms served by high-court judges, the number of judicial appointments made over a thirty-year period, and the frequency of changes in procedural rules, had a positive impact on real economic growth per capita (Feld and Voigt, 2003)[2]. (It has to be noted that this survey was restricted to supreme courts. The inclusion of others, such as commercial courts, might reveal a different relationship between judicial independence and economic growth.) So it is not enough to know that a country has the right rules in place. Whether judicial independence is actually respected is what counts for economic development.

The importance of formal rules is shown by a 28-country study of Latin America and South-East Asia which compared average rates of per capita GDP in the 1980s with levels of predictability in judicial decision-making experienced by representatives of the private sector, NGOs, government and journalists. The key question was whether judges enforced the law objectively according to transparent rules. It was found that: 'An arbitrary judiciary is an important factor in overall political predictability and has significant costs in terms of economic performance' (Weber, 1995: 25).

There are, perhaps inevitably, methodological problems of which advocates of the rule of law should be aware when making assessments of its significance in specific contexts. One question which immediately arises is: in which direction does causality run, from the rule of law to economic growth, or from economic growth to the rule of law? There may be a virtuous (or vicious) circle here. Do institutions such as the rule of law increase a country's wealth, or do rich countries have better institutions because they can afford them? It might be that a large volume of commerce is needed before the protection of property rights becomes possible. Or more might be spent on the protection of property rights in courts when their value warrants it. Higher levels of economic development might permit greater expenditure on the judicial system generally, or both the rule of law and development may be the result of common factors such as the political culture, or social capital. Statistical analysis has confirmed that improving the quality of institutions such as the rule of law is important for economic growth, but also that there is a circle of causality in which economic growth itself improves institutional quality (Messick, 1999; Chong and Calderon, 2000).

Then there is the question of how the quality of institutions should be measured: by formal laws (for example, on credit or shareholding); by proxy measures (such as the frequency with which governments lose court cases when challenged, as a measure of judicial independence); or by highly subjective expert evaluations (for example, the prevalence of corruption)? Some studies have tried to measure the effect of legal institutions by proxy variables such as political instability. The International Country Risk Guide includes the quality of the bureaucracy and the level of corruption, as well as the risk of expropriation, the repudiation of contracts by the state, and the rule of law, defined as 'the degree to which the citizens of a country are willing to accept the established institutions to make and implement laws and adjudicate disputes'. The rule of law index also includes variables such as 'sound political institutions' and 'provisions for an orderly succession of power', which again are questionable proxies for the rule of law. Rule of law variables have also been confused with policy variables such as the credibility of a government's commitment to property rights, arbitrary changes in taxation, and changes in regulation policy (Knack and Keefer, 1995; Henisz, 2000).

Combining aspects of the rule of law with other measures such as 'nationalization potential', 'infrastructure quality' or 'bureaucratic delays' in order to construct overall measures of institutional quality not only makes it difficult to gauge the significance to economic development of rule of law factors alone. It can also introduce an element of tautology if legal variables are tainted by indicators of economic performance which are supposed to be the dependent variables. The fact that the effect of legal institutions may be felt in different, and possibly conflicting, ways makes it all the more important to isolate their independent significance. For example, the credibility of legal institutions may be important for creating investor confidence, but not if those institutions prevent policy-makers from responding to a financial crisis (Messick, 1999; Chong and Calderon, 2000).

Methodological ambiguity has additional political significance arising from the use of a controversial element in definitions of the rule of law, namely the protection of *private* property. For example, a comparative study of the importance of law in Asian economic development between 1960 and 1995 (Pistor and Wellons *et al.*, 1999) defines 'law' as a combination of public policy (here referring to whether the state or market is primarily responsible for allocating resources) and judicial procedures (referring to whether decisions are rule-based or discretionary). This identification of the rule of law with the substance of public policy needs to be isolated from those aspects of the rule of law which have to do with the justice of the legal system and relationships between the citizen and the state. Unfortunately many statistical examinations of the relationship between the rule of law and economic development fail to do this.

Identifying the rule of law with free enterprise may hamper the contribution which the rule of law can make to social development and the amelioration of poverty (Shklar, 1998).

The rule of law and poverty alleviation

The rule of law is relevant to another development objective, the alleviation of poverty. The poor are in particular need of the protection of life, personal security and human rights which the rule of law can provide. Lawlessness also contributes to poverty when officials flout the law and are not held accountable for their actions. For the poor, the rule of law can help prevent official violence which leaves them unable to earn a living, or forced to incur unproductive expenditure for self-protection. Without the rule of law the poor are also vulnerable to corruption, loss of property to government officials, and insecurity. Public services and the judicial process become things to be avoided (Anderson, 2003).

The poor should also benefit from the contribution which the rule of law makes to economic development, assuming (heroically) that this 'trickles down' to the poor. Politically and economically the absence of the rule of law exacerbates a sense of powerlessness on the part of poor. Consequently, without the protection of human and property rights, and a comprehensive framework of property, contract, labour, bankruptcy, and commercial laws effectively, impartially and cleanly administered by an honest judiciary, no equitable development is possible (World Bank, 2001b). The rule of law also requires equality before the law, rather than bias and discrimination in legal procedures and interpretations. This is of particular benefit to the poor.

But there are many impediments faced by the poor and other disadvantaged groups when seeking justice. The costs of litigation, as well as cultural and language barriers and physical inaccessibility, are of particular significance for the poor. In Bangladesh the level of poverty means that less than 15 per cent of the population has access to the regular courts (Messick, 2000). Dependence on landlords, employers, husbands and others with economic and social power constrains people from demanding their rights. Low educational and literacy levels mean that laws (which are often unclear, inconsistent and outdated) are poorly understood by disadvantaged groups. Understanding is further undermined when laws are drafted, and cases conducted, in an incomprehensible language, as in Pakistan and the Philippines, where English is used. Legal information is rarely adequately disseminated among the poor and those who face discrimination because of gender or ethnic identity.

The attitudes of the legal profession towards the poor constitute another barrier to justice. Traditional attitudes often undermine legal provisions designed to assist disadvantaged groups, such as those outlawing polygamy, child marriages, and 'honour' killings, for example. New laws protecting human rights often remain unimplemented. Patronage, kinship and other social connections, rather than legal rules, influence the decisions of judges to the disadvantage of those not well placed in the social hierarchy. Legal traditions sometimes emphasize social control and the suppression of dissent rather than the protection of rights. Consequently the poor and other marginalized groups view the law with resignation, scepticism or indifference, and as something traditionally used against them and in the interests of the wealthy. So even when the rule of law is given prominence in the development objectives of aid donors and national governments, 'it remains an alien concept to the majority of the world's poor' (Asian Development Bank, 2001: 30).

Improving access to justice for the poor has thus become a component of donors' anti-poverty strategies. One objective of law reform is to reduce the delays and costs associated with the formal judicial process. The most favoured means are legal aid, public interest litigation, alternative dispute resolution (ADR) mechanisms, and legal 'empowerment'.

Legal aid entails using public funds to help low-income litigants to afford the costs of lawyers and court procedures. It is, however, unusual for adequate resources to be devoted to such schemes, leading, as in the case of India, to substantial gaps 'between aspiration and reality' (Cranston, 1997: 237). Legal aid also runs the risk of being construed as political subversion if used to support human rights claimants.

Public interest litigation, sometimes known as class action law suits or representative actions, can reduce legal costs by the application of a single remedy to all relevant cases. But this can have the effect of changing priorities and therefore public policy, a development likely to be opposed by governments.

Alternative dispute resolution seeks to offer quicker, cheaper and socially acceptable justice through the use of less formal mechanisms than the regular courts (see Chapter 9). This encompasses a wide range of institutions, both modern and traditional, including informal tribunals (such as India's Lok Adalats), arbitration clauses in contracts (for example Malaysia), mediation procedures (for example Sri Lanka's conciliation boards), and the thousands of 'conciliation groups' in Vietnam which mediate in small-scale civil disputes between neighbours and family members (Cranston, 1997). In Bangladesh the *shalish* is another informal method of dispute resolution used for family and land disputes, preferred to the 'corruption, delay, indifference and physical distance of the courts' (Golub, 1993: 19).

An alternative to the adaptation of traditional methods of resolving disputes is to create special tribunals and small claims courts which dispense justice cheaply and quickly, but in ways which nevertheless preserve the rules of natural justice. Such tribunals can be particularly effective in resolving disputes between the citizen and public authorities, as well as between employer and employee or landlord and tenant.

The risk with some traditional dispute resolution procedures is that they lack essential qualities required by the rule of law. For example, the *shalish* of rural Bangladesh are biased against women and the poor, consisting as they do exclusively of male village leaders. They lack credibility for a number of other reasons: the influence on them of patron–client relations; the involvement of Muslim clerics with an inadequate understanding of the law; the general ignorance of the law of their members combined with harmful interpretations; corruption; and the deliberate misinterpretation of the law in favour of local elites such as landowners. In Pakistan, *jirgas*, or village courts, have been responsible for issuing verdicts that target the innocent (especially when women), favour the rich, and demand honour killings and even rape. However, NGO involvement has shown that improved justice can be obtained by the provision of training, legal advice and advocacy to court members and litigants. Corruption and patron–client influences can also be discouraged, and the implementation of decisions can be monitored (von Benda-Beckman, 2001; Golub, 1993).

Development agencies have also initiated legal empowerment projects which typically combine educational programmes with practical assistance in the use of legal procedures and litigation, such as counselling, representation and advocacy. So while many rule-of-law initiatives focus on legal institutions and personnel, legal empowerment projects concentrate on those who, from a socially and economically weak position, seek to use the law in defence of their rights and interests, and who wish to engage with the legal system. Information about laws affecting the poor is disseminated through the print and broadcasting media, for example using posters against domestic violence or radio broadcasts informing women of their voting rights. Lay persons can be trained to offer legal advice and assistance to people unable to engage lawyers. For example, NGOs in the

Philippines have trained farmers to guide land reform applicants in their dealings with the Department of Agrarian Reform, and provided repre-sentation and advocacy before administrative tribunals such as those set up by the Department of Labour (Asian Development Bank, 2001). Since it is in the interest of the poor for public officials to be more aware of their needs and entitlements, legal empowerment includes training courses for public servants in their obligations under social programmes designed to alleviate poverty. Empowerment also carries with it the idea of raising awareness of bias within the law, and mobilizing pressure for institutional reform.

Aid and judicial independence

It has long been recognized that the rule of law is dependent on measures which 'prevent the executive and its many agents from imposing their powers, interests, and persecutive inclinations upon the judiciary' (Shklar quoting Montesqueiu, 1998: 25). Before any of the principles embodied in the rule of law can be made operative it is essential to have a judiciary that is as far as possible free from all kinds of external interference (Frischtak, 1997).

Many donor-supported legal and judicial reform programmes are specif-ically aimed at establishing judicial independence in developing and tran-sition economies. International efforts have included the specification of standards to which nation-states are expected to agree among the objec-tives of judicial reform. The most important was produced by the World Conference on the Independence of Justice held in Montreal in 1983, at which representatives of 26 international bodies, including the United Nations, the International Commission of Jurists and the four international courts, unanimously adopted a Universal Declaration on the Independence of Justice. This was followed in 1985 by the Basic Principles on the Independence of the Judiciary promulgated by the 7th United Nations Congress on the Prevention of Crime and the Treatment of Offenders.

The meaning of judicial independence

Judicial independence means, first, *impartiality*: that is, that judicial deci-sions are not influenced by any personal interest that a judge might have in the outcome of the case. Judges provide a 'neutral third', detached from those involved in litigation, and thus placing all on an equal footing before the law. This is especially important when the government is a party to a dispute. Judicial independence requires judges to eschew commitment to party, race, class, caste, community, tribe and religion when exercising judicial powers. An impartial judiciary is one which bases its decisions exclusively on the law rather than fear of the government or a predisposition to declare its actions legal (Larkins, 1996). In 1981 the International Commission of Jurists defined judicial independence as meaning that 'every judge is free to decide matters in accordance with his assessment of the facts and his understanding of the law without any improper influences, inducements or pressures, from any quarter or for any reason' (quoted in Vyas, 1992: 135). To this end international declarations require the political executive to guarantee the physical security of all lawyers when engaged in litigation (Frankel, 1993).

The discharge of judicial function subject only to the law is buttressed by a number of rules, including judicial immunity, the *sub-judice* rule, the disqualification of judges from serving as members of the executive or legislature, the regulation of other political activities, and the exclusion of judges from hearings in which they have an interest. It has even been advocated, for example in the 1983 Universal Declaration and by lawyers from countries with regional and cultural divisions based on ethnicity, that the social composition of the judiciary should reflect society 'in all its aspects' (Shetreet, 1985: 633–5).

Second, judicial independence means *insularity*: that is, independence from the executive and legislature, and with jurisdiction over all issues of a judicial nature. The judiciary has to be free from interference for political gain in the composition of courts, the tenure of judges, their methods of appointment, and their remuneration. Judicial insularity also means collective independence, enabling the judiciary to act as a corporate body with a role in the management of budgets, court personnel and premises (though there are many variations in the way such responsibilities can be shared with the executive). Ideally, executive control should be limited to the minimum requirements of executive accountability to the legislature. There are a large number of choices to be made in this respect, such as how to make judicial appointments, which disciplinary procedures to adopt, and how to ensure judicial accountability. However appointments are managed, it is essential that judges are not selected because of their political views but on merit.

Other conditions necessary for judicial independence have been proposed, including respect for decisions once rendered; independence from judicial colleagues who might seek to exert influence over the administrative, procedural or substantive stages of adjudication; and freedom from pressures of public opinion, especially that mobilized and articulated by the mass media (Shetreet, 1985; Domingo, 1999). To understand the full significance of judicial independence it may also be necessary to consider the scope of the judiciary's authority, especially when adjudicating on the decisions of the government.

Any given judiciary is likely to vary in the extent to which the different conditions for independence are present. Judges may be impartial, but not insulated from political interference and with little scope to challenge the actions of state agencies. Or there may be little political interference, but equally little impartiality or scope of authority, so that judges are inclined to act in support of political power (as in Pinochet's Chile). Or courts may be given wide scope, but lack impartiality and insularity (Larkins, 1996). The rule of law is fully served only when judicial independence is enjoyed by judges with the authority to adjudicate in all areas of public and private law.

It is in effect difficult to measure how independent a judiciary is. The constituent elements of judicial independence do not necessarily all move together. Weighting the different elements is difficult (for example, highly politicized judicial appointments yet minimal post-appointment interference, compared with selecting judges on merit but promoting them on political criteria). Judicial independence within a single country may also vary depending on the type of case, especially since formal and technical provisions (such as the judicial budget, the selection process, and tenure) are routinely ignored or manipulated in many countries. Nevertheless the International Commission of Jurists has produced a list of indicators by which the judicial independence of different countries can be compared, including direct efforts by governments to influence judicial decisions and the executive's role in the 'personnel management' of the judiciary (Widner, 1999).

Attacks on the independence of the judiciary

Countries in transition from authoritarianism have to remove violations of the rule of law from the statute books and constitutional documents to put an end to practices by the political executive which undermine the independence of the judiciary. These have included merging the judiciary and the executive (in Uruguay in the 1970s), changing the terms of employment in order to remove uncooperative justices (as in Bangladesh in 1977), omitting to adjust judicial salaries and transferring judges to 'punishment posting' (as in India in the 1980s), suspending the operation of courts, refusing to execute court judgements, pre-empting judicial reso-lution of disputes by legislation of constitutional amendment, passing retroactive legislation to reverse judicial decisions, using ad-hoc tribunals which ignore the protections offered by the ordinary courts, and allocat-ing cases in order to affect their outcome (Shetreet, 1985).

Unsurprisingly, protecting the independence of the judiciary has proved to be one of the most intractable problems facing societies in transition from authoritarianism to democracy. The Centre for the Independence of Judges and Lawyers (part of the International Commission of Jurists) regularly conducts annual surveys which reveal attacks on the indepen-dence of the judiciary, ranging from physical violence to an absence of job security. In 1999, for example, the Centre found instances in 49 countries, many of them supposedly trying to consolidate democracy, of attacks on the guardians of the rule of law by state agents, paramilitary groups, mili-tias and armed opposition groups. A total of 412 jurists suffered reprisals for carrying out their professional duties, included 16 killed, 12 'disap-peared', 79 prosecuted, detained or tortured, 8 physically abused, 35 verbally threatened and 262 professionally obstructed. Violence against jurists included physical attacks, threats and intimidation against 31 judges and prosecutors and over 100 others associated with the adminis-tration of justice in Colombia, and the arrest of lawyers defending oppo-nents and critics of the government in Belarus. Zimbabwe has become notorious for the harassment of judges, illustrated by the arrest of High Court Justice Benjamin Paradza in 2003, a judge with a history of passing judgements unfavourable to the government, such as ordering the release of opposition members abducted by supporters of the president, and ruling as illegal the eviction orders served on some white farmers.

Other tactics include suspending judges before challenges to executive action can be heard, appointing temporary judges who are more vulnera-ble to political influence (as in Pakistan), and even biasing housing allo-cations to penalize magistrates ruling against city officials (as in Ukraine). The overwhelming power of the executive in transitional regimes also constitutes a persistent threat to judicial independence, illustrated by deci-sions to 'pack' the Supreme Court in Argentina under Menem in 1991 and in Mexico under Zedillo in 1995 (Domingo, 1999).

Judicial independence is undermined in other ways, including impunity rules inhibiting lawyers from pursuing justice, as in Chad, where no action was taken against members of the security forces who had committed human rights violations. The use of exceptional courts undermines the principles of natural justice, including allowing military tribunals to hear civilian cases as in Peru and the Democratic Republic of the Congo. Improper political interference includes improper selection procedures as in Kenya where a chief justice was appointed despite not being a practising advocate or sitting judge as required by the constitution, and despite having been dismissed twice previously from judicial offices on disciplinary grounds. He had, however, been active as deputy public prosecutor in prosecuting critics of the government. Lack of security of tenure also makes it easier for politicians to obtain favourable treatment from the judiciary, raising concerns about Peru where 80 per cent of judges were working in 1999 on temporary contracts. Under-funding by governments leaves the judiciary vulnerable to corruption and improper political influences from local authorities to which the courts have to turn for resources, as in Russia (Rishmawi, 2000).

There are three major reasons for this continuing harassment of jurists. First, there is the legacy of earlier authoritarianism. Remnants of the authoritarian regime (whether military, single-party or communist) still frequently hold judicial office, especially when others do not have the requisite qualifications. In Central and Eastern Europe it has been difficult to replace the old ruling-class members of the judicial branch, with its links to the totalitarian system, by a new class eager to introduce new values consistent with the need to keep the judiciary independent and subordinated exclusively to the law. In Bulgaria, where priority had been given to political appointments of magistrates, rather than to favouring their professional qualifications, a ruling was issued by the Constitutional Court to prevent parliament from changing eligibility criteria as a way of removing troublesome members of the judiciary. In the Czech Republic, resorting to criteria for selection or confirmation in office based on a candidate's legal preparation, means those who can boast of experience acquired during the communist era are clearly favoured. Consequently the anti-democratic traditions in the judiciary are likely to persist. For example, Chile's supreme court which supported the Pinochet regime has shown leniency towards human rights violations during military rule, leading to the possibility that judicial independence may imperil democracy.

Second, judicial independence is not always regarded as a top priority in key sections of society. There may well be resistance to legal reform in political cultures in which patronage, clientelism, predatory rule and circumventions of the law are institutionalized, and when judges and politicians fear that past corruption will be disclosed and punished.

Interest groups may have stronger incentives to push for deviations from existing policy than to push for the protection of judicial indepen-dence. Lawyers themselves may be neither sufficiently powerful nor sufficiently motivated to protect judicial independence. Judges may find it difficult to resist the influence of powerful economic and political inter-ests, including their own class or corporate values and preferences. Judges have sometimes shown a bias towards the executive's interest in public order rather than individual rights to freedom of expression, assembly, association or movement. They may also exhibit a bias in favour of private property rights when governments seek to restrict these in the public interest (Vyas, 1992). Legislators have stronger incentives to bypass the judiciary than to support its independence, and governments may feel that the judiciary is blocking policies democratically arrived at by usurping the power of parliament. It is difficult to strike the right balance between an independent judiciary and rule by judges

The ideological position of senior judges can compromise their inde-pendence *vis-à-vis* parties in dispute, especially the government. For example, there was no need for Pinochet to purge the Supreme Court in Chile following his coup d'état in 1973 because the justices were ideo-logically disposed towards his policies and against those of the legitimate government, so that 'the rulings of the Supreme Court supported or strengthened Pinochet's reign', including his terrorizing of the opponents of the military and supporters of the previous government (Fiss, 1993).

Third, the constant revision of constitutions undermines continuity and the stability of the judiciary, preventing new institutions from becoming established. This is a particularly important consideration for new demo-cratic regimes trying to reinstate the rule of law after a period of authori-tarianism. At first sight it might seem that a complete purge of the judiciary is needed to ensure that democracy is supported by judicial inde-pendence rather than bias in favour of the *ancien régime*. However, the institutionalization of judicial independence may require stability rather than disruption, making the gradual removal of authoritarian remnants the preferred option, as in Chile in 1993 when three justices were impeached by the Chamber of Deputies for supporting the transfer of an important human rights case to a military tribunal. For the judiciary to be fully insti-tutionalized as an independent branch of government it may be better to remove judges for specific infringements of the constitution or common jurisprudence, rather than for a general association with a particular regime. In other words, there should be 'precise cause' for the removal of judges if there is not to be a long delay in the institutionalization of judi-cial independence and thus the rule of law (Larkins, 1996).

Protecting judicial independence

Arguably the most important prerequisite of judicial independence is political competition. This explains the paradox of executives and legislatures not limiting the power of judiciaries even when the courts frequently find *against* executive and administrative action, and when the judiciary is ultimately dependent under the constitution upon politicians for organization, appointments, funding and enforcement. Politicians may be prepared to share rule-making with judges, allowing them to elaborate on the details of legislation, or develop a whole area of law. Such 'delegation' is likely when politicians calculate that they will be able to claim the credit for policies from their supporters while shifting blame from opponents on to the judiciary. It is in the interest of political decision-makers to delegate powers to an independent judiciary because 'this delegation assists in maximizing their political support and chances of re-election' (Salzberger, 1993: 350).

Political support for an independent judiciary flows from the expectations of governing parties under competitive, compared with dominant, party systems. Politicians in some democracies have incentives to support judicial independence because of the long-term pattern of electoral politics. Where political parties expect elected government to continue with the likelihood of regular transfers of power from one party to another, politicians will support judicial independence. But if a party expects to remain in power indefinitely despite regular elections, its leaders will calculate that there will be 'lower risk-adjusted costs to nonindependent judiciaries'. So states with dominant parties are less likely to find that independent courts are respected (Ramseyer, 1994: 747).

Strong and stable political competition also guarantees the independence of the judiciary, when formal constitutional protections cannot, because of the incentives for mutual restraint which it creates for both government and opposition. A political party in power has incentives to respect judicial independence because of the constraints this would impose on the opposition, should it come to power (Stephenson, 2003). Judicial independence thus has part of its origins in the desire of politicians to avoid the risks of sustained political competition under which political actors who anticipate alternating in power over a sustained period of time will adopt a pro-independence perspective. Though judicial independence reduces the benefits a party can accrue while in power, it also reduces the costs of being out of power, since its opponents are also constrained. Equally, politicians continue to 'play' the political game even when they are not in power, because they know they will have the opportunity to punish violators of judicial independence once they return to power. Politicians may also be favourably disposed towards judicial independence because of concerns about corruption in government and business, the effect of a collapse of the rule of law on party cohesion, or the need to establish a new regime's legitimacy.

So while instances may be found in Africa where judicial independence seems to be increasing despite the persistence of single-party systems, it is also important to note the example of Kenya where a lack of incentives for reform is explained by government oppression of opposition; and that senior African judges believe multi-party democracy is the best safeguard of judicial independence (Widner, 1999).

Judicial independence also requires the backing of public opinion. This is likely to be available, even though sections of the public may have a vested interest in redistribution of wealth to which the judiciary may be ideologically opposed. This is because there will be stronger preferences for the protection provided by judicial independence against the illegal acquisition of wealth and power by politicians and their cronies. Sections of the public may benefit from state interventions with redistributive objectives, but still prefer this to be achieved within the rule of law.

In order for public opinion to support judicial independence, and in particular keeping judicial recruitment on a professional, not political, basis, resources need to be devoted to legal education among the public generally, and not just professionals, as well as consciousness-raising with the help of legal watchdogs.

The influence of legal professionals is also likely to be a prerequisite of judicial independence. While the history of authoritarianism shows that a subservient judiciary can suit the interests of the profession, once a democratic regime is in place the judiciary will have a vested interest in a system which values their expertise, a quality not held in great regard when the judiciary is politically subordinate. The actions which can be taken by the judiciary to underpin its own autonomy include encouraging, through more efficient court procedures, appeals against biased decisions taken in lower-level courts. Senior members of the judiciary can also influence public opinion and opinion-leaders on the rightness of autonomy, including promoting 'legal literacy', or the educating of people in the law and legal procedures. They can develop jurisprudence in the direction of judicial review in order to demonstrate to the public their independence from politics. They can call on international organizations (governmental and non-governmental) to support law reform.

International organizations have other roles to play in laying down basic principles to ensure the independence of the judiciary, governing such things as: the need for objective criteria when selecting and permanently placing judges; the assignment of administrative tasks to the relevant judicial bodies; transparent procedures; a competent independent body to carry out any advisory functions needed; and disciplinary functions, so that when these are not assigned to judicial bodies they are entrusted to agents of special competence under the control of a superior judicial organ. The Basic Principles on the Independence of the Judiciary adopted at the Seventh United Nations Congress on the Prevention of Crime and the Treatment of Offenders, 1985, are an example, as are the recommendations of the Ministers' Committee of the Council of Europe, 1994.

The politics of law reform

The main obstacles to law reform in support of the rule of law are political. In order that laws and constitutions can be rewritten, judges and bureaucrats retrained and institutions restructured, elites have to be motivated to accept the ensuing constraints on their behaviour, such as refraining from interfering in judicial decision-making. The problem is to know how to create incentives for political leaders to respect the rule of law. Making their decisions transparent is obviously crucial, as is permitting appeals to the judiciary against what are perceived to be illegal decisions by politicians and bureaucrats. An active civil society, including a free press, is a further requirement. Together with regular and free elections, these conditions make it clear to politicians that they risk losing office if they try to place themselves above the law. Incentives to support the rule of law are thus derived ultimately from transparency and accountability in politics. So the internal political will to reform is more important than external aid, which often has little impact. One of the reasons why foreign aid concentrates on the rewriting of laws and the retraining of judicial and administrative personnel is that breaking down entrenched political interests and developing new kinds of political leaders are such difficult and long-term remedies (Carothers, 1998).

Poor understanding of political conditions, and ignorance of how existing judicial arrangements serve the interests of specific economic, political and professional groups, have meant that many rule of law projects have failed to improve the quality of justice. Group interests in the *status quo* go beyond legal professionals and political elites to include business interests and other powerful economic groups. For example, wealthy people in Bangladesh who were heavily in debt to the state banks made sure that an alternative enforcement procedure was fatally flawed. Reformers thus need sound information about the interests of powerful groups. Consequently, the World Bank has initiated research to provide this, starting in Argentina, the Dominican Republic, India, Mexico and Slovakia (Messick, 2000).

Judicial reform is in effect a highly political process, affecting the distribution of power between state institutions (the executive, legislative and judicial branches of government) and between social strata. It requires changes in cultural values and norms, as well as long-term improvements in institutional capacity. Changes in political leadership can reduce levels of political support for reform. All this means that 'improvements in quality and effectiveness will tend to be slow in developing' and that gradual and incremental changes are more likely to have lasting beneficial effects than interventions designed to produce quick results (Biebesheimer and Payne, 2001: ii; Faundez, 1997).

Because of the powerful political interests at stake, and despite assistance from donors, legal systems have not been reformed enough in many transitional countries to fulfil the requirements of the rule of law. For example, in Russia judges and court officials still receive poor salaries and inadequate education and training, leading to incompetence among judges and prosecutors, corruption (especially in the provinces and ethnic republics), conflict between laws or judicial procedures and the constitution or the new criminal-procedural code, and undue influence exerted by government authorities over court decisions, all leading to 'the deeply cynical view of the legal system held by millions of Russians' (Aron, 2002: 10). Ukraine was slow to pass new criminal, civil, administrative and procedural codes. Foreign aid has had little impact in countries supported by the USA, with the rule of law actually deteriorating in some cases (USGAO, 2001).

Recipient governments rarely express an interest in reform before donors offer support. Nor can it be assumed that the judiciary will be supportive – supreme courts have rarely been allies in pushing for reform. Civil society groups cannot be guaranteed to support reform, often being more involved in partisan and ideological conflict and competition with each other and with state institutions. Public demand has rarely initiated reform, public dissatisfaction with the judicial system has never directed the course of reform, and the involvement of the public in reform efforts has been minimal. So donor resources and presence have usually had to substitute for political will (raising questions about how lasting reforms will be), and 'constituency-building' has tended to focus on increasing the interest and knowledge of the legal professions and building support in public institutions (Hammergren, 1998).

Conclusion

The rule of law is a complex constitutional principle comprising different conceptions of justice – as regularity, as equality, as ubiquity and as natural. It is most obviously a foundation of democracy. But additional importance attaches to it when it is shown that it is necessary for economic as well as political development, reflecting the assumption in economic theory that economic growth is dependent on non-interference by governments in private property rights. The rule of law is relevant to social development, meaning the alleviation of poverty. Reforming institutions to strengthen the rule of law is intensely political, and requires the creation of incentives for political leaders, and for different sections of society to be convinced that the rule of law is preferable to the *status quo*.

The rule of law is mainly secured through judicial independence, making it important to understand what this means and why it is so difficult to guarantee. Countries in transition from authoritarianism have to put an end to practices by the political executive which undermine the independence of the judiciary. Arguably the most important prerequisite of judicial independence is political competition, but formal safeguards are also crucial, as are favourable public opinion, the influence of legal professionals and the role of international organizations.

It is unavoidable that politicians, especially members of the executive, should have some role in managing the judicial branch of government. Senior judges have to be appointed, and expenditure on the judiciary – its personnel, buildings and supporting facilities – approved. The judicial branch cannot be totally immune from intervention by the executive. So a crucial constitutional question is how legislative or executive involvement can be made compatible with an independent judiciary.

The lesson for the international community is that if it wishes to support the rule of law there are indirect as well as direct ways of doing so, namely fostering stable political competition and correlative values such as a long-term perspective, a willingness to compromise, political stability and judicial doctrines that are attractive to all political parties (Stephenson, 2003). Resources should also be devoted to establishing strong political parties, and free and fair elections.

While there is probably no procedure that can guarantee total immunity from political manipulation, formal safeguards are crucial, needing aid donors to ensure that constitutional rules protect security of tenure, so that judges cannot be removed from office arbitrarily at the displeasure of the executive, or transferred from one jurisdiction to another for political ends rather than in the public interest (locating expertise in the most appropriate places). Support should be given to the creation of rigorous procedures for the removal of a judge, such as an inquiry by a specially appointed tribunal as in Zambia and Tanzania. Other procedural rules protect independence, including judicial immunity, fixed remuneration, *sub judice*, and the law of contempt (Vyas, 1992). Effective parliamentary scrutiny of ministers and departments of justice is also of great importance. Lack of transparency, preventing public scrutiny of executive action, especially appointments to supreme courts, has frequently been associated with political interference in judicial decision-making. Executive power, especially disproportionate in developing countries, needs to be balanced by a legislative capacity to exercise effective oversight and accountability.

The rule of law protects the individual against the state by preventing the concentration of power. Another way to do this is to fragment state power into a territorial hierarchy of governments, making it easier for political elites to be held accountable. Decentralization as a constitutional part of good governance is the subject of the next chapter.

5

The Decentralization of Political Power

Decentralization and good governance

The division of political and administrative powers territorially between different spatial entities in society is as important a constitutional matter as the allocation of powers between branches of government and the creation of rules within which they operate. Though the decentralization of power to territorial units is given varying degrees of constitutional status in different countries, it has been adopted as part of the democratization process in all regions of the world (Turner, 1999b) and as a response to pressures from spatially defined minority groups for a measure of self-determination. Demands for unity following civil war (as in Uganda and Mozambique), state reconstruction in post-communist countries and improved service delivery (in parts of East Asia and Latin America) have also prompted the creation or reform of decentralized government in the 'third wave' of democratization.

Such trends have been supported by the donor community. There seems to be a consensus among them that democratic decentralization is an essential part of good governance and a key aspect of political and administrative reform. Some donors, especially USAID, emphasize the contribution which decentralization can make to democratization, while the main multilateral agencies stress the importance of decentralization for social development generally and poverty reduction in particular (Blair, 2000).

USAID claims that 'effective decentralization can provide exciting opportunities for democratic change at the local level and can help improve national democracy as well' (USAID, 2000: 1). The World Bank looks to decentralization for increased administrative efficiency and political stability: 'successful decentralization improves the efficiency and responsiveness of the public sector while accommodating potentially explosive political forces' (World Bank, 2000: 107). According to the deputy director of the IMF's Western Hemisphere Department, 'decentralizing spending responsibilities can bring substantial welfare gains' (Ter-Minassian, 1997: 36). The UN urges governments everywhere to consider decentralizing the political system to make it more responsive to the political demands of citizens (UNDP, 1997b).

Decentralization and development

Aid donors tend to emphasize three major benefits to be derived from decentralization to local government institutions. The first is that public policies will be more responsive to local needs. Democratic decentralization should be a more effective way of meeting local needs than centralized planning. It provides a mechanism responsive to the variety of circumstances encountered from place to place, thereby improving allocative efficiency. Local politicians and bureaucrats are more responsive and accountable to the local population. Decentralization enables the benefits from government intervention to the citizens being served to be 'internalized'. It may even be possible for mobile citizens to 'vote with their feet' by moving from one local jurisdiction to another, thereby instilling competition within the structure of local government (UNDP, 1997b; World Bank, 2000b; OECD, 2004).

This claim is supported by the economic argument that different preferences for public services will produce spatially differentiated patterns of demand that can be efficiently met only by responsive local governments (Bird, 1990). Thus decentralization is designed to reflect unique local circumstances in development policy-making and implementation. These local circumstances include the local resources that are available in addition to contributions made to local and regional development by national agencies. When decision-making is decentralized, political demands for goods and services become tempered by resources. Participation in local government makes local knowledge of local conditions available to decision-makers (for example, on soil conditions and water courses in the case of irrigation policy and management), especially if user-groups are given a role in management (as with forests and irrigation projects in India and Nepal: Osmani, 2001).

The second major aim of decentralization for new democracies is securing the legitimacy of the new regime and so consolidating democratic stability. The World Bank has noted that national unity is being sought through decentralization in both South Africa and Uganda. It can assist with deflating secessionist tendencies in countries as diverse as Ethiopia, Bosnia Herzegovina and Russia. It can help governments gain local support in areas under rebel control, as in Colombia. 'A primary objective of decentralization is to maintain political stability in the face of pressures for localization' (World Bank, 2000b: 107–8).

Finally, decentralization is now frequently linked to poverty reduction in policy prescriptions by international agencies. When the majority of the population are poor, and all but excluded from national politics, it is natural to think that decentralization will help the poor by positioning power at the local level where they have a chance of capturing it, or at least making it more responsive to their needs and interests.

Consequently, the argument that decentralization has a part to play in poverty reduction has two dimensions: one to do with participation, the other with responsiveness. When decision-making power is located close to poor communities, and the poor are organized to lobby for their interests, officials will be encouraged to respond to their needs. At the same time widespread popular participation 'helps increase the voice of poor people in local affairs' (World Bank, 2001b). The poor benefit particularly from decision-making based on local information. Governments which are well informed of local needs are best placed to help the disadvantaged, because they can direct resources to services of benefit to the poor, such as health and education.

Aid projects

Donor support for decentralization takes three main forms (OECD, 2004). First, technical support is given to help create a favourable legal and political environment through legislation and policy. For example, in Sierra Leone the World Bank has helped the government to design and implement a sustainable fiscal decentralization strategy. The aim is to strengthen the ability of the decentralization secretariat in the Ministry of Local Government and Community Development and the Local Government Finance Department of the Ministry of Finance to provide policy advice on decentralization and to manage the central government's responsibilities. The aid covers the cost of specialist personnel, equipment, vehicles, technical assistance and training in both agencies.

Second, assistance is given with the early implementation of reforms and reorganization, including the framing of legislation for specific delegations of power, such as local powers of taxation. Training is also provided for the elected members and officers of newly created local government councils.

Third, there is a wide range of reforms, assisted by overseas aid, to 'deepen' and sustain new structures of decentralized governance. Interventions here aim to: strengthen policies for particular sectors such as health care or poverty reduction; build management capacity at the local level; and strengthen civil society to make public participation more effective. Municipalities have been helped by UNDP to create community development departments (in Thailand), undertake participatory district planning (in Nepal), and design income generating activities for designated groups (in Tanzania).

Aid to strengthen civil society focuses on the mobilization of group interests through community organizations. In the Philippines, for example, the local government code of 1991 requires a quarter of local council membership to come from the non-governmental sectors. Christian Aid, the Ford Foundation and other donors have established national networks of NGOs with resources to provide training and organizational development for bodies representing women's interests, farmers, fishermen and other social and economic groups.

Fourth, capacity-building seeks to strengthen the ability of local bureaucracies in the performance of their management functions, including financial management and policy planning. For example, the World Bank, the Inter-American Development Bank and the German aid agency GTZ have provided Ecuador with US$2000 million in loans to spend on increasing the administrative capacity of municipalities to plan and implement housing and urban infrastructure projects. In Uganda, UNDP has supported the decentralization programme by funds to develop the capacity of district resistance committees to plan and manage policies related to poverty reduction, including the development of small-scale enterprises.

Experiments in decentralization have often produced disappointments. Assessments are frequently catalogues of failures, difficulties, obstacles and frustrations. However, the very real shortcomings of much decentralization should not be allowed to obscure the benefits that have been achieved. Most decentralist reforms have wholly or partially achieved at least some of the theoretical benefits ascribed to them, if not all of them (Crook and Manor, 1998). The problem areas discussed here relate to the previously identified objectives of decentralization: responsiveness, state legitimacy and poverty reduction.

Responsiveness

Opposition from within government

Responsiveness presupposes the accountability of local public servants to locally elected representatives, and from elected representatives to local citizens. However, decentralization initiatives often encounter opposition from civil servants who, because of career aspirations, life styles and professionalism, wish to retain their links with the central government. Consequently decentralized governments often lack full control over the personnel responsible for providing local services such as agricultural extension, health care and education. For example, teachers in Pakistan have successfully opposed a reorganization of education that would place them under local authority control because it was felt that decentralization would reduce career opportunities in other local government areas, and damage the prestige of their profession. Elsewhere, the accountability of local officials to elected bodies has been weakened by opposition to the localization of employment from professional administrators, in whose interest it was to remain part of a national public service and to whom central governments deferred, not least because of reluctance among members of the central political executive to see power devolved (Blair, 2000).

There will always be political costs to those at the centre – politicians and bureaucrats – in the loss of control over local decision-makers and resources. Patronage, privilege and elite interests are not easily relinquished. And political interests hostile to decentralization are also often well represented in those supervisory agencies at national level responsible for ensuring local governments perform their statutory duties effectively. For example, attempts have been made in Colombia to make decentralized governments more accountable by delegating tax powers to local councils. But this has been impeded by clientelism, where spending on local services is regarded as a favour to be obtained from local political leaders. Attempts to mobilize local revenues are politically difficult under clientelist political relations (Merat, 2004).

The political and ideological concerns of national elites often in practice outweigh their interest in decentralization, including protecting the

power of local political allies (in Bangladesh), the pursuit of national inte-
gration (in Indonesia), the redress of special inequalities (in Laos) and (in
Vietnam) the creation of an autonomous state under the rule of law
(Turner, 1999a).

Participation

For elected members of local councils to be responsive to local needs and
demands, there need to be mechanisms for accountability. To make
accountability effective, additional opportunities for participation on a
continuing basis are required. In Latin America the extension of citizen
participation, together with stable and predictable financial arrangements
for local government, has been a common factor in successful decentralization initiatives (Peterson, 1997). Additional forms of political participation include: strong opposition parties with incentives to expose the
actions and policies of the governing group to public scrutiny; public
meetings so that citizens can at least be consulted before major policy
decisions are taken (for example, the open town meetings being convened
by some municipalities in El Salvador and Honduras, and 'participatory
budgeting' practised in the Brazilian city of Porto Alegre); formal procedures for the redress of grievances; and opinion polls to gauge satisfaction
with public services. All such activities need to be backed by information
from independent media disseminating news and investigating suspected
malpractices. Studies of city governments in the Third World show that
though such participation is often seen by local councillors as a threat to
their authority, community consultation in drawing up municipal budgets
increases the number of people with experience of how decisions are
made, making the process of selecting priorities more transparent (Devas
et al., 2001).

   While it may be necessary for central and local governments to create
formal institutions in which citizens can participate, the existence of
decentralized governance itself can under some circumstances encourage
the development of grass-roots activism through NGOs, community
groups and social movements. For example, in the 1990s the existence of
stronger municipalities in Mexico provided political space for the emergence of civic participation and the development of civil society in the
form of pressure groups, human rights organizations, NGOs and electoral
monitors (Santin del Rio, 2004).

   One danger for decentralized government is that participation is sometimes institutionalized in order to mobilize support for national elites. For

example, structures for participation from the village upwards in Zimbabwe have been used to help the ruling party maintain control of local-level politics, rather than to make local democracy and self-government a reality (Masuko, 1996). One aim of the system of decentralization introduced in 1985 by the military government of Bangladesh was to co-opt powerful local groups in support of the Ershad regime. This focused the attention of local elected representatives on the benefits to be had by responding to the central authorities rather than on accountability to the poor, thus undermining any chance of decentralization alleviating poverty. Indeed, decentralization 'intensified the marked inequalities which existed' (Crook and Manor, 1998: 129, 279).

Local participation has also often been hampered by the attitudes of local authority personnel who have not been supportive of more direct forms of participation (Hay *et al.*, 1990; Gboku, 1993). Elected representatives do not always see it as important to make themselves accessible to their constituents. They may also find it difficult and risky to spend from tax revenues while mobilizing self-help activities (Crook, 2003.

Participation may also not be enjoyed equally by all sections of the community. The participation of some local groups can be more effective than others. When considering the responsiveness of decentralized governments to local needs it is important not to adopt a socially homogenous model of the local 'community'. Such communities consist of different interests, and it is unlikely that local governments will respond to all equally. Elections often marginalize some groups within local society, notably women, minorities and other vulnerable people. Some parts of civil society, such as organizations representing the business community, have far more political influence than others. Evidence from Kenya and Uganda indicates that before participation and accountability can function effectively 'the capacity of both local governments and civil society organisations need to be strengthened' (Devas and Grant, 2003: 315).

In developing countries women are particularly weak at effectively articulating their political demands, even when they are well represented numerically on local councils through quotas, as for example in the Indian state of Karnataka. The results for disadvantaged groups are mixed. While geographically concentrated ethnic minorities are sometimes empowered by democratic local government (in Bolivia and the Philippines, for example), scheduled castes in most of India are still too weak politically to promote their economic interests, despite forty years of mandatory representation within Panchayati Raj (Blair, 2000).

Central controls

The benefits of responsiveness to local demands and needs have frequently been further limited by centralist tendencies in development planning and management. Decentralist reforms have often been negated by central controls which make local policies respond more to central direction than to local needs and popular preferences. Restricted autonomy is a feature of many post-communist regimes. Recentralization has taken place throughout much of Eastern and Central Europe following early legislation to decentralize power (Elander, 1997; Regulska, 1997; Zsamboki and Bell, 1997). Continuing centralization on the part of governments using participatory and decentralizing rhetoric can occur because central governments require local institutions to be bound by national policy aims and directives, as in Kenya, Mongolia and Senegal for example (Osmani, 2001).

Continuing centralization is also found in Africa, despite efforts over a long period to decentralize power. Capital investment is planned by national ministries, leaving local authorities 'discouraged by the absence of real decisions'. Local financial autonomy is undermined by shortages of technical personnel and direct, often arbitrary, control of local budgets by central departments, especially ministries of finance. Botswana, Ghana, Kenya and Swaziland are examples of countries where local authorities are unable 'to act independently of central direction, or to respond to their constituents' wants and needs' (Wunsch, 2001: 278–80). A comparative study of the health and road sectors in sub-Saharan Africa found that the level of responsiveness of locally determined needs is reduced by oversight from central ministries, their control of day-to-day management (especially personnel and procurement), dependence on central allocations of resources and resistance from within the civil service. Consequently statutory arrangements for decentralization are often not reflected in the actual management of public services (Andrews and Schroeder, 2003).

Central policy control can be imposed by appointments to key positions locally and also by dissolutions (Boukhalov and Ivannikov, 1995; Campbell, 1995b). In Romania the National Salvation Front government appointed its members as mayors of cities where the party had received less than 50 per cent of the vote in 1990 (Gallagher, 1996: 215). Appointed executives at republic, regional and local levels were used in President Yeltsin's conflict with the Russian parliament, with senior officials and whole councils being dismissed and dissolved until eventually all councils had experienced suspension. The new representative local governments have also had a struggle to constrain the corruption and illegalities of officials who are the political clients of the president (Campbell, 1995c; Gelman and Sentanova, 1995).

Administrative incapacity

Responding to local needs is made additionally difficult when local governments do not have the administrative capacity required. Administrative incapacity is widespread. A comparative study of Bulgaria, the Czech Republic, Hungary and Slovakia found financial resources to be inadequate to maintain existing levels of social care, and personnel to be lacking in experience and skills. Shortages of financial and human resources have also incapacitated local government in Romania (Campbell, 1995a). Because of chronic under-funding in Ugand, 'service delivery in urban areas, where it exists, has been effectively, if not legally, privatized', if only by default (Gombay and O'Manique, 1996: 95). Administrative incapacity reduces the willingness of governments to decentralize (Elster *et al.*, 1998).

Such incapacity has a destructive effect on local government's standing in the mind of the public, and on its ability to take on new roles, including dealing with growing demands resulting from the poverty, unemployment and inflation caused by structural adjustment policies. Interest in public participation is likely to wane further if resources are insufficient for preferences to be implemented (Devas and Grant, 2003).

Financial dependence

Dependence on central authorities for resources has further reduced the political autonomy of local institutions and therefore their responsiveness. For example, Poland's new local authorities are 'highly dependent on fiscal transfers, with limited discretion in taxation and therefore little accountability to the electorate for revenue decisions' (Hicks and Kaminski, 1995: 15–17). Local dependence on tax-sharing and transfers for resources characterizes local democracy throughout Eastern and Central Europe (Bird *et al.*, 1994). Overall, subnational governments account for a small share of total public expenditure (unless regional budgets in federations such as Argentina and India are included), and local governments raise a small percentage of total government revenues. Decentralized spending increased through the 1990s as a percentage of

Table 5.1   *Fiscal decentralization, 1990–97 – developing world and post-communist Europe, sub-national government share (%)*

	Total public expenditure		Total tax revenue	
	1990	1997	1990	1997
Latin America				
Argentina	46.3	43.9	38.2	41.1
Bolivia	17.7	36.3	15.1	19.1
Chile	7.2	8.5	6.4	7.0
Nicaragua	3.5	9.6	2.5	8.3
Peru	9.8	24.4	1.2	2.4
Africa				
Botswana	7.9	3.8	0.1	0.6
Kenya	3.4	3.5	2.2	1.9
South Africa	20.7	49.8	5.5	5.3
Asia				
India	51.1	53.3	33.8	36.1
Indonesia	13.1	14.8	2.9	2.9
Malaysia	20.2	19.1	3.7	2.4
Thailand	7.5	9.6	4.4	5.5
Post-communist Europe				
Bulgaria	18.9	15.7	22.4	11.8
Estonia	34.8	22.4	26.5	14.2
Hungary	20.6	23.7	7.6	8.9
Lithuania	30.4	22.6	14.4	16.2
Romania	15.4	13.3	12.8	9.2

SOURCE: data from World Bank (2000b), Table A1, pp. 216–17.

NOTE: Reliable fiscal data for sub-national governance is notoriously difficult to come by. Even the World Bank was only able to muster full data for just over a third of the entries in its tabulation for the *World Development Report 1999/2000*.

total public expenditure, but the share of total tax revenues raised by subnational governments remained constant on average (see Table 5.1). Latin American countries have done the most to increase subnational government's share of revenues and expenditure (Peterson, 1997).

The fact that the spending of decentralized governments is increasing globally does not necessarily mean that the spending bodies are exercising autonomy in relation to the policies the expenditure supports (Selee and Tulchin, 2004). More important for autonomy are: the proportion of

local revenues that comes from central allocations; the form the allocations take (whether they are contributions to the local authority's general
funds to be spent at its discretion, or are assigned to specific areas of
expenditure such as roads, education or health care and requiring centrally
determined standards to be achieved); whether subnational governments
have powers and opportunities to raise revenues from other sources such
as charges and rents; and whether transfers take the form of grants or a
share of centrally collected revenue.

State legitimacy

The view that vibrant local governance can enhance national democracy by
legitimizing the state in the eyes of its citizens has been confirmed by
observers in all regions with democratizing states. Establishing the legitimacy of government nationally can be helped by legislation to redress the
'institutional deficit' under earlier regimes (Naim, 1995). In Colombia, for
example, it is through the democratization and strengthening of local
administration that 'government legitimacy lost or at least called into question is being regained. Such reforms ... forge new ties between the state
and civil society' (Rodriguez, 1995: 169). In Central and Eastern Europe
democratic decentralization has helped the state to respond to the resentment felt towards the mode of local administration under the previous
regimes – hierarchical, centralized, lacking in electoral choice, and without
the proper separation of judicial and executive powers (Davey, 1995b: 44).

Decentralization also becomes a 'source of democratic vitality' when it
gives people experience of democracy. It can serve democratic consolidation by removing barriers to participation, strengthening the responsiveness and accountability of government, preventing politics becoming a
'winner takes all' game, and giving minorities opportunities to share
power, learn the complexities of government, and obtain credibility and
responsibility (Diamond *et al.*, 1995: 46).

Legitimacy can also be served by democratic decentralization under
conditions of ethnic pluralism. Transitions from highly centralized authoritarian regimes provide opportunities for a measure of autonomy demanded
by ethnically, linguistically or culturally distinctive areas. Political decentralization can help by giving ethnic groups a degree of autonomy, by
protecting such autonomy against recentralization, and by protecting the
rights of minorities in quasi-autonomous areas. An equitable intergovernmental fiscal system may be crucial if ethnically diverse societies are to

recognize the state's legitimacy (Schmitter, 1992; Bird *et al.*, 1995; Przeworski, 1995). Botswana is but one example of local government contributing to the legitimacy of the state by its acceptance of the boundaries of the Tswana tribes and their cultural distinctiveness (Holm, 1988).

The nation-state can benefit from the legitimacy that subnational political authority enjoys in the local political culture. For example, decentralization in Uganda, including the National Resistance Movement's ten-point programme of 1986, was in part a response to a resurgence of support for traditional kingdoms and other forms of regional autonomy (Gombay and O'Manique, 1996: 99–101). In both Zimbabwe and Namibia local government reorganization was prompted in part by the need to correct the illegitimacy of areas defined racially and ethnically by whites-dominated regimes (Tordoff and Young, 1994: 286). In Hungary communities have claimed municipal status as an assertion of ancient rights of local self-government (Davey, 1995a: 69).

What the democratization process shows is that a significant consensus about democracy among national elites is necessary before local democratization can be initiated. A culture of democracy supports decentralization and participation rather than the reverse (Aziz and Arnold, 1996). For example, in South Korea democratization instigated 'the introduction of a local self-government system' because there was enormous public support for more participation and responsive government, especially within the middle class. Local democracy was a consequence of the democratization movement against a government party anxious about losing control of the localities. Experience in Central and Eastern Europe was that 'decentralised administration is a product of a pluralist society and not a method to achieve pluralism' (Seroka, 1996: 318). Similarly in Mexico, 'only with consistent social and political forces committed to democratic change in prevailing structures and policies, will municipal empowerment become a real possibility' (Massolo, 1996: 247).

Conversely, democratic decentralization will be delayed if confidence and trust in the democratic process at the national level are weak, as in Mozambique, where one objective of the Local Government Reform Programme launched in 1991 was a 'deepening' of democracy. Mutual distrust between government and opposition at the centre disrupted the process of democratic decentralization. Local elections were boycotted and repeatedly postponed. Reform legislation was delayed because of conflict over electoral procedures, the administration and supervision of elections, the designation of areas to receive municipal status, and the form of state tutelage. Candidates engaged in, or were the victims of, politically motivated violence and detention (Weimer and Fandrych, 1999). Democratic decentralization thus needs an 'enabling environment' which may, as in Paraguay, need donor support to counterbalance opposition (Rojas *et al.*, 1998).

The use of democratic decentralization to accommodate ethnic aspirations and so help legitimize the existing nation-state is risky. In some ethnically complex societies decentralization may turn national minorities into local majorities and give them the power to discriminate against those who find themselves in a minority within the reorganized territorial structure of subnational government. There is a limit to the extent to which power can be devolved to ever smaller units in an attempt to achieve homogenous populations.

Another possibility is that decentralization, initiated from a central government motivated by objectives to do with efficiency, security and the exploitation of under-utilized resources, can generate mobilization and protest in places where no regional cultural identities previously existed. Chile is a case in point. Similarly, elite fears of 'balkanization' in Bolivia delayed the introduction of democratic decentralization. If decentralization exacerbates political tensions between areas with different resource endowments, economic activities and public services might be disrupted (Nickson, 1995; Slater, 1995; von Braun and Grote, 2002).

Poverty reduction

Though the arguments and assumptions about the poverty-reducing potential of decentralized governance seem plausible, there are powerful theoretical and empirical reasons for doubting that a redistribution of political power or material resources can be achieved by the decentralization of political authority. The history of decentralization in developing countries suggests that the participation of, and responsiveness to, the poor have rarely been achieved in this way. This is because local elites tend to dominate processes of political participation, and capture resources that otherwise might respond to the needs of the poor.

Elite domination

Democratic decentralization undoubtedly creates opportunities for the poor to obtain representation on local councils. However, elections usually produce a membership dominated by people from elite occupations such as teachers, civil servants, wealthy farmers, businessmen and traders, rather than representatives from the poor. For example, in Ghana, educated people and professionals (mainly male) have been over-represented on district assemblies. Where decentralization has brought in people from formerly excluded, low-status groups, such as farmers, artisans and small traders, as in Côte d'Ivoire, the poorest groups have remained unrepresented. Even in the Indian state of Karnataka, where about a fifth of council seats have been reserved for scheduled castes and tribals, councils remain dominated by landowning castes. If the poor do manage to become well represented on district and village councils, their contributions to debate and decision-making tends to be extremely limited, reflecting cultural subordination (Crook and Manor, 1998; Crook and Sverrisson, 2001; Osmani, 2001).

Participation between elections in lobbying, advocacy, consultations, campaigns, investigations and petitions is important if solidarity and self-confidence among the poor are to be built up, empowering them both psychologically and materially (Crook and Sverrisson, 2001: 8). So empowering the poor means more than providing the formal institutions and procedures of representative government. Empowerment recognizes the importance of the 'political agency' of the poor and their ability to use the opportunities for local participation to their own benefit (Engberg-Pedersen and Webster, 2002).

However, the poor in developing countries find themselves disempowered by a wide range of economic and social factors which limit the effectiveness of their participation: material inequality, the risks from political activism, and competition (see Chapter 7). In addition, a range of organizational factors block the effective participation of the poor in local government, and constrain the capacity for delegated authority to empower people. Local officials may be reluctant to undermine their own professional status by making their activities more intelligible to the poor and uneducated. Elected officials are also often reluctant to share their representative role with other participants or permit officials to forge direct links with community and group activists.

Unsurprisingly, then, a survey of decentralization programmes in a selection of African, Asian and Latin American countries led to the conclusion that 'it is naïve to imagine that simply introducing elections for local offices will transform the relationship between governments and citizens or empower the mass of the poor'. Most forms of political participation tend to be dominated by urban or rural elite minorities (Crook and Sverrisson, 2001).

Responsiveness and elite capture

Political decentralization frequently gives more power to socio-economic elites. Decentralization may mean a redistribution of power and resources from centre to periphery, but this does not mean that power and income redistribution between classes will follow, as the Brazilian case shows (Souza, 1994). Greater local autonomy to manage local resources from whatever source is likely to create greater opportunities for capture by local elites. Elite capture is still very prominent in less-developed and post-communist countries, including Bolivia, Honduras, India, Mali, the Philippines and Ukraine. Poverty reduction by local governments is severely constrained. Elite control over the allocation of resources ensures that existing patterns of power and wealth are not disturbed (Blair, 2000).

Even where decentralized policy-making has reflected the felt needs of local people, and where there has been some redistribution towards poor or marginalized groups, as in Karnataka district councils, statutory requirements to direct resources at the poor have not always been followed. Expenditure gets deflected towards local elites under the influence of patronage, corruption, electoral manipulation, fraud and misappropriation. For example, financial mismanagement in Guinea's communes has meant that tax revenues are 'often appropriated by members and local notables' (Charlick, 2001). Central government priorities also deflect expenditure from pro-poor policies, which are anyway often beyond the capacities of local councils, as in Côte d' Ivoire. Local authorities rarely have the legal powers or resources to do other than implement national programmes. They are generally unable to contribute to pro-poor economic growth by making changes to levels of economic activity, wages or prices (Crook, 2003). Where they do have powers to support economic development, local authorities spend 'a minor fraction' of their budgets on it (Helmsing, 2003: 75). Consequently, even the most successful and responsive cases such as those examined by Crook and Manor 'showed little evidence of having been particularly responsive to "vulnerable groups", the poor and the marginalized' (1998: 301).

There is also the theoretical question of whether local government is suitable for the performance of distributive functions, rather than the allocation function of the public sector. Interpersonal equity may be inconsistent with local autonomy. This is because an out-migration of firms and households would undermine the policies of a local government attempting to redistribute income from rich to poor. Even if the rich remained, poor people would be attracted by the redistributive quality of the services being offered, such immigration then significantly reducing the resources available to meet social needs. Mobility is a strong discouragement to positive redistribution. Since local authorities are unlikely to be given power to control migration, redistribution is usually considered a role for central authorities (Bailey, 1999).

Indeed, decentralization has sometimes been used to enable the wealthy to protect their privileged economic and social position by separating their communities territorially from poor areas needing high levels of local service provision, expenditure and revenue-raising. Decentralization may allow those who can afford it to move into exclusive jurisdictions, isolating themselves in municipalities where a high standard of limited services can be provided. Low tax rates and levels of social expenditure further attract the rich and repel the poor. The high cost of services in poor areas then falls on those with the highest levels of need but least able to pay. This raises questions about the territorial design of decentralized government and the size of areas, though again it is generally assumed that central governments are more likely than local to be successful in redistributing income from richer to poorer neighbourhoods (Prud'homme, 2003).

Consequently, very few decentralization programmes have alleviated poverty. The optimism of the *World Development Report 2000–1* is somewhat undermined by one of the background papers commissioned for it which concluded that the 'notion that there is a predictable and general link between decentralization of government and the development of more "pro-poor" policies or poverty-alleviating outcomes clearly lacks any convincing evidence' (Crook and Sverrisson, 2001: 52). In a recent study for the OECD of 18 developing countries and 3 Indian states, more than two-thirds of the cases were found to have had negative effects on poverty reduction. Only in 3 cases were the effects positive: Bolivia, the Philippines and West Bengal in India (Jutting *et al.*, 2004).

However, there clearly are actions that can be taken, and in a few cases have been, to strengthen the participation of the poor in local democracy, and to make local decisions, plans and expenditure more responsive to the poor's needs. After itemizing the reforms needed to make decentralization pro-poor, the likelihood of finding governments in the Third World willing to undertake such measures will be assessed.

Promoting the participation of the poor

Central government support is necessary if decentralization is to be pro-poor (Jutting *et al.*, 2004). It has to be support which recognizes the economic and political obstacles to effective participation by the poor, and the risks of elite capture of devolved powers and resources, including those targeted at the poor. To make pro-poor participation effective, state support has to be directed at the poor's material deprivation and their capacity for group action. How the empowerment of the poor might be supported is explored in Chapter 7. Within many systems of decentralization there are also administrative barriers to political participation which need to be removed by central governments that seek genuine decentralization.

First, the professional values and practices of local government staff can be reoriented towards the empowerment of the poor. Power disparities and other inequalities need to be recognized and understood by local officials. Second, collective action by groups of service users and other citizens can be supported with status (for example, from legal entitlements to consultation) and resources, perhaps following the example of the Philippines where the local government code of 1991 requires that NGOs be incorporated into advisory bodies at local and provincial levels. NGOs have also to be represented on local development councils, school and health boards, and other special-purpose agencies. They can nominate members to council seats reserved for representatives from specified sectors (women, ethnic minorities, workers and certain occupations) and take the lead in legislative 'initiatives' and public 'recall' (Brillantes, 1994; Turner, 1999a).

Third, resources and powers can be devolved to enable local authorities to initiate administrative procedures which encourage the participation of the poor, such as participatory budgeting (as in Entebbe, Uganda), surveys of consumer needs (as in Ghana and Senegal) and complaints procedures (such as the local ombudsmen in Benin and Nigeria). 'Charters' can be provided specifying standards by which service users can judge the performance of local authorities. Financial management can be made more transparent, especially income generation, intergovernmental transfers, and expenditure flows (Olowu, 2003).

Strengthening responsiveness to the poor

Strengthening the participation of the poor locally obviously goes some way towards preventing the capture by local elites of institutions and resources designed to alleviate poverty. But other interventions by the central government are needed to support the poor in their conflicts with other strata and ensure the responsiveness of local authorities to their needs and interests.

Disempowering local elites

In the very few cases, such as West Bengal, where decentralization has produced poverty-alleviating outcomes, there has been strong commitment to pro-poor policies within the dominant party at central government level. Its local activists have challenged resistance from local elites and supported pro-poor organizations. The responsiveness of decentralized government to the poor has been found to require the mobilization of local anti-elite alliances between small peasants, sharecroppers, agricultural labourers and some white-collar employees such as teachers and clerks. The mobilizing force is usually an ideologically motivated national party with the power to prevent hostile local elites from sabotaging the programmes of social and economic redistribution mentioned earlier. Central governments may bypass local authorities under the control of local elites if the patron–client system obstructs the initiation of pro-poor projects. In other words, there needs to be a departure from the normal forms of local party politics in the Third World, in which local elites are incorporated into support for national leadership by patronage and clientelism, thereby intensifying inequalities and poverty (Crook and Sverrisson, 2001).

Efforts can also be made to identify and support pro-poor factions among local elites. Wealthy members of a community might calculate that a measure of redistribution could be to their advantage. They might gain satisfaction from altruism or, more likely, a sense of increased security from the reduction of poverty (for example, if they associate it with crime). They may benefit generally from the enhancement of the quality of community life which follows from the increased consumption by the poor of goods such as education. For example, local government reforms by the state government in Ceara, Brazil, enabled different elite positions to emerge, with some in favour of pro-poor policies, for example retailers concerned about unemployed beggars 'on the doorsteps of their establishments' (Tendler, 1997: 153–4).

Devolving redistributive functions

The devolution of significant and relevant powers is needed if decentralization is to be pro-poor. First, this helps to avoid elite capture by making it more worthwhile for poor people to spend time and resources acquiring information about local politics. Second, the production of goods and services by local governments can be expected to lead to income redistribution. Many local government services are conventionally regarded as redistributive, such as primary and secondary education, housing, and social services, particularly those designed for children. Regulatory policies such as land use planning and rent controls can also have significant distributional effects. The transfer of natural resources management to local authorities can operate to the advantage of the poor by protecting rural livelihoods, generating incomes, and thus alleviating poverty and increasing equity. But again it has to be recognized that this increases the risk of hostility from, or capture by, existing economic elites such as logging companies in the case of forest management (Larson, 2003).

Second, redistribution has even been classed as a local public good in its own right, since it produces benefits that are both non-rival (available to all) and non-excludable (non-payers cannot be excluded from consumption). Those bearing the cost of provision live in the local government area itself. Since the optimal level of redistribution will vary from locality to locality according to the values and wealth of taxpayers, redistribution could be completely decentralized (Pauly, 1973). Local altruism may lead local governments to target poverty more effectively than central governments, because a higher level of altruism is likely to be found towards one's immediate community than towards society generally, again suggesting that 'there may be more scope for redistribution at subnational levels' (Jimenez, 2000: 178).

Third, with sufficient powers and resources local authorities can take more specific action designed to alleviate poverty. Local 'safety-nets' can be budgeted for to protect incomes and security when economic crises threaten the vulnerable. The standards of settlements can be upgraded (especially housing, water and sanitation). The position of the poor in local market transactions can be strengthened by vocational training and contracting with small enterprises. Investment in public information programmes, for example about HIV and AIDS, can improve the poor's life chances (Helmsing, 2003). Local governments can also help implement redistributive policies by targeting the intended beneficiaries of central government's anti-poverty programmes.

Fourth, the consumption of merit goods can also be encouraged by local governments. Housing, education, food, public transport and other services can be subsidized. (Though it has to be remembered that in the case of public utilities subsidies are likely to benefit the better off whose consumption rises with income.) Territorial inequalities can be addressed. The need, cost and ability to pay for public services vary according to geographical location. Distributional inequities reveal themselves in the geographical location of amenities such as hospitals and in the incidence of disbenefits, such as pollution. The costs and benefits of life are usually unevenly distributed among neighbourhoods which in their turn are specific to different income groups. Spatial inequalities such as these are found in most developing countries. In Zimbabwe, for example, health and extension services are unevenly distributed (Rakodi, 1990: 138). In Tanzania spatial planning has specifically targeted such inequalities and has increased spatial equity in access to clean water, health facilities, primary education and roads (Maro, 1990). It is important that powers to provide services of benefit to the poor are properly devolved so that local councils are not ruled *ultra vires* if they try to help the poor, as happened in Colombo over initiatives to improve low-income settlements. Central government also needs to supervise the allocation of funds for poverty alleviation to ensure that legal requirements are not ignored, as has happened in most districts of Ghana (Devas *et al.*, 2001).

Policies are also needed to protect the poor from the adverse effects of economic development. Local authorities may find themselves struggling to prevent the livelihoods of the poor from worsening, rather than engaging in poverty reduction, especially in urban areas. A study of the relationship between urban governance and poverty in 10 cities in developing countries found that effective pro-poor policies included preventing industrial development from forcibly removing poor people from their homes, adopting supportive policies for the informal sector, flexible land-use planning, and the provision of safe and affordable water, sanitation and solid-waste collection to all neighbourhoods (Devas *et al.*, 2001).

If the poor are concentrated in areas that are economically disadvantaged, local governments will be unable to raise the resources locally that are needed to alleviate poverty. Intergovernmental transfers are needed which do not exacerbate spatial inequalities and which encourage the mobilization of local resources. Grant arrangements can be made to effect geographical and social redistribution. In theory a central government could devise an equalization scheme that would pay extra grant to authorities that undertook redistribution and thereby encouraged the emigration of the rich and the immigration of the poor, with the consequent adverse effect on the local per capita tax base. However, a consequence may be that local governments will lose a measure of autonomy, bringing poverty reduction into conflict with the aim of responsiveness. While it may seem uncontroversial to require local authorities to target central grants on the poor, it has to be recognized that conditional or hypothecated grants put local autonomy at risk. It is extremely difficult to strike the right balance between conditional and unconditional grants, and between respecting local autonomy and maintaining standards of service in the interest of distributional objectives (Ter-Minassian, 1997).

Decentralized poverty reduction requires an appropriate system of transfers from central government to ensure that sufficient resources are available for the 'right' objectives. Expenditure will have to be targeted on the poor, either as income support or to develop human capital and productivity through health, education and housing provision. The choices here are likely to be embodied in national policies backed up by conditional grants. Nevertheless, spatial equalization will have to deter-mine allocations from the centre, even though not all poor people are concentrated in poor regions (Bird and Rodriguez, 1999).

Experience in many countries, including Argentina and Bolivia, indi-cates that success in targeting the poor requires central governments to provide most of the funding and to monitor expenditure, while local governments deliver the services, drawing on their superior information about social needs in their areas (World Bank, 2000b). Intergovernmental allocations need to be based on a formula which reflects the needs of poor areas and poor people, but adopting such a formula may be opposed by powerful political interests in wealthy localities. For example, in Tanzania, local governments are highly dependent on central allocations based on budget requests driven by the current supply of services (for example, enrolment levels in education) rather than the level of local demand (for example, the number of school-age children in the locality). This favours well-endowed urban localities, despite the official pro-poor objectives set for decentralization by both the Tanzanian government and aid donors (Boex, 2003).

While equalization grants may go some way towards allowing poorer *areas* with small tax bases to provide at least a minimum if not equal level of service, income inequality and poverty are found in all areas. So measures to promote horizontal equity will go only part of the way towards reducing the impact of poverty on people's lives, as the cases of India and Indonesia show (World Bank, 2000b).

The migration problem that might arise following redistribution efforts can also be overcome to a certain extent if the units of local government are geographically large. By reorganizing the structure of local govern-ment in this way, central governments make it theoretically possible for local governments to initiate policies of progressive redistribution between social classes and neighbourhoods. This has been tried in Johannesburg (Devas *et al.*, 2001). In developing countries even more than in developed ones, mobility is restricted anyway by cultural factors and economic opportunities. And mobility across jurisdictions is rarely driven by the quality of public services.

It has also been noted that where decentralization has helped the poor there has been a hierarchy of regional and district authorities large enough to support lower tiers and, ideally, providing a 'policy elite' sharing central government's commitment to poverty alleviation and immune to the power of local elites (Belshaw, 2000; Crook and Sverrisson, 2001). However, opinion on the structure of areas for decentralized governance is not unanimous. It may be better, for the sake of participatory democracy, to keep the basic units of local government as small as possible, using joint coordinating committees, interauthority management agreements, side contracts, and support from regional field offices for dispersed rural settlements for the delivery of services which the smallest authorities cannot afford to provide individually. Then upper-tier authorities are not needed for large-scale operations (Bennett, 1994).

Central governments are not necessarily the sole sources of redistributive policies. It is true that they can compensate for differences *between* localities in incomes, capacities to tax and spend, and political willingness to address inequalities. Yet there is no conclusive evidence that differences between the sources of money for redistributive public services such as education and health affects equity of access or outcomes in the same way. For example, Brazil, Chile and Colombia rely heavily on local authority spending on basic education, but with very different equity outcomes. Nevertheless, decentralized service provision supported by central government funding can meet equity objectives; and local governments have information advantages when it comes to targeting poverty. For example, in Albania local authority targeting of social assistance to poor households is more effective than national government's targeting of poor districts because local authorities have better information on social conditions in their areas (Jimenez, 2000).

The state and poverty

The general picture in developing countries is one of limited devolution, rather than the extensive empowerment of local authorities required for poverty alleviation. Decentralized governments tend to play a minor role in the provision of social services and other redistributive functions. Historical traditions of centralization leave central governments reluctant to empower either local governments or civil society. Local autonomy and therefore accountability to all sectors of local society, and not just the rich and powerful, is further undermined by central controls and tutelage designed to restrict mismanagement at the local level (Charlick, 2001).

Even when there is extensive decentralization it is rare for this to be accompanied by measures specifically designed to strengthen the voice of the poor. For example, the radical decentralization under Uganda's Constitution and Local Government Act 1997 contains extensive devolution of potentially redistributive powers, including nursery, primary, secondary and technical education, and health services (including maternity and child welfare). The reform is also intended to involve the participation of under-represented and disadvantaged groups. But these are identified as women, young people and the disabled, who may or may not be poor. The constitutional principles of decentralization make no reference to poverty (Mitchison, 2003). The central government sees its job as ensuring that local councils are effective, efficient, honest and providing value for money. It does not supervise them to ensure they are pro-poor.

Any redisributive aims of central government action may be further compromised by irresistible political pressures. Equalization by fiscal transfers may be negated by political considerations such as the need to retain the political support of richer areas, or for discrimination among equally poor areas to favour sensitive frontier regions, as in Indonesia and Argentina (Bird and Vaillancourt, 1998: 29–30).

There is no doubt that decentralization could serve the aim of poverty alleviation in poor countries. But for it to do so requires a national political context that is supportive, a context that is all too often lacking.

Prerequisites of successful decentralization

The many years of donor involvement in the reorganization of decentralized governance have provided numerous lessons on how foreign aid and technical assistance can be deployed to best effect (see for example OECD, 2004). Perhaps the most important lesson, and the one most difficult for donors to deal with, is that decentralization is a political process affecting the distribution of power within the structure of government in particular and society in general. Consequently donor interventions are affected by the political environment, including existing power structures, democratic traditions (or the lack of them), the presence and strength of party competition, patronage, and the status of civil society.

Successful decentralization requires among other things its status within the national system of governance to be clarified with explicit, stable and coherent rules. Such rules affect the power of different interests within government (bureaucrats, professional and technical personnel, and politicians) as well as within different areas of the country. They specify how local interests are to be represented and how local decision-makers are to be recruited. They determine the powers to be exercised at subnational levels, and the resources to be made available to support those powers. The choice of institutions for decentralized government, and the level of autonomy devolved, will reflect political interests represented at the centre. The response at the periphery of a change in relationships between centre and subnational levels (such as recentralization) will depend on how local interests are affected politically and economically. This is why it is common for national political elites to favour centralization when in power, only to find decentralization attractive when in opposition, leading in some countries in Latin America to cycles of decentralization and recentralization (Peterson, 1997).

Decentralization requires commitment on the part of national governments. Administrative support is needed to ensure that local institutions are adequately staffed, empowered to raise revenues in ways consistent with the objectives of decentralization and other government policies, and efficiently provided with the technical and financial resources that cannot be obtained locally. Central governments need to free controls from bureaucratic delays and political disputes. Central government's own capacity for efficient monitoring and support will almost certainly need to be strengthened as an integral part of a programme of decentralization, especially if there is a serious intention to change the relationships between levels of government from one marked by hierarchy and subordination to one more characterized by partnership.

Any lack of government commitment will impede donor support because the work of donors and the different government organizations affected by decentralization will not be coordinated. Close cooperation between donors and government agencies appears to be related to the strength of government commitment to implement reforms. Commitment must extend to planning decentralization in a coherent way with long-term objectives in mind, rather than using it as an ad-hoc solution to a sudden crisis, or as a means of offloading difficult responsibilities (Conyers, 2003).

Conclusion

There is a consensus among donors that decentralization is an essential part of good governance and a key aspect of political and administrative reform. Three major benefits to be derived from decentralization to local government institutions are emphasized: public policies become more responsive to local needs; the legitimacy of a new regime is made more secure, so consolidating democratic stability; and poverty alleviation is assisted by greater participation in decentralized institutions.

Attempts to empower local political institutions encounter opposition from within government, administrative weakness at the local level, and financial dependence. State legitimacy will be served only if people trust the motives of those who initiate reforms. Poverty reduction can be served if the power of local elites can be moderated and the participation of the poor encouraged by their economic and political empowerment.

The effective articulation of the interests of the poor has been recognized as an essential part of any poverty reduction programme in poor countries. The next chapter examines how political pluralism and collective action in poor communities can be supported.

6

Political Pluralism

Pluralism and civil society

As an objective of international support for good governance, political pluralism is the most difficult set of principles to engage with. Involvement in the key institutions of a pluralist state – political parties and organized interests – is vulnerable to the charge of interference in the internal politics of a sovereign state. While all governance conditionalities involve the imposition of reform from outside, the requirements of political pluralism can easily draw the aid donor into the most sensitive areas of national politics.

To get round this potential hazard, donors focus their attentions on civil society, a concept which partly obscures the political significance of the organizations involved, and which is capable of being addressed in politically neutral terms. The major multilateral donors have adopted a 'civil society empowerment' approach, partly to appear distanced from the internal politics of recipient states, but also because many associations within civil society are believed to be well placed to act as economic and social service providers, self-help bodies, and employment creators. However, different agencies interpret civil society in different ways, some more coherently than others (Stiles, 1998; Ottaway, 2005).

Encouragement and support to parts of civil society which to varying degrees engage in political activism can also be given indirectly via charitable non-governmental organizations such as Oxfam in the UK, the Netherlands Organization for International Development Cooperation, the Friedrich Naumann Stiftung in Germany, and World Vision International in the USA and Canada, which again helps fend off accusations of political interference. There has been a consequent increase in the proportion of bilateral aid flowing either via Northern NGOs or directly to organizations in recipient countries, which have rapidly increased in numbers as a consequence (Edwards and Hulme, 1996).

Aid to pluralism

Aid to civil society to enable groups to participate in policy-making takes three main forms. First, recipient governments are required by some donors to demonstrate that relevant groups have been involved in formulating public policies. The most important examples are the 'poverty reduction strategies' (PRS) on which the World Bank bases its assistance to individual countries. A PRS has to recognize that the poor and other marginalized groups lack political influence, or 'voice', and show that non-governmental organizations are involved in poverty reduction efforts.

Second, donors consult civil society organizations over a range of development policies, and local activists themselves have been influential in securing such consultation (Ottaway, 2005). Third, technical assistance is provided to help governments involve civil society in policy-making, and to strengthen the capacity of representative organizations to take part. For example, the World Bank provides training and financial assistance to help recipient countries strengthen public participation in policy-making and implementation for poverty reduction. It also requires governments to increase the capacity of poor people to participate by removing legal and other barriers to group formation and influence on public policy, and by providing 'an administrative and judicial framework supportive of such associations' to empower people with 'the means to articulate their needs and demands in public forums and in political processes' (World Bank, 2001b: 109–11).

The UN's Development Programme also provides policy advice and technical assistance on capacity development, advocacy, public information, and networking to share knowledge of good practice (UNDP, 1997b: 17).

The USA's Agency for International Development targets funding on organizations that 'enter the public policy arena, the so-called "politically active" or advocacy civil society organizations'. It specifically supports associations which 'give voice to citizens and expand their influence on the political process' in order to counterbalance the power not only of governments but also of economic and political elites (USAID, 2005).

The European Community provides civil society groups with office equipment, accommodation, training, subsidies for publications, and advice through seminars, conferences and exchanges (Robinson, 1996).

The UK's Department for Intenational Development (DFID) helps governments and civil society organizations to communicate with each other on public policies, and promotes the involvement of groups representing the poor and socially excluded in policy-making and implementation. DFID also supports the political activities of pro-poor civil society organizations via NGOs such as CAFOD, CARE, Christian Aid and the CTUC.

Pluralism and development

A plurality of autonomous political associations contributes to political development in a number of important ways, so that freedom of association is more than a fundamental right. It is also a means of supporting democracy. Democracy is dependent on the existence of a plurality of political groups, organized to influence policy-makers, mobilize public opinion, hold governments at all levels to account, and make governments responsive to the expression of demands and needs (Diamond, 1997).

The first benefit to be obtained from the freedom of organized interests to engage with the political process is an extension to the monitoring of state power. Political pluralism subjects democratic government to scrutiny from competing perspectives, leading to pressures for reform, such as when corruption is exposed, overlooked policy options are canvassed, or neglected social costs of policy choices are revealed. In this way pluralism redresses the imbalance of power between state and society which is so common in newly democratizing countries, and so provides a basis for the limitation of state power. Accountability and transparency are also enhanced by demands for better performance by the state, whether ethically or instrumentally.

Second, freedom of association stimulates political participation and provides a source of political leadership. The empowerment of associations and increased popular participation makes it more difficult for elites to manipulate democratic institutions (Luckham and White, 1996). Such participation can also create links between reformist politicians and poorer classes, bypassing political institutions which are dominated by elite interests (such as congress in the Philippines). By providing an alternative to clientelism, associational autonomy allows people, especially the poor, to move from being clients of local and national elites to being citizens (Diamond, 1997). By 'organizing the unorganized', pluralism empowers rural workers, women, the poorer members of religious congregations (in Latin America), victims of state oppression or environmental degradation, and the intended beneficiaries of state policies, to challenge the power of economic and religious elites (Clarke, 1998). Participation extends beyond the organizations themselves when people engage in electoral politics by registering candidates (local elections in Chile), support party candidates in national elections (as in Brazil) or fill co-opted places on local councils and committees (as in the Philippines).

Third, by educating people in democracy and disseminating political information, pluralism contributes to 'democratic deepening' or the infusion of institutions with democratic practices. If an association's own internal decision-making is democratic this will help to sustain democratic norms within the wider society. As de Tocqueville recognized long ago, it is the politics that goes on within and between associations, especially those with overt political objectives, that socializes society into norms and practices that allow conflicts to be resolved by democratic means. Hence the need for aid to develop more democratic internal governance and accountability, especially when aims include justice, equity, democracy and accountability (Edwards *et al.*, 1999).

Experience of political association also stimulates awareness of the rights and obligations of citizenship. There is thus reciprocity at work in the relationship between political associations and democracy, with democracy providing the freedom to associate and associations, through their internal activities and external relations with other associations and the state, educating people in the values and practices necessary for successful democratic government (Foley and Edwards, 1996).

Fourth, the functional representation of interests creates cross-cutting allegiances so that groups hitherto excluded from political power, such as women, the urban and rural poor, and ethnic minorities, become fully represented in the political process. Pluralism thus provides opportunities for the poor and disadvantaged to redress injustices (Diamond, 1992: 123). It contributes to political equality by redistributing power to the benefit of those formerly marginalized or excluded because of social and political discrimination.

Finally, pluralism increases the growth of social capital and a 'civic community' in which relations between political associations are founded on trust, cooperation and reciprocity. Repeated interactions and exchanges between associations also encourage participation and collective action. As the 'civic community' grows stronger, so the effectiveness of democratic government increases, which in turn broadens support for democracy. Thus a plurality of political associations makes a major contribution to the consolidation of democracy (Fukuyama, 2001).

Pluralist democracy

The pluralist model of political power is composed of a number of inter-related elements. In advocating pluralism, donors are in fact setting formidable standards which few if any democracies completely achieve. For pluralism to contribute to political development, a number of conditions have to be met, some of which do not fall within the limited support to civil society which aid donors are able to give.

First, pluralism implies formal *political equality*, protected by the fundamental political rights to vote, to free speech, and to association for political ends. Representative institutions and the rights of opposition also protect individual and sectional interests against unfair and arbitrary discrimination. Access to political power is guaranteed by freedom of electoral choice, by lobbying and other forms of pressure group activity, and by politically independent mass media.

Second, pluralism requires a *two-party or multi-party system*, offering electoral choice, legitimate and effective political opposition, and accountability to the interests ranged in support of them electorally. Arguments in support of the one-party state by reference to the threat of tribal factionalism (as in Zimbabwe), the need to concentrate on economic development rather than democracy (Tanzania), Asian values (Singapore), the dictatorship of the proletariat, and the lack of society's readiness for democracy (Kenya) are indefensible in pluralist democracy. Parties must also have autonomy from the state, and not be created by or subordinate to it, as has been the case with dominant parties in many developing countries, such as Golkar in Indonesia and the Kuomintang in Taiwan.

Third, pluralism places great emphasis on *functional representation*. This is where aid to civil society becomes most pertinent. Political pluralism can only be institutionalized by adherence to the fundamental political rights of freedom of speech and freedom of association. The law has to give protection to these rights. The two rights are closely related. They need each other. Freedom of association is meaningless if people are not free to express their views (if, for example, they are likely to be prosecuted for uttering criticisms of the current political leadership, as in Singapore or Zimbabwe). And freedom of speech is empty if the expression of views and criticisms cannot be backed by organization and mobilization.

Pluralism enables the political weakness of the individual citizen in mass society to be compensated for by the right and ability of all freely to organize for political ends. Interests can be mobilized and made politically effective by processes of functional representation. Power is diffused among groups. So while political parties *aggregate* interests, so that majorities can be formed and governments created, interest groups *articulate* political demands between elections, enabling political leaders to respond with alternative legislative proposals or adjustments to their election manifestos designed to broaden their appeal to voters.

A pluralist model of functional representation is thus different from that of corporatism, under which representative producer groups are used by the state as instruments of mobilization, control and legitimation. Under corporatism, groups do not spontaneously articulate a plurality of political demands from all sections of society. The state controls the selection of groups for inclusion in, and exclusion from, the processes of policy planning. In return for recognition, the representatives of sectional interests secure the required decisions by their constituents (for example, on investment, employment and prices on the part of employers, and pay claims on the part of unions).

Under pluralism, a rough equality of power between groups produces a *balanced competition* for resources in democratic policy-making processes. Equilibrium between groups is maintained by the countervailing power of different groups with different power bases, and by the existence of cross-cutting interests which moderate demands from people who have much to lose in one aspect of their lives from excessive demands on behalf of another aspect (for example, producer vs. consumer interests).

The sources of power on which groups in a pluralist polity can draw are seen as *non-cumulative*. Some groups will have money, some expertise, and some sanctions which they can deploy, such as influence over groups of voters. But no group is able to accumulate all sources of power. Thus no interest is consistently successful in securing its aims across the whole range of public policies. Groups may not have the same degree of political influence, but none is completely powerless. All can hope to win some of the time. Policy issues tend to be resolved in ways generally compatible with the preferences of the majority of the public.

Fourth, *the state* in a pluralist democracy is regarded as a neutral set of institutions for adjudicating between conflicting interests. In pluralist interpretations of politics, it is clear that the state is thought of as an 'umpire', rather than a set of institutions which defends a particular class and its privileges, or exhibits a marked bias towards particular interests, or has interests of its own (for example, within its bureaucracy) to defend. Thus pluralism implies a theory of the state which differs significantly from other conceptualizations.

Finally, while it is recognized that all political systems are to some degree elitist, the pluralist political system is characterized by a *plurality of elites*. In mass democracy power may inevitably be concentrated in the hands of political leaders rather than the electorate or even the rank-and-file members of political organizations. Under pluralism, positions within the elite are open to people recruited on the basis of merit or open political competition. Elites do not form a cohesive social stratum by the restriction of access to membership of a ruling class. Different social, economic, political, professional, administrative and other elites lack the social cohesion to turn them into a ruling class. Elites recruit from diverse socio-economic backgrounds. Competition between political parties is further evidence of elite plurality.

Political parties

Political associations constitute the foundation of pluralist democracy, whether for interest aggregation (political parties) or interest articulation (civil society acting as pressure groups). The importance of political parties in any pluralist reform is indicated by the electorate's need for alternative programmes and leaders if representative and accountable government is to function properly. Political parties are also the most important institutions of political mobilization in the context of mass politics. A party mobilizes and controls support so that power can be captured and the legitimacy of constitutional office secured.

Political parties perform a number of crucial functions in democratizing states (Smith, 2003). They endow regimes with legitimacy, act as a medium for political recruitment, and provide opportunities for the formation of coalitions of political interests sufficient to sustain a government.

However, under some circumstances parties can impede political integration by aggregating primarily ethnic and regional interests. One problem in countries seeking to consolidate pluralist democracy has been that societies deeply divided along ethnic lines have had difficulty in creating political parties whose membership, leadership and programmes cut across ethnic divisions and unite people on the basis of nationwide identities such as class or ideology. Ethnic parties have encouraged conflicts which have proved difficult to manage within existing constitutional arrangements. Rather than aggregate interests into organizations capable of providing stable majority government, they have when in power governed to the exclusion of other minorities. Thus parties can contribute to the disintegration of the state if they represent deep ethnic divisions and appeal for support only to the members of vertical cleavages, as in the Ukraine and elsewhere. For integration to be achieved parties have either to mobilize horizontal social strata cutting across ethnic lines, or be willing and able to negotiate in a democratic context a solution to fundamental conflicts about the integrity of the state itself, as in the peaceful division of Czechoslovakia.

Interest aggregation may be difficult to achieve for other reasons. In many post-authoritarian states parties have emerged from aggregations of political movements and action groups representing different interests and policy orientations. For example, the Polish Democratic Union was established in 1990 by the Forum of the Democratic Right, the Civic Movement for Democratic Action and the electoral committees supporting the presidential candidacy of Tadeusz Mazowiecki. It brought together factions identifying with social-democratic, liberal, Christian, secularist and environmentalist ideologies (Lewis, 1995). In the early 1990s, citizens in Eastern and Central Europe found that political parties often represented their interests better than interest groups such as trade unions, the church, environmental groups, farmers' organizations and business associations (Toka, 1996). But the skill of coalition-building has been tested as party systems have become highly fragmented, as has happened in parts of post-communist Europe, perhaps most notably in Poland's 'hyper-fragmentation' (Cotta, 1996). Divisions within political parties have sometimes delayed the consolidation of democracy, as in Bulgaria.

Parties also act as the conduits of upward pressure from individual members, affiliated organizations (such as women's groups, youth movements or trade unions), and the electorate. They should have a major influence on public policy by applying ideologies to social and economic problems, though in developing countries their impact on policy formation and implementation has generally been weak (Randall, 1988). However, parties in new democracies can be relevant to policy outcomes, especially poverty reduction, by empowering the poor. Experience in parts of India and Latin America suggests strongly that the opportunity to elect pro-poor parties to office makes a significance difference to the strength of public policies designed to alleviate poverty, especially if parties are not fragmented organizationally, and have coherent ideologies and programmes (Moore and Putzel, 1999).

The difficulties in providing conduits of influence from the rank and file can be illustrated by the experience of some post-communist regimes, where party elites have dominated parliamentary politics to the exclusion of other modes of participation, as in Hungary (Lomax, 1996). As measured by party membership and electoral turnout, parties have not contributed as much to political participation as might in theory have been anticipated. When parties have few members, weak organizations, and 'little grass-roots activism', it leads to the emergence of 'half-democracies' and a growing gap between party elites and ordinary citizens (Agh, 1996: 54–5; Pridham, 2001). The significance of parties to participation sometimes lies in the opportunities they provide for choice which people are free to ignore, perhaps in favour of other modes of participation (Lewis, 2001b).

Parties need to develop beyond the small associations of elites, which characterize many of the new parties of post-communist Europe, into mass organizations that identify with socio-economic interests and ideologies. Pluralism needs more than the mobilization of people during elections. Parties have to offer opportunities for political participation in the development of political programmes, rather than

> make it more difficult for society to articulate and express specific group and class interests, and so function in a way that serves to preserve, rather than to bridge, the gap between the political elite and society. (Lomax, 1995 : 186)

Parties also contribute to political socialization, sometimes socializing people into opposition to the regime, or at least a significant part or parts of it, such as its approach to the economy. It depends on the type of party. For example, the communist successor parties in Eastern Europe (such as the Hungarian Socialist Party, Social Democracy of the Republic of Poland, and the Party of the Democratic Left in Slovakia) can be divided into, on one hand, 'mass' parties with large memberships, coherent ideological positions, and internal discipline in support of policy, and, on the other, 'cadre' parties which rely on the leadership to attract voters, have smaller memberships, fewer activists and more flexible positions on policy. The more cadre-like have supporters that approve of democratic changes and are helping to consolidate democracy through the socialization of their followers. The 'mass' type, because of their stronger resemblance to the parties and ideologies of the communist era, tend to attract supporters hostile to economic and political reforms (Ishayama, 2001).

Finally, parties can contribute to political stability by absorbing increasing political participation, and organizing it in constructive and legitimate ways (Smith, 2003). However, the way parties respond to potential sources of political instability, such as the relationship between the state and religion, continuing support for the old order, growing inequality, or economic crises, is highly relevant to the acceptability of a regime to its citizens. The legitimacy of a new regime is also dependent upon parties offering opportunities for the peaceful transfer of governmental authority through procedures regarded as fair even by the losing side.

How far political parties are able to perform the roles necessary for the establishment of political pluralism in post-authoritarian states depends on contextual factors, such as stability of membership and electoral support, the existence of democratic traditions within the political culture, and continuities in elites and parties from the authoritarian past. Historical experience of parties in a democratic setting has not always been available to newly democratizing states, and there has been a tendency everywhere for parties to lose some of their erstwhile functions to other institutions such as the media. The case of Eastern Europe suggests strongly that parties have not always been dominant in the management of conflict, the mobilization of participation, the integration of society and the securing of legitimacy. Doubts remain as to how far political parties can provide functions without which pluralist democracy cannot survive. But further consolidation of pluralist democracy cannot take place without sustained party competition (Pridham and Lewis, 1996; Lewis, 2001a).

Party systems and pluralism

It is clear from the role played by political parties that their significance for political pluralism is immense. Parties provide the most revealing indication of how far a political system is pluralist. For political parties to ensure pluralist democracy there needs to be competition between sustainable organizations. Pluralism entails a particular type of party system as well as a particular type of organization. The success of democratization depends in part on the existence of institutionalized parties and party systems of government. These requirements pose two of the most intractable questions in politics: what sustains a multi-party system, what kind of organization is likely to sustain parties capable of supporting democracy?

The consolidation of democracy is conditional upon the institutionalization of regular electoral competition between parties which can adapt to new constitutional rules, even if the transition from authoritarianism was dominated by socio-political movements such as the African National Congress in South Africa, Civic Forum in Czechoslovakia, and Solidarity in Poland. Such political movements have to 'institutionalize' themselves in readiness for electoral competition (Ware, 1996).

The institutionalization of a pluralist party system depends on stringent requirements that are not easily satisfied. The rules governing party competition need to be commonly observed, widely understood and confidently anticipated. There should be stability in the number of parties competing for office. Parties should be strongly rooted in society, affect political preferences, attract stable electoral support, and demonstrate continuity in ideological terms. Parties that fail to develop ideologically so that they are unable to offer voters a coherent set of social and economic goals, as in Poland, present two threats to good government: governmental instability, and political apathy on the part of citizens that can increase the appeal of less pluralistic alternatives (Wesolowski, 1996).

Institutionalization also requires political elites to recognize the legitimacy of electoral competition as the route to office; and party organizations need to exist independently of powerful leaders, with well-resourced nationwide organizations, and well-established internal procedures for recruitment to party offices. The more party systems are characterized by these qualities the more institutionalized they are. The fewer the qualities, the more 'inchoate' the system is likely to be (Mainwaring and Scully, 1995).

Unfortunately, parties and party systems in poorer countries tend to be inchoate and associated with personalism, weak accountability, electoral volatility, uncertainty, and low levels of legitimacy (Mainwaring, 1998). In Africa the majority of countries fall into the 'inchoate' category. There is some evidence of a virtuous circle: an institutionalized party system is a 'requisite for democratic government', and the more experience a country has of democracy, the higher the level of party system institutionalization (Kuenzi and Lambright, 2001: 463). But on the whole democratization has been held back in Africa by the inability of new movements to develop an appeal to new constituencies and distance themselves from the tactics of their authoritarian predecessors. The appeal of new parties has been limited by elitism, urban bias, identification with ethnic groups, and a failure to articulate policies which respond to the needs of the masses. Tactically new parties have too often been vehicles for opportunistic politicians with less interest in pluralist democracy than in gaining or regaining power – many had close associations with the previous regime until removed from office because of corruption, incompetence or abuse of power (Ihonoubere, 1998).

Weak legitimacy has also been found in the post-communist states of Europe and the former Soviet Union. Survey data has revealed a lack of public confidence in and respect for parties, leading to weak party attachments. (In a Polish survey conducted in 1994 over half the respondents (53%) were of the opinion that 'nobody needs political parties except their leaders and activists' and 65 per cent could find no party that represented people like them: Wesolowski, 1996: 248–9.) It has even been suggested that the nature of pluralism in new democracies has reduced the role parties play in structuring electoral competition, shaping political identities and aggregating interests (Diamond and Gunther, 2001).

The institutionalization of pluralism also raises the question of how many parties offer the best prospects for stability. This has involved a comparison of two-party competition with a multi-party system. A multi-party system might be thought to be less stable because of the uncertainties associated with the formation of coalitions. Equally, a multiplicity of parties might ensure that all interests are represented, creating incentives to engage in lawful political action rather than violence. A multi-party system in some post-communist countries (for example, the Czech Republic and Hungary) has not prevented the legislative process from functioning or extremist movements from being marginalized. A comparative study of developing countries found some support, though 'weak and fragmentary', for the hypothesis that democratic consolidation was more likely under a multi- than a two-party system (Power and Gasiorowski, 1997). This is significant when countries emerging from authoritarianism have a propensity to spawn a multiplicity of political parties. It is also relevant to the dilemma built into pluralist politics of allowing anti-democratic parties to compete, as in parts of post-communist Europe which have seen the emergence of authoritarian, right-wing nationalist parties.

Sustainable political parties

An important element in the institutionalization of party systems of government is the strength of parties as organizations. Strong parties tend to be adaptable (for example, in moving from opposition to government), autonomous from narrow socio-economic interests, founding personalities, the bureaucracy and the military, and coherent in their decision-making procedures (Dix, 1992). However, generalizations such as this must be offered with the utmost caution.

The sheer variety of political parties explains why it is so difficult to identify organizational features that will prolong their lives. Parties vary according to level of organizational development, the origins of their policies (ideology, religion, populism, ethnicity), the interests they represent, the internal distribution of power and their level of commitment to pluralist democracy (Gunther and Diamond, 2003). However, comparative studies have identified a number of recurring characteristics associated with stable organization.

To survive parties need elaborate internal structures which are effective in nominating candidates, communicating manifestos and mobilizing support for both candidates and policies (Yanai, 1999). A mass organization also enables the party to create a sense of national legitimacy by developing an ideology and communicating it to society. Such an organization provides an approach to the management of society and economy as well as political education, indoctrination and control.

The lack of such well-developed organizations accounts for the instability of many of the parties in post-communist Europe which represent genuine pluralism (as distinct from those of authoritarian disposition). East European parties are characterized by 'weak institutionalization', which means they lack autonomy, identity, legitimacy, organizational stability and social roots. The personalized nature of politics, especially in smaller states, such as those of the Baltic region, has encouraged a 'continuing fluidity of party structures, the tendency of parties to split and reform with disconcerting frequency, and the dominance of individuals and political leaders over party structures' (Lewis, 2001a: 200). Having a mass membership has been seen as irrelevant by dominant party leaders who rely on the state, not party members and supporters, for resources and have no incentive to create links with supporting affiliates such as trade unions or women's groups. With some notable exceptions, especially among the successor parties to those of the old regime, the idea of a mass membership found little favour, largely because of its association with the communist past.

There has consequently been little interest within the political elite in building organizations in which rank-and-file members played a continuing role between elections. Party membership offered few attractions to political activists. Parties lack clear identities in the minds of voters and so do not appeal to clearly defined socio-economic interests (Kopecky, 1995). They have tended to be 'cadre' parties, that is, lacking a mass organization and with leaders who appeal directly to the electorate. Voters and paid-up members are less important than votes which are sought by means of vague 'catch-all' slogans. Consequently, there might be elite pluralism, 'but that involved little conception of broader political participation or a more active form of mass democracy ... and provided few incentives for developing the party's organization'. Such factors have produced 'a low level of party institutionalisation in Eastern Europe' (Lewis, 2000: 104, 121).

A decline in 'attachment to party' may reflect disillusionment with a particular type of party (perhaps based on class or ideology), resulting in support for parties based on other identities, such as ethnicity, territory, religion or cause (for example, environmental protection). The most dramatic example in post-communist Europe was Czechoslovakia in the early 1990s when Czech and Slovak voters supported parties 'whose appeal was directed exclusively to the electorate within one of the two republics' (Wightman, 1995: 60). Parties which did not see themselves as exclusively Czech or Slovak had little success. This quickly led to the 'velvet divorce' of 1993 and the establishment of two sovereign states.

Throughout the Third World the organizational development of political parties has also been hampered. Here the main constraints have been shortages of funds (for example, opposition parties in Malaysia), the domination of ambitious leaders (for example, in Brazil and South Korea), factionalism, and clientelism (Randall and Svasand, 2002). The strength of party organization in developing countries has often been dependent upon the distribution of rewards, in the form of allocations of state resources and appointments within the military and bureaucracy, to supporters and clients on a personalized basis. Factionalism within political parties is one manifestation of a more fundamental dimension of politics in many new democracies, namely clientelism (Smith, 2003).

Factionalism refers to an informal aspect of party organization which is an inevitable consequence of alliances and coalitions between leaders and followers that have no ideological foundation but which are designed to secure electoral support. Relationship between leaders of factions and their followers are based on a range of social and economic conditions, such as feudalistic tenure systems (when a landowner can guarantee electoral support from tenants because of their economic dependency), cultural loyalties (tribal, linguistic or caste-based) and other traditional obligations.

Hence party fragmentation, disintegration, disorder and realignments are commonly found in the early stages of democratization as parties search for effective forms of organization. Fissions within parties easily develop into factions which in turn become new parties (Olson, 1998). However, some parties are organizationally viable. For example, the organizations of the former communist parties helped them adapt to the vastly different political circumstances of pluralist democracy, including to varying degrees the loss of material assets and members, especially when supported by trade unions with their own mass organizations. 'To have a headquarters in a locality, with its communications equipment and its human networks, stood for something more than just the cash value of buildings' (Waller, 1995: 485). The Hungarian Socialist Party has 400 local offices, plus over 2000 settlement units and 16 functional organizations of teachers, women, religious groups, young people, and business men and women. Local and regional levels enjoy a measure of autonomy, and internal democracy permits some control over the leadership by party activists. It has been able to draw support from all sections of Hungarian society, and has the largest membership of all parties (Agh, 1995).

The non-successor parties have also begun to move away from their original positions, in which the 'party in public office' (the members of legislatures and executives) focused on parliamentary and governmental life, and on mobilizing voters, rather than on the party as an extra-parliamentary organization and building a mass membership. Some parties in parts of post-communist Europe, notably Hungary and the Czech Republic, have developed central organizations which exert considerable influence over parliamentary groups and party policy. While the holders of legislative and executive offices are well represented on party executives, they are no longer as dominant as they once were (van Biezen, 2000).

The recent political history of Eastern and Central Europe is instructive because despite the generally low level of party institutionalization, political pluralism has survived in some countries. Even without deep social foundations and plentiful resources, parties can under some conditions demonstrate 'a reasonably strong capacity for responsible political behaviour and surprisingly high levels of commitment to democratic norms' (Lewis, 2000: 159).

Organizational survival also depends on having a party leadership that is representative of a broad and balanced range of interests, social elites, members and activists (Randall, 1988; Graham, 1993). A strong party organization also requires consistency (especially in ideological position, discipline, internal organization, rules of leadership succession and methods of mass mobilization), and significant financial and human resources, including professional staff (Mainwaring, 1998; Stockton, 2001). A party's relationship with voters is another factor contributing to the stability of party organization. Linkage with voters has been of great significance in post-communist Europe, with three main types evolving. Charismatic parties offer voters personalities rather than programmes. Clientelist parties provide distinct groups of voters with personal advantages. Programmatic parties offer collective goods. The latter face the huge organizational task of providing information which will convince voters of the desirability of their policies and objectives, but they are likely to be the most stable. Charismatic parties are unstable because support is associated with unique personalities. And clientelist parties become less appealing as voters become more educated and as economic development creates social and economic interests that cannot be served by clientelist incentives (Kitschelt, 1995).

Organized interests

In order to understand the contribution which organized interests make to pluralism it is useful to distinguish sectional interests from altruistic causes. Sectional interests form associations to defend and advance the social or economic position of their members who are united by virtue of their common position in economy and society. Examples are trade unions, professional associations of doctors, lawyers, teachers, journalists and engineers, employers' organizations, chambers of commerce, and water-user associations. Organizations to defend the interests of peasants, landless labourers, forest workers, war veterans and workers in the informal sector also fall into this category.

Sectional interest groups may only occasionally become involved in political activism. Their main purpose will often be to provide services to their members, such as training, negotiations to improve employments conditions, recruitment, conducting research, and enforcing codes of conduct. The Psychological and Educational Association set up in 1990 in Vietnam is an example (Harper, 1996). Such groups become political when they find it necessary to bring advocacy and pressure to bear on governments in order to influence public policy.

Cause groups are associations of people pursuing ethical objectives or the interests of people too weak politically to defend their own material position in society. Causes entail some perception of the public good and originate in ideological, humanitarian, religious or ethical values. This category of pressure group contains a wide variety of organizations, ranging from those with precise and limited remits, such as child welfare, to political movements which combine a number of broad objectives, such as greater democracy, with more specific aims such as opposition to violence against women, illegal waste dumping, or corruption, as in the case of the political movements active in parts of the former Soviet Union in 2002, including Azerbaijan, Georgia, Ukraine and Uzbekistan.

Groups promoting a cause are not always representative, at least in terms of membership, of those whose interests they wish to advance. Fairly typical is Latin America, where many cause groups are 'composed of middle-class, educated and professional people who have opted for political or humanitarian reasons to work with (or on behalf of) the poor and marginalised' (Pearce, 1997: 259).

Causes can also be promoted by non-governmental organizations which seek to promote the interests of the people they serve through different kinds of political involvement. Even organizations without explicit political roles can empower their members and so contribute to the development of political pluralism. For example, voluntary bodies which exist primarily to satisfy economic, recreational, spiritual, social or cultural needs through self-help projects, credit schemes, cooperatives and not-for-profit businesses, can impart political skills and raise political awareness through their internal decision-making and their relationships with state and economy (Fowler, 1996).

The action groups and social movements which have received much attention from observers of Third World politics include both sectional interest groups and cause groups, many of which combine political activism with self-help projects to further the developmental, social and political aims of people who suffer subordination and discrimination because of poverty, gender, religion or ethnicity. Some action groups wish to change the political system fundamentally – for example, the Muslim Brotherhood in Egypt. Some exert political pressure to change part of the political process – for example, to give indigenous people more opportunities to participate in politics. Others have limited policy objectives, such as improving the quality of housing and municipal services in poor neighbourhoods (such as the Basic Christian Communities in Latin America), saving forests from commercial exploitation (for example, the Chipko movement in India), or increasing resources for women's health (for example, Women in Nigeria) (Haynes, 1997). Sectional interest and altruism are difficult to distinguish among movements engaging in struggles to alleviate poverty, bring about social justice, and protect the environment.

So the line between sectional and cause, or promotional, groups is inevitably blurred. Sectional interests may simultaneously seek to protect livelihoods and promote the public interest. For example, organizations protesting against the social and economic effects of dams or mining operations may be motivated by concerns about both the livelihoods of poor people and ecological damage. India's Self-Employed Women's Association, in addition to acting as a sectional interest group, has also promoted new methods of child care to enable all working women to have careers without risking the welfare of their children (Edwards and Sen, 2000).

A pluralistic political system will be composed of groups and associations which are autonomous from the state and formed voluntarily by their members (White, 1996a). The rough balance of power between organized interests assumed by pluralism is a model rarely matched in reality. The real world of interest groups is distinguished by inequality – of power, of independence from the state, and even of level of voluntary association.

In terms of power, some groups are better organized and resourced than others (for example, rural workers versus international agri-businesses). In many countries struggling to democratize, the urban areas are much more pluralistic than the rural, whose poor are left unorganized and under-represented. Some governmental policies and interventions depend on the cooperation of private interests (such as farmers in the case of agricultural extension programmes). Such dependency confers political influence when organized interests can demand a say in the formation of public policy in return for cooperation. By involving groups within civil society in service delivery, governments create additional opportunities for people to influence the development of public policy, and may endorse this by creating formal mechanisms for involving community groups in the design of policies (as with Colombian primary health care: Clarke, 1998). It is widely believed by development professionals that while civil associations can offer a cost-effective means of delivering services to communities, their most important role is enabling formerly excluded groups to become involved in policy-making.

However, governments are more likely to be dependent on sectional interests than on promotional organizations. Since the latter often seek to protect those who are politically weak (such as the poor or the aged) they are unlikely to represent interests on which governments are dependent. In addition, those who promote a cause on moral grounds have few resources which they can threaten to withhold if they want to promote legislation. There will be promotional groups on both sides of a moral argument, again making it easier for governments to resist pressure. Cause groups, like sectional interests, can, however, develop expertise beyond that which resides within the government's own bureaucracy. For example, representatives from environmental NGOs in Sri Lanka have been co-opted on to the National Environmental Council. In Venezuela the Federation of Environmental Organizations has been appointed technical adviser to the Congressional Commission on the Environment.

Appearing to be responsible, rather than 'extremist', may also be necessary for an organization to obtain good access to ministers and civil servants, a perception which works to the disadvantage of radical cause groups. Militant forms of protest may have to be abandoned in favour of close working relationships with, or even access to, officials. Long-term relationships with government may require 'correct' methods of political influence through the 'proper channels'. Being part of the planning stage of policy formulation is much better than being left to react against something designed by others. Hence the importance of access to officials and ministers. Wishing to present a responsible image may thus deter groups from engaging in campaigns to influence public opinion or from using direct forms of political action and protest, such as demonstrations. However, there will be occasions when there is no other way to challenge something that is regarded as wrong, such as when marginalized groups are denied a full part in the political process. A promotional group may have to start with an appeal to public opinion and hope that it can move on to negotiations with government officials. A sectional group is likely to be part of the official network, using direct action (such as a strike) only as a last resort.

Being seen as 'responsible' may depend on being 'representative'. This can work against the promotional group whose activists do not come from the sections of society whose interests they wish to promote, or whose demands make them seem deviants from dominant values and social mores. The more a group can demonstrate cooperation, expertise, respectability and representativeness, the more likely it is to gain access to decision-makers. In Chile, for example, organizations that chose to endorse the state's liberal economic model 'benefited from close access to the government, often in advisory roles', while those who challenged the current orthodoxy in the interest of poor communities 'remained marginal to the mainstream economic and political developments in the country' (Pearce, 1997: 270). Such developments have led some observers to query the value of non-governmental organizations in developing countries, since 'they now have the social grace not to persist with awkward questions and the organizational capacity to divert the poor and disadvantaged from more radical ideas' (Hulme and Edwards, 1997: 3).

Some groups have more autonomy from the state than others. Though a close relationship with political institutions can be mutually beneficial, a loss of autonomy can work against the interests of the group. In Latin America social movements have been vulnerable to 'capture' by governments through the medium of clientelist politics, when the leadership has been co-opted by the state. Political demands then reflect what the state is prepared to offer, public resources become instruments of political control, and group leaders place their political careers above the interests of their associations (Cavarozzi and Palermo, 1995). A lack of autonomy also characterizes organized interests in Bangladesh. In most Arab countries it is also difficult for political associations to enjoy freedom from co-option by the state. Civil society groups are used to indoctrinate society into the wisdom of government plans and decisions, broaden support for political elites, and reinforce authoritarian values: 'only where the state is weak (as in the examples of Lebanon and Palestine) have NGOs been able to play a significant social and political role' (Marzouk, 1997: 199–200). While market reforms in China have created opportunities for the formation of groups not affiliated to the Communist Party, such as the Taxi Drivers Association, the Association of Private Entrepreneurs, and the Disabled Persons Association, there is great variation in the degree of autonomy from the state and party. Some groups owe their origin to the state while others spring from spontaneous voluntary action (for example the Chinese Poverty Research Association). Some groups, both sectional and promotional, are among the organizations which either are not registered with the authorities or are actually illegal (such as the Chinese Christian Association and some women's groups) (Howell, 1996).

Even when political associations are pro-democratic it may not be easy for them to move, during the transition from authoritarianism, from protest and political confrontation to constructive dialogue with governments, a problem encountered in some Latin American countries (Hernandez and Fox, 1995). Pluralism will be weak when authoritarianism is deeply rooted culturally, political representation a novel phenomenon, and organizations traditionally monopolized by and subordinated to political parties. For example, the 'democratization of social life' creates a counterpoint to the state in Vietnam, when in the past social organizations (trade unions, youth movements and women's organizations) have been integrated into government and party. New social organizations have emerged to support the urban poor in their quest for housing, work and health care. But such participation has been limited because 'the constraints of the old centralized planning system still exist; the elements of civil society are still underdeveloped; and ways to attract and operationalize people's participation are as yet unreliable and ineffective' (Luan, 1996: 189; Reilly, 1995). In parts of Eastern and Central Europe it has also proved difficult to develop the political culture necessary for pluralism to flourish and for respect for others, recognition of responsibilities, toleration, civic engagement, and willingness to deal with conflict through 'mediation and discourse' to become established patterns of political behaviour (Pietrzyk, 2003: 41).

Inequalities between interests arise in other ways. Some groups are in a position to ensure that current conditions are not seen as problems, thereby excluding them from the political agenda. Bias can be mobilized so that questions are not asked or alternatives sought, leaving those who benefit from the existing structure of assumptions, beliefs, institutions and social relationships to retain their privileges at the expense of others. Some issues are organized into politics, while others are organized out. Powerful interests can define the social and political structure to their own advantage. They can prevent disadvantaged groups such as the poor or women from questioning the system. The rules of political life are not unambiguous. They can be interpreted, used and misused in the interests of participants. The powerful then become the 'unconscious beneficiaries' of bias built into the system even when they do not consciously dictate the agenda.

Freedom of association and the poor

Since all societies fall short of the pluralist ideal of equally distributed power, there are concerns within the donor community about the political power of the poor. The effective articulation of the interests of the poor has been recognized as an essential part of any poverty reduction programme in poor countries. The World Bank claims that the state will deliver more effectively to all citizens and poor people in particular, and generate political support for public action against poverty, if a government creates a climate favourable to 'pro-poor actions and coalitions, facilitating the growth of poor people's associations, and increasing the political capacity of poor people' (World Bank, 2001b: 99).

The idea of 'pro-poor coalitions' stems from the belief that poverty reduction is a public good. Governments can encourage the formation of pro-poor coalitions in which wealthier groups recognize a common cause with the poor. Governments can make society aware of the common interests of the poor and non-poor: in ending the mass migration of the rural poor to urban areas; in the beneficial consequences for economic development of reduced poverty; and in the control of communicable diseases by improving the health status of the poor. Pro-poor alliances can be mobilized by presenting poverty in different ways: as deprivation rather than income level; as threatening to people's 'respectability'; and as a problem whose solution is politically feasible (Moore and Putzel, 1999). The state can introduce into public debate 'the notion that poverty reduction is a public good and can further the well-being of the non-poor' (World Bank, 2001b: 109).

The poor's own associations and organizations also need to be encouraged so that they become more effective at demanding pro-poor policies. Disadvantaged groups must have opportunities to mobilize political pressure, including becoming an effective electoral force and direct action by trade unions, peasant associations, urban social movements, landless groups, ethnic associations, and indigenous groups such as the tin-miners and peasants of Bolivia and Ecuador, whose mass protests forced changes on the white ruling classes in 2005.

Improving the capacity of the state to respond to demands should also stimulate the effective political organization of the poor. Government schemes and projects can create an enabling environment for mobilization by such devices as building incentives for collective action into development projects, and creating legally binding rights (see Chapter 7). In the longer term democracy itself should contribute to the empowerment of the poor, since it necessarily upholds political rights and civil liberties.

Pluralism can also be encouraged if the state makes it easier for local communities to interact with local governments, with the aim of making public services more accessible. Collaboration between community groups and local governments can improve the living conditions of the poor, improve health care, deliver relief efforts, and support production for export markets (as in Taiwan), thus building up the poor's economic assets.

Pluralism receives further encouragement from efforts to strengthen the rule of law and reinforce the independence and effectiveness of the judiciary, so that citizens are equal before the law and the state is subject to the law. This should help remove the illegalities which the poor encounter when they seek to exert political influence or enforce their rights.

There are other policy changes which are of benefit to all political associations. These include legal protection for freedom of association, tax advantages for voluntary bodies, and the use of partnerships between government and the voluntary sector. Governments can also generate social capital through education policies and the protection of property rights (Fukuyama, 2001).

Conclusion

Pluralism implies formal *political equality*, protected by the fundamental political rights to vote, to free speech, and to association for political ends; a *two-party or multi-party system*, offering electoral choice; and *functional representation*. Political associations are the most important organizations in pluralist democracy, whether for interest aggregation (political parties) or interest articulation (civil society acting through pressure groups).

Parties perform a number of crucial functions in pluralist democracy, which in turn requires a particular type of party system and a particular type of party organization. Consequently, the sustaining organizational characteristics of party systems and organizations should be of particular interest to aid donors seeking to influence governance.

The mobilization of civil society through organized interest groups cannot guarantee that all interests in society will have equal power. Hence concerns within the donor community about the political power of the poor, and how best to encourage participation in those political organizations most likely to promote poverty reduction. An objective of aid to governance has been to increase participation generally, and especially that of the poor, so the next chapter examines the contribution which political participation makes to development.

7

Participation

Donors' views on participation

Participation is understood within the donor community as both an end in itself and a means to other political and administrative objectives. For example, both the UNDP and DFID regard participation as a human right. UNDP includes participation along with equality and representation as principles underpinning its work, while DFID endorses the rights of all citizens 'to participation in, and access to information relating to, the decision-making processes that affect their lives' (DFID, 2001: 86). At the same time participation is seen as a means to the greater effectiveness of development projects, the mobilization of resources, and the empowerment of people hitherto excluded or marginalized by the prevailing power structures within society (Chambers, 1995: 30).

Within the international aid community, participation is accepted as contributing to development in two main ways: increasing the effectiveness of state interventions; and empowering people, especially the poor.

Participation and development

The World Bank exemplifies the belief that participation improves the *effectiveness* of development projects and programmes. The objective of participation is stronger state capacity (World Bank, 1997: 110). Participation improves state capacity by endowing it with credibility when citizens can express opinions and demands, by reducing information problems, and by plugging gaps in state provision. Therefore the state must bring 'popular voice' into policy-making by opening up ways for groups in civil society to 'have their say' and encouraging wider participation in the design and delivery of goods and services. Participation is necessary to ensure the long-term sustainability of projects and programmes. By strengthening ownership, transparency and accountability, it 'enhances effectiveness of development projects and policies' (World Bank, 2005). Within British aid policy, too, participation is believed to make it more likely that aid will be effective and sustainable (World Bank, 1995: 6).

UNDP also stresses how development requires a contribution from public participation through civil society organizations because governments 'cannot on their own fulfill all the tasks required for sustainable human development. This goal requires the active participation and partnership of citizens and their organisations' (UNDP, 1995: 2).

The second main aim of participation is *empowerment*. For the World Bank, participation in monitoring and evaluating projects empowers the beneficiaries through the learning which occurs as people analyse problems, reflect, and take action to correct mistakes. The Bank sees participation as providing 'social accountability' in which citizens, communities and civil society organizations hold government officials to account. For the OECD too, the empowerment of the poor is dependent upon the right to participate (OECD, 2001: 46).

Supporting participation

All the major bilateral donors support the principle of participation as an element of good governance, and have funded ways of strengthening it, including education and training, support for grass-roots organizations, and the involvement of all stakeholders in the design, operation, monitoring and evaluation of development projects (OECD, 1997: 6).

Efforts to include the participation of intended beneficiaries in the development initiatives of aid donors started in 1980. In 1981 Sweden decided that participation was a basic right to be included in all its aid projects. In 1986 the German aid agency GTZ made the participation of the poor one of the principles underlying its work in the field. The World Bank set up a Learning Group on Popular Participation in 1990 to advise on how participation should be incorporated in Bank operations. The UK's Department for International Development began to include 'stakeholder' participation in its development projects in the first half of the 1990s. Over the same period NGOs also extended the use of participatory techniques for research into development, the appraisal of needs for projects, the evaluation of project outcomes, gender analysis, and the application of local knowledge to community problem-solving (Long, 2001).

The focus of aid is on the creation of an 'enabling environment' which removes obstacles to participation. This consists of strategies that governments can adopt to strengthen 'voice and participation' in all areas of governance. Voting rules can be changed to make the outcome of elections more representative, and to strengthen incentives to vote. New institutional arrangements can be created for providing public goods through partnerships between the public sector and the private sector or organizations in civil society. Deliberation between the public and private sectors, such as between governments, unions and employers in economic policy-making, can facilitate participation in development projects. Rights to associate and organize, gain access to information, enter into contracts, and manage economic assets can be safeguarded with legislation. Public agencies can be required to consult clients and service users through hearings, forums and surveys. Legislation can be passed requiring the involvement of users and clients in the management of public resources (for example schools, grazing lands, water resources, forests, health care).

Forms of participation

From the different kinds of activities that are labelled 'participation' by aid donors, it is clear that this concept has different meanings in different settings and among different advocates. There is a convenient ambiguity about the term when incorporated into aid policy. Some forms of participation are more politically significant than others. They do not all permit the same level of citizen involvement in and influence on public policy. The weaker forms have sometimes attracted hostile reactions from critics for being tokenistic, inauthentic, incorporative and even repressive (Smith, 1998). Evaluation is made difficult by the fact that conflicting arguments about participation rarely refer to the same type of activity, making it especially important for advocates and critics to specify precisely what type of individual or collective behaviour defines the participation under discussion.

What different conceptualizations have in common is the aim of involving more people in politics than is allowed by the formal institutions of representative government. A *participatory* view of democracy contrasts with a *procedural* view which concentrates on decision-making procedures rather than the extent of public participation in them. Voting is the most significant form of political participation in the procedural model of democracy, whereas the participative model prescribes as much direct involvement in the making and implementing of decisions as possible. This then makes it possible to correct the social bias that occurs in levels of participation, with higher levels generally recorded among those with higher income, educational attainment and social status. Participative democracy is thus associated with political equality. There is an assumption behind the participative model that the more people practise decision-making, including in settings outside government such as the workplace, the more effective they become in articulating political demands.

Consultation

The weakest form of participation in the planning and provision of public services is consultation. This may be indirect, as when a group of actors who are designated the representatives of a larger group or community are merely consulted by authoritative decision-makers before plans are finalized and binding decisions taken. For example, in Sri Lanka officials of the Integrated Rural Development Programme consult local MPs and, to a lesser extent, members of Development Councils (Perera, 1987). If such actors are elected by the people they are taken to represent, the form of participation created is stronger than if the representatives are chosen by outsiders, such as national political leaders or bureaucrats involved in the planning and delivery of services to the local community. A more direct form of consultative participation is when the public generally can comment on local plans.

But in all cases, the right which the participants exercise is merely the right to advise, not to decide. Decision-makers are obliged only to seek and listen to advice. They are not obliged to follow it. In the case of the Rural Initiatives and Poverty Relief Project in Argentina, for example, consultations with 'primary stakeholders' – women, migrant workers and indigenous people – were extensive, but 'the only proposals from beneficiaries which were accepted by the programme were those meeting the conditions set beforehand by the Bank' (from a local NGO report, quoted in Long, 2001: 73). The Tarai Research Network (TRN) set up by the Nepalese Ministry of Agriculture is another example of generating information for policy-making from consultations with farmers in the Tarai agro-ecological zone (part of the northern floodplain of the Ganges). It was found that the exercise was basically extractive:

in that villagers who provide the information can expect no direct benefit in return. At the same time, the underlying motive behind the exercise is to provide accurate and timely information to policy-makers, and if this later feeds into better practice, some indirect benefit should ultimately accrue. (Gill, 1998: 13)

Other examples of consultation are the 'report cards' based on social surveys of random samples of households in different categories, including slum-dwellings, in which the clients of public services such as health care, education, housing, and water supply assess administrative performance and express views on the quality and adequacy of services, indicate priorities and identify problems, especially for the poor. Such reporting may be organized by a non-governmental policy research organization, such as the Public Affairs Centre in Bangalore, India, or a government agency, such as the Department of Budget and Management in the Philippines. Questionnaires are usually finalized only after focus group discussions with service users, citizens and clients. Social auditing, as found for example in Rajastan, India, is another method of consultation.

Representation on managing bodies

A stronger form of participation is when representatives from designated groups can become members of the managing bodies of local institutions such as recreation centres, hospitals, day-care centres, communal homes for the elderly or disabled, schools, and clinics. Participation of this kind may combine the management of services with the organization of productive activity and the exercise of influence on planners and decision-makers responsible for the allocation of resources. It may also include accountability to the community or groups of beneficiaries from which the board members are drawn. The WHO sees this as a method for 'promoting greater responsiveness to consumer preferences' in health care (WHO, 1993: 51).

Such organizations can develop long-term plans, monitor the quality of care, appoint, pay and assess the staff, assess the adequacy of resources, recommend fee levels and criteria for exemptions, purchase equipment, develop channels of communication with users, and organize education programmes. Self-managing bodies can also be a way of involving hitherto excluded sections of the community in decision-making and implementation, empowering them by increasing their knowledge and status.

Though the boundaries are inevitably blurred, it is possible to distinguish user participation in the management of public service facilities and projects from other kinds of direct participation, such as user representation on community or neighbourhood councils, neighbourhood action groups, community self-help, consultative procedures, or cooperatives, all of which may be supported in one way or another by public agencies: the recruitment and funding of community development workers, grants, premises, training, technical advice, administrative support, or statutory status.

A major benefit of this type of participation is that it can build up the assets of the poor. For example, community participation in the conservation and management of forests in India and the Gambia has improved soil conservation, increased agricultural production, reduced timber smuggling and increased employment. Wildlife management and bushfire control in Côte d'Ivoire have also created new assets for the poor. Elected committees for soil and water conservation in Kenya have 'improved productivity; decreased land degradation; increased local resilience and decreased vulnerability to external natural and socioeconomic shocks and stresses; and increased capacity of local groups to manage their own productive resources' (Thompson, 1995: 1530). In Nigeria, where women account for 60 to 80 per cent of the agricultural labour force, women's groups have been formed in farming communities with the support of technical specialists from state agriculture departments to initiate enterprises such as cassava processing, groundnut oil production and livestock fattening.

In the Philippines, local irrigation associations have been set up to manage dams, canals and ditches. They can own property, enter into contracts, collect fees, impose sanctions, negotiate rights of way, obtain inputs of labour, materials and land from the community, and repay the interest-free loans provided by the National Irrigation Administration. The economic benefits from the participative management of water resources include increase rice yields, the cultivation of previously arid land, new assets such as mills and storage facilities, and credit schemes (World Bank, 1996).

Managing public services

Participation in the management of an institution is distinguishable from participation in service delivery, or the representation of a community on functional boards or committees to manage the service of which the institution is a part. This kind of participation brings citizens and service users into the management of projects or programmes such as elementary education or employment creation schemes. Examples are Sri Lanka's school development boards, and school management committees in Bangladesh. These ad-hoc bodies may have been set up for quite important development programmes, including the local infrastructure of water supplies, roads, and sewage systems. The type of 'representation' involved is relevant to the quality of participation that this sort of managerial device permits.

Action groups

Participation can also refer to the creation of action groups and voluntary organizations to articulate the needs of people that government programmes are intended to serve. This is one of the roles performed by many NGOs. The participation involved may combine the management of services or the organization of productive activity with the exercise of influence on planners and decision-makers responsible for the allocation of resources. Participation is thus of the pressure-group variety. It involves the articulation of political demands. Action groups often represent important opportunities for the mobilization of political pressure and action on behalf of disadvantaged groups, sometimes escalating to direct and even illegal action, as in the case of some peasant and trade unions, squatter groups, urban social movements, landless groups and ethnic associations (Cornwall, 2002).

'Interest-oriented participation' may feed into other kinds, such as communications between officials and dependent groups, the management of community facilities, and involvement in formal structures of local government and political parties through voting and office-holding. If the identification of needs and priorities can be backed up with resources to carry out a project then participation has moved beyond sharing decision-making authority with bureaucrats to a power of initiative which may be regarded as qualitatively different from a capacity to act or decide on matters proposed or assigned by others (Paul, 1987).

NGOs are frequently credited with offering better opportunities for participation than state agencies. In so doing, they increase support for development, and raise political awareness. They should therefore not only be better at defining needs, but also show greater commitment to the poor than conventional state organs. Participation in the organization itself is very important. In Manila, for example, the political socialization brought about by participation in the Tondo organizations taught people the significance of collective action, class solidarity, and the origins of their underprivileged economic and political circumstances, whereas before they had experienced only small-scale solidarity based on vertical clientele relations, bringing them into conflict with each other over what they believed to be fixed amounts of very scarce resources (Ruland, 1984).

Representative government

Finally, participation may involve creating formal structures of representative government at different levels in the spatial hierarchy, perhaps including the lowest levels possible of wards and neighbourhoods. An important example (because it entails an unusual degree of devolution) is Bolivia's Law of Popular Participation, 1994, which not only devolves new powers to municipalities. It also requires them to engage in participatory planning, management and auditing with local institutions such as peasant communities, indigenous groups, neighbourhood councils and, for auditing, vigilance committees. In effect this amounts to a further devolution of responsibilities to submunicipal areas for a range of social, infrastructural, productive and environmental powers (Blackburn, 1998).

The participation that the majority of the inhabitants of the area covered by the tier of government will engage in will be voting periodically to choose their representatives to sit on decision-making assemblies and councils. However, some will obviously seek office. Some of these will be successful. The lower the tier of elected government involved, the greater the proportion of the community that will participate in a more active sense than just voting.

Elected representation on statutory decision-making bodies as in a system of local government may be thought to be a strong form of participation, especially if the area is small enough for accountability and responsiveness to be strong. It is likely to be regarded with growing approval as expectations increase that political pluralism will apply to all levels of government. But it may also be argued that there should be additional forms of participation such as those described earlier if development projects and programmes are to be really successful. 'Delegated' rather than 'direct' participation may be seen as alienating if there is a long line of delegation between the people and the decision-makers. From Zimbabwe's experience it would seem that important intervening variables are the extent to which local representatives become instruments of top-down rather than bottom-up planning; the way new structures for participation interact with traditional and other local elites; and where in the hierarchy budgetary powers and technical skills are located (de Valk, 1990).

Full participation comes when all forms are used in unison. This seems to have been recognized in India where a working group on district planning was set up to find ways of ensuring that participation means that people can make their needs known and ensure that the benefits of plans and projects go to the deserving target groups. The group recommended that participation should occur at every stage of planning, that advantage should be taken of the experiences of voluntary agencies, that district planners should interact with people in their villages and with their representative organizations, and that consultations should take place with beneficiary groups through open forums consisting of the representatives of local agencies. Indirect representation on district planning bodies was no longer regarded as sufficient (Thimmaiah, 1987).

Participation will be affected by the pattern of areas created for local representative government, though the evidence is inconclusive. Large subnational governments may be no less satisfactory than small ones in encouraging participation, though there may be positive disadvantages for poor people in smaller communities, notably in Third World countries. But it remains uncertain as to whether biases in effective political participation can be overcome by the creation of larger units of government in which, perhaps, more effective coalitions among the poor can be organized. It is likely that the persistence of patronage and the dependency of the poor upon the rich will be more important factors than size of local government area in the level of effectiveness of political participation among different socio-economic groups. There is also some fragmentary evidence that a complex structure of tiers causes confusion and alienation (Norris, 1983).

The range of powers devolved is also significant for participation, because it determines both the rights of participants and the matters in which they can be involved. So it is logically possible for the citizens of a locality to have full decision-making powers in some trivial area of public policy. Functions then undermine participation. Alternatively, participants may merely have a right to be consulted on major issues that directly affect their lives, such as the priority to be given to important development projects. Unfortunately these two logical possibilities have been reality in many newly democratizing countries. If participative institutions are given trivial powers and functions then the objectives of participation may not be realized. There can also be significant local discretion without participation when plans are formulated at district level by teams of central government officials.

There is also a relationship between the financing of representative community government and participation, determined by whether local accountability is undermined by inadequate local sources of revenue as compared with central grants-in-aid. Participation is by no means automatically restricted if funds come from outside. There can be popular participation in the choice of priorities whoever provides the funds if they come free of conditions. But it is unlikely that they will. And full accountability requires that participants in the local political process should have some say in how money is to be raised as well as spent.

Participation can be further adversely affected if, as frequently happens, responsibilities are not matched by adequate resources. A crisis of confidence in local leaders and elected representatives is likely if basic services cannot be provided nor basic needs met because of insufficient funding of local government. This may be reflected in abnormally low levels of turnout in local elections or in other indicators of disaffection.

Participation and the effectiveness of development projects

As we have seen, it is often assumed that participation will lead to improved project design. Felt needs are more likely to be served. Outside planners will not be as successful in designing projects that meet the specific needs of beneficiaries as the beneficiaries themselves. Projects have been found to be more easily sustained when community participation is involved. Community involvement in design and implementation strengthens project maintenance and increases cost recovery rates (Bamberger, 1987).

The benefits of consultation arise from the access to local knowledge which it allows decision-makers. If beneficiaries are able to provide genuine feedback to project managers, then the design, implementation and outcomes of projects can be improved. For example, in health care patients are an important source of knowledge about illness – how it is reacted to, and the effects of the environment on it – that health professionals badly need. Information sharing at consultative meetings facilitates collective action among beneficiaries and has a positive effect on community development projects by enabling people to carry out their responsibilities better. Such information is also a source of power by raising the consciousness of people generally, or providing specific insights into planning and development processes and who wields power within them.

A review of World Bank experience with community participation in urban housing, population, health, nutrition, and irrigation projects found that understanding beneficiary needs and attributes helped improve project design, even if participation just means information gathering and consultation. Community participation meant that new services or activities were introduced, or existing ones modified, in line with beneficiary preferences; and that potential clients were motivated to use project services, thus mobilizing demand. A significant saving was made in time and money as a result of smooth implementation of tasks that are normally prone to conflicts and delays. Another significant contribution of community participation towards project efficiency was through sounder operational maintenance and better day-to-day management, particularly in the irrigation projects (Paul, 1987).

Evidence from 121 rural water supply projects also showed that those with high levels of beneficiary participation had a 68 per cent success rate, while among those with low levels only 12 per cent were successful (Long, 2001). A review of 52 USAID projects found similarly that beneficiary participation contributed to project effectiveness. However, it was not found to be the most important factor. Other factors, such as adequate funding, and the skill and motivation of the implementing team, were found to be more important in most cases. Indeed the participatory model was found to have significant benefits in the richer countries rather than the poorer. A lot depended on the type of participation involved. The more direct forms of participation were found to be less significant, while the variables with strong correlations with project effectiveness were adequacy of communication, beneficiary commitment, increased community capacity, and local control of outputs. Participation in implementation and maintenance was more important than participation in the earlier stages of a project. Participation increased in importance as projects progressed, as did the importance of utilizing local skills and knowledge, the degree of ownership and control of outputs, and community capacity (Finsterbusch and Van Wicklin, 1987).

Other studies have shown that participation works better for project effectiveness under some conditions than others, and especially when it is based on already existing local communal institutions and systems of collective management perhaps associated with kinship, traditional leadership or other traditions of rural cooperation. It also helps when the projects involved require less complex technologies and are relatively small in scale (Useem *et al.*, 1988).

Other conditions necessary for successful participation were revealed in a study of the Southern Thailand Experimental Project between 1982 and 1985, the primary objective of which was to create village problem-solving groups to work on development projects of their own choice. Despite equal amounts of government assistance to the poor villages taking part, success varied widely. Some villages initiated only modest projects that generated little momentum and soon faltered while others mounted extensive projects for sanitation, rubber production, cooperative enterprise, fish farming and poultry production. It was found that mobilization was more intense in villages that were relatively isolated from competing alternatives in urban centres, had already accumulated some development experience, and had confidence in traditional village authorities and local government. Leadership was given by village heads and extension agents. The first two factors were more important than the third for the success of village projects, but all were more significant than levels of poverty or distribution of wealth (Useem *et al.*, 1988).

In Nicaragua, however, the relationship between local governments and the local people was very significant for the mobilization of the population behind community improvements such as health centres, wells, bridges and schools, as well as public health and literacy campaigns. Local government was an 'articulate interface' between the organized population and the state agencies that generally have what few resources there are for community projects (Downs, 1987). Again we see the importance of different kinds of participation working in combination.

Participation in the management of services through community management committees has been found to improve performance by strengthening the accountability of providers to clients. The involvement of diverse groups based on kinship, ethnicity or culture facilitates the expression of grievances and collaboration in problem-solving. Participation encourages a sense of ownership of and support for ways of solving local problems. Empathy and trust between service providers (for example, in health care) and their clients is encouraged (World Bank, 1994). In the field of health care, experience also suggests that discussions of health costs by managing committees not only contributes to a more cost-conscious level of provision and utilization of health care, but also encourages efforts to find health-promoting alternatives such as water supplies and diets (Kasongo Project Team, 1984).

The benefits of such participation may be felt by the participants themselves or the public officials responsible for the management of the service. An example of the former is when the quality of service becomes more responsive to consumer preferences (one of the World Health

Organization's aims for community involvement in the management of facilities in the field of health care: World Health Organization, 1993); or when the involvement of diverse groups based on kinship, ethnicity or culture facilitates the expression of grievances and collaboration in problem-solving (World Bank, 1994). An example of the latter is the 'compelling evidence that arrangements that promote participation by stakeholders in the design and implementation of public services or programmes can improve both the rate of return and the sustainability of those activities' (World Bank, 1997: 117).

However, participation in public management can encounter obstacles which it may not be in the interest of the state to remove. First, in their attempt to maintain credibility with the agency, participants are likely to become incorporated into the agency's perspective on the service, especially if representing an apathetic 'constituency'. The sponsoring agency is also likely to be dominant in schemes involving the delegation of authority (making the rules and controlling the procedures).

Second, there may be insufficient community organization to support this form of participation. It requires exceptional political abilities for people of low status (such as the landless) to relay to the authorities the experiences of those without power and avoid betraying their constituents by adapting to the norms of 'responsible' authority. Finding qualified people to participate can be very difficult, as was found with Botswana's school boards.

Third, service users often experience poor communication with professionals. It can be an obstacle to empowerment if the language, and especially the jargon, of professional practice create a veil of 'expert knowledge' which users find hard to penetrate.

Fourth, community workers involved with the project seek ends (for example the development of community awareness and integration) to which the community's ends (for example a cleaner environment) are merely means. As some health programmes have found, different interests may have different and not necessarily compatible objectives: donors will want to make interventions more effective; project managers will want cheap labour; and hitherto 'silent' groups, and particularly women, will want to gain some political influence (Eyben and Ladbury, 1995).

Clients may prefer consultation to control, fearing the responsibility involved in managing public facilities. In the case of hearings in connection with the environmental impact of public works in Brazil, 'the socio-educational profile of most citizens means that they feel unable to discuss public issues as equals with formal authorities'. Consequently, participants preferred to delegate decision-making rather than to exercise power themselves. The hearings then functioned as channels of information from the authorities to local residents, legitimizing decisions taken in government offices, rather than gathering information and preferences from the public (Alonso and Costa, 2004). However, if participation just means consultation or merely information absorption, the evidence suggests there is an unmet demand in many areas of public policy. What is not so clear is whether there is an equally strong demand for stronger forms of involvement in local policy-making, including the management of facilities such as clinics or schools.

There are certainly conditions under which participants have been happy with the involvement of outsiders, such as project managers or government professionals, especially if participation exacerbates existing social divisions, whether based on gender, caste or class. For instance, in the management of forests by user-groups in Nepal the role of the district forest officer was crucial in ensuring that the conflicting interests of castes did not undermine the participatory scheme. Caste conflict also threatened water-users' management of tank irrigation in Tamil Nadu, India, requiring the supporting non-governmental project team from the local university to reconcile opposing interests, and challenge local power relations to ensure that Harijans were recognized as equal partners in the project (Eyben and Ladbury, 1995; Gronow, 1995; Mosse, 1995)

Professionals may be reluctant to implement the empowerment of users of their services, fearing that their jobs will be 'deskilled' and believing that power is a zero-sum game where they can only lose if users gain. It is difficult for advocates of user involvement to convince them that empowering users also empowers professionals, even if the professionals accept that service standards can be improved by user empowerment. For example, community-managed schools were introduced in El Salvador to provide primary education in areas of rural poverty, but administrators and teachers resisted the involvement of parents in school management, and 'the hoped for participation of the poor was not realised' (Long, 2001: 147). The case of water-tank rehabilitation in Sri Lanka's dry zone showed that members of NGOs can also find 'the full-blown use of a participatory methodology' threatening (Samaranayake, 1998).

Community workers may obstruct empowerment by reflecting their government employer's perceptions of problems and needs, and by throwing communities back on their own limited resources, thus reinforcing social inequalities. Lay members of management bodies (for example for schools, clinics, natural resources) may feel marginalized in decision-making and unable to challenge professionals through a lack of expertise, confidence and experience. Community or group representatives may be unable to communicate effectively with their 'constituents' because of isolation, poor communication facilities, or official restrictions on the right to report back. Class, ethnic and religious divisions among lay members of governing and managerial bodies restrict effective participation in management.

Even if they do not fear a loss of power, professionals may refuse to accept laypersons' knowledge as valid. They may see themselves as teachers rather than facilitators, especially in projects requiring technical expertise, such as agricultural extension work or public works. In the 1990s attempts to introduce farmer participation in the development of new agricultural practices in a province of Zimbabwe found that 'In a hierarchically structured society, where hierarchy is based mostly on the level of formal education, it is difficult for formally educated staff to accept farmers' traditional and experience-based knowledge systems as equal, and to learn from them' (Hagmann *et al.*, 1998: 54).

Whether the development that is generated through projects and programmes involving participation makes poor areas more prosperous will depend on the quality of the projects initiated for those areas. Inequalities will be perpetuated if participation favours villages that are better able to produce workable plans (Finsterbusch and Van Wicklin, 1987). Whether the development is redistributive between classes and income groups will depend on who benefits from the opportunities to exercise power and influence created by participation.

Unfortunately, the commonest form of participation, consultation, is often no more than part of the information-gathering process in bureaucracies such as rural planning departments and project offices. It is often regarded as more a formality than a genuine opportunity for people to control the decisions that will affect their own environments or standards of living. For example, the professionals involved in slum improvement projects in five large Indian cities (engineers, doctors and community development workers) used participatory techniques more to extract information from slum-dwellers rather than to give them a role in planning urban redevelopment (Kar and Phillips, 1998). A review of 24 countries in which the World Bank sponsored participatory poverty assessments found not a single case in which the participation of the poor amounted to anything other than 'information sharing' (Holland and Blackburn, 1998: 201–10).

If consultation is to be effective in altering official perceptions of local realities (for example, agricultural methods, access to health care and education, the costs of corruption, the use of forest resources, or the strategies for coping with scarcity and crisis adopted by the poor), policy-makers need to be brought face-to-face with people whose lives their policies are supposed to improve. Equally, bodies representing and mobilizing the opinions of recipients of government policies need a good understanding of how the policy process works (Holland and Blackburn, 1998: 153–7).

Information sharing can then facilitate collective or individual action among beneficiaries and can have a positive effect on the success of projects if it means that beneficiaries can carry out their responsibilities better. Such information sharing can be critical in programmes such as family planning and nutrition. Information can also be a source of power either by generally raising consciousness of local conditions or by providing specific insights into the planning process and who wields power within it.

There may be costs as well as benefits to projects from participation. The costs include delays in starting a project, staff increases, pressure to add to the scope of the project, and 'capture' of project benefits by unintended beneficiaries leading to political conflict. Gaining a clear idea of such costs as well as the benefits of participation needs diagnostic studies, analysis of constraints, flexible project design, appropriate technology, the promotion of local leadership and organization, two-way communication, and attention to feedback on emerging problems. Participation is not always seen as consistent with the efficient delivery of aid or the political and organizational imperatives of development projects (Finsterbusch and Van Wicklin, 1987; Bamberger, 1991).

One controversial view, that runs contrary to the confidence of enthusiasts for participation in the beneficial effects of community knowledge, is that low levels of participation should reduce the adverse effects of ignorance, irrationality and extremism. Birch summarizes this argument as follows: 'populist theories of democracy involved unnecessary and unrealistic assumptions about the political interest, knowledge and rationality of the average citizen' (Birch, 1993: 83). In development work there is 'a danger of swinging from one untenable position ("we know best") to an equally untenable and damaging one ("they know best")' (Cleaver, 1999: 605).

This is a concern about participation that would not be shared by most members of the development community, where it has become an article of faith that participation makes critically important knowledge available to policy-makers: knowledge about local social and economic circumstances, about political power structures, about indigenous and affordable technologies, about experience of past successes and failures, about environmental conditions and so on. Some long-standing beliefs in poor, rural communities might well impede progress, such as misplaced confidence in the abilities of traditional healers, religious fatalism that prevents farmers from adopting new techniques and seeds, or the traditional oppression of members of the community (notably women), but others that appear strange to Westernized technocrats often reflect rationalities derived from local circumstances. It might also be pointed out that irrationality and ignorance are not the exclusive preserves of people who have hitherto been without voice, as the views on AIDS expressed in the past by some South African leaders go to show.

Empowerment

Participation has an effect on projects carried out in that particular mode. But it also has an effect on the people who participate. It should make them more effective both politically and administratively.

Politically people become more conscious of their strengths when engaging with the authorities. Dealing with one set of agencies enhances the ability to deal with others and to articulate demands beyond those associated with the original project. Participation also produces leadership. It means the development of political skills among individuals and groups as a preparation for action. The poor become empowered when they develop a capacity to share ideas, experiences, problems and judgements about what action might be taken. Consciousness-raising is also part of the empowerment process, demystifying the social and economic position of the poor and their relationships with other social strata. Developing negotiating skills and an ability to cooperate are central to the process of empowerment. Internal individual and group skills include listening, assertiveness, exploiting expertise, dealing with difficult people, enabling newcomers to get involved, broadening the basis of involvement, accumulating knowledge, creating organizations, and ensuring organizations are accepted as representative of the group interests they have been created to promote.

There is evidence (albeit mainly from established democracies) that participation in relatively small groups, including those that are simply deliberative, such as citizens' juries, results in the participants being better informed, more sophisticated politically, more committed to solving policy problems, and better able to empathize with whatever vulnerable group is intended to benefit from the policy in question. But participants need to feel that their deliberations can have some effect. Otherwise they are likely to become frustrated with participation for participation's sake. Participation can then become counter-productive (Segall, 2005).

Administratively, people become better at making decisions and managing projects. Skills and knowledge should be strengthened to enable beneficiaries to take responsibility for managing projects, organize further self-help efforts, negotiate with local governments for community services, motivate other users of local services, and generally contribute to the social education of the community. For example, participatory approaches to natural resource management in semi-arid and drought-prone areas in Adhra Pradesh, Karnataka and Tamil Nadu built up group solidarity and administrative skills such as book-keeping, managing bank accounts, negotiating rebates on bulk purchases, monitoring the quality of results, and devising and enforcing rules and regulations (Blackburn, 1998).

Empowerment is likely to be more effective if there is a high level of literacy in the community and if 'countervailing power' has been nurtured among weaker sections of society, so that the powers of vested interests are roughly in balance in terms of resources, expertise, educational levels, social status and size of membership. In such circumstances, which legislation can help bring about, the domination of decision-making by powerful interests can be ameliorated. Effective participation is more likely to be found if there has already been some empowerment of local groups representing the poor and disadvantaged sections of the community (Fung *et al.*, 2003).

It is often argued that participation will enable groups that have been politically weak to exercise the power that their numbers and needs justify. Participation is supposed to facilitate access to benefits and so ensure a more equitable distribution of benefits. However, it has frequently been shown that local institutions have been easily captured by those already rich and powerful, and used to further entrench their privilege within local communities (see Chapter 5). For example, water supply points become sited near influential households in parts of rural India despite being funded under anti-poverty programmes. Such capture by local elites must count as a 'cost' of participation that may or may not be included in any evaluation.

NGOs are also vulnerable to capture by local elites. A participative, egalitarian style is always threatened by oligarchic forms of leadership in the hands of socio-economic or even traditional elites. Government officials may play important roles, especially in NGOs that have been initiated as part of a government development programme. Studies of many NGOs also reveal that the poor tend to be under-represented, experiencing access problems similar to those encountered with government agencies. Patron–client relations may extend into NGOs.

Action groups, especially those representing the interests of the poor, can expect to encounter resistance from local and regional elites such as important landowners and merchants who dominate the formal structure of local government, and from national government leaders and administrators who regard local organizations as a challenge to their authority and bureaucratic convenience. NGOs are often perceived by central governments as their most active critics, presenting an alternative political voice, and capturing a growing share of overseas funding (Bowden, 1990). Once they become vehicles for movements that threaten the *status quo*, NGOs must expect the same degrees of hostile response from the authorities as any other opposition movement.

Spontaneous local action groups are also vulnerable to internal conflicts of interest, leadership problems and divisions on caste, kinship, ethnic, partisan, religious and even gender lines. Internal factionalism is rarely absent. Shortages of political, organizational and technical skills frequently exacerbate such problems (Esman and Uphoff, 1984).

Inequality, exclusion, dependency and cultural patterns also make political participation difficult for the poor and especially poor women. Consequently, there are great risks in political participation for people who live in a precarious position as regards both life and work. In rural areas land-rights are generally weak, and threatened by dispossession, leading to landlessness and possibly destitution. There is also the risk of alienating the people upon whom one is dependent – landlord, employer, moneylender, and persons of higher status. These are all participants in the political process whose interests may be threatened by successful political participation by the poor, and explains why political participation may provoke severe repression by the state.

For example, research into village-level participation under Uganda's local government system found that villagers were reluctant to participate in village governance, seeing participation as risky: 'In a context where political culture dictates obedience and deference towards people in positions of power and authority, years of oppressive rule have rendered avoidance of politics the sensible way to ensure personal safety and survival' (Golooba-Mutebi, 2004: 301–2). There was also a feeling that elected officials should carry the responsibility of government, leaving people free to get on with the business of earning a living. Among many factors deterring the participation of the poor in the community groups set up under the health sector reform of 1998 in Bangladesh were fear of reprisals, and the low priority given by the poor to participation that is costly and brings few returns (Mahmud, 2004).

Risks of a different sort confront participants in the violent urban areas of Jamaica. Following participatory research on violence and poverty, the urban poor could not take part in the dissemination of the findings from consulations with focus groups:

> [O]pen participation of potentially vulnerable community members was not possible; in addition, the divided nature of Jamaican society meant that previous initiatives for the poor to talk directly to policy-makers had been highly conflictive. (Moser and Holland, 1998: 55)

Political participation among the poor is further inhibited by relationships of dependency, economic isolation, clientelist and populist modes of political incorporation, competition between the rural and urban poor, and the tyranny of work. The poor have to devote their energies to making ends meet and are likely, as in Ethiopia, to find participation 'a time-consuming and tedious task that does not do much for them' (Wordofa, 1998: 16).

Cultural obstacles include low levels of literacy and education, extreme parochialism, and respect for traditional authority, religion and custom. Consequently, people of low status may have little incentive to partici-pate, knowing that it will have little impact on their position in the social hierarchy. For example, women are often reluctant to participate in community-based health and population projects, even though they are the intended beneficiaries, because they 'lack the power and skills to participate in collective decision-making' dominated by high-status men (Eyben and Ladbury, 1995: 195).

Women, and especially poor women, are widely repressed by religion (especially dominant interpretations of Islam), patriarchal societies, family responsibilities and lack of education – of the 960 million illiterate people in the world, two-thirds are women. They consequently tend to be under-represented on all mechanisms of participation, sometimes, as with forest management groups in parts of India, because rules allow only one household member to participate, thus effectively excluding women because of cultural discrimination. Where women did participate, they were restricted by traditional deference to men, fear of reprisals for even speaking at meetings, and lack of time within an already overburdened life. In many settings, women's participation becomes meaningful only in all-women groups, which gradually spread confidence that women can participate alongside men (Mohanty, 2004).

It is difficult for the poor to organize and unionize when there are substantial reserve armies of labour available to much better-organized employers. Women may feel reluctant to join male-dominated organizations such as trade unions. Participation through pressure groups and other forms of political association may be uninviting (for example trade union activity may be discredited through association with the previous authoritarian regime in newly democratizing countries). Civil society, independent social organizations and cooperative spheres of social autonomy may be weakened by the profit motive and market relationships: while it is often argued that a free market is a prerequisite for civic freedoms, competitive democracy, and arbitration between and reconciliation of conflicting interests, it can also dissolve and weaken civil society. Apathy and ignorance can undermine collective action, and participatory institutions can degenerate into bureaucratization, technocracy and oligarchy (Lewis, 1997; Fung *et al.*, 2003).

Thus participatory approaches to development projects should not assume that individuals can be separated from their existing social networks, economic relationships, and power structures. Whether new arrangements empower people already marginalized and excluded because of poverty or gender bias will depend on much more than decision-making structures. Studies of the collective management of water resources, as one instance, have revealed a failure to recognize the effect of social structures on participation, such that the evidence for empowerment has been 'partial, tenuous and reliant on assertions of the rightness of the approach rather than convincing proof of outcomes' (Cleaver, 1999: 597).

Advocacy of participation as a means to empowerment is also confronted by the fact that politics is elitist, in the sense that only a small proportion of the population will join political organizations or engage in other forms of political action. Power in a representative system of democracy is delegated to a relatively small group of office-holders. Government is an activity reserved by necessity to the few (though direct democracy and mass participation are more feasible than we are often led to believe). For the majority, political action constitutes a very small proportion of their total range of activities. Only a small minority hold legislative office in central and local government. An even smaller group occupy executive and judicial offices. Public services employ large numbers directly occupied in the business of government, especially if the police, teachers, health service employees are included. But only a small proportion of these are in a position to influence the choice of public policies and items for political agendas.

Empowerment through participation can even be undermined by aid donors themselves, whose latest discourse risks losing its earlier focus on the needs of the poor. It is now common for donors to make reference to 'stakeholders' when advocating participation, a habit which is far more controversial than is generally acknowledged. For example, the World Bank defines participation as 'the process through which stakeholders influence and share control over priority setting, policy-making, resource allocations and access to public goods and services', thus including as 'participants' all those with an interest in project outcomes – government officials, representatives of national and international NGOs, financial institutions, businesses and professional bodies – as well as the recipients of policies and services, including and especially the poor. This fashion for 'stakeholder' participation has also influenced British aid policy.

Unfortunately, such euphemistic attempts to convey inclusiveness are unhelpful to the participation of the poor. If 'stakeholder' refers to the various stakes that people have in the outcomes of policy initiatives, or risks that are taken with assets that may be lost, then what may be trivial for one group can be crucial to the well-being of another. If a project goes wrong, the livelihoods of the poor may be seriously harmed while the interests of bureaucrats may be unaffected, or even improved if corruption has caused the policy failure. A distinction between 'primary' and 'secondary' stakeholders goes nowhere near identifying different interests, often conflicting, in the outcomes of a development project. A concept which fails to acknowledge the vastly different 'stakes'people have in a development activity is virtually worthless for the analysis of the politics of poverty, even though it has a fine rhetorical sound in political declarations.

If participation is to empower the poor, governments need to focus on the constraints imposed by material deprivation, limits to freedom of association, and official attitudes.

Material deprivation

Many of the obstacles to effective political participation by the poor are the result of low incomes. Improving the poor's material conditions would make involvement in political as well as other social activities easier. But this requires policies designed to have a redistributive impact. Action by central governments is needed to increase the poor's access to economic resources, including infrastructure projects (such as rural roads, irrigation and electrification), markets (for example, by legalizing street vendors), technology, and finance (such as 'seed' capital for small-scale producers) (Gupta *et al.*, 2002). Land reform, protection of the rights of sharecroppers, and credit programmes have also been effective, as in the case of West Bengal. Implementing minimum wage legislation, tenancy reforms, and other measures to reduce the dependence and vulnerability of the poor also weakens local elites (Engberg-Pedersen and Webster, 2002). 'Core' labour standards have to be enforced to eliminate forced labour and discrimination in employment practices. Market failures in the financial, health, education, housing and water sectors have to be addressed by the state with public expenditure programmes and subsidized consumption of private provision, since these all add to the poor's assets (World Bank, 2001b).

Before the poor can be empowered their extreme economic insecurity needs to be reduced and livelihoods secured so that political dependence does not so closely follow economic dependence. The more that overseas aid can be directed towards income-generating activities, as for example the UN's Community Development Investment Funds and Community Loan Funds, the more it will have an impact on the political bargaining position of the poor in local governance, as well as on family livelihoods (Osmani, 2001).

Supporting group action

Empowering the poor so that their participation in politics is effective needs to be supported by strong central government action which removes legal and other barriers to freedom of association and the mobilization of groups aiming to influence public policy. Support needs to be given to grassroots organizations such as unions and cooperatives in ways that overcome the impediments to political organization that specifically affect the poor (such as lack of time, resources, information, and external help). This can include support for NGOs which act as links between community groups and national agencies as well as providing technical assistance and organizational skills.

There is also a need for state intervention to protect the legal rights of the poor. Strengthening the rule of law by reinforcing the independence of the judiciary makes citizens more equal before the law as well as subjecting state officials to the law. This should help remove the illegalities which confront the poor and their representatives when they seek to exert political pressure or enforce their rights: arbitrary arrest, police harassment, bureaucratic discrimination in the allocation of entitlements, and intimidation and murder by illegal paramilitary groups employed by economic elites such as landlords and companies. The state can also support the poor locally through enabling rules that permit legal service organizations to improve legal literacy, provide legal aid, create a culture of rights, organize legal advocacy, and campaign for legal reform. Such changes not only assist the poor in securing their legal rights and entitlements but also empower them politically (World Bank, 2001b).

Measures to uphold the rule of law and protect the rights of the poor also help ensure that elections are competitive and fair, and that the abuse of power is restricted. Local decision-making is thus made more accountable to the public. Local officials are subject to legal rules, making them more accountable to elected representatives. If the law supports the principle and practice of political opposition, the voice of the poor can be backed up by electoral sanctions against corrupt councillors and parties that abuse their powers of patronage, misdirect funds, or otherwise distort policy implementation. Political competition is essential for the effective operation of procedures to curb patronage and corruption, so it is essential that party politics is allowed into local government (Echeverri-Gent, 1992).

Such reforms need to be accompanied by a political discourse on poverty which changes perceptions associating it with shame or fate, or which simply deny its existence. Such a discourse is an important part of a pro poor political environment (Webster, 2002).

Official attitudes

The mobilization of the poor requires leadership that will often have to be drawn from other social strata. The poor need help so that the disadvantages of illiteracy, economic insecurity, dependence and low levels of confidence can be overcome. Sources of successful initiative and leadership have included municipal health officers, community development workers (sometimes funded with external aid, as in Nepal), mayors (for example, in the Philippines), chairpersons of local councils (India), field officers from the centre (as in India's Rajiv Gandhi Missions), midwives and NGOs.

However, the poor regularly encounter harassment, abuse, criminality, corruption, arrogance, rudeness and disdain when seeking services from state administration. So governments need to train and motivate staff to adopt pro-poor attitudes and methods of working. Better personnel (recruited on merit, rewarded for good performance, and insulated from political pressure) would go some way towards solving this problem. In addition, the professional values and practices of community workers and other development professionals (such as social workers) can be reoriented towards empowerment by recognizing and building on the poor's skills, understandings and abilities. Accepting the rights of users to be involved in the definition of problems and the planning, management and delivery of services can also be encouraged. Public servants can be trained to adopt practices that are non-elitist and non-oppressive, and to recognize that language is a form of power, creating a need for interpreting and translating facilities (Braye and Preston-Shoot, 1995). The existence of power disparities and other inequalities in social and personal relationships can be acknowledged. Personal and organizational commitments to empowerment and to learning from service users can be developed. Local officials can be given the duty of putting people in touch with sources of advocacy.

Conclusion

Despite the emphasis since 1980 in aid policy on participation, the achievements are less than hoped for. An examination of projects supported by the World Bank, the DFID and the German GTZ revealed that participation of the poor 'seldom occurs' in the first stage of project cycles – the identification phase – when the idea for a project is considered from the point of view of economic development, poverty alleviation, or reform in a particular sector such as health care or education (Long, 2001: 66). There tends to be more participation of the poor at the design stage, though still in a minority of cases. While participation in the implementation phase is more substantial, it includes contributions of cash, labour or materials. Participation then falls off in the later stages of monitoring and evaluation. So while participation is firmly on the list of donor concerns about the quality of governance, their own development projects do not set a particularly impressive example.

The problem has been to get development agencies, both governmental and non-governmental, national and international, to adopt participation as a philosophy, culture and working practice. Solving this problem is difficult, not least because it requires recognition that the participation of the poor is likely to be ineffective unless power structures that perpetuate poverty are recognized and challenged, something that by definition local and national political elites are reluctant to do, unless they spot that participation can be used to manipulate and co-opt potential dissenters. This conclusion applies even when participation means little more than listening to the intended beneficiaries of development projects as they analyse their needs and evaluate outcomes.

Incorporating the participation of the poor in policy-making and administration is a long-term process (taking up to twenty years before becoming fully effective), and requires extensive organizational change. Case-studies of the rural development division of the Sri Lankan Ministry of Policy, Planning and Implementation, the Soil and Water Conservation Branch of Kenya's Ministry of Agriculture, and the National Irrigation Administration in the Philippines show how administrative procedures and cultures of formerly centralized and bureaucratic organizations can be altered, but only over a long period (Thompson, 1995).

8

Eradicating Corruption

Introduction: the cost of corruption

The problem of corruption came to feature prominently among the governance concerns of the international development community in the 1990s, eventually forming part of the anti-poverty efforts of both multilateral and bilateral aid donors. There can be no doubt as to the seriousness with which the aid community views corruption. Every facet of development is believed to be harmed by it. It is regarded as a particularly significant adversary in the fight against poverty (Doig and McIvor, 1999).

The scale of the problem certainly warrants such concern, though by its nature corruption is hard to quantify. Total values of corrupt transactions are difficult to compute, and much reliance has to be placed on evidence which indicates the cost of corruption to individual countries and regions. For example, in Latin America corruption accounts for the loss of 10 per cent in GDP each year, and 20 per cent of the funds earmarked for government procurement are lost through corruption. The African Union estimates that corruption costs African economies more than US$148 billion each year, or 25 per cent of Africa's GDP, and increases the cost of goods by up to 20 per cent.

International agencies are loath to calculate the scale of corruption lest they offend recipient governments and compromise reform efforts. Nevertheless, recent research by the World Bank Institute concluded that US$1000 billion is paid in bribes each year worldwide – and this does not include embezzlement and the theft of public assets. An extreme example is Russia, where in 2006 the deputy prosecutor general estimated that bureaucrats receive £125 billion in bribes annually.

What are also clear are the bad reputations which far too many countries have among those who have commercial dealings with their govern-

Table 8.1   *Perceptions of corruption, 2002 – regional averages, with highest and lowest scores*

Regions	Scores
South Asia	2.6
Sri Lanka	3.7
Bangladesh	1.2
Middle East	3.9
Jordan	4.5
Egypt	3.4
Latin America	4.0
Chile	7.5
Paraguay	1.7
Eastern Europe/Central Asia	4.1
Slovenia	6.0
Azerbaijan	2.0
East Asia/Pacific	3.0
Hong Kong	8.2
Indonesia	1.9
Africa	3.4
Botswana	6.4
Nigeria	1.6

SOURCE: data from Transparency International, 2002.

NOTE: the higher the score, the lower the perceived corruption.

ments. Of the 102 countries surveyed by Transparency International in 2002, 70 scored less than 5 out of a possible 'clean' score of 10, based on the perceptions of business people, risk analysts, and residents, both local and expatriate. Corruption is perceived as 'rampant' in the 7 countries that scored less than 2: Angola, Bangladesh, Indonesia, Kenya, Madagascar, Nigeria and Paraguay. The highest levels of corruption in developing and post-communist states are found in South Asia (see Table 8.1).

Agency views on corruption

All leading multilateral agencies have formulated detailed assessments of corruption on which they have built strategies for reform. The UNDP sees corruption as inimical to every aspect of development – economic, social and political – and as especially damaging to the interests of the poor. It also recognizes that corruption has a gender dimension: 'It widens the gender gap because corrupt payments are in exchange for breaking the rules of fairness in employment and procurement. Corruption also worsens gender inequalities because it is often redistributional from the poor (mostly women) to officeholders (mostly men)' (UNDP, 1999: 10).

The World Bank also stresses the harmful effects of corruption on the poor via its damaging consequences for economic growth, and public services, as well as its direct costs (World Bank, 2001c). The IMF concentrates on the economic and public financial aspects of corruption, and its harmful effects on both taxation and public expenditure which lead to greater income inequality (IMF, 2002).

Bilateral donors also seek to curb corruption because of its economic and social costs. For example, the UK's Department for International Development notes how corruption is something from which the poor in particular suffer, since the looting of public assets leads to distorted decision-making, discriminatory application of regulations, tax evasion and resources wasted on poor projects – all of which damage the prospects for development and poverty reduction and the ability of poor countries to compete in a global economy (DFID, 2000: 26).

Donor assistance

The anti-corruption work of the international donor community falls into five categories. First, international agreements are sought obliging the governments of member states to take action against corruption. For example, the UN Convention against Corruption requires member states to embody anti-corruption measures in legislation. The OECD has hosted diplomatic negotiations to make bribery by international businesses based in OECD countries a criminal offence. It has pressured member states to build the control of corruption into their aid procedures. Some donor states have agreed to take action against their national and international companies that engage in corrupt transactions with officials in developing and transitional states. Examples are the Council of Europe's Criminal and Civil Law Conventions on Corruption, and the 1998 anti-bribery convention endorsed by OECD countries which makes it a crime to offer, promise or give a bribe to a foreign public official in order to obtain or retain business.

Second, information is generated and disseminated among governments and civil society about the causes and costs of corruption, and the strategies most likely to be effective in combating it. The World Bank has carried out numerous surveys of households, firms and public agencies. The IMF carries out research into the causes, consequences and reform of corrupt behaviour. Research into the causes and consequences of corruption, together with analysis of anti-corruption efforts in developing and transitional countries, forms the basis of OECD policy recommendations to aid agencies and recipient governments.

Third, advice is given on how to tackle corruption. UNDP has advised governments on effective policies (for example in Tanzania) and the structure of effective anti-corruption commissions (for example in Honduras). It funds consultative processes to develop anti-corruption policies (for example in Tanzania and Mongolia) and advises civil society organizations and the media on how best to monitor areas of governance prone to corruption (for example in Georgia). The World Bank advises governments on how to address corruption in their country assistance plans and specific projects. It has developed diagnostic methods for assessing whether recipient governments have appropriate arrangements in place to identify the prevalence of corruption and to deal with it, such as institutional and governance reviews, public expenditure reviews, and poverty reduction strategy papers. The IMF gives policy advice in areas of public management likely to have a beneficial impact on corruption (for example, on financial accountability in the public sector). The Fund has also developed standards and codes of best practice on the dissemination of economic and financial data, on fiscal transparency in all aspects of budgeting, and on the accountability of central banks and other financial agencies.

Preparations for EU membership have provided the Council of Europe with an opportunity to help Eastern European states meet accession criteria relating to corruption (Kpundeh, 1998; World Bank, 2000a; Heidenheimer and Moroff, 2002; Holmes, 2003). Bilateral donors also place the eradication of corruption high on their governance agendas, mainly through investigation and policy advice. For example, USAID funds research and sponsors conferences (in Latin America and the Caribbean), symposiums, (Senegal)and workshops (Ukraine).

Fourth, resources are provided to strengthen the capacity of anti-corruption agencies. UNDP supports civil society organizations, as well as bodies responsible for drafting anti-corruption laws and codes of conduct. The IMF has provided technical assistance to strengthen financial organizations responsible for public expenditure management and tax administration.

Finally, aid is sometimes made conditional upon efforts being made to combat corruption. For example, the IMF requires minimum standards in the control, accounting, reporting and auditing systems of the central banks in countries to which the Fund lends. Measures to redress corruption have become part of the formal conditions for the disbursement of IMF loans. Financial assistance is denied to countries where corruption is judged to threaten economic recovery (Abed and Gupta, 2002; IMF, 2002).

Corruption and development

Corruption is generally seen by economists and political theorists as harmful to development, whether political, social, or economic.

Corruption and politics

Politically, corruption erodes the legitimacy of the state and government. Trust and confidence in state institutions evaporate as corruption strengthens clientelism, or offers political protection to organized crime. It undermines political legitimacy by attacking fundamental principles of democracy, particularly equality of citizens under the law and transparent decision-making. Public policy is made in secret networks and negotiations rather than in open and accountable institutions. The significance of the political opposition is reduced when it is seen as a symbol of failure in the competition for the spoils of office, rather than as a necessary part of constitutional government.

Corruption destroys trust in public officials, including members of the judiciary. As the rule of law is eroded, encouraged by corrupt judges, trust in the whole system of government declines to dangerously low levels (Johnston, 2002). The case of Uganda shows how political leadership can lose credibility when constantly engaged in a fight for corruptly acquired 'spoils' (Ouma, 1991).

The unequal distribution of political power is worsened by corruption as those with money buy more privileges and favours to which they are not legally entitled. Yet the poor have too much at stake to risk speaking out against corruption. They find themselves at an even greater disadvantage than normal when trying to seek judicial remedies against powerful political and criminal elements that can more easily afford the bribes required to secure favourable decisions. Human rights are more easily undermined if violators can bribe their way out of prosecution.

Eventually corruption can lead to political instability. According to the chairman of Ecuador's Anti-Corruption Commission, the pernicious effects of corruption include violence, increased social polarization and political alienation, all of which contributed to the uprising in 1997 (Doig and Riley, 1998).

Corruption and social development

Socially, corruption is associated with lower per capita incomes, higher levels of poverty, greater income inequality, higher levels of infant and child mortality, and higher school dropout rates (Abed and Gupta, 2002). It can lead to a brain drain of scarce professionals without contracts – or with scruples – especially doctors, teachers, engineers and economists in the case of Uganda (Ouma, 1991). Cross-national comparisons show that reducing corruption from Indonesia's level to South Korea's in 1997–8 would have produced between a twofold and a fourfold increase in per capita incomes and decrease in infant mortality, as well as improvement in literacy of between 15 and 25 percentage points (Kaufmann *et al.*, 2000). A strong correlation is found between human development as measured by the UNDP's Human Development Index (HDI) and levels of corruption: 'as levels of corruption increase HDI levels decrease more and more precipitously' (Johnston, 2002: 780). Human development is further harmed when corruption undermines state regulation of economic activities which endanger health and the environment.

Corruption's damage to social development operates in part through its effect on the composition of public expenditure. For example, statistical comparisons of 90 countries revealed a 'negative, significant and robust relationship between corruption and government expenditure on education' (Mauro, 2002: 243). A possible explanation is that there are fewer opportunities for bribery within educational projects compared with high-technology purchases made from oligopolies by government's investing in large-scale capital expenditure, such as defence procurements and construction projects. Corruption encourages this latter type of budgeting. Since educational attainment increases the rate of economic growth in poor countries, this is another route by which corruption has adverse economic consequences. One concern here is that by skewing expenditure towards large-scale capital expenditure corruption encourages political elites to indulge in 'white-elephant' projects such as grandiose official buildings. While there is no conclusive evidence that corruption leads to higher levels of expenditure on wasteful projects, an improvement in a country's level of corruption is associated with an increase in current expenditure as a ratio of GDP and a fall in capital expenditure (Mauro, 1995, 1997a, 1997b).

The social costs of corruption include the injustices caused when those who pay bribes receive fast decisions, or benefits to which they are not entitled, and drive those who do not (or cannot) into even slower and less efficient bureaucratic queues, or lose them their entitlements altogether. The citizen suffers further when bureaucrats have incentives to work slower and reduce the number of access points, when government performance and effectiveness are undermined, and when the morale of the public service is destroyed. Inefficiency in public service provision follows from the misallocation and misappropriation of very scarce resources, the loss of government revenues, the resentment caused by the absence of the merit principle, and loss of staff to more lucrative departments, for example, from Labour and Education to Inland Revenue and Customs and Excise (Ouma, 1991; Ades and Di Tella, 1997).

Corruption is a major obstacle to poverty reduction programmes. All forms affect them directly or indirectly. The lower levels of public expenditure brought about by corruption are of special significance to the poor (such as health care, education and water). When corruption levels are high the poor pay more in bribes for what services there are. In 2004 it was estimated that the annual burden of corruption on households in Bangladesh amounted to US $1096 million. The highest levels of corruption were in land administration, the police and the lower levels of the judiciary, but corruption was also high in education, health care, power supply, local government and pensions.

Not surprisingly, the poor everywhere pay a higher proportion of their income in bribes than the rich – in Cambodia, for example, between 2 and 3 per cent compared with 0.9 per cent,. In Romania, the poorest third of those paying bribes lose 11 per cent of their income in this way, compared with 2 per cent of the richest third. Tax systems are also made even more regressive when the rich pay bribes to evade taxes. Then a greater tax burden falls on the poor who, unable to compensate for the lost revenue, receive fewer and inferior services. In general, when corruption worsens, inequality and poverty increase (Gupta *et al.*, 2002; World Bank, 2004).

Resources targeted at the poor are often misallocated or misappropriated as a result of corruption, as in the case of South Africa's social security payments. The decisions of officials in charge of resources designated for the alleviation of poverty become arbitrary and uncertain, even when the law itself is clear about rights and entitlements. Corruption means that the poor face additional obstacles when trying to secure justice from the courts, or their entitlements to publicly provided goods and services from the bureaucracy. Corruption reduces the impact of development assistance on poverty by diverting funds from development projects, increasing their cost, enabling poor-quality firms to secure contracts, sanctioning poor performance, falsifying accounts and payrolls, and misappropriating inputs (Tanzi and Davoodi, 2002).

The poor also suffer from the effects of corruption on their economic activities. Poor farmers suffer when middlemen bribe officials to obtain monopoly control over agricultural distribution. The development of small-scale enterprises, a way to provide some relief from poverty, especially for the urban poor, is limited by corruption in the relevant state agencies, thus restricting the availability of financial support. Because economic growth increases the incomes of the poor, corruption holds back this form of poverty alleviation by reducing growth levels (see below). Corruption creates incentives for capital rather than labour-intensive projects of benefit to the poor, and harms small businesses and petty traders who pay twice as much in bribes as large firms.

Corruption and economic development

The adverse economic effects of corruption are felt mainly as losses of economic efficiency and economic growth. As regards efficiency, corruption inflates business costs (for example when widespread bribery is required to obtain public works contracts). Bribes enable environmental rules to be broken, and criminal prosecution to be evaded. Bribery means excessive payments by the state for large-scale procurements, over-expenditure on projects, and a loss of efficiency from the creation of private monopolies by corrupt privatizations (though the creation of such monopolies *without* corruption will also produce losses of efficiency in the use of resources). Corruption also distorts public demand for the allocation of public resources.

Corruption raises the cost of public provision if the most efficient firms are not selected for contracts (or contractors lack qualifications, equipment and expertise). There is a progressive loss of efficiency by firms supplying goods and services to the public sector when efficient firms are excluded – a form of 'dynamic inefficiency' (della Porta and Vannucci, 1997). Bribery also increases transaction costs because of the need for increased secrecy and anti-bribery policing, plus the time wasted seeking access to officials (Rose-Ackerman, 1999).

Corruption adversely affects economic growth by diverting large sums which would otherwise support investment in enterprises, infrastructure and public services. Empirical studies using cross-national regression analysis show that an improvement in a country's corruption index of one standard deviation will produce an increase of 4 percentage points in the investment rate, and nearly half a percentage point in the annual growth rate of per capita GDP (Mauro, 1997a).

By creating uncertainty in the administration of laws and regulations governing transactions, creating an arbitrary tax, increasing the cost of doing business, and making property rights and contracts insecure, corruption deters investment (Tanzi, 1998). It stifles initiative and enterprise, not only because of the added costs of gaining permission to invest, but also because of threats to property from political instability engendered by corruption. If corruption spreads to the judiciary it destroys the rule of law, with serious economic consequences. When the resolution of disputes is no longer the outcome of impartially applied law, incentives to invest are again weakened. In this way, corruption also discourages direct foreign investment, so often crucial to economic development in poor countries.

Corruption further reduces economic growth by lowering the productivity of public investments, and by diverting them away from existing infrastructure, such as roads, power supplies and telecommunications, thus leading to its deterioration (Gupta *et al.,* 2002; Tanzi and Davoodi, 2002). It is also associated with a higher proportion of public expenditure and GDP devoted to spending on the military. So it is reasonable to expect that an improvement in corruption should produce a higher level of government spending on more productive investments.

Thus we find that countries with higher levels of economic development, as measured by per capita GNP, have lower levels of corruption, as measured by the survey of perceptions of corruption in 102 countries carried out by Transparency International (see Table 8.2). However, there is considerable variation in levels of corruption within each group of economies, with the least-corrupt country in each scoring better than the average for the next highest group, with the exception of upper-middle-income Chile, which does not quite reach the average for high-income economies.

So corrupt countries can have different levels of growth, and countries with the same growth levels can be rated differently in terms of corrup-

Table 8.2   *Corruption and economic development, 2002 – groups of economies by levels of corruption, with highest and lowest scores per group*

Economies	Median score	Country score
Low-income	2.6	
Ghana		3.9
Bangladesh		1.2
Lower-middle-income	3.3	
Namibia		5.7
Angola		1.7
Upper-middle-income	4.3	
Chile		7.5
Venezuela		2.5
High-income	8.0	
Finland		9.7
Greece		4.2

SOURCES: data from World Bank, 'Country Groups by Income', www.worldbank.org/data/countryclass/classgroups.htm; Transparency International (2002).

tion. It may be that the effect of corruption on economic development is not as influential as theory suggests, especially if development is not limited to growth rates. Comparative data from 25 transition economies between 1994 and 1998 showed that the effect of corruption on economic performance as measured not only by growth, but also by inflation, fiscal balance and foreign direct investment, showed the effect of corruption to be relatively minor compared with the effects of economic structural reforms, such as privatization, the reform of state-owned enterprises, reliance on markets to set prices, and the creation of a sound regulatory system (Abed and Davoodi, 2002).

Variance in growth rates among corrupt countries might be explained by variations in the form, disposition and impact of corruption. The *form* of corruption refers to a distinction between 'looting' and 'dividend-collecting' (that is, transferring a percentage of the profits of private firms to officials in exchange for policies and services enabling them to earn higher profits). The *disposition* of corruption refers to what is done with bribes (for example kept at home, invested, consumed, or sent abroad). And the *impact* of corruption contrasts dividend-collecting, which creates incentives for pro-growth policies, with looting, which is economically very suboptimal. Comparing Zaire and South Korea in these terms, Wedeman (1997) found that high levels of 'looting' in the case of Zaire led to capital starvation of export industries, insecure property rights, and low growth; while in South Korea high levels of corruption in the form of 'dividend-collecting' led to high rates of economic growth via big indus- trial conglomerates being given access to cheap capital. This helps to explain how under some circumstances rapid economic growth increases opportunities for corruption, as in South Korea in the 1970s and 80s (Quah, 1999).

There is also the seeming paradox, if corruption impedes economic growth, of some successful South-East Asian economies. China, Indonesia, Thailand and Vietnam are ranked among the most corrupt countries in the world, yet have achieved impressive rates of growth and levels of foreign investment. Something would seem to cancel out the negative influence of corruption. This might be the predictions which investors can make about attempts to corrupt, that is, whether there is confidence from past experience that corruption will produce the favours being sought. When the outcome of corrupt transaction is more predictable, corruption will have a less adverse effect on investment. This was tested with cross-national empirical data for 69 countries, confirming that 'corruption regimes that are more predictable – in the sense that those seeking favours from governments do obtain those favours – have less negative impact on investment than those that are less predictable'. However, the results also show that even with predictability, investment would be higher were corruption levels lower. Therefore 'more corruption necessarily means less investment'. It is better to have a low level of corruption than a high level even when it does less harm than in some other countries (Campos *et al.*, 1999: 1065).

Furthermore, even if some corrupt countries experience high rates of growth, a widening spiral of illegal payoffs will eventually undermine development by shifting activities from productive to unproductive, and entrenching corruption so it is difficult to shift. In the long run, corruption becomes a deterrent to investment and economic growth.

Beneficial corruption?

Corruption is not always seen as a problem. There is a 'revisionist' view which sees it as beneficial because it speeds up cumbersome procedures, bypasses inefficient regulation enforcement, buys political access for the excluded, or even produces more effective policies than those emerging from legitimate channels. Knowing that bureaucracies are often slow-moving and inefficient, it is natural to ask whether corruption might offer some benefits to set against its more obvious costs. If bureaucratic red tape is very pronounced, might the adverse effect of corruption be partly offset by 'oiling the wheels' of administrative decision-making (Nye, 2002)?

While there is evidence that 'in countries with high levels of red tape corruption has less damaging effects on investment' (Ades and Di Tella, 1997: 501), it was not sufficiently conclusive statistically to dispel concerns that corruption provides officials with incentives to create scarcity, delays and more red tape. The consensus now is that a bribe may lubricate the wheels of bureaucracy for those individuals who have the resources, but at the same time it strengthens incentives within the bureau-cracy to delay decisions and fight other agencies for access to corrupt payments, thus undermining the effectiveness and morale of the adminis-trative system for society as a whole. Officials inevitably exercise varying degrees of discretion in implementing public policy, so 'instead of corrup-tion being the grease for the squeaky wheels of a rigid administration, it becomes the fuel for excessive and discretionary regulation'. And even if greasing the wheels by bribery speeded up decision-making, it would also accelerate the accumulation of the economic costs of corruption. In fact, much time is actually wasted by bribery, because of the negotiations, secrecy and caution needed, far more than is the case with legal relation-ships between private sector managers and officials. Bribery comes 'at the expense of productively running firms and governments'. In surveys, policy-making elites in developing countries have unanimously expressed the view that corruption, 'far from being a lubricant of development, was a most formidable impediment to it' (Hutchcroft, 1997; Kaufmann, 1998: 66–70).

Another theoretical possibility is that bribery improves the allocative efficiency of bureaucratic decisions by creating auction-like conditions, so that favours go to the most efficient producers who can afford the highest 'prices'. Corruption may thus improve the allocation of resources and make their use more productive. However, efficient producers may not engage in the 'auction' for ethical reasons, thus making the outcome worse than properly regulated allocations. Officials are also likely to water-down the auction-like conditions and allow some legal regulation so as not to alienate all applicants. So those excluded from the official rationing (by lack of information or limited access) will not necessarily be the least-efficient producers. Auctions also need freely flowing information which is blocked by the risks associated with bribe-taking (Alam, 1991).

An even more radical proposition is that corruption encourages investment and innovation by reducing uncertainty about how the future will be affected by bureaucratic decisions: 'graft can provide the direct incentive necessary to mobilize the bureaucracy on behalf of entrepreneurs' (Leff, 1989: 11). The weakness in this argument is that comparisons of Asia and Africa do not reveal expected contrasts: far more stable economic environments (such as in East Asia) have not made corruption levels significantly lower than in Africa, where economic uncertainty has been much higher. Furthermore, incentives to invest are reduced by the need to buy permission. And because bribes cannot be deducted from taxable income, they are 'particularly harmful for risk-taking in the context of innovation' (Bardham, 1997: 1329; Sindzingre, 2002).

Explaining corruption

Explanations of corruption as a political phenomenon identify five sets of factors, namely social and political structures, motivations, political economy, institutions and culture (Heywood, 1997).

Political structures

Explanations that focus upon social and political structures see corruption arising from relationships between the state and the citizen which are embedded in clientelist networks and communal ties, rather than impersonal transactions governed solely by law. Where state interventions are not driven by policies that can be justified in the public interest, but by promises made to client groups in return for their loyalty and support, the boundary between the private and public becomes blurred, and public resources are at risk of being appropriated for private gain. Formally the citizen is the client of the state, but informally is expected to make an additional payment for what is offered as a legal entitlement: (Philp, 1997; Shah and Schacter, 2004).

However, this is at best only a partial explanation of corruption, since the incidence and forms of corruption vary independently of the extent to which politics is dominated by personalistic relationships. Nor does it explain why the reciprocity entailed by clientelism should necessitate bribery as distinct from the use of public resources to reward communities for their political support with roads, schools, clinics and so on. However, it may be that clientelism encourages the development of administrative dysfunctions that in their turn facilitate corruption (Kurer, 1997).

Motives

A number of factors are thought to provide motives for public officials to behave corruptly. One is a level of pay for public servants too low for subsistence (for example Bangladesh), which can be brought about when high inflation erodes the real incomes of civil servants, as in Indonesia (Robertson-Snape, 1999). Budget austerity can lead to a decline in the real wages of civil servants, even to below the poverty line, as in Mozambique (Harrison, 1999). Alternatively, civil servants may be motivated to behave corruptly when their wages do not reflect those in comparable private sector jobs. Inadequate remuneration can also affect the judiciary. Incentives for corrupt inducements are strengthened when inefficient court administration leads to delays and backlogs in the processing of cases (Rose-Ackerman, 1999: 155).

Such motives may be strengthened when the risks of detection, prosecution and punishment are low, as they are likely to be when the forces of law and order are also corrupt, including anti-corruption agencies such as the Philippines Presidential Commission on Good Government in the 1980s. Alternatively, members of the political elite may be protected by their seniority against prosecution so that where corruption is a capital offence, as in Vietnam and China, junior officials are executed while senior officials receive prison sentences or no punishment at all. Other conditions which reduce the risks attendant upon corruption and so strengthen motivations include government secrecy, docile or captive media, and weak political and administrative accountability (Quah, 2002).

Political economy

The political-economy explanation of corruption, one which is favoured by most international agencies, claims that state intervention, especially in the economic sphere, affords too many opportunities for corruption. According to this view, governments increase the opportunities for corruption by 'interfering' in economic decision-making through trade restrictions, subsidies and price controls, thereby increasing the incentives for private interests to gain the necessary state approval by bribery. Restrictions on trade create incentives for importers and manufacturers to seek special privileges through bribes, while price controls attract bribes from those not entitled to goods at artificially low prices. So if government restrictions on economic activities are eased, countries should become less corrupt as there will be fewer bureaucratic powers for officials to abuse. If markets, rather than states, allocate resources, corruption could be significantly reduced (Mauro, 1997b).

Such claims will be assessed later. Suffice it to say at this point that it is the organization of the state, rather than its scope, which is relevant for corruption: whether there is the rule of law, administrative recruitment and promotion on merit, effective prosecution and punishment of corruption, effective management supervision and audit, properly formulated laws and regulations, and transparent anti-corruption mechanisms: 'the way the state operates and carries out its functions is far more important than the size of public sector activity' (Tanzi, 1998: 566).

Institutions

Consequently, much emphasis has been placed on the institutional causes of corruption, leading to the conclusion that the more the exercise of political and administrative authority is transparent, accountable and open, the more difficult it is to hide corruption. A major cause of corruption is weak constitutional controls over public spending.

A lack of effective scrutiny by the media, pressure groups and organized interests is further encouragement to corruption by reducing the risk of exposure. For example, in Uganda freedom of speech and association, and active media, would make public institutions more responsive to the public good by deterring the abuse of power and trust (Ouma, 1991). The institutional breeding-ground for corruption often also includes weak sanctions against those exposed as corrupt, and weak commitment to eradicating corruption on the part of political leaders. When the system of justice does not act as a deterrent, corruption is likely to flourish (World Bank, 1997).

Regular and predictable changes in political leadership through the democratic process are also needed to impose integrity on the conduct of public affairs. Comparative studies have tested the hypothesis that weak political competition makes corruption possible because public accountability is enfeebled, the concealment of corruption easier, the oversight of bureaucracy less effective, and the threat of electoral sanctions less credible. Only when political parties are engaged in meaningful electoral competition do they have incentives to expose corruption among their opponents. Cross-national comparisons have found that 'extensive, organized competition tends to coincide with lower levels of corruption', mainly because when political competition is weak, other institutional causes of corruption come into play (Johnston, 2002: 789). However, the process of democratization in transitional states may itself encourage corruption by creating new financial needs, such as funding election campaigns by political parties, lobbying parties by organized interests, and securing livelihoods for elected representatives. Hence the importance of rapid democratic 'deepening', in which opponents and victims of corruption can mobilize effectively, and institutions of accountability can exercise effective oversight. In this way democratic politics can make the costs of corruption outweigh the benefits (Harriss-White and White, 1996).

Culture

Finally, there has been much debate on possible cultural causes of corruption. It has been seen as representing a cultural obligation to give gifts, as for example among the Javanese (Robertson-Snape, 1999), or respect for family loyalties, leading officials to rate their duty to family or community higher than duty to one's office. There may be a cultural heritage in the exchange of gifts between local communities and public officials. In Uganda, for example, 'from an African perspective it is perfectly in order to exchange gifts: what is important however, is the motive behind the exchange and the subsequent expectations' (Ouma, 1991: 477).

Gift-giving can be carried over from private into public life in societies which see no distinction between public and private roles (Rose-Ackerman, 1996). Or the idea of corruption as payment for favours may be absent from a society's set of values, as in Thailand where such transactions are regarded as a way of life, to be expected and not seen as contrary to the public interest (Quah, 1999).

However, the extent of popular protest against corruption shows it is not universally endorsed by cultural values and practices. Corruption in many non-Western societies is regarded as unacceptable, regardless of social background. In India, for example, 'opinion polls regularly suggest that regardless of caste, ethnicity, gender or religion voters perceive politicians as corrupt' (Singh, 1997: 638). Surveys of public opinion, as well as popular protests, 'suggest that widespread tolerance of corruption is not the rule in most countries' (Rose-Ackerman, 1998: 36). In many developing countries corruption is seen as marking a decline in public ethics. Levels of tolerance of corruption vary between countries, but even if it is sometimes seen as a necessary evil (simply for getting things done) it is still regarded as evil. Variations in levels of tolerance may indicate no more than citizens in different countries vary in the confidence they have that the authorities will do something about the problem. In Eastern and Central Europe, for example, what varies is not tolerance but levels of despair and resignation. And in Nigeria, the shame of corruption is made worse by the feeling that there is no alternative means of survival (Holmes, 2003; Apampa, 2005).

People in most cultures are generally able to distinguish between appropriate and inappropriate public behaviour by the servants of the state: for example, 'pure' gifts in countries such as Tanzania and Kenya do *not* precede a *quid pro quo*. It is insulting to developing countries to assume that gift-giving sanctions kickbacks to politicians or bureaucrats (Rose-Ackerman, 1996, 1998). So a tradition of gift-giving should not be seen as condoning corruption. And it is certainly not the case that only in Westernized societies is a clear distinction made between public and private roles and property. Historical and comparative inquiry provides 'scant evidence' for this; on the contrary, 'the public–private distinction is ancient and not specifically western' (Kurer, 2005: 229).

Anti-corruption strategies

Much thought has been given to designing strategies that will do most to reduce if not eliminate corruption. Some of the reforms advocated are based on a priori reasoning, such as assuming that more transparency in government will deter corruption. Others are based on observations of actual reforms, such as the operation of different types of anti-corruption agency. The ways in which governments, assisted by the donor community, can tackle the problem of corruption may be considered under three headings: civil society, economic policy, and institutions.

Civil society

It is now generally recognized that anti-corruption strategies will fail unless they are linked to measures to strengthen the ability of civil society to challenge corruption (Gillespie and Okruhlik, 1991). This means increasing society's opposition to and awareness of corruption through education, public vigilance, and the scrutiny of political and administrative behaviour. Organizations within civil society, especially human rights groups, trade unions, business associations and religious congregations, can raise public awareness of corruption through surveys and other kinds of feedback on the quality of public services, and conferences to disseminate the information collected. They can also lobby for legislative controls, new institutions, judicial reform, freedom of information, and reform of public procurement procedures. The 'Clean Hands' campaigns in Bulgaria, the Czech Republic, Poland, Russia and Slovakia in the second half of the 1990s illustrate what can be done to raise public awareness of corruption and the state's record in dealing with it (Holmes, 2003).

In the private sector, professional bodies can insist upon the observance of ethical codes, and industrial organizations can oblige their members to refrain from bribery. Companies can form 'islands of integrity' where members sign up to anti-bribery pacts, agreeing not to obtain business through bribes. Such agreements get round the problem that any company unilaterally refusing to pay bribes will lose out to competitors. The first such pact was agreed within the energy sector in Ecuador, when the government instructed procurement officials to accept bids for public contracts only from companies that had given a commitment not to offer any form of inducement (Eigen, 1996).

Civil society organizations can also monitor political and administrative processes that are vulnerable to corruption, such as privatizations, procurements, housing allocations, social security payments, agricultural extension services and poverty reduction schemes. Watchdog groups within civil society can expose wasteful projects and demand official justifications for seemingly excessive expenditure. Examples include the Public Affairs Centre in Bangalore, India, Nigeria's Zero Corruption coalition and the national branches of Transparency International (Rose-Ackerman, 1999). Such activity is important for identifying where corruption is located (central or local government, the police, judiciary or public utilities) so that appropriate countermeasures can be adopted (World Bank, 2000a). The media make a particularly important contribution to scrutiny by civil society, assuming that they can survive an often repressive environment of censorship and intimidation (including the imprisonment and murder of journalists for exposing corruption, as in Russia); and assuming that the media do not harbour corruption themselves, as in the case of 'envelope journalism' in Indonesia. The media have been particularly important in exposing corruption in Poland and Hungary (Holmes, 2003).

There is much evidence that before any strategy to deal with corruption is likely to be effective, it has to be backed by strong political will on the part of a leadership that is willing to devise reforms that are technically and politically feasible, adopt credible sanctions, and allocate significant resources, including expertise, to the campaign. (Political will is clearly problematic if, as is alleged, Nigerian legislators had to be bribed to pass an anti-corruption law: *The Guardian*, 24 January 2004, p. 16.) This is only likely to be forthcoming if there is sufficient effective political demand within society to convince politicians that it is in their interest to eradicate corruption. Civil society groups can help build political demand by collecting and disseminating information about the experiences which individuals, businesses and households have of corruption, and by mobilizing activists to expose it. The eradication of corruption becomes yet another reason for increasing political participation within civil society.

Economic policy

Economic approaches to corruption usually demand changes in public policy which reduce state intervention and bureaucratic regulation, leaving the distribution of resources in the economy to market forces in the belief that this will reduce the opportunities for corruption. By removing powers and property rights from state officials the market for corruption should be destroyed. The assumption here (and particularly within the World Bank and IMF) is that the more there is state management of the economy, the more opportunities there are for private interests to seek benefits in the form of permits and licenses from public officials. Deregulation, liberalization and privatization are thus leading instruments in the fight against corruption.

There is no doubt that relations between the state and private interests, brought about by regulation, taxation, procurement, contracts and subsidies, create opportunities for corruption. But high levels of state intervention are found in countries with the lowest levels of corruption, such as Canada, Denmark, Finland, the Netherlands and Sweden.

Also, liberalizing and deregulating the economy has not ended corruption in countries where pro-market reforms have been introduced. In Latin America, the comparative and historical evidence on high-level corruption 'offers scant support for the simple binary opposition between rent-seeking interventionists and profit-seeking markets postulated by neo-liberal theory' (Whitehead, 2002: 811). In Mozambique rapid and unstable economic liberalization arising from structural adjustment policies in the late 1980s legitimized acquisitiveness and self-interest. Consequently privatization led to the acquisition of property by families of government ministers, while increased cross-border flows led to embezzlement and corruption among customs officials (Harrison, 1999). In Russia, despite economic liberalization, the ability of powerful lobbies to *avoid* taxation places an unbearable tax burden on the rest of the private sector, which encourages corruption to *evade* tax obligations (Varese, 1997). Neo-liberalism in the transition to democracy of the post-communist states of Central and Eastern Europe has proved extremely conducive to corruption, with the attendant risk of a culture of corruption developing (Holmes, 2003). Corruption continued to thrive during South Korea's liberalization. Indeed, corruption in countries which liberalize their economies is likely to increase, as newly formed private economic interests seek to recruit the support of the state in their attempts to defeat their competitors. For example,

> Chinese market reforms have created an environment in which an official has greater freedom to abuse his or her position, has more motivation to do so and less motivation not to, has an expanding variety of channels and opportunities, and has many well-resourced people willing to join the transaction on terms which offer security as well as material advantage. (White, 1996b: 45)

Since there are states where governments regularly supervise economic activities without corruption, it is likely that transparency in economic policy-making and implementation will be a more important anti-corruption measure, especially with regard to privatization, competition policy, monopolies, trading standards, banking law, and the rules of corporate governance. If regulatory agencies can be made to operate openly, consistently and accountably, they will form an important part of the institutional measures used in the fight against corruption.

Institutions

An institutional structure to tackle corruption takes the form of stronger legal rules prohibiting corruption and regulating political and administrative behaviour; agencies with more or less exclusive anti-corruption remits; civil service reforms to reduce incentives to behave corruptly; and political competition which increase the risks and political costs of exposure.

Anti-corruption laws need to specify clearly the nature of the offence, the penalties incurred, and their relationship to the size and type of bribery. Rules and codes of conduct can be formulated governing the disclosure of assets from non-governmental sources, conflicts of interest, and lobbying by elected representatives on behalf of private interests. Specific anti-corruption rules can be accompanied by a more general commitment to make all laws and regulations clear, explicit and, where possible, limited in the discretion conferred on public officials. When official discretion is necessary, decision-making should be both transparent and subject to appeal and adjudication procedures, such as specialized administrative tribunals and public inquiries (see Chapter 9).

Investigation and prosecution under anti-corruption laws will obviously be made more effective if there is an independent judiciary. A judiciary that is not itself corrupt makes it possible to prosecute corrupt officials. So judges have to be appointed on merit and held accountable, with judicial codes of ethics governing the behaviour of all court officials. Law societies and bar associations can help promote professional standards. Requiring judges to declare their assets is a further deterrent to bribery.

One of the most important pieces of anti-corruption legislation is a freedom of information statute which gives citizens access to government records. Freedom of information makes those who engage in corruption more vulnerable to detection. It can be used to disclose choices made after bids for contracts have been received, showing who has been successful and where in government their contracts are located. The press can be allowed access to information about the resources supporting conspicuous consumption by politicians and officials. The prices charged by government agencies, compared with the private sector and overseas governments, can be publicized. All competitors for government contracts should have equal access to relevant information (Klitgaard, 2000). When freedom of information is combined with the routine publication of accounts, budgets and revenues it becomes a formidable deterrent to corruption.

Publicity can be extended to judicial decisions. Statutory protection can also be given to 'whistleblowers' to prevent the harassment, intimidation and sanctioning of staff who call attention, whether internally or in public, to irregularities in decision-making.

Independent *anti-corruption agencies* are a familiar part of anti-corruption strategies, with many models from which lessons may be learned. Evidence from Hong Kong and Singapore indicates that to be effective anti-corruption agencies, whether general-purpose or service-specific, need to be given strong, long-term support by political leaders, be empowered to act independently of the police and political executive, be endowed with broad mandates, and be allowed to target 'high' corruption. Parliamentary oversight and judicial review of agency work are essential. In multi-ethnic societies it may be necessary to ensure that the agency's leadership is fully representative if it is to have credibility, as the case of Benin's *Cellule pour la Moralisation de la Vie Publique* shows (Heilbrunn, 1999; Johnston, 1999).

Effective agencies are also likely to combine investigation and prosecution with public education and prevention, as with Botswana's Directorate on Corruption and Economic Crime. Hong Kong's independent commission against corruption also has a structure and staffing policy designed to ensure that the agency develops preventive, educational and advisory functions, as well as powers of investigation and prosecution (Doig, 1995; Quah, 1995; Skidmore, 1996; Doig and Riley, 1998). Preventive work can include policy advice, training, managerial reforms, educational campaigns, and openness to complaints from the public. An advisory role enables an agency to help government ministries improve their own anti-corruption procedures.

The accountability and liability to prosecution and punishment that are essential to an anti-corruption strategy generally are equally applicable to anti-corruption agencies themselves. Steps have to be taken to ensure such agencies do not succumb to corruption, such as making them answerable to parliament and guaranteeing the prosecution and of staff suspected of corruption. Guarding the guardians is an essential element of anti-corruption work (Quah, 2002).

State audit, supported by parliamentary committees, can also be regarded as an anti-corruption institution. Independent audit is an indispensable weapon against corruption, especially when conducted by genuinely independent professional auditors serving the legislature in a truly transparent manner. Independent audit must be extended to all governmental financial data, so that there are no secret funds to be used for corrupt purposes (Rose-Ackerman, 1999). However, tracing the route taken by items of expenditure is more likely to reveal, and therefore deter, theft and fraud rather than bribery.

Civil service reforms can increase the benefits of probity and the costs of corruption. The motivation to act corruptly on the part of public servants can be reduced by strengthening formal incentives against corruption, such as improvements to officials' salaries, and informal incentives such as career opportunities and reputations. The removal of incentives for corruption may be necessary in the judiciary, too, with better pay and working conditions, more systematic monitoring, wide publicity for delays in hearing cases, an improvement through training and organization in the professionalism of judges, and well-drafted laws which make it clear when judicial discretion is being used arbitrarily (Heywood, 1997; UNDP, 1997a).

Increased wages could prove very expensive for poor countries and certainly cannot be the sole measure against corruption. Furthermore, higher wages might lead to demands for higher bribes because of the higher cost of losing one's job if caught out (Tanzi, 1998). However, evidence from case-studies of pay reforms in tax administration, and regression analysis of wage data and corruption for 31 low-income countries, led to the conclusion that 'paying wages that ensure low corruption may not necessarily be very costly ... and paying wages that ensure an honest civil service may be cost-effective' (Van Rijckeghem and Weder, 2002: 79).

The effects of higher wages on corruption will not be immediate, and other policies, particularly to strengthen the rule of law, are also needed. Unsuccessful anti-corruption efforts in Tanzania's Revenue Authority show that a significant increase in wages will not reduce corruption unless monitoring is effective, sanctions are strong, corrupt networks are destroyed, tax laws are simplified, discretion is reduced and relations between collectors and taxpayers are made transparent (Fjeldstad, 2003).

Other managerial changes can be put in place to serve anti-corruption purposes, such as a transparently merit-based system of recruitment and the objective monitoring of performance. The establishment of benchmarks and performance measures which can be compared with actual policy outcomes, such as procurement costs, constitutes another anti-corruption civil service reform. It may even be possible to turn bribes into standardized fees for faster access to entitlements, with the proceeds used to reward good performance with bonuses. Management reforms, including new incentives, the dismissal of corrupt officials, the professionalization of staff, stronger management controls, and modern forms of staff assessment, have helped reduce corruption in the Philippines' tax administration and Argentina's social security system (Kaufmann, 1998; Rose-Ackerman, 1999).

Democratic political competition makes it harder for corruption to be hidden from political opponents who will have strong incentives to expose it among their competitors for legislative and executive office at all levels of government. The assumption that political competition offers a deterrent to corrupt behaviour is given some support by empirical evidence that corruption is more prominent in countries where democratic culture and institutions are weakest (Bull and Newell, 2003). The average corruption scores of countries grouped into the categories used by Freedom House to rate civil liberties and political rights (see Table 8.3) also support an association of democracy with lower levels of corruption, though the 'free' countries of neither the developing world or Eastern and Central Europe manage to average above a corruption score of 5 (out of a possible 10). There are some notable exceptions to the patterns found here, notably a corruption score of 4.8 by the 'not free' state of Belarus, the 'partly free' Singapore with a corruption score of 9.3 (better than any Western European country), and Bolivia and Romania, 'Free' countries but with corruption scores of 2.2 and 2.6 respectively.

When competition between strong political parties is organized according to stable rules with predictable outcomes, government parties facing loss of office have no incentive to loot the public purse since they will want to fight on as part of the legitimate opposition in the hope of returning to power constitutionally. However, this is an optimistic theoretical scenario requiring conditions that are far from easy to guarantee, even in well-established democracies: fair competition, decisive outcomes, a small number of well-institutionalized parties, and developed interest groups offering parties stable support. In addition, electoral penalties for corruption may be weakened if corrupt politicians know, because of constitutional rules, that they have no chance of re-election. Competitive elections alone will not deter corruption. Additional checks on power are

Table 8.3   *Corruption and democracy, 2002*

	Average corruption scores	
Freedom House rating	*Developing countries*	*Post-communist states*
Free	4.4	4.1
Partly free	3.2	2.4
Not free	2.7	3.3

SOURCES: data from Freedom House (2002); Transparency International (2002).

NOTE: based on ratings for the 57 developing countries and 19 post-communist states of Central and Eastern Europe and the former USSR included in Transparency International's survey for 2002.

needed, such as the separation of powers, the rule of law, and transparency in decision-making in all parts of government (Rose-Ackerman, 1996; Johnston, 2002).

There has been some debate over whether the introduction of investigative mechanisms, sanctions, and new incentives is enough to curb corruption. Experience of policy reforms indicates that systemic corruption can be tackled effectively with piecemeal changes which, if successful, can support more holistic reform. (Brinkerhoff, 2000). But because corruption is a symptom of governance failure, the higher the corruption the more an anti-corruption strategy should focus on the governmental context, such as the rule of law, institutions of accountability, and citizens' rights of appeal. Only when corruption is relatively marginal, and the general context of governance sound, should the emphasis be on salaries, anti-corruption agencies, financial controls, public awareness campaigns and high-profile prosecutions. Similarly, support for 'whistleblowers' may be negated if the rule of law is weak. Consequently, increasing the penalties for corruption may work better in richer countries, while in poorer countries an approach which concentrates on building institutions of government is more likely to create 'powerful antidotes' to corruption, such as high administrative standards, citizen empowerment and governmental transparency (Shah and Schacter, 2004; de Maria, 2005). There is empirical evidence in support of this conclusion. Institution-building, such as efforts to strengthen the rule of law, has been shown by econometric analysis to be more effective in controlling corruption in less-developed countries (Leite and Weidmann, 2002).

Obstacles to reform

None of these bulwarks against corruption will be erected unless there is political will to do so, and the lack of this has been among the most difficult obstacles which anti-corruption efforts have encountered. There has been too little determination within the political leadership to punish corruption at all levels in the political and administrative hierarchies, and too many cosmetic gestures such as creating toothless anti-corruption agencies (Quah, 2002). In Central and Eastern Europe a contributory factor is a form of 'path dependency', or constraints imposed by historical legacies, which require current leaders to disassociate themselves from the communist regime: 'many politicians and state officials have been reluctant to use what they consider to be excessively draconian measures for combating corruption, on the grounds that this would be too reminiscent of the authoritarian past' (Holmes, 2003: 197).

Anti-corruption agencies are also vulnerable to political interference, denied adequate resources, or given no power to prosecute. In Uganda, for example, the Inspectorate of Government (one of whose tasks is to eliminate corruption in public offices) has been impeded in its work by insufficient funding, inadequate staffing, shortages of vehicles, computers and investigative equipment, and a lack of training in investigation and prosecution (Kpundeh, 2002). Needless to say, lack of independence affects the credibility of anti-corruption agencies with the public.

Numerous obstacles can be placed in the way of social movements that try to expose corruption. Civil society can be excluded from the design of anti-corruption strategies. Access to information can be impeded. In Rajasthan, India, for example, the right-to-information movement has fought to gain access to official documents that have revealed fraud and corruption. The movement has encountered obstructive officials and a reluctant state legislature. Activists have been harassed and intimidated. Village-level development workers have taken strike action in opposition to public scrutiny. There have also been delays in investigating corruption exposed by the movement's public hearings (Jenkins and Goetz, 1999).

Sometimes the power of economic interests is just too great for governments to be able to move against their wishes. A striking case is that of the corrupt business conglomerates in South Korea, where 'businessmen have been repeatedly pardoned and investigations soft-pedalled to avoid adverse effects on the economy' (Moran, 1999: 582). Globally the picture is that 'the rising number of anti-corruption initiatives being developed is running up against a massive wall of corrupt practices' (Pope and Vogl, 2000: 6).

Conclusion

All leading multilateral agencies have formulated detailed assessments of corruption on which they have built strategies for reform. The anti-corruption work of the international donor community revolves around generating information (for example, by research into the causes of corruption), disseminating it among governments and civil society, and advising recipient governments on the laws and institutions that constitute their campaigns against corruption. Donors draw support from both economists and political theorists who find corruption to be harmful to the development of democratic politics, social equality, economic growth, and administrative capacity.

Understanding how to deal with corruption entails understanding its causes, which have been identified as arising from social and political structures, the incentives motivating the behaviour of public servants, the structure of the economy and government's role in it, the strength of political and legal institutions, and cultural attributes which are sometimes used to present corruption in a favourable light. The ways in which governments, assisted by the donor community, can tackle the problem of corruption involve reforms to civil society, economic policy, and institutions, but reform in this area of politics encounters formidable political obstacles.

9

Transparent and Accountable Public Administration

'Horizontal' accountability

Administrative accountability is sometimes referred to (rather misleadingly) as 'horizontal', to distinguish it from what is perceived to be a more vertical relationship between state and society entailed by political accountability (see Chapter 2). Horizontal accountability occurs when one part of the state is entitled to explanation (answerability) from another on which it can impose sanctions if not satisfied (enforceability). So administrative agencies (ministries, departments, bureaux, boards) are answerable to ministers and legislatures, sometimes via regulatory bodies, auditors, anti-corruption commissions, and ombudsmen. Within agencies, management hierarchies are made up from chains of command and control entailing internal accountability of public servants to their superiors. The judiciary then subjects both political and administrative decisions to judicial review.

Horizontal accountability thus means that

> governments constrain themselves, at least in theory, through a complex web of accountability relationships in which the right of seekers to demand information and explanation is matched by the obligation of targets to provide them, under threat of sanction. (Goetz and Jenkins, 2005: 12)

While the relations of subordination found in all such forms of accountability call the label 'horizontal' into question, it is important, especially for technical assistance from aid donors, to identify accountability within state institutions which subsequently flow on through the political relationships between state and society.

Aiding accountability

Administrative accountability is not always clearly distinguished from political accountability in aid programmes supporting administrative reform, and is usually included among the aims and objectives of reforms designed to enhance the efficiency of public services. For example, the UN, through its Development Programme, includes accountability and transparency of the work of public officials and their departments, public enterprises and quasi-governmental bodies, among the foundations of good governance. It sees its remit as helping to build public services that are not only efficient but also accountable to the needs of citizens. To strengthen accountability the agency provides technical assistance to public procurement systems and funding to help NGOs demand accountability from public services.

The creation of accountable public sector institutions is one of the aims of the World Bank's assistance to the financial management systems of recipient states, especially public spending controls. Here the Bank has identified a widespread need to ensure that all budgets are audited and accounted for, as well as to improve how budgets are drawn up and to make fully transparent any adjustments to expenditure plans made after legislative approval.

USAID also includes accountability for public funds in its remit, but concentrates on the legislative scrutiny as a mechanism for holding government agencies to account. For example, it has supported the development of legislative committees in Bolivia, Malawi, Namibia, Palestine and Peru and with technical assistance, particularly training, in order to improve the quality of legislative oversight of administration, including public accounts and budget committees.

Administrative accountability and development

It is now generally accepted, following a period of hostility to the state on the part of the major multilateral aid agencies, that the state has an important role to play in the development effort, even when economic liberalization has been pursued with vigour and the state is seen primarily as 'partner, catalyst and facilitator' rather than direct provider. As the World Bank expressed it in 1997:

> An effective state is vital for the provision of the goods and services – and the rules and institutions – that allow markets to flourish and people to lead healthier, happier lives. Without it, sustainable development, both economic and social, is impossible. (World Bank, 1997: 1)

The importance of the state means that the power of administrative agencies is of particular significance. Yet democratic political development requires policy decisions to be taken by the people's elected representatives. They need to hire officials to carry out their decisions, but such officials should be the servants of the politicians, otherwise the form of government would be bureaucracy rather than democracy. Presidents, ministers and, at the local level, councillors take policy decisions authorized by elected status, and their paid officials offer professional advice and take the necessary executive actions.

However, this still leaves state bureaucracies many sources of power, some of which are unavoidable if democracies are to be served by professional experts recruited on merit following the acquisition of relevant qualifications. A formal description of democracy conceals the potential power at the disposal of permanent and professional civil servants. A complete separation of the political and administrative processes is a fiction. Public servants are political, though not necessarily partisan, actors in all systems of government. In democracies, the challenge is to control this power through accountability mechanisms without damaging the contribution to the public good which a strong bureaucracy can make.

The political power of officials stems from their experience of government, their professional and technical expertise, and their relative permanence in office. Their authority as policy advisers is strengthened by the secrecy surrounding much decision-making and the organizational complexity of departments of state.

Complexity has been increased by the fashion for organizations staffed by bureaucrats who are at the very best only indirectly accountable, such as executive agencies, management boards, autonomous institutes, state-owned enterprises, regulatory agencies, and other satellite bodies, to which the management of services is delegated by 'core' departments. Their chief executives, who may or may not be career civil servants, are responsible for implementing policy in a managerial way (with powers of recruitment, dismissal, promotion, pay and conditions, grading, organization, use of IT and so on).

In every state the scope for arbitrary bureaucratic action, misuse of state powers and the promotion of public officials' private interests constitutes a threat to democracy. This is why 'sustainable development generally calls for formal mechanisms of restraint that hold the state and its officials accountable for their actions' (World Bank, 1997: 99).

Accountability is also concerned with limiting administrative inefficiency, incompetence and failure to achieve declared official objectives. It arises in part from the importance of ensuring that money allocated by political decision-makers (usually legislators) to fund specific activities actually reaches the intended beneficiaries (for example, local authorities, hospitals or schools). Accountability at its most basic ensures that the wishes of elected representatives are actually carried out through administrative practice.

The importance of this function of accountability is graphically illustrated by the case of Uganda, where the World Bank, in collaboration with the government, carried out a Public Expenditure Tracking Survey of primary education between 1991 and 1995. It was found that no more than 2 per cent of allocated capitation grants had actually reached schools in 1991, rising to only 26 per cent by 1995. Improving accountability by making budget allocations publicly transparent and strengthening financial procedures made it possible by 1999 to ensure that 100 per cent of capitation grants reached the target schools (World Bank 2001d).

Administrative accountability also poses the question of whether policies are being implemented as intended and resources being used for the purposes specified by the law-makers. Here the problem is not that expenditure budgeted for has not occurred. It is that money has been spent, but not on the activities budgeted for. This is a form of misappropriation by service managers, not for their own personal gain, but to provide additional resources for alternative purposes not itemized in the budget. For example, health policy in Kenya has emphasized the importance of preventive measures. Expenditure, however, has fallen below budgetary targets, with the bulk of spending going on curative health care (Oyugi, 1992). In Tanzania, most of the money allocated to regions for irrigation purposes under agricultural policy was used for other purposes (Mukandala, 1992). The role of accountability is to expose and explain such anomalies so that pressure can be brought to bear on the political executive to take corrective action.

Accountability also tests whether public resources have been used efficiently – in other words, whether better value for money could not have been obtained by adopting an alternative way of tackling a social or economic problem. This entails looking for obvious signs of waste, or making comparisons with previous experience of the same activity, such as highway maintenance or vaccination programmes. For example, the inefficiency of the public sector in many African states has long been of concern, especially to the donor community. In Ghana civil servants, teachers, doctors and nurses have had to compensate for poor salaries and job insecurity by taking on additional employment, resulting in low productivity in the delivery of services and growing dissatisfaction among service users. Property tax in Indonesia is another example, realizing only 40 per cent of its potential. Another case is that of Sri Lanka's poverty alleviation programme from 1990 to 1995, when a policy of consumption grants underestimated problems of implementation and 'proved to be both a very costly experiment ... and ... also ineffective for the majority of the poor' (Gunatilleke, 2000: 176; Lewis, 2003; Owosu, 2005).

In addition to efficiency, accountability is also intended to identify effectiveness by assessing whether policies have achieved their intended outcomes. As with inefficiency, public bureaucracies in developing countries too often have a poor record when it comes to achieving objectives. For example, the 1996 Forestry Law in Bolivia empowered municipalities to manage municipal forest reserves to which local community groups would have access in order to exploit forest resources. However, only an insignificant area of municipal forest reserves has received central government approval, mainly because politicians are reluctant to upset the small number of large and politically powerful forestry companies which dominate the sector (Gordillo and Andersson, 2004). The effectiveness of China's anti-poverty policy of 1994 was undermined by the concentration of poverty alleviation resources – low-interest loans from the Agricultural Development Bank, a food-for-work programme, and training – on 592 poor counties, when between a third and a half of the rural poor live in areas not designated 'poor' (Riskin, 2000).

Such policy review cannot be left to internal managerial procedures. It has to be subjected to external scrutiny in order to reflect the democratic principle that public administration is carried out on behalf of the people's elected representatives. For this purpose the political executive has to be regarded as part of the state's administrative structure. When publicity is given to administrative accountability, opportunities are created for political interests to mobilize against the forces constraining improved policy implementation.

Factors affecting accountability

Achieving stronger accountability as part of good governance has become far more complex than implied by basic democratic constitutional principles governing the relationships between legislatures, executives and bureaucracies (Elcock, 1998). A number of political developments have produced this complexity. These need to be understood if development assistance is to be effective, especially when there are contradictions between the principles involved in competing conceptions of accountability.

First, the problem of deciding how best to enforce administrative accountability is complicated by the organizational complexity of the state. New and unique organizational forms have been set up, with their own styles of direction and control, often in response to international development assistance which reflects current trends in managerialist thinking as applied to the public sector (see Chapter 10). This organizational development collectively represents the different political values to which contemporary public administration has to respond. The conduct of public officials is governed by conflicting principles of accountability embodied in the constitutional rules of representative government, the need to be able to justify decisions before the courts, political demands to consult the representatives of service users, procedural tests of reasonableness, quasi-judicial tests of appropriate discretion, financial tests of economy and efficiency, commercial tests in the case of state-owned enterprises, professional codes of conduct, and, for subnational governments, the demands of local and national politicians. Public officials are required to accommodate these different principles in their work or, more likely, jettison those that conflict with what they see as their primary duty or responsibility. There is no simple answer to the question: to whom should those responsible for the implementation of public policy on behalf of the political executive be accountable?

The most visible conflict in contemporary public administration is between traditional (constitutional) accountability and demands for more efficient management. Current fashions in public sector management insist upon freeing public servants/managers from the political controls upon which accountability has traditionally been founded. 'New public management' restricts political control of public services to the strategic level, leaving service managers to operate within organizational structures appropriate for their type of activity. Managers are given autonomy to respond to feedback from their 'markets' and 'customers'. They are encouraged to deliver by means of contracts which separate purchaser from provider in the hope that the taxpayer will benefit from competition between would-be providers. At the same time, 'consumers' of public services should be empowered by opportunities for 'exit' and redress. This way of managing public services entails agency self-evaluation using performance indicators as well as external evaluators (for example, auditors). Evaluation will then be de-politicized when performance is measured against 'objective' criteria.

Regrettably, the accountability of 'marketized' and privatized providers of collective goods (for example water and sewage disposal) is obstructed by such managerialism. There are usually restrictions on the powers of intervention by elected representatives into service standards by contractors. Information can be withheld from those seeking accountability on the grounds of commercial confidentiality. Attempts to turn service users into 'customers' by citizens' and customers' 'charters' guaranteeing standards of service not only weaken citizenship and the right to participate in communal decision-making, but also depict traditional forms of accountability as interference in consumer choice. Delegation to quasi-autonomous agencies (development corporations, health boards, marketing boards) in order to deepen managerial autonomy further creates uncertain lines of accountability. The introduction of private sector accountability measures into public services (performance indicators, contracting mechanisms, and incentives such as job insecurity) also conflicts with traditional accountability, which concentrates on errors rather than achievements.

Second, the complexity and scope of modern public services and regulation make it difficult, if not impossible, to identify the contribution of different individuals to particular outcomes, and then assign responsibility, both of which are required by traditional forms of accountability which individualize the relationship between public officials and those to whom they are required to answer for their decisions. Both the scope of government and the professionalization of public services make it possible for politicians to evade responsibility

Third, party politics can undermine traditional forms of accountability by lending the support of majority groups in legislatures to politicians whose custody of a department has been found wanting, or whose personal public actions have violated established codes (for example, about conflicts of interest).

Fourth, it is sometimes claimed that competitive tendering strengthens the accountability of providers to the public and their representatives. The separation of client and contractor functions, together with improved procedures for monitoring performance, facilitate accountability by making staff more keenly aware of, and better able to respond to, the requirements and concerns of the public. Service users may feel that their views will have more effect if there are several competing suppliers needing to listen to the public if they are to win contracts in the future (Struyk, 2002).

Unfortunately, the costs of contracting out are never considered as frequently as the theoretical benefits. First, if accountability is to be protected, agencies need to be permitted to specify the *means* of service delivery as well as *outputs*. Otherwise accountability to voters and taxpayers is weakened by leaving agencies responsible for activities over which they have limited control. Accountability is further weakened if information about the value of contracts currently awarded by agencies, or about the contracts won by direct labour organizations, is limited – and companies regularly cite commercial confidentiality as grounds for withholding information.

Furthermore, one of the aims of contracting out is to insulate service providers from politics in order to get round the problem of political interference in the routine work of public servants, as frequently happens in developing countries. By separating the roles of provider and purchaser in this way, a 'much simpler and less ambiguous accountability for the provider organization' is created (World Bank, 2004: 98). But this means that the provider is accountable to the government agency purchasing the service, not that it will listen to the views of service users. So users have to make their views felt through the political process, just as they had to when the service was provided 'in house'. If their elected representatives actually lose control over aspects of the service as a result of contracting out, accountability is weakened, not strengthened.

The use of 'third-sector' bodies in the provision of public services (not-for-profit, voluntary, mutual aid/self help, community bodies and so on) in the social welfare field creates problems of accountability which need to be set against the benefits of this type of service provision (Taylor, 1996). The sheer diversity of providers (advocacy groups, self-help bodies, philanthropic groups) diffuses power and responsibility, and thus blurs accountability (Schwartz and Sharkansky, 2000). There are likely to be conflicting accountabilities to different 'stakeholders' (service users, volunteers, professional managers, and contracting agencies). The complexities of contracts also blur accountability, making it easier for decision-makers to evade blame if contracted services go wrong. The capacity of third-sector organizations to scrutinize government agencies, thus aiding accountability, may be compromised by a contractual dependency relationship. Variable relationships with government agencies (collaborative, contractual, or grant-receiving) complicate accountability further, as does the explicit distancing from governmental control, and therefore conventional mechanisms of accountability, that lies behind the use of this form of service delivery. And funding agencies may receive 'kickbacks' from community organizations (such as jobs for political cronies or family members) which act as a disincentive to scrutinize recipient bodies too closely (as in Israel, for example).

Finally, the aid conditionalities imposed by donors do not always improve administrative accountability. The case of structural adjustment programmes for public expenditure reform in Jamaica warns that reforms can have conflicting effects on accountability, some positive, some negative. On the negative side accountability has been undermined by a centralized and less accountable style of government adopted to push through unpopular, externally imposed policies. An important conclusion for aid agencies which impose expenditure targets is that they need 'to devote considerable effort to forging commitment to such targets from the recipient Government in order to ensure that such targets do not lead to unaccountable modes of behaviour' (Harrigan, 1998: 19).

Mechanisms of accountability

In order to provide support for administrative accountability the democratic state uses a number of principles and institutional devices designed to protect a special relationship between the state's administrative apparatus and the different branches of government – executive, legislature and judiciary. These principles, with their attendant institutions, are the 'service' bureaucracy, scrutiny, and appeal.

Service bureaucracy

The concept of a 'service' bureaucracy refers both to public service as the motivator of public officials and the subjugation of officialdom to political leadership. An ideological element is involved by making a distinction between politics and administration. Though there are many ways the roles of public servants, especially at senior level, bring them into politics broadly defined, the service bureaucracy needs an ideological device which denies any moral foundation for bureaucratic autonomy, such as claims to represent the public interest or the integrity of the state. The distinction between administration and politics underlines the theory (something of a fiction in practice) that the task of the public service is to carry out the decisions of politicians made according to prescribed democratic practices, such as representative and majoritarian government. In the 'service' model of bureaucracy, importance is attached to the *political* leadership of administration.

A fully accountable administration within this model of political–administrative relationships then requires political neutrality among officials, protected by appointment, not election, to office, selection by an impartial body, recruitment on merit, and security of tenure. The 'neutrality' of public officials has become something of an ideological myth because professionalization may compete with loyalty to political leaders, especially when administration is dependent upon professional specialization and expertise. Furthermore, public officials have individual values and even ideological dispositions. This may become problematic if the social background of senior public servants is narrow, unrepresentative and exclusive. Any interpenetration of bureaucracy and business interests might influence the policy choices and frameworks of thought and action within administrative agencies. Providers of technical assistance to administrative reform programmes as part of overseas aid need to be aware of such tendencies, which can dilute the 'service' bureaucracy.

The anonymity of public officials, at least at senior levels, may be necessary to secure accountability, as it leaves politicians to answer for the performance of their agencies (ministries and departments) so that officials cannot be personally identified with commitment to a party position or policy. Anonymity protects continuity, so that a newly elected government can have confidence in the willingness and ability of the public services to implement new policies. The danger here is that anonymity and confidentiality may be waived if it suits politicians to shift the blame for administrative errors. There is also the possibility that it will be in the public interest for public servants to 'blow the whistle' on their political 'masters' if they feel that accountability is being compromised by a politician's behaviour, such as lying to parliament.

A 'service' bureaucracy also implies managerial discipline in the form of the superior–subordinate relationship within administrative agencies. Senior officials have to be able to account to ministers for the actions of their subordinates. This may be compromised by the existence of relatively weak sanctions (especially if the fault is over-zealous adherence to rules, or bureaupathology). Sanctions may also require long and elaborate 'hearings' by peers rather than outsiders, as with some police forces. Managerial discipline may have to take account of public service union-ization, the impulse to cover up scandal when in conflict for resources, and *esprit de corps* among colleagues.

In fact, attempts to create a service bureaucracy face many obstacles. Ministerial responsibility to parliament can be weakened by the sheer scale and complexity of modern government, as well as by partisan support for errant colleagues (as in India). The merit system of recruit-ment and promotion is undermined by traditional and ascriptive ties supporting nepotism and patronage (as in the Arab states). Patron–client relationships in politics turn administrative positions into rewards for political favours. Party political connections undermine anonymity and protect incompetence, indolence and criminality (as in Zambia). Corruption destroys impartiality in the application of legal rules to indi-vidual cases (throughout the Third World and much of post-communist Europe). Social superiority and self-interest lead officials to behave without sensitivity towards the interests, rights and well-being of citizens, and make them impervious to community participation (for example, in India and Brazil). Political interference in administrative processes can force officials into inflexible, rule-bound, and other bureaupathological patterns of behaviour (Jabbra and Dwivedi, 1988). Thus administrative reform in support of a service bureaucracy needs to be shored up by cultural and institutional changes that bring administrative behaviour into line with democratic expectations, indicating the enormity of the task facing the donor community and technical assistance.

Scrutiny

The dependence of administrative accountability on scrutiny explains why accountability is so often linked to transparency, implying that public actions are open to public inspection. Freedom of information legislation is thus needed to support transparency. The media obviously have an important role to play here. Publicity should support accountability through its deterrent effect: administrators will do only what can be publicly justified.

Scrutiny also requires the development of civil society, especially those parts of it concerned with the interests which specific groups have in public policies and their modes of implementation (see Chapter 6). Some governments have come under pressure to create 'opposition' bodies to subject policy implementation to scrutiny. These consist of a wide range of participatory bodies involved with budgeting, auditing and service standards. There is a 'new accountability agenda' with international development thinking covering a wide range of policies, and varying in scale, depth and reach. Activities include consultation, information-sharing, monitoring and auditing: 'Citizens are combining electoral accountability and participation with what would traditionally have been considered the official accountability activities of the state' (World Bank, 2004).

Interesting recent developments have seen people being provided with an effective voice rather than merely being consulted by decision-makers and planners on their terms and according to their agendas (see Chapter 7). This means reducing participants' dependency on government agencies for information, so that consultation becomes interrogation, and the threat of sanctions becomes a reality (for example, against corruption). Such scrutiny empowers citizens to demand answers, not just supply information (Goetz and Jenkins, 2005). However, such accountability will always depend to a certain extent on access to official documents – financial records, cost estimates, employment registers, receipts, invoices, expenditure plans, payment records and lists of beneficiaries under anti-poverty schemes – especially when civil society is unable to command knowledge and expertise equal to that found in government bureaucracies.

Monitoring is further complicated when outcomes are determined by a multitude of interactions between public service professionals and their clients (for example, teachers and their pupils, or doctors and patients). It may also be difficult to attribute outcomes to the actions of public officials rather than other factors outside the official's control, such as nutrition levels, employment opportunities, or environmental changes. Accountability through the generation and dissemination of information (as in report cards) may provide information on outcomes, but not on the decisions which contributed to those outcomes. So it is difficult to know who to hold accountable. Citizens also need some benchmark against which to evaluate services. Nevertheless, government agencies may be sufficiently concerned about their reputations as revealed by information on the quantity and quality of their services to make this mechanism of accountability effective.

A further difficulty here is that users may be reluctant to complain about abuses if the only alternative is more expensive private provision. Also, any benefits following from a complaint being made are felt by a much wider group than those who complain, who may be taking risks in so doing (World Bank, 2004).

Scrutiny is also dependent upon the existence of legislative institutions capable of delving into the financial and administrative details of administration. Investigation can be through questions to ministers, reflecting the duties of elected representatives to their constituents. But the most useful legislative device for administrative accountability to the legislature is the functionally specialized scrutiny committee. To provide the strongest possible accountability to the legislature, such a body needs expertise in areas of public policy, whether relating to individual public services, such as health or energy, individual central government departments, or public expenditure generally, in a context which is free from the restrictions imposed by partisan politics. This means providing committees with professional support staff, and entitling them to call for papers from both within government and civil society, and take oral evidence from ministers, civil servants, representatives of organized interests, and independent experts.

There is no reason why sufficient scrutiny committees should not be set up to cover all areas of public policy, examining how well policy has been administered and with what level of efficiency and effectiveness. By extending the range of parliamentary scrutiny they deepen accountability. Committees may sometimes be restricted by what civil servants are free to talk about – they should not be seen to endorse or oppose government policy – but there is an important educative function to be performed here. Scrutiny committees can increase the influence which back-benchers exert over government policy. Recommendations may be rejected or ignored by the executive, yet later appear as a policy proposal. Their investigations can stimulate new perceptions in the policy community of which they form part, encourage new approaches within departments, and raise the political profile of a policy issue. By widening the public policy debate they provide groups within civil society with opportunities to express views on policy options.

The most important parliamentary committee for accountability is likely to be the public accounts committee, which follows up reports on matters of concern submitted to the legislature by the auditor general. Increasingly, public accounts committees add tests of efficiency and economy to their traditional functions of ensuring that government accounts are technically correct, that there have been no fraudulent transactions, and that expenditure has been in line with legislative authorization.

Legislative procedures need to provide opportunities for the proper deliberation of committee reports. This is to ensure that the whole of the legislature benefits from the expertise acquired by small groups of elected representatives. Accountability has to feed into policy-making via evaluation, as well as ensuring that policies have been fully and properly implemented. It is equally important to expect governments to respond rapidly when parliamentary scrutiny reveals the misuse of funds or administrative authority, and not, as in India, delay action until incriminating evidence is lost and personnel move on (Jain, 1988: 132).

It follows that parliamentary scrutiny should be supported by independent audit provided by the office of auditor general. Independence usually means making the state auditor an officer of the legislature rather than of the executive. Under the Polish constitution, for example, the president of the Supreme Chamber of Control is appointed by parliament for a fixed tenure of six years. Special conditions of service (procedures for appointment, removal, immunity, and internal management) have been created to secure independence. Alternatively, the office may be separate from both legislature and executive, as in India, where the comptroller and auditor general is appointed by the non-executive president to ensure not only that the executive complies with the laws passed by the legislature, but also that subordinate authorities comply with the rules and orders issued by the executive. The CAG can be removed from office only on the grounds of misbehaviour or incapacity, by both houses of parliament supporting a motion with a two-thirds majority.

It is important for accountability that the state audit office be not only independent of the executive, but also empowered to assess more than just the probity of public expenditure. Traditionally state audit offices were concerned with certifying the accounts of administrative agencies under their jurisdiction. To this control of financial regularity is now usually added assessments of efficiency and economy. This means audit offices are allowed to make public judgements (for the benefit of the public as well as the legislature) about whether public money has been spent in the most effective way and with the greatest possible economy. They venture into the realm of public policy to assess whether expenditure plans are achieving the desired results efficiently. The financial policies of administrative agencies are thus brought within the purview of state audit. Audit then seeks value for money as much as, if not more than, financial probity, as in Ghana, for example. In India the CAG supplies parliament with performance reviews of systems, projects and programmes, as well as comprehensive appraisals of public enterprises and other bodies substantially financed from union or state revenues.

Appeal

Finally, accountability can be strengthened by a variety of appeals mechanisms offering the citizen a review of an administrative decision. Such reviews vary greatly in the formalities involved, and range from reconsideration by a more senior official within the department to the full judicial process initiated by appeal to the courts against the use of administrative powers.

The simplest form of appeal occurs when administrative procedures allow a complainant to ask for a decision to be referred to higher authority within the bureaucratic hierarchy of the responsible department. *Internal review* may even be enshrined in a constitution, as in Estonia, where an internal administrative appeal may be set in motion by a memorandum or petition to the appropriate agency. Officials are required to respond within a month. Appeals may not be referred internally to the officials whose decision gave rise to the complaint (Galligan and Smilov, 1999: 83).

A quasi-judicial *public inquiry* is a more formalized internal review of an administrative decision. It is conducted by a specialist official following an appeal by a citizen against a decision which they feel harms their personal interests, even though the policy aims to promote a wider public interest. The grievances for which such an inquiry might be thought appropriate arise when a person feels that their livelihood, environment or amenities are threatened by the application of public policy to their individual case or circumstances. The aggrieved citizen may be entitled to appeal against a proposal arising from government plans – to construct a road or dam, extend a publicly owned airport, or designate an area as a national park, for example. Or the citizen may have been refused permission to take some action of their own on the grounds that it is contrary to public policy, such as constructing buildings on agricultural land, increasing the discharge of effluent from a factory, or planting new varieties of seed.

Public inquiries are generally held by an inspector appointed from a specialist cadre within the agency responsible for the policy that has given rise to the appeal. Alternatively, an independent agency may be set up to organize inquiries, and in such cases the inspectors may have the power to make binding decisions, against which there is likely to be a right of appeal to the courts. Placing inspectors in separate agencies under the supervision of the ministry of justice increases their independence without sacrificing knowledge and experience of a particular area of public policy.

Procedural rules governing inquiries vary, but generally veer towards the informal. Views and information are gathered from all interested parties during hearings at which witnesses can present evidence and be cross-questioned by representatives (not necessarily lawyers) of the various interests affected by the outcome of the appeal. Rules of procedure may need tightening to ensure fairness to all concerned, such as when a witness is clearly being 'led' when giving evidence. As the name implies, inquiries are open to the public, thus increasing the transparency of decision-making, with consequential beneficial effects on accountability.

The procedure at the inquiry is basically inquisitorial rather than accusatorial, leading to a recommendation to a minister or a legally binding decision from the inspector. Ministers will not necessarily be bound to follow the inspector's advice. However, the positive contribution to administrative accountability comes from the attention to individual rights and natural justice induced within the department, and the need to justify departmental action before an inspector who is supposedly impartial. Even when inspectors are appointed by the department against which the appeal is being made, they are obliged to give all interested parties a full and fair hearing. Failure to do so can result in an appeal to the courts if the law connects the public inquiry system to judicial review.

The implementation of public policy may also give rise to cases where the citizen feels aggrieved at how an official has exercised discretion and wishes to challenge the decision without contesting its legality. The application of general policy to individual cases creates the possibility that differences of opinion will occur over how well the citizen's circumstances have been understood by the official charged with making a decision. When considering entitlement to a claimed benefit (income support, pension, bursary, permit, grant, credit, tax relief and so on) the official has to decide whether the claimant is eligible under the policy. When a claim is rejected the claimant may feel that something relevant has been misunderstood or overlooked, and that a correct understanding of the circumstances would lead to a favourable decision.

The importance of bureaucratic allocations to the welfare of individuals and households has prompted some governments to provide means of adjudication in the form of an independent body which hears both sides of a dispute before making a legally binding decision which either endorses that made by the administrative agency or substitutes its own. In order to reflect the principles of adjudication and substitution involved, a quasi-judicial entity is required in the form of an *administrative tribunal*, an informal court which arrives at an impartial, open and fair judgement following an appeal against a discretionary decision by a public authority.

Tribunals should in principle provide specialized, inexpensive and informal adjudication as an alternative to the ordinary courts, where challenging the authorities usually proves expensive, protracted and, for some, intimidating. Tribunal procedures can also reflect the particular nature of the public policies giving rise to appeals. Nevertheless, it will usually be thought important that procedures at hearings should observe the rules of natural justice and culminate in reasoned and transparent decisions.

As their name suggests, administrative tribunals usually consist of a panel of three adjudicators drawn from different walks of life to ensure a balance of attitudes and opinions. So a tribunal in the field of industrial or employment policy might consist of one representative of business and one of labour, with a lawyer in the chair. At hearings, representatives of the agency against which the appeal has been made and of the appellant present their respective sides of the case, with the rules of evidence applied flexibly so that both interested parties feel that everything of relevance to their case has been heard. Appellants may wish to present their own cases or be represented by someone from a support group such as a trade union or voluntary body, rather than a lawyer. In such ways costs and formalities are reduced, which can be of particular benefit to poorer appellants.

A growing number of developing and post-communist countries have adapted the institution of *ombudsman* to their own legislative procedures. The basis of the institution lies in the need for an independent investigator empowered to look into an individual citizen's grievance against the state. Beyond this the powers of the investigator, known variously as the citizen's defender, public defender of rights, complaints commissioner, public grievance investigator, public advocate, or public defender of rights, or, generally, as the ombudsman – a reference back to the eighteenth-century Swedish institution – vary greatly. There is plenty of scope for donor assistance here, especially in training and capacity-building.

The commonest form of ombudsman is entitled to investigate grievances arising from the application of public policy to individual circumstances. Individual injustice or hardship may also arise from defects in the process of policy implementation. The term 'maladministration' has been coined to denote a defect in the conduct of officials and their administrative procedures. Maladministration ranges from corruption, malice and bias at one extreme, to carelessness, negligence, delay and inefficiency at the other. An appeal against maladministration does not necessarily accuse the official of the wrongful exercise of discretion. It may just be concerned with failure to adopt proper standards in the exercise of administrative powers. It does not seek a review of the merits of a decision, but an investigation into an alleged misuse of administrative authority.

The task of an ombudsman is to receive complaints from members of the public, investigate legitimate complaints, and seek a remedy if justified. The benefits of this from of accountability are informality, speed and impartiality. The latter requires the investigator to be an officer of the legislature, like the auditor general (as it is in the majority of cases) rather than of the executive. For example, the Czech public defender of rights is appointed by parliament and reports to the chamber of deputies.

There is plenty of scope for variation on this basic theme. Some ombudsmen are empowered to become far more involved in politics than is assumed under the concept of maladministration, considering fundamental matters affecting the citizen's human rights. The Polish commissioner for citizens' rights protection is one such example, being concerned with legality rather than just maladministration, and having a role in lawmaking. Similarly, under the Argentinian constitution (s. 86) the public defender is empowered to protect human rights 'and any other rights, guarantees and interests protected in this Constitution and the laws, against the acts, actions and omissions of the Administration', in addition to protecting the citizen against maladministration, or the exercise of administrative functions found to be 'illegitimate, defective, irregular, abusive, arbitrary, discriminatory, negligent, seriously inconvenient or untimely'.

Another decision to be made when setting up the office of ombudsman is how to deal with cases of hardship that occur despite official behaviour and procedures being impeccable. The line between the quality of administrative procedures and the quality of a decision can become blurred. So an ombudsman may be empowered to investigate the quality of decisions taken without maladministration but which are nevertheless anomalous or perverse in some way. Flexibility may be necessary if the institution is to attract popular support, such as taking a supportive attitude towards complainants whose grievances fall outside the ombudsman's jurisdiction. This was found to be the case in southern Africa (Ayeni, 1997).

Then there is the question of whether an ombudsman should be entitled to investigate complaints from members of the public who have not themselves been harmed but who feel that some aspect of the administrative process is a cause for concern. Acceptance of this principle gives the Ugandan office of Inspector General of Government the constitutional power to investigate any act, omission, advice, decision or recommendation occurring in the exercise of administrative functions on its own initiative or upon complaint made to it by any member of the public, whether or not that person has suffered any injustice. In this way the inspectorate is able to investigate a wide range of complaints, such as whether public officials have the required qualifications, or are abusing their powers for corrupt purposes. The Inspector General can also take up complaints by public servants themselves, including police officers, when there is concern about the way colleagues have exercised their powers.

It may also be felt that the ombudsman should be allowed to comment on proposed administrative rules and procedures, and to make recommendations about existing procedures when the investigation of an individual complaint reveals cause for concern. For example, the Czech Public Defender of Rights can propose remedial measures to remove the cause of maladministration, so that investigation of a complaint can lead to administrative reform. When reporting to the Chamber of Deputies the Public Defender can also draw attention to legislation giving rise to public dissatisfaction and preventing the recognition of citizens' rights.

Usually the powers of an ombudsman will apply generally to a wide range of government agencies. The Argentinean Public Defender has the power to investigate, either at the request of a complainant or on his own initiative, any agency of public administration, including private companies which deliver public services. But it may be felt necessary to appoint specialist ombudsmen for specific institutions, such as prisons, the army, local government, or health services. Hungary has special ombudsmen on data protection and minority rights. Specialization by area is another possibility: South Africa has 10 ombudsmen, 1 national and 9 provincial.

There are generally few sanctions at the disposal of ombudsmen. They usually have no power to force government agencies to change a decision or make reparation to someone affected by maladministration. The assumption is that publicizing the matter will normally produce a remedy if the fault is clear. Beyond that, it is for the legislature to exert pressure on the executive for a better decision. But it is possible to give an ombudsman greater powers in relation to the more serious forms of maladministration. The Ugandan Inspector General of Government, for example, is empowered by the constitution to 'arrest, cause arrest, prosecute or cause prosecution in respect of cases involving corruption, abuse of authority or of public office'. Even here, however, there is no authority to substitute a decision for that which led to the initial grievance.

Finally, accountability may require appeal to the courts. *Judicial review* tests administrative decisions for *ultra vires* (that the authority has acted beyond its statutory powers) and rules of natural justice. It asks whether public powers have been exercised fairly, reasonably, in good faith, on relevant grounds and for proper purposes. Judicial review may also be sought when a complainant feels that the decision-maker has not followed a procedure required by law (such as allowing time for representations to be made) or has acted negligently (James, 1996: 614).

Under judicial review appeal may be made to the ordinary courts or specialized administrative courts (as in the French tradition), Thailand being an example of the latter. Many developing and post-communist countries have no specialized administrative courts, leaving appeals against administrative action to be dealt with by the ordinary courts. For example, in the Czech Republic administrative law cases are decided by the ordinary courts or the constitutional courts. The right to appeal against administrative decisions is provided for in the Charter of Fundamental Rights and Liberties. There is no settled doctrine on whether or not courts can decide on matters of fact or merit as well as on matters of law.

In Hungary the civil courts also deal with disputes arising from administrative decisions, though such a decision cannot be contested if it falls within the scope of statutory discretion. Apart from a few exceptions (for example, military matters), every administrative decision can be appealed against if it is thought to violate a legal rule. The procedural rules of the civil courts are followed in administrative cases. If a court finds against the administration, the agency concerned must come to a new decision based on the court's reasoning.

Such right of appeal is usually protected by constitutional provision. For example, in Slovakia, art. 46 of the constitution guarantees that

> any person who claims to have been denied his or her rights through a decision made by a public authority may turn to a court of law to have the legality of the decision reviewed, unless otherwise provided by law. The review of decisions in matters of fundamental rights and freedoms shall not be excluded from the jurisdiction of courts of law. (Quoted in Galligan and Smilov, 1999: 335)

An alternative to a hierarchy of specialized administrative courts is the use of administrative law panels within the ordinary civil courts. For example, in Estonia appeals against administrative decisions are heard by the administrative sections found at each level of the hierarchy of courts, up to and including the supreme court. Administrative law panels are also able to review legislation and declare it unconstitutional if it is found to violate a right or freedom protected by the constitution. Administrative panels within the civil courts are also found in Latvia (Galligan and Smilov, 1999).

When found in favour of the appellant, the results of the court's decision will be to cancel the original decision giving rise to the appeal. The decisions of the courts may also serve to guard against future injustice by forcing a review of policy or procedure, restricting future policy development or the use of existing powers.

Clearly judicial review, though generally costly and slow, provides opportunities for grievances to be redressed and justice to be done in matters of great relevance to people's livelihoods and welfare. However, problems for governance can occur through the power which judicial review places in the hands of judges.

First, the values of judges may conflict with those of politicians as to what is in the public interest. Judges are drawn into politics by shaping social and economic developments through rulings on the *merits* of decisions (for example, the economic viability of an infrastructure project). Furthermore, judges, in controlling the executive branch, claim a legitimacy equal to that of elected representatives, 'developing a parallel channel of accountability' (James, 1996: 627), evading 'ouster' clauses in statutes, and publicly criticizing ministers' broad discretionary powers. Judicial decisions can also have the effect of entrenching the role of pressure groups in public policy-making by such means as extending the duty to consult, or abandoning the *locus standi* rule. For example, the World Development Movement was given leave to challenge the British government's decision on the Pergau Dam on the grounds that it was a pressure group devoted to improving overseas aid.

Second, judicial review of administrative action can create a certain amount of uncertainty about public policy. Litigation is inevitably sporadic, yet it is from this that judges develop common law as applied to administrative decisions. Judges may also be inconsistent in their approach to public policy or the administrative process (for example, what judges count as 'unreasonable' can vary greatly). Decision-making in the administration may be inhibited in anticipation of judicial challenge if judicial intervention creates a legalistic and defensive ethos in policy implementation.

Administrators may feel that the expectations of judges require a model of rationality in decision-making that is hard (if not impossible) to emulate in practice. Or agencies may be obliged to carry out functions for which they may not have the resources. Judicial review also affects administrative practice by prescribing procedural consistency if a 'legitimate expectation' has been created

Where there is an independent judiciary these drawbacks need not be unduly threatening to the consolidation of democracy. Judges should be more concerned with the procedural qualities of executive decisions than with their substantive content, especially when those decisions have a quasi-judicial quality themselves. Judicial review 'controls' administration not in the sense of determining individual decisions, but in the sense of directing administrators to do their duty as laid down in statute. It limits the scope of discretion only by enforcing procedural preconditions if any; and ensuring powers are exercised by the correct body (guarding against improper delegation). The courts do not dictate the results of the exercise of discretion, only that the decision is within the permissible range of an authority's power.

Legislatures can also (and regularly do) nullify judicial decisions which cause administrative difficulties by passing laws which have retrospective effect. The extent to which the judiciary can correct things thus depends on the wishes of those who are to be corrected. Public administrators will not necessarily be overly inhibited by judicial review, mainly because the principles of administrative law developed by the courts are often insufficiently precise to offer clear guidance. Very few of the often small number of cases coming before the courts raise principles of general application.

Judicial review tends to concentrate on a narrow range of administrative activity and covers only an infinitesimal percentage of the millions of decisions taken daily by public authorities. Even when the scope of judicial review is extended it will not necessarily have a direct marked effect on administrative practice. For example, the rules of 'natural justice' leave administrators considerable discretion in deciding when they should be applied and what procedures would be regarded as complying with them. And while judges may see their role as 'curbing' or 'controlling' the state through judicial review of administrative action, the *availability* of judicial review may actually legitimize state controls.

Conclusion

There are close interrelationships between the administrative accountability demanded by Western aid donors and pro-democracy organizations and the other facets of good governance. Indeed, a discussion of administrative accountability leads inevitably into important political considerations. Strong accountability is not just a matter of managerial controls, procedural technicalities and judicial scrutiny. It requires effective representative institutions and these in their turn require political accountability and pluralism, so that there are serious consequences in terms of power and office for those who are seen to abuse their position. Parliamentary accountability needs to be so organized that there is a threat to the political credibility of those in power if faulty implementation (ineffective, uneconomic, inefficient, fraudulent or corrupt) is revealed by legislative scrutiny. Effective accountability is also dependent on an informed (and literate) public, as well as effective political competition between leaders and elites.

The key instruments of accountability are: a performance-oriented, neutral civil service; legislative committees with the power to call bureaucrats and ministers to account for the progress of policy implementation; strong investigatory commissions with the power to reveal administrative deficiencies and enforce sanctions; and quasi-judicial institutions to which appeal can be made for impartial adjudication. These also have to compete with new vogues for managerial independence in the belief that public sector managers can deliver good services only if they are free to respond to quasi-commercial incentives. Accountability to their 'markets' takes precedence over accountability to their political masters, who in any case are usually divided in their assessment of what constitutes good administration.

Real administrative accountability thus needs institutional development, especially political institutions which enable the bureaucracy to be subjected to scrutiny and control. Parliamentary democracy, accountable government, and accountable administration are interrelated. Accountable public administration requires the preservation, possibly by constitutional provision, of autonomous political organizations, especially political parties, that can provide support for institutions responsible for holding the bureaucracy accountable. Civil service neutrality in recruitment, deployment and promotions, and strict respect for merit in all career decisions, have to be protected so that public confidence in the civil service as an impartial institution operating under parliamentary control and within the rule of law, and in fairly elected parliamentarians, is preserved.

Politics in developing and post-communist states is too often dominated by the executive. Partisan advantage outweighs determination among legislators to hold the executive to account, and interference in the judiciary removes the threat of independent review of grievances. Statist traditions make it unlikely that governments will willingly concede authority to external agencies and procedures, such as inquiries, tribunals and ombudsmen. Administrative accountability needs its focus to shift from the executive to the legislature, with parliaments empowered to scrutinize executive action and administrative performance (especially through select committees) and to enforce sanctions against ministerial impropriety, especially with regard to public expenditure. The protection of judicial independence, so that recourse to the law can serve to protect private interests against the abuse of public power, is another precondition.

10

Efficient Public Management

Introduction

A number of the governance reforms discussed so far affect public administration: combating corruption, enforcing the rule of law, providing a foundation of law and property rights, ensuring public servants are accountable; and decentralization. This chapter focuses on the question of administrative efficiency, and in particular the essential requirements for a capable public sector as understood by international development agencies.

After a decade of denigrating the state in favour of the private sector, the leading international aid bodies rediscovered that the state is an important service provider that shapes the institutional context in which markets function. State institutions matter for economic growth and the capacity of the state is important for economic and human development. State agencies have important roles: investing resources, directing credit facilities, procuring goods and services, negotiating contracts, and providing, directly or indirectly, public services (such as water supply, sanitation, public health, security, education and health care) which have a profound effect on the quality of life and the reduction of poverty.

Public management and development

If public management is defective, the consequences can be severe, especially for the developmental objectives sought by the international development community. Poorly functioning bureaucracies impede efforts to promote economic growth and reduce poverty. When the influence of public servants on policy-making lacks technical expertise it will eventually work its way through to the economy, constraining the accumulation of human and physical capital. Countries with weak state capability and

226

poor policies experience slow growth in per capita incomes. Social objectives, such as the reduction of infant mortality, are made more difficult to achieve. Vital economic assets can be lost if maintenance work is inadequate (for example, in irrigation schemes).

When the policy-making bodies at the centre of government are weak, plans are ill-informed and uncoordinated. Budgets are based on unrealistic and unsound assumptions, and are further undermined by extra-budgetary expenditure and delays in the production of audited accounts. Funds allocated to official priorities are deflected elsewhere. Spending by donors can lead to insupportable recurrent costs. Accountability and transparency are destroyed. The result is 'incoherent strategic policies and macroeconomic instability' (World Bank, 1997: 81).

The consequences of badly managed public services – services that are inaccessible, unaffordable, disorganized and of low quality – are especially severe for poor people. Inaccessible health services mean higher mortality rates, especially for children. Inadequate and incompetent maintenance deny poor children access to education. Understaffed and under-resourced clinics deny people basic health care. Limited access to clean water, sanitation, and rural transport adds to the vulnerability of the poor, and compounds inequality. If the poor cannot find or afford more expensive alternatives to disorganized services lacking sufficiently qualified staff, with high levels of absenteeism, or without adequate supplies (such as medicines in clinics or teaching materials in schools), they either go without or else suffer the consequences of incompetent treatment (particularly dangerous in the case of health care).

Poor standards of public administration are far from being the only explanations of harmful outcomes for the poor. Cultural, religious and social practices and values also play their part. Economic inequalities are of paramount significance. Nevertheless, public provision, especially in education, health care, communications, water supply and sanitation, can compensate for the social and economic disadvantages caused by poverty, and so alleviate some of its burden.

Supporting better public management

Hence the consensus among the leading aid donors is that to make the management of the public sector more efficient and capable, three sets of reforms are needed: a strong central government capacity for formulating and coordinating policy; efficient and effective delivery systems; and motivated and capable staff.

The World Bank bases its interventions in support of public management reforms on the assumption that the first stage is to create an effective policy-*making* process, so that what is implemented produces the desired outcomes:

> [E]ffective public sectors the world over have generally been characterized by strong central capacity for macro-economic and strategic policy formulation; by mechanisms to delegate, discipline and debate policies among government agencies; and by institutionalized links to stakeholders outside government, providing transparency and accountability, and encouraging feedback. (World Bank, 1997: 81)

So, for example, in Mozambique the Bank has a US$35 million public sector reform programme which includes strengthening the capacity of the Offices of President and Prime Minister for policy-making through the provision of new staff, training and equipment. Of particular importance here and elsewhere is making sure policies are closely linked to resources, especially within poverty reduction strategies.

If and when good policies are formulated, they need to be implemented, and it is here that developing countries have too often failed:

> Some developing countries lack the most basic underpinnings of a professional, rule-based bureaucracy. Even reform-minded leaders cannot translate their goals into reality because the machinery linking policy statements to action has ceased to function. As a result, a vast gap has opened up between what the state says it will do and what it does. (World Bank, 1997: 97)

Hence the emphasis placed by the donor community on reforming institutions for service delivery. For example, the United Nations Development Programme links administrative reform to the Millennium Development Goals because if the efficiency of public administration can be increased in poor countries, then more resources can be made available and the chances of success increased:

> In societies undergoing rapid change as an effect of globalization or other forms of transition, a strong administrative capacity offers much-needed clarity and coherence for the implementation of national priorities, including those connected with MDG targets. (UNDP, 2006: 3)

The World Bank supports a very wide range of public sector management projects. Some are components of sectoral programmes. Then interventions to change the organization of, say, the civil service form part of reform in agriculture, transport or economic policy (Mukherjee and Manning, 2001). For example, 20 per cent of a grant to finance poverty reduction in Uganda was allocated to the reform of public administration and the system of justice. In Poland, a rural support project attempted to increase the efficiency of the agricultural insurance fund by strengthening its management capacity. Some projects include interventions designed to alter the size, remuneration arrangements and career structures of the civil service, others emphasize organizational structures, and some concentrate on accountability and service delivery. Most projects combine a wide range of managerial changes, as in Tanzania, Bolivia and Jamaica .

UNDP has been particularly active in the field of civil service reform in a large number of countries over the years, concentrating on training both public service managers and analysts in policy development, evaluation and implementation. Other aspects of human resource management have been supported. Reform efforts have been heavily influenced by 'new public management' advocacy. In 2003 UNDP supported 380 projects in 112 countries, mostly in Europe and the former Soviet Union. Over 70 per cent were concerned with civil service reform (through training, changes in conditions of employment and legal status, and the introduction of performance management). The remaining projects addressed management processes and structures, including the use of information technology.

Policy-making capacity in government

The policy-making 'capacity' of governments refers to mechanisms providing political executives with the costs and benefits of competing proposals, adequate information (especially budgetary), and coordinated policy debate between the political heads of agencies. Organizational arrangements are needed to produce decisions that are well-informed, with the costs and benefits of alternative policy options identified, and responses to problems coordinated.

Policy-makers also need to be able to obtain feedback from external 'stakeholders' and experts, monitor implementation and evaluate outcomes. The annual 'dialogues' with trade associations convened by Malaysia's Ministry of International Trade and Industry are an example (Kaul, 1996). The contributions from external interests to the policy-making process have been found to be crucial, especially in East Asia, where consultative arrangements supported by technical expertise are widely regarded as having enabled the governments of South Korea, Malaysia, Singapore and Thailand to formulate coherent and effective public policies.

The types of mechanism for good policy-making capacity vary, and range from Secretariats for presidents, prime ministers and cabinets (for example, Poland's Secretariat General of the Government), and interministerial coordinating councils (as in Romania), through Ministries of Finance, Economic Planning Boards (South Korea), and Presidential Economic Councils (Georgia), to independent groups of eminent citizens (for example, Hungary's 'Blue Ribbon' Commissions or Bulgaria's Economic Transition Project: Collins, 1993). The Policy Analysis and Coordinating Division of the Zambian Cabinet Office established in 1993 is one model. It was designed with more 'open government' in mind and a more democratic policy formulation process, involving policies initiated by ministers after consultation with civil society (especially NGOs and the private sector). In order to design policies likely to be implemented, advice is taken from civil servants and affected citizens. Much importance is attached to monitoring implementation by policy-making bodies, such as the cabinet (Garnett *et al.*, 1997).

The common need is for central agencies and deliberative councils with technical capability. However, cabinets and councils of ministers have frequently been hamstrung by inadequate staff, information, logistical support and procedures, especially for financial planning. Skills in drafting legislation have also frequently been inadequate (Collins, 1993; Bardill, 2000). Transitional countries have also experienced a loss of managers, economists and planners to the private sector, aid agencies, NGOs, or overseas, because of low pay, bad personnel management, social disruption or political repression (for example, Kenya). The availability of sources of non-governmental policy analysis, such as academic institutes, is highly variable. Experience of deliberative councils, especially African experiments with 'economic and social councils', reveals the danger of making them too exclusive.

Problems of coordination can be severe, causing conflicting decisions and delays, as with departmentalism in Poland (Taras, 1993). There may be internal resistance to open relationships between ministries, or to working as teams which openly exchange information (though in Zambia a more open management structure was supported by younger staff). Aid donors have been known to further fragment central policy-making capacity through bilateral deals with ministries and departments. This can lead to unaffordable recurrent costs (for example, road repairs, school equipment, or health centre drugs and medicines). Ministries of finance need to be integrated into the process to ensure better coordination in the preparation of economic policy.

Policy-making arrangements at the core of government have been the most difficult area of reform in transitional countries with formerly centrally planned economies. Devising new ways of analysing the need for change and producing new policy options are particularly important in post-communist states where centralized planning systems have been replaced by government policy-making in the context of capitalist relations of production, market forces, private property and competition. New types of economic information are required in the context of economic restructuring, privatization, new financial institutions, and support for the private sector. The significance of the rule of law (as distinct from the will of the party), newly democratized political institutions, and new political processes (such as the reactions of private sectional interests) has to be built into policy-making. Something has to fill the institutional vacuum for policy coordination left by the removal of Communist Party organs (Collins, 1993).

Efficient service delivery mechanisms

Currently the solutions to administrative inefficiency most frequently discussed are the contracting out of service delivery to private firms or NGOs, managerial autonomy through performance-based agencies, and a 'customer' orientation towards users of public services.

Contracting out service delivery

Rather than provide services directly through their own organizations and with their own staff (or direct labour), government agencies are urged to put services out to tender and take bids from non-governmental organizations, including commercial firms, not-for-profit organizations, voluntary bodies and community groups. The competition between providers, which can include in-house organizations, is expected to improve value for money. Contracts commit government agencies to greater clarity in their objectives, predictability in service standards, and effectiveness in monitoring the consequences for users. Contracts also offer the potential benefits of extra resources being made available, fewer subsidies having to be paid to loss-making activities, and increased tax revenues from the new profits made by private enterprises.

Competitive tendering, which may be made compulsory for some public services, can secure significant efficiency gains by bringing about savings while standards are maintained or even improved. Competition for contracts can improve productivity in direct labour organizations, which may be successful with their bids. The community then benefits from increased efficiency in that the taxpayers' money goes further or less of it is needed. The assumption that the private sector can provide public services at less cost to the taxpayer with no loss of quality has proved popular in a number of the transitional regimes of Central and Eastern Europe (Lember, 2004).

Some serious problems have to be solved before contracts are likely to save the taxpayer money. First, competition cannot be guaranteed. The effective regulation of market mechanisms is difficult to achieve (for example, in the case of private health care). The private sector may be weak. Both factors limit the extent to which fair competition between bidders can be assured. Contracts are also prone to corruption and mismanagement, especially if the rule of law is not well established (Hughes, 1998).

Political patronage has to be kept out of the contracting process, as shown by the case of solid-waste management in Accra, Kumasi and Tema in Ghana, and Kampala in Uganda. Poor contract management meant little improvement in the quality of service, but a large increase in service charges, and so no efficiency gains for households. Political patronage was allowed to infect the tendering process. Improper tendering procedures left contractors with monopoly powers. Their excessive profiteering increased costs to the taxpayer. In Kampala the local authority lacked the managerial and supervisory personnel needed for it to carry out its responsibilities effectively. Late payments, incompetent personnel, disruption of work-schedules, weak supervision of the contractor's work, and rent-seeking resulted in little improvement in a city with very severe problems of sanitation (Golooba-Mutebi, 2003; Aworti, 2004).

Second, contractual arrangements threaten the public service ethos (where this exists). Employees of private companies, especially if taken from public services and given inferior terms and conditions of employment, may well adopt the attitude: 'If I am to be treated as a mercenary, I might as well act like one' (World Bank, 2004: 102). Countries trying to create a public service ethos as part of the transition from authoritarianism might find that contracts with the private sector produce unwelcome outcomes.

Third, writing contracts requires specialized and scarce skills, essential if government agencies are not to be left vulnerable to unscrupulous or incompetent commercial firms. Clear objectives need to be set so that the providers know what the agency expects of them. Good information must be available so that incontrovertible conclusions can be reached about whether the contractors have done what they were paid to do. Politically and administratively acceptable measures have to be agreed upon so that a judgement can be made about whether the contract has achieved greater efficiency than is possible by the use of in-house or direct service units within the parent ministry or local authority.

The administrative skills required to define standards of performance, prepare legally sound contracts, run a fair tendering process, evaluate bids, monitor the work of the contractors, and enforce agreed standards are rare in countries in transition from authoritarianism. Analysis of a range of contracts in the field of health care across six countries showed how difficult it can be for developing countries to manage the process of contracting out effectively. The administrative demands are formidable, and when not met weaken every stage of the process. This puts government agencies at a disadvantage, leading to the conclusion that

> given the somewhat mixed evidence on the effectiveness of contracting in promoting greater efficiency or higher quality, developing country governments may be well advised to restrict contracting-out to those services where it is clear that they have the capacity to manage contracts and that contracting out will be beneficial. (Bennett and Mills, 1998: 325)

Ministries of Health frequently lack the administrative capacity to design, negotiate and enforce contracts with private and non-governmental providers (Hecht *et al.*, 2004). States which have had trouble financing services directly, whether because of inadequate revenues, shortages of qualified personnel, administrative inefficiency, civil unrest or corruption, are unlikely to be well placed to fund and monitor the contractual obligations of private providers (Robinson and White, 1998).

While contracting out may be appropriate for technical services, where it is relatively easy to identify what is needed and whether it has been provided to specification, there are many public services where it is hard to judge the relative importance of the numerous factors that contribute to eventual outcomes. The subjective nature of much quality assessment in public services makes it difficult to control contracts and contractors to ensure that real efficiency has been achieved. It may also be thought that there are some controls which only governments should be allowed to impose on their citizens, such as the exercise of coercion, incarceration, and powers affecting fundamental human rights, though this has not deterred some countries such as Estonia from contracting prisons out to commercial enterprises (Lember, 2004).

Finally, it cannot be assumed that contracting out will always produce value for money. When government agencies are required to accept the lowest bid there is a risk that money will be wasted if the result is inferior goods or services. For example, in Bangladesh the government wished to distribute treadle pumps as a form of irrigation following a drought. Acceptance of the lowest bidder led to pumps being supplied that fell short of the required specifications. The rehabilitation programme was subjected to delay and waste when over 13,500 pumps had to be rejected (Lewis, 1993).

Contracting with the third sector

Contracts with the 'third sector' of non-governmental and non-commercial organizations deserve special attention, since it is often held that partnerships between the state and the bodies in this sector are particularly significant in the struggle to alleviate poverty. The 'third sector' consists of business associations, youth groups, women's organizations, voluntary bodies, community associations, religious foundations, professional bodies and autonomous non-governmental organizations providing economic and social services such as agricultural extension, vocational training, social welfare, irrigation and credit. The state is seen as an enabling body, mobilizing the participation of civil society in the satisfaction of demands and needs.

The relationships between government agencies and organizations within the 'third sector' vary, and do not necessarily involve contracts or service agreements. A public body may support a non-governmental organization financially, leaving it to provide a service which fills a gap in public provision. In this way the state tacitly approves of what the organization does without wishing to engage it in a contractual relationship. This happens when NGOs find a 'niche' that is brought about by a congruence of their specialized skills, the needs of specific and usually disadvantaged social groups, and gaps in state provision.

When the activities of such bodies do not conflict with the policy objectives of governments, it may be very cost-effective for the state to provide financial backing. An example would be an NGO which organizes a savings scheme from which poor women can obtain loans to acquire livestock, following this up with training and vaccination programmes, as in the case of Proshika in Bangladesh. In India, many NGOs are involved in this way in government programmes for social forestry, ecological development, primary health care, the provision of safe drinking water, education, rural housing, land reform, minimum wage legislation and bonded labour rehabilitation. Consequently, government allocations to NGOs can be very substantial (Robinson *et al.*, 1993).

Alternatively, a central or local government may wish to make an NGO an extension of one of its own departments by contracting with it to provide part of the service in a manner jointly agreed by the two organizations involved (as eventually happened with the agricultural extension services run by Proshika). Contractual arrangements with NGOs have been recorded in the policy areas of agricultural extension (Uganda and Mozambique), rural water supply, sanitation service (in Bolivia and Chile), educational assistance and foster care for Roma children (in Albania), tube well installation for landless irrigation groups (in Bangladesh), training home visitors in child health for the Ministry of Health in Brazil, forest conservation in Nepal, the distribution of government-subsidized food in Mexico, primary health care in Kazakhstan and Kyrgyzstan, child health and family planning in Haiti, rural water supply and sanitation in Bolivia, and therapy under India's national tuberculosis programme. In Guatemala, nearly 100 NGOs are under contract to provide health care to about 3.7 million people, leading to an increase in immunization rates from 69 per cent in 1997 to 87 per cent in 2001 (Hecht *et al.*, 2004).

There are also hybrid forms of service delivery that combine features of non-governmental provision to communities that would otherwise go without (such as when communities organize services through self-help, or religious foundations provide education for the children of poor families), with activities that involve NGOs becoming extensions of national and local government departments through contractual relationships. Such hybrids have been labelled 'institutionalized co-production', when civic bodies provide a government agency with important services on a largely voluntary basis. Examples include the Citizen–Police Liaison Committee in Karachi, the Ghana Public Road Transportation Union, urban sanitation arrangements in the poor neighbourhoods of some Brazilian cities, and small-scale irrigation systems in parts of Asia. The incentives which attract cooperation of this type are not always financial, but rather to do with the honour, status, discretion over the use of resources, political influence which can be gained from participation in the scheme, and ability to make services responsive to different needs (Joshi and Moore, 2004).

A further variation, one that has been labelled 'contracting in', occurs when donors support local organizations which then hire extension workers paid for by the government. The organization then meets the operational costs – on-farm demonstrations and trials of new seeds in the case of agricultural extension services in Uganda and Mozambique, for example. This clearly requires NGOs to provide services which conform to the government's agriculture policies (Anderson and van Crowder, 2000).

How far government agencies will be prepared to delegate service delivery to third-sector bodies depends on a range of political and administrative circumstances, such as the level of pluralism in the political system, the state's capacity to provide services itself, and how NGOs see their own political roles – in Asia 'non-radical NGOs have for obvious reasons found more favour with governments' (Farrington and Lewis, 1993: 327). Relations between NGOs and government agencies range from equal partners at one extreme to virtual absorption at the other, the latter occurring in Chile when local community organizations became 'absorbed and co-opted by the local health department' (Brinkerhoff, 2002: 26).

There are obvious advantages for government of contracts with third-sector organizations. The supply of specialized and dedicated expertise can be increased, costs lowered, efficiency raised, bureaucracy reduced, and political patronage avoided. 'Consumer' choice can be strengthened, and potentially difficult trade unions bypassed. Involving this sector in service delivery can also help a government to demonstrate its commitment to accountability and participation, as in the Philippines. At the same time, one attraction of such bodies for governments is that they can easily be discarded when politically necessary (Ganapin, 1993; Edwards and Hulme, 1996).

Governments may also be able to 'scale up' the *ad hoc* innovations of third-sector bodies, universalizing them beyond the area of operations of individual organizations, as with new technologies for hill farming in the Philippines, and the dissemination of information on rice-fish farming in north-eastern Thailand. Governments may be able to obtain training for their staff from NGO specialists. The specialized knowledge of distinct client groups, such as the landless or the disabled, help governments to 'customize' services (Farrington and Lewis, 1993; Brinkerhoff, 2002).

There are also potential advantages for the non-governmental sector in cooperation with government agencies. It can provide access to funds (especially from aid donors), raise their profile and create opportunities to influence public policy (a powerful motivation for Indonesian NGOs in the 1990s). Being part of a contracting organization may lead to volunteers being more valued, and better able to obtain stronger support from their organization in terms of training, supervision, rewards, consultation and evaluation. Paid staff may obtain greater job security. Contracts with governments can help local organizations overcome problems encountered in their work with the poor, such as weak legal rights, scarce resources for new economic activities (for example, vaccines for livestock management), and inadequate research capacity.

There are however risks with contractual relations between government and the third sector. These arise from the administrative complexity caused, and conflicts of organizational culture.

Governments may find contracts administratively cumbersome. Third-sector bodies may be poorly organized, unreliable (because of the optional availability of volunteers), expensive to supervise, and difficult to negotiate with when they are also campaigning as pressure groups. Government agencies may find it difficult to ensure that minimum standards are maintained by organizations which have their own priorities and ideas about how best to look after the interests of their client groups. While some community bodies have good reputations for the quality of their provision (for example, mission schools in Africa and Asia), others suffer from staffing difficulties, operational inefficiencies and unstable organization. Government agencies may find that organizations operating on a break-even basis have different organizational values, priorities, cultures and management styles from their own.

There are also potential costs to the third sector. First, volunteers may be deterred, not wishing to work with government bodies, or be controlled in what they do and when they do it by the rules implicit in contracts. They may be put off by the increased bureaucracy which a contractual relationship will almost certainly require. Participative styles of management may be threatened by contracts. There is evidence from Asia and Latin America that 'time and space for reflection and innovation are reduced as NGOs become contractors to donors and/or governments' (Edwards and Hulme, 1996: 963). Civic organizations risk becoming professionalized, bureaucratized and dependent, rather than voluntary, creative and autonomous (White and Robinson, 1998). For example, government procedures imposed damaging limitations on how the Bangladesh Rural Advancement Committee (BRAC) could operate after it signed a contract with the Agricultural Development Corporation to install and service tube wells so that landless irrigation groups (formed by BRAC) could sell water to local farmers. It was also found that among the landless there was little trust in the officials who had done nothing in the past for this section of the rural population (Mustafa *et al.*, 1993). If contracts lead to a growth in the number of paid officials, that too may be objectionable to the voluntary worker who feels that the whole ethos of the organization is being pushed away from the philanthropic ideal towards an income-earning imperative.

Second, cooperation with governments may strike at the independence of non-governmental bodies, especially to campaign politically as pressure groups. Government agencies may define politically acceptable behaviour, forcing groups into a 'responsible' mode, leading to a loss of credibility among clients if the organization is seen as having been co-opted by government into a more conservative stance on social problems and how to deal with them. AGRARIA, the Chilean NGO which acts as a contractor under the state's agricultural technology programme, has experienced internal tension between those devoted to its original pressure group role concerned with rural poverty alleviation, and those keen to maximize the financial advantages of contracts. In the Philippines, tension within the radical Haribon Foundation following involvement with the Department of Environment and Natural Resources was resolved when an agreement on the purpose of the policy was accepted, showing that 'it is difficult to collaborate with NGOs that are critical of sensitive policy issues or belong to "anti-government" coalitions. No matter how rational such criticisms are, they will still be perceived as biased and irrational' (Ganapin, 1993: 269). Governments are likely only to be interested in NGOs as service providers, not as sources of new ideas about public policies (Robinson, 1997).

States may impose a restrictive environment of laws, taxes, controls, bureaucratic resistance and even political repression on civic organizations and other parts of the third sector (White and Robinson, 1998). Public accountability for contracts can, and probably should, mean extensive intervention and veto by statutory authorities.

Third, small organization may be marginalized as a result of having neither the resources nor skills to comply with the legal requirements specified in contracts and the tendering process. Government agencies are more likely to want to enter into contracts with the bigger, more established bodies, leaving small community groups vulnerable unless they have organizers who are capable of meeting government officials on equal terms. Contracts can lead organizations to commit unachievable standards in order to be competitive. Dependence on one-off contracts can increase financial insecurity, a problem exacerbated when government agencies fail to pay their bills in a timely fashion, as has happened with local authorities in a number of Eastern European countries (Struyk, 2002). Small local organizations, such as self-help groups, with commitment to a cause, have to continue unfunded work while trying to meet contract targets. Competition for funds and contracts can also generate reluctance to share information and resources, with the risk of duplication of effort.

The use of the third sector in service delivery is constrained by other factors. The coverage provided by non-governmental bodies is often quite limited, as in Bangladesh where it has been estimated that only between 10 and 20 per cent of landless households are reached, indicating that 'primary responsibility for the welfare of the population will always remain with government' (Lewis, 1993: 55). Non-governmental resources are unevenly spread spatially and socially. If governments as direct providers have trouble ensuring equity in service provision and standards, will they be better at achieving these objectives via the funding of community and other non-governmental bodies? (See Robinson and White, 1998.) Furthermore, NGOs are not necessarily accountable to those to whom they provide services, a further reason why they should not automatically be seen as cheap substitutes for state provision.

Government officials and group workers do not always see eye-to-eye on the implementation of public policies. Conflicts of interest can occur when local officials are closely allied socially and politically with local economic elites, yet have to collaborate with an organization that is attempting to extend the economic opportunities of the poor, as has happened in Bangladesh with Proshika's involvement in social forestry (Khan *et al.*, 1993). In many parts of Asia, NGOs work with women and the landless, while officials from departments of agriculture traditionally work with male farmers.

Performance-based agencies

Delegated management is another principle of new public management. It entails separating operational units from their parent ministries, leaving the latter responsible for policy-making, while the executive agencies concentrate on implementation and service delivery. The managers of the agencies have considerably more autonomy than they had as members of ministerial hierarchies, especially in relation to personnel and financial discretion, but remain accountable for outputs and outcomes to the ministers of their parent departments. Chief executives are given performance contracts specifying measures of output and performance standards. By creating specialized managements for limited sets of tasks, it should be possible to establish clear objectives and evaluate precisely how well the tasks have been performed. Staff can then be judged on their performance against agreed objectives, with consequences for pay, promotions and job retention (Caulfield, 2002). Thus the distinction between the purchasers and providers of services is brought into the organization of government departments. The aims are to improve efficiency and make services more responsive to the demands of 'consumers'.

Another aim is to insulate management from political interference, making managers more responsive to the preconditions of effective service delivery. For example, according to the head of the Ghanaian civil service, ministers set strategic targets for government policy and delegate to implementing agencies 'the day-to-day operational targets required for effective management ... to ensure that our Ministers do not get involved in routine operational decisions' (Dodoo, 1997: 120).

Examples of this form of managerial delegation are found in tax collection (Uganda), health care (Zambia) and water services (Ghana). At least eight African states use agencies for tax collection. Uganda's Ministry of Gender, Labour and Social Development has twelve agencies under its supervision. Agencies are also found in Bolivia, Estonia, Jamaica, Pakistan, Tanzania and Thailand. The creation of executive agencies in newly democratizing countries has been motivated by a wish rather than an obligation to follow the new public management agenda adopted by some industrialized countries. In Tanzania the Executive Agency Programme launched in 1997 was prompted by the political benefits which different groups of politicians and officials saw coming from it – reducing the size of the public sector for members of the government, better remuneration for bureaucrats, and additional departmental income for Permanent Secretaries (Caulfield, 2002). In Central and Eastern Europe, where 'agencification' has been applied to government businesses, higher education, government research, support for culture, the state media, regulation, and special funds (for example, for pensions or agriculture), it has been favoured by politicians seeking increased patronage and lower expenditure, civil servants seeking greater autonomy, pay and job security, and foreign donors seeking improved performance and greater professionalism (Beblavy, 2002).

While some aid agencies have urged caution, especially in countries with 'inadequate controls over inputs and weak capacity' (World Bank, 1997: 90), executive agencies as alternatives to traditional bureaucracies are derived from assumptions consistent with other aid conditionalities such as structural adjustment, market imperatives, and incentive systems in government. Agencies in Tanzania and Ghana are modelled on those in the UK and were introduced with support from the Department for International Development.

Politics in transitional countries throws up obstacles which have to be overcome before 'agencification' can take place. Those who benefit from the existing system, especially professionals in technical divisions, are powerful and well placed to sabotage reform. Awarding special privileges to staff as part of managerial autonomy can cause resentment in the departments from which policy execution has been 'hived off'. Examination of Ghana's Health Service, an executive agency under the Ministry of Health, revealed inertia, resistance to change and continuing centralized control over policy and resources, including personnel (Larbi, 1998).

Delegation has often been negated by persistent central ministerial intervention in staffing, contracts and borrowing. There are strong pressures leading to centralization rather than agency autonomy in developing countries. This is prompted by the need to reduce civil service numbers, depoliticize the civil service, stamp out nepotism, or combat corruption. Such reforms tend to call for the enforcement of uniformity across government, rather than agency autonomy (Polidano, 2001). External pressures, such as structural adjustment programmes, may also run counter to agency autonomy (for example, demands from the IMF for tight fiscal control).

Analysis of agencies in Tanzania and Uganda shows that, by reducing political interference in management, the creation of agencies alienated politicians who lost opportunities for patronage as well as control over administration. They then withdrew badly needed political support. One concern is that the delegation of powers over staffing matters can lead to recruitment and promotion on particularistic criteria – ethnicity, regional identity, or clientelism. In Uganda the significance of patronage led to

an undermining of board appointments on merit principles, in favour of political and even ethnically biased appointments. The URA's [Uganda Revenue Authority's] governing board is now dominated by Ministry of Finance officials, even though the point of the reform was to grant more operational independence to the authority. (Caulfield, 2006: 23)

Political traditions may also prove too strong for real delegation of managerial authority to take place. For example, agencies in Thailand, such as the Office for National Educational Standards, the Community Organisations Development Institute and the Agricultural Research Development Agency, have been unable to evade the highly unified administrative system, the hierarchical structure of government, prime-ministerial control, and bureaucratic red tape (Bowornwathana, 2006).

Autonomous agencies create risks for public administration, particularly when viewed from a democratic perspective (Minogue, 1998). Accountability through the democratic process is clearly at risk when public servants are judged by criteria that relate to their accountability to senior officials only, and have deliberately been distanced from the process of legislative scrutiny in the interest of managerial autonomy. Furthermore, a lack of independent legal personality can prevent judicial review. Imprecise relationships between agency executives, ministerial staff and ministers also impede accountability. In Uganda and Tanzania, where constitutional forms of accountability have been deliberately weakened as part of executive autonomy, other mechanisms become doubly important, such as national audit and departmental monitoring. But these mechanisms have been incapacitated (not least by the transfer of professional staff from departments to agencies), leading to a further weakening of parliamentary oversight, as auditors and ministers are unable to provide adequate reports on agency performance (Caulfield, 2006).

The costs of lost accountability are considerable. Comparisons of executive agencies in health care, urban water supply, agricultural marketing and business development services in ten countries in Asia, Africa and Latin America revealed that if managerial autonomy is not balanced by accountability to service users or elected representatives, policy becomes fragmented, transaction costs increase and managers become more self-serving (Batley, 1999).

There is a further risk that agencies will become dominant in policy-making as well as execution, and that original mandates will be exceeded in the absence of full oversight. The national budget can become 'balkanized'. For example, in Central and Eastern Europe executive autonomy has enabled agencies to block policy changes which they oppose, creating 'policy entrenchment' as agencies obtain greater policy-making capacity than parent ministries (Beblavy, 2002). Fragmenting the bureaucracy may be the last thing developing and transitional countries need, rather than a unified, professional and competent civil service, as well as strategic coherence and capacity for coordinated policy-making.

Executive agencies make huge demands on management capacity at the centre (in the form of support services, resource allocation, performance indicators, policy formulation, and information systems) as well as in the autonomous agencies themselves. For executive agencies to bring the promised benefits to administrative efficiency there need to be management and information systems in place that are rarely found in transitional countries. Financial information systems need to be capable of tracking, controlling and auditing expenditure (Caulfield, 2002). If performance indicators are poorly developed, monitoring goes by default. Analysis of the Estonian Health Insurance Fund, Tax and Customs Board, Consumer Protection Board and Environmental Inspectorate, in a country where agencies spend about half of the total state budget and employ 80 per cent of civil servants, found performance evaluation to be 'chaotic', leaving agencies with far too much autonomy (Tavits and Annus, 2006: 8).

The success of what appears at first glance to be a technical device needs institutional and administrative developments that are lacking in many transitional countries. Giving managers discretionary powers to recruit staff and spend money can be a dangerous strategy in countries without a properly organized public sector. It requires the rule of law to be well established, rules governing the spending of public money and the management of personnel to be workable, and probity in government business to be enforced. If used as a 'quick fix' imported from abroad, as in some Central and Eastern European countries, the task of creating an appropriate legal, constitutional and financial framework might be neglected (Beblavy, 2002).

Without such institutional development, what is seen as a solution to one problem is likely to exacerbate others without necessarily achieving its own aims. Executive agencies should not be seen as correcting managerial deficiencies, but as requiring sound public management before they are introduced: 'The greater the shortcomings in a country's established management practices, the less suitable the reforms' (Schick, 1998: 124).

A customer orientation

Another popular notion is to treat citizens as 'customers' of public services, rather than the 'passive recipients of monopolistically provided state services' (Kaul, 1997: 16). Public services have been criticized for lacking information on consumers' views of providers; for serving producer, not consumer, interests; and encouraging low expectations of public service. A consumerist approach involves strategies to counter these tendencies.

First, the articulation of views by users and community groups through neighbourhood committees, co-opted representatives, and advisory bodies is encouraged. Second, accessibility is improved by 'one-stop shops', computer technology and training in customer sensitivity. Third, governments should 'speak to the consumer' through marketing and advertising to improve public awareness of the services available. An example is South Africa's Batho Pele (People First) project, designed to make the delivery of public services more user-friendly, and requiring government departments to provide service guarantees, redirect resources to hitherto neglected groups, and develop a culture of 'customer care' which is sensitive to needs originating in race, gender or disability (Ncholo, 2000).

Public bodies are expected to compensate the 'consumer' for any lack of choice by providing contracts specifying standards of service and means of redress, statements of citizens', customers' or clients' rights, and information on performance levels, as in Malaysia's Clients' Charters, for example (Chiu, 1997). Guaranteeing standards and offering compensation if goods and services do not come up to a prescribed standard are supposed to substitute for the power to take custom elsewhere found in the classic model of the sovereign consumer.

A consumer orientation also seeks to enlarge of the range of services available. Choice may be increased by a variety of means. First, the resources available to the user may be increased so that they can 'exit' the system of public provision and exercise effective demand within the private market for, say, education or health care. Or choice may be facilitated by the creation of a variety and range of public provision. This introduces a quasi-consumerism in which providers have to be more responsive to user demand or see their resources withdrawn. Finally, the range of services can be extended by 'market development', or the stimulation of new sources of provision within the private, voluntary and informal sectors.

There are some bold assumptions behind this view of public services that raise important questions. First, can it be assumed that public servants can be trained to treat the citizen as a consumer? At best, it will take some time, especially in transitional states where cultures of bureaucratic officiousness linger on. The values, methods and behaviour of professionals in public bureaucracies run counter to a consumerist perspective on public service users. Officials tend to be predominantly male, urbanized, educated and Westernized. They are thus more likely to be accessible to the wealthier middle class than to the poor.

Second, even if officials can be given incentives to treat citizens as consumers with all that that implies, the vast majority of service users will not be able to take their 'custom' elsewhere. At best they will be clients of the administration, and at worst dependents who have no alternative but to use the services on offer. For the user to have a benchmark to compare with their own experience, charters and 'contracts' should specify standards in detail. But these usually contain vague intentions rather than firm promises. And the promises have to be enforceable, entailing a relationship between the state and the citizen that is rarely found.

The assumption about diversity of provision confuses the benefits of competition for the consumer with its effects on the government agency. It does not follow that competition among private providers to which services might be contracted out will increase the choice open to the 'consumer'. Consumer choice is not strengthened when a government agency chooses between firms bidding for a contract. Why should the choice of a contractor make a service more responsive to the wishes of users than if it is provided directly? Even if the number of firms in the relevant market increases, 'consumers' still have to convey to the government what it is they seek from the service concerned.

Finally, the advocates of consumerism use diametrically opposed concepts of accountability. On the one hand, 'accountability' means 'consumer-responsive', when the users of an agency's services are presumed to have the power of the consumer in a competitive market of suppliers. On the other hand, there is the more traditional understanding of accountability, involving the responsiveness of governments to voters who can replace decision-makers at elections if they find fault with the services on offer. The debate about accountability cannot be resolved while such different understandings persist. The latter form of accountability requires stronger consumer groups than are usually found. The former concept is based on a misrepresentation of the relationship between the state and the citizen.

Reforming public servants

In trying to ensure that public servants are motivated and competent, numerous problems which undermine the integrity and effectiveness of public services are found in transitional states: nepotism in recruitment, partisan interference in staff deployment, and technological changes which increase workloads, reduce opportunities for promotion, and marginalize unions and professional associations (Hubbard, 1997).

Because providing government jobs for graduates with nowhere else to go has long been a political necessity (Turner and Hulme, 1997), wage bills frequently outpace expenditure on operations and maintenance. Even though revenues are often insufficient to pay competitive salaries, they are still a major cause of public deficits. As the private sector develops, large disparities open up between public and private sector remuneration, pensions, working conditions, and holidays, leaving incentives in the public sector too weak to secure needed commitment, or prevent a 'drain' of talent. Public sector pay has also been eroded by inflation. And there is evidence that countries with low levels of civil service pay perform worse than others (Klitgaard, 1997).

The development of effective non-material incentives (such as organizational missions and identity, or clear policy orientations) has been limited by uncertainty over the future role of the civil service. Fundamental political and economic changes in transitional countries have meant a lack of clear policy orientations following rapid turnovers in leadership, political conflicts between governments and parliaments, difficulties in securing parliamentary endorsement in the absence of reliable majorities, lack of information about future resources, and uncertainty about the allocation of powers and finance between different levels of government.

The main solutions proposed are meritocracy, proper compensation, the cultivation of *esprit de corps*, and more effective incentives.

Meritocratic recruitment and promotion is needed to create neutral, professional and depoliticized civil services, particularly in states anxious to replace a totally politicized public service with one that is neutral and independent, and capable of supporting a democratic government. This has been a guiding principle behind reforms in the Czech Republic, for example (Vidlakova, 1993: 72). Throughout Eastern Europe there has been basic rethinking about who should make appointments, what qualifications staff should have, how they should be trained, how the service should be structured and graded, how staff should be appraised, what procedures should be established for disciplinary action and appeal, how codes of conduct can be institutionalized, and how civil servants should be remunerated (Collins, 1993).

Adequate compensation to attract and retain well-qualified personnel should be feasible if surplus posts can be eliminated by the removal of 'ghost workers' and unfilled positions. However, increasing the wages of remaining staff may not solve the problem of salary bills crowding out recurrent expenditure. It has also been noted that the IMF has often imposed wage *freezes* as part of loan agreements (Turner and Hulme, 1997). Systematic evaluations of staffing needs in government agencies are rare. Senior civil servants have been known to resist 'retrenchments' because of possible implications for their department's status. Increasing unemployment when the state is 'employer of last resort' is politically unpopular, especially if the savings made are insufficient to have a significant effect on salaries (as in Kenya: Cohen, 1993).

Improving *esprit de corps* is difficult, and is likely to need a change of political ethos as much as administrative innovations, such as new training programmes, new devices for conferring prestige (for example, the Malaysian Public Services Innovation Awards), worker participation, self-managing teams, or multi-tasking (Kaul, 1996).

Stronger incentives to improve performance (such as bonuses, performance allowances, or budget increases) have great support among donors, though there are obstacles and risks. These include unfavourable contexts (such as risk-averse employees), and difficulties in measuring effort and results. Over-ambitious managers may 'ratchet up' performance requirements, and their subordinates may focus on what is measurable to the exclusion of what is not. Competitive incentives may be negated by cultural values such as security of employment, highly personalized administrative procedures (as in Kenya), kinship and tribal networks, the importance attached to leisure and celebrations, and respect for consensus and equality (Klitgaard, 1997).

Conclusion

Administrative reform has been found to be a slow and sometimes painful process. It has been inhibited by a number of factors that have often proved intractable. Some failures can be explained by shortcomings in the way donors have planned their interventions in support of administrative reform.

First, not enough attention has been given to the context of reform. Failures to link them to broader governmental, economic and social objectives, to limit objectives to what can be managed at any one time, and to provide the necessary resources, have meant that changes have not produced better public services, greater citizen satisfaction, stronger accountability, or better policy-making capacity. Civil service reform is unlikely to produce the desired results unless there are sufficient resources to attract well-qualified professionals and improve state audit. This in turn means tax reforms to increase revenues in the long run, and donor assistance (grants, loans and debt relief) in the short term (Kiggundu, 1998; Olowu, 1999).

Second, the appropriateness of new public management thinking is questionable in the context of underdevelopment. It is 'oriented more to the cost-cutting, tax reducing concerns of northern states than the capacity-building and developmental concerns of southern states' where the need is for well-resourced, professional, 'steel frame' civil services capable of high-quality policy formulation and implementation (Minogue, 1998: 33).

Third, it is generally accepted that committed political leadership at the highest levels (perhaps a cabinet minister as in Trinidad and Tobago, or a public service review commission as in Uganda) is essential if change is to be supported at all levels: 'most successful reforms are politically driven at the highest level' (Kaul, 1996: 149). Yet such support may be lacking because reforms produce few benefits for politicians and high costs, encounter hostility among officials who fear for their jobs and livelihoods, and are seen as originating from donors (who fund a substantial proportion of them) rather than domestic interests (Therkildsen, 2000).

Finally, reformers usually concentrate on formal organizations and institutions, to the neglect of informal relationships, political values, and social attitudes which are much more difficult to change, especially by foreign agencies. Such foundations upon which formal administrative structures rest are most difficult to address during the volatile politics of democratic transition. This was found in South Africa, when disappointing progress with an impressive raft of reforms produced yet more recommendations for institutional reforms from the Presidential Review Commission without 'a more thoroughgoing reorientation of underlying values, attitudes, behaviour and power relations'. During periods of fundamental and, for some, painful political and economic restructuring, public service reform is likely to be 'ad hoc, fragmented and un-coordinated as the consolidation of power and prestige takes precedence' (Bardill, 2000: 115).

11

Economic Reform and Poverty Alleviation

Introduction

It was noted in Chapter 1 that 'good governance' is sometimes taken to mean 'good government' plus 'public policy'. We have seen that it is not easy to obtain agreement on what 'good' government entails. With public policy, however, a consensus has emerged among donors that economic liberalism is required, replacing state-led development by free markets, private ownership, and international competition. In other words, development is now seen to demand capitalism (Cammack, 2002). When such economic restructuring has severe consequences for the poor, the role of the state is to give capitalism a 'human face' by 'empowering' the poor in both markets and politics.

National economic planning

After constitutional independence in most developing countries, the preferred route to economic and social development was centralized state planning. This was encouraged by a range of factors (Turner and Hulme, 1997): the USSR model for regimes of a Marxist persuasion; the success of state planning in the UK and USA during the Second World War; and theories of economic development which gave a leading role to the state (to redress market failures and to allocate resources to public goods). In addition, access to international finance usually depended on having a national plan in place.

Political legitimacy and national unity were also sought through plans for economic growth. New elites had confidence in the state as the main driver of economic and social development. There were shortages of capital and skills in the private sector, and political demands for state control of foreign owned businesses were often strong. Public ownership through state-owned enterprises (SOEs) was an important part of this mode of planning, having its origins in colonial forms of infrastructure investment (for example, railways) and control of exports (for example, marketing boards). It was also believed that without state intervention the quantity or quality of the goods available through the market would be inadequate.

Such ideological positions were bolstered by the conviction that incomes should be redistributed (perhaps so that vulnerable groups could acquire the necessities of life), that the state should control the 'commanding heights' of the economy so that the whole economy (and therefore society) is not at the mercy of a small minority of corporate property-holders, that state ownership is preferable to foreign ownership, and that private property owners should not be allowed to exploit natural monopolies. Furthermore, in less developed countries the private sector was often too underdeveloped to raise investment capital.

New policy directions

Eventually it became clear that such centralized planning was failing. Plans were over-optimistic about the speed of development, the availability of resources, and governmental capacity to manage the economy. Too often plans had to rely on poor data, and analytical models did not reflect economic complexities. Poor communication between planning units and line ministries with weak administrative capacities provided further impediments. National plans were found to be unable to deal with unanticipated crises (especially the oil price rises of 1973–4 and 1979), and short-term political objectives led to frequent deviations from plan priorities and implementation, especially in African states (Tangri, 1995).

As the so-called 'third development decade', the 1980s were years of reappraisal in development thinking. The dominant ideology, neo-classical economics, began to have a major impact on development policy. The state and national development planning were rejected as economically inefficient. In their place the free market was embraced through deregulation, privatization and budget cuts. These perceptions of development came together in the belief that the poor need economic opportunities and new institutions through which they can participate in growth, rather than be incorporated into national plans designed by modernizing elites (Esman, 1988). Consequently the 1980s proved extremely receptive to a 'counter-revolution' in development thinking.

The argument of the counter-revolution was that the centralized state planning favoured by many newly independent governments and their Western advisers in the 1950s and 60s failed because it discouraged self-reliance and experimentation, impeded the movement of resources to where they would be most productive, and inhibited the establishment of new enterprises and the expansion of efficient productive capacity. Standardized decisions under central planning could not adjust to changes in conditions of either supply or demand. In its fundamentals, the counter-revolution was directed against an overextended public sector, an overemphasis on physical capital formation to the neglect of human resources, and a proliferation of distorting economic controls aimed at social equality to the detriment of economic efficiency (Toye, 1987).

Ideology combined with economic forces to produce a fundamental shift in development policy and practice. The recession in the world economy during the early 1980s led to reductions in the levels of both official aid and private investment in less-developed countries. Adverse terms of trade resulting from a loss of competitiveness combined with this to produce a crisis of investment. Foreign exchange shortages and domestic budget deficits resulted from domestic policies that increased demand too rapidly relative to the productive potential of the economy, causing distortions in relative prices. In Central and Eastern Europe, with ex-communists still in positions of power and the political fortunes of the Left revived by hardships caused by other reforms, it was necessary 'to secure the irreversibility of the reform process'. The new political leadership also had to create an entrepreneurial class committed to a market economy, and manage conflicts between the industrial working class and managers of SOEs (hard-hit by inflation and unemployment), the peasantry, and small businesses (Estrin, 1994). In the former communist states privatization was also an attempt to restore confiscated property to original owners or their descendants.

Lower demand and prices for primary products, with a consequent loss of foreign exchange earnings and increased borrowing to pay for imports, was a further problem. Increased interest rates in the early 1980s left some countries unable to service debts. Structural adjustment programmes (SAPs) made IMF and World Bank financial help available to poor countries suffering from protectionism in the West, the sharp increase in oil prices in 1973 and 1979, and difficulties in raising loans for investment, industrial inputs, oil and food.

Structural adjustment meant that development assistance would be available only if certain conditions were met in the recipient country, typically trade liberalization, the reduction or abolition of market distortions (such as subsidies on production and consumption and interest rate ceilings), the reorganization of para-statals, reform of the food distribution system, the direction of public investment towards exports and import-substitution, and privatization (Sarris, 1987). The International Monetary Fund specified reductions in government expenditure; increases in taxation, interest rates and producer prices; policies to raise investment levels; trade liberalization; and wage restraint (Khan and Knight, 1986).

Structural adjustment also usually included budget 'rationalisation' (usually meaning the allocation of resources to the so-called 'productive' sectors of the economy and away from 'unproductive' social services), and reductions in the size of the public sector generally (while targeting those in need). Cuts in the public sector were required, even though there is less scope for these than in developed countries. (Governments in less-developed countries already spend less per capita; absolute spending on social services is very low; and budget cuts can mean the collapse of social provision, especially in health and education). As recently as 2004 the IMF's insistence on a budget ceiling meant over 8000 qualified teachers were left unemployed in Zambia, because the IMF claimed that an 'excessive' pay agreement carried the threat of inflation.

Governments were further expected to raise revenues by fees and charges for public services; correct price distortions by devaluation (to improve balance of payments); and raise interest rates (to weed out bad investments). They were urged to create a climate for investment and private enterprise by 'deregulation' (that is, removing barriers to the free operation of market forces), and control inflation to ensure macroeconomic stability. Third World governments accepted, more or less willingly, depending on the ideology of their current leadership, the conditions that increasingly throughout the 1980s and 1990s were the price that poor countries had to pay in order to obtain multilateral and sometimes bilateral assistance with their balance of payments problems, foreign exchange crises and international indebtedness.

Economic policy thus had to be oriented towards marketization. Governments were expected to 'roll back' the state in favour of the private sector, limiting it to public goods (such as defence), merit goods (for example, education), infrastructure, economic information, and scientific and technological research. Government regulations were to be reformed in order to control private monopolies created by privatization, protect consumers, workers, the environment (vulnerable to cost-cutting production methods), and society (against the undesirable distributive effects of privatization and deregulation), and foster competition and innovation to make markets work more effectively.

A central part of structural adjustment involved public enterprise reform and/or privatization. During the 1980s state ownership of productive enterprises came under strong attack as the advocates of the free market, private property and free enterprise came to dominate key positions in international development agencies, the governments of some bilateral donors, and some Third World governments. State-owned enterprises were criticized as economically inefficient in production, as incurring unnecessarily high costs, as lacking innovation, as delaying deliveries, as suffering from political 'interference' in the management of production and distribution, and as employing poorly motivated managers, undisciplined by the profit motive. State-owned enterprises were also claimed to be unaccountable through the political system and bureaucratically inflated, contributing to budget deficits, industrial conflict, and political unrest over corruption and the abuse of patronage. Management failures (to produce profits, job satisfaction, corporate direction, technological development or service to the community) were seen as a consequence of structural and financial constraints imposed by governments. Public enterprises often formed an integral part of the patron–client relationships that characterize many Third World political systems.

A large number of countries subsequently engaged in privatization programmes, though often on a fairly limited scale. Different forms of privatization have been adopted. Divestiture by selling to the private sector has sometimes been accompanied by 'liberalization' so that competition and market forces affect the behaviour of all enterprises. Enterprises have been leased to the private sector or have entered into management contracts to strengthen unsuccessful corporations.

Between 1980 and 1994 over three and a half thousand privatizations took place in less developed countries, with transactions valued at US$30 billion in 1992. These were mainly concentrated in Latin America and East Asia. Between 1988 and 1996 the proportion of state-owned enterprises privatized ranged from 83 per cent in the Philippines to 1 per cent in Tunisia. Even when governments were committed to privatization, large enterprises remained in public ownership (for example in Hungary and Poland). Privatization has been concentrated in a small number of middle-income and former communist states: 'what remains under state ownership in many countries is substantial enough to frustrate ardent supporters of privatization such as the World Bank' (Ramamurti, 1999: 142).

Consequences of economic liberalism

It seemed, then, as if the state was in the process of withering away, to be replaced by a system in which ownership for the purposes of production is left in the hands of the private capitalist firm, and the market is left to play the dominant role in the allocation of resources and the supply of goods. However, reviews of progress showed that the achievements of the 'development revolution' in the less developed countries were disappointing.

The deregulation of markets revealed how far markets are not simple but complex relationships between producers or sellers and buyers or consumers, varying in terms of their information and power. Deregulation has frequently increased inequality, leading to political crises, and market-led growth has not necessarily 'trickled down' to the poor. Market transactions caused new vulnerabilities by undermining existing patterns of security (based on kinship, traditional dependencies and obligations, or mutual aid) and threatening entitlements (through price rises, lower wages or loss of employment). Food security for the poor worsened. The impact of natural events has been reinforced (for example, when floods cause job losses *and* increases in food prices). A reduced role for non-market institutions and public provision in health care, social assistance, education and training, has meant that society's security has been reduced and early gains in poverty reduction lost. Targeting public expenditure on the poor and vulnerable (such as children under five, nursing mothers, or pregnant women) proved administratively expensive, and prone to corruption and 'capture' by those not legally entitled to the benefits.

Too often reformers have misunderstood the operation of markets in poor countries. Economies cannot always provide the skills, investments, and infrastructure to replace state trading institutions such as marketing boards. Some participants in the market have less access to information, credit, and transportation than others. And state intervention remained necessary to target food subsidies at most vulnerable groups, stabilize food prices, and regulate trading (for example, the provision of market sites, the maintenance of traders' safety, the enforcement of quality standards, the standardization of contracts, and the provision of information about prices and supplies).

Consequently, structural adjustment has often been damaging for the poor, being associated with a slowing down in the decline in infant mortality, increases in malnutrition and disease among children, and declining school enrolments. Charges and indirect taxes hit the poor hardest. The poor have experienced declining incomes from employment and a deterioration of their material conditions. The phasing out of subsidies (for example for utilities) and the introduction of fees (for example for health care, education, piped water, and electricity) hurt poor families most. Increased prices caused great hardship, as in Niger where hunger for the poor is the result of free markets in which the price of grain has increased as it has been exported to wealthier countries. In China, the cost of health care is such that a growing number of poor people are unable to afford hospital treatment, rising from 10 per cent of patients in small towns in 1993 to 42 per cent in 1998. Health care has become both less equitable and less efficient. Women are forced to add more paid work to domestic chores (to compensate for less state assistance and more expensive food), leading to deteriorations in health, child care, and school attendances, especially by girls. When Uganda removed fees in 2001, visits to health facilities rose by 80 per cent, with the poorest 20 per cent of the population benefiting most.

The poor are often unable to afford services which are not fully funded by tax revenues and demand payment from the user at the point of delivery. The burden of service charges falls more heavily on the poor than the well-off, partly because a higher proportion of the poor's income is taken in charges, and partly because the lack of availability to the poor forces them to take a more expensive alternative (for example, from water-sellers) while the rich receive public provision (from public utilities). For example, in parts of India the poor pay up to 30 times more for water than middle- and upper-income households. Charges for public services (such as education) and community financing were found not only to reduce service use, but also to shift the burden of financing provision from the state and general taxation to communities that were already in need.

The poor have also been adversely affected by the increased costs faced by small farmers (for water, fertilizer, pesticides and seeds). The small transactions of poor people become less profitable and significant to other participants in markets (such as banks). Financial reforms have tightened credit restrictions, closed rural banks, and reduced the availability of credit.

Privatization has also benefited the rich at the expense of the poor. It concentrates wealth in fewer hands unless action is taken to reform the prevailing income distribution (and it is not easy to see why those with the political power and will to privatize should want to redistribute). Since the income benefits of privatization will be to bond-holders, not taxpayers, and since taxpayers will belong on average to a lower income bracket than bond-holders, privatization is regressive (unless offset by relief from the tax burden of unprofitable or inefficient public enterprises). If, as frequently happens, public assets are sold off at below market value, the taxpayer loses exchequer income, again leading to inequity.

Income disparities are highly likely to be intensified by share ownership because even if shares are spread (as in the Czech voucher system), large numbers will hold shares but their shares will not account for a large proportion of share ownership (Estrin, 1994). Free or concessionary shares to privatized workers or pensioners will not necessarily lead to distributional equity. The more monopolistic the privatized firm, the less distributional equity will be achieved. And distributional benefits are lost if privatization means that the distributional objectives of public enterprises are dropped. The loss of government revenues from state marketing has also led to higher inflation and fewer public services – of particular significance for the poor.

Some private companies (for example, supplying water) have been accused of profiteering, corruption, excessive secrecy, and ignoring obligations to serve poor neighbourhoods. Governments are increasingly reluctant to meet the companies' demands for protection against risk and for profit guarantees. Alternatives are being sought which are more likely to deliver services such as clean water and effective sanitation to poor communities.

Other economic and political benefits of economic liberalization failed to materialize. Real growth of GDP averaged 4.3 per cent from 1980 to 1989, slowing to 3.3 per cent in the latter year. Debt continued to be a major obstacle to growth. Changes in interest rates and the terms of trade reduced real incomes. On average interest rates in the 1980s were more than double what they had been in the 1960s, and nearly six times higher than in the late 1970s when developing countries borrowed heavily. Inflation in the severely indebted middle-income countries exceeded 100 per cent between 1980 and 1987, compared with 8 per cent in South Asia and 5 per cent in East Asia. During the early 1980s growth in developing countries' exports fell as world growth slowed and industrial countries' imports declined, though after 1983 exports from developing countries began to expand again. But prices for many primary commodities fell during the decade to their lowest levels since the Second World War, hitting many of the poorest developing countries hardest (World Bank, 1990).

Investment in key social sectors was inadequate. $1 per capita on public health was spent on average in poor countries, when $4 was needed. Millions of primary school children were not enrolled in school (including a disproportionate number of girls). Health spending was concentrated in urban areas and on facilities used by the middle classes. Education expenditure was biased towards higher education and not basic schooling. And a disproportionate percentage of education expenditure went to the education of boys.

Experience of trade liberalization has exposed some of the fallacies in arguments underpinning policies to open up economies to competition by reducing trade barriers. Free trade is supposed to boost productivity and per capita incomes. However, trade barriers are not necessarily an impediment to growth, if the right domestic policies are in place, as the examples of Taiwan and South Korea show. Mexico has achieved a growth rate of about 1 per cent per year since joining the North American Free Trade Agreement, while Vietnam's economy has grown by 5 per cent annually during some twenty years of trade restrictions. This suggests that premature free trade for countries with industries that are trying to compete from a position of weakness could lead to large parts of the manufacturing sector being destroyed, as happened in Senegal. Protection for 'infant industries' has been used very successfully in the past, calling into question the neo-liberal orthodoxy and going some way to explain the difficulties experienced by the World Trade Organization when trying to broker trade liberalization (Chang, 2005).

The greatest failure was in relation to poverty. Despite economic growth and improvements in incomes, consumption, life expectancy, educational attainment and infant mortality, over a billion people, or roughly a third of the population of the developing world, remained in poverty – defined as those struggling to survive on less than US $370 a year. Of these, 630 million were extremely poor, with annual consumption valued at less than US $275. During the 1980s – the 'lost decade' for the poor – the incidence of poverty in Latin America and sub-Saharan Africa actually increased. Incomes fell in absolute terms in many developing countries. The living standards of millions in Latin America and sub-Saharan Africa were lower than they had been in the early 1970s. The picture in South Asia, with nearly half the developing world's poor, including almost half of those living in extreme poverty, was equally bleak.

The indicators of well-being that showed rising trends still fell below satisfactory levels: 50 years for life expectancy in sub-Saharan Africa; infant mortality in South Asia at over 170 deaths per thousand; more than 110 million children in the developing world without access to primary education. In the least-developed countries about a third of the population would not survive to 40 years of age. Growth in consumption had not accelerated fast enough in many countries, and in sub-Saharan Africa consumption per head declined by 2.1 per cent a year between 1980 and 1997, and rose by less than 1 per cent in Latin America, the Middle East and North Africa (UNDP, 2000b).

A further consequence of economic liberalization was growing inequality. The trend through the 1980s and 1990s was towards greater inequality in all regions of the world, regardless of economic growth rates, though income inequality varies greatly from region to region. The Gini coefficient compares the shares of national wealth captured by the poorest section of society, so that the higher the coefficient, the lower the share of national income going to the poorest people, a value of 0 representing perfect equality, and one of 100 perfect inequality; South Asia has a Gini coefficient of 33.4 compared with sub-Saharan Africa's of 72.2 (UNDP, 2005: 55).

Such large-scale inequality is objectionable on both moral and economic grounds. Inequality means injustice by condemning the poor and victims of discrimination to shorter lives, worse health, less education, lower social status, fewer life chances and less political influence than wealthier members of society. Inequality limits or removes opportunities. In particular, inequality of educational opportunity is strongly correlated with low levels of income, health and political influence.

The harmful economic effects of inequality include losses in productivity and investment by limiting the poor's ability to borrow and invest. Political inequality impedes the emergence of institutions conducive to economic growth, such as property rights, economic infrastructure, and financial institutions. For official development planners to claim that equity, defined as equality of opportunity and avoidance of absolute deprivation, 'is of immense importance for development, both on intrinsic grounds and as the result of a hard-headed analysis of the development process' (Ferreira and Walton, 2005: 37) is a significant development in aid policy.

Hence the importance of redistributing income from the richest to the poorest fifths of the population. This can be done in two ways. First, the transfer of relatively small shares would raise millions above the poverty level: 26 million in Brazil and 12 million in Mexico by a transfer of 5 per cent of the income of the richest 20 per cent, for example. But this would require a much greater tax effort than many governments are prepared to make. The second option is to ensure the poor benefit disproportionately from economic growth, by receiving more from future growth than their present percentage of national income. This would have a major impact on poverty in low- and middle-income countries. It requires public policies to increase the assets of the poor, through education and training, stronger rights to land, and reduced transportation costs. If the income of the poor grew at twice the national rate the number of people in the world living in extreme poverty would fall by a third by 2015 (UNDP, 2005: 67).

Poverty alleviation

A change in approach to international development assistance was brought about by a combination of factors which weakened confidence in structural adjustment policies as the means to economic development. The success of the Asian 'tigers', the failure of adjustment reforms in Africa to prevent living standards, real wages and employment opportunities from declining dramatically, economic crisis in Mexico in 1994 despite the adoption of the World Bank's economic strategy, and a rising chorus of criticism from leading economists, NGOs and campaign groups, forced a revision of aid policy. In 1998 the focus switched to alleviating poverty, defined not in narrow income terms, but as a combination of factors which limit the well-being and capabilities of people: poor nutrition, low health status, restricted educational attainment, vulnerability and powerlessness.

Government action is now called upon to combat poverty and strengthen the access of the poor to public services. It has been rediscovered that poverty can be removed only by different forms of collective action. Countries that ensure people, and especially the poor, have access to health care, education, potable water and sanitation do so through public services. The critical factor in advances in human welfare such as increased literacy, lower infant and maternal mortality rates, and equality of educational opportunity in such countries as Sri Lanka, Costa Rica, Cuba and Botswana has been 'concerted action by governments in organising and providing public services for all' that are free or heavily subsidized for poor people, and funded through progressive taxation (Emmett *et al.*, 2006: 32).

The incidences of countries which have been able to achieve better social conditions than their economic circumstances would suggest possible have enabled analysts to identify the conditions necessary for the formulation of public policies which are effective in achieving success in key areas of human development. The state is of paramount importance. Despite diversity in population size, political regime, culture, dominant religion, level of economic development, and historical legacies in the provision of social services, countries such as Chile, China, Costa Rica, Cuba, Sri Lanka and Vietnam have two features in common which are related to their social progress.

First, at crucial times they have had political leaderships committed to improving people's status in terms of health, education, adult literacy, employment, social security, sanitation, and food security. Such leadership has responded to pressures from civil society or ideological imperatives such as social and economic equality. Policies in these areas have been universalistic, and not targeted solely on the poor.

Second, public provision has been mobilized by the state, either directly through its own public services or via commercial firms and voluntary bodies. This draws attention to the importance not just of well-devised policies but also of administrative resources and capacity to implement them, including professional and technical staff. Social policies need to be supported by public policies for communications so that physical access is available to all (Ghai, 2000: 16).

A 'new poverty agenda' has been adopted by aid agencies (Green, 2002). Policies that promote the productive use of the poor's most abundant asset – labour – supported by basic social services, especially health care, family planning, nutrition and primary education, are now advocated by the donor community. They will have to be *public* policies involving *public* spending. Providing the poor with access to social services requires a firm commitment by governments to the provision of the infrastructure and organization of social services and the way they are financed. These are not the sentiments of radical agitators; they are the advocacy of the IMF, the World Bank and most bilateral donors.

The recipients of aid now have to produce 'comprehensive development frameworks' (CDFs) consisting of public policies to promote good government and human welfare as measured by health status, educational levels, the availability of clean water, sanitation, energy supplies and transportation, cultural preservation and the physical environment. CDFs represent 'a substantially transformed conditionality', no longer focused on economic growth, but on 'the subordination of society's resources to meeting the perceived requirements of the poorest' (Pender, 2001: 409). One IMF concessional loan – the Poverty Reduction and Growth Facility

– is directly and explicitly conditional upon borrowing governments taking steps to reduce poverty.

Governments are also required to write Poverty Reduction Strategy Papers (PRSPs). These are plans drawn up by national governments in consultation with local communities, civil society organizations (trade unions, producer groups, religious bodies, indigenous groups, and research institutes) and aid donors. The papers are expected to show how public policy is to make a contribution to reducing poverty. They describe how participation was organized, diagnose poverty and existing obstacles to its reduction, identify targets and indicators to show how these will be monitored, and specify the policies and related budgets which are designed to meet those targets.

Progress in drawing up PRSPs has been slow. Civil society groups have been hard-pressed to cope with technical economic questions. Some parts of government, notably legislatures and party leaders, have not been sufficiently involved. Some strategies have been based on unrealistic assumptions about economic growth, or have taken no account of vulnerability to external factors such as fluctuations in the balance of payments. Governments also find it difficult to set priorities in the context of budgetary uncertainties, or show how their policies will affect poverty for the better (Ames, *et al.*, 2002). Fewer than a third of developing countries have set targets for reducing poverty. Many governments have no explicit plans for reducing poverty, and those that do are vague about budgets and organization, and are based on monetary measures alone, without explicit targets for other dimensions of poverty, such as nutrition, literacy and life expectancy (UNDP, 2000a).

Pro-poor policy falls into four broad categories of public action: investing in people (mainly through education and health care); protecting the poor's economic assets; protecting the vulnerable (that is, the poor and other groups experiencing deprivation and discrimination); and reforming governance.

Investing in people

Social investment has both direct and indirect effects on poverty. Social expenditure has the direct effect of providing access to services such as health and education which improve the ability of people to obtain higher incomes. It also produces a more equal distribution of incomes, ensuring that economic growth is accompanied by less, rather than more, inequality.

Indirectly social investment helps reduce poverty via its economic consequences. Social security not only contributes to social justice and individual freedom. It also supports economic development by building human capital, securing economic and political stability, and dealing with market failures (and so increasing economic efficiency: Barr, 2004). Social provision, perhaps funded by savings on economic subsidies, contributes to economic growth. Productivity is increased by improvements in levels of education and health. Investments in education, health, water supply and sanitation, as well as roads, ports and energy supplies, are needed if a country is to develop a capacity to manufacture goods for export, a major way in which low-income countries have raised economic growth levels. Growth then has a beneficial effect on income poverty. For every 1 per cent of increase in average per capita income the poverty rate declines by 2 per cent – but only if growth is accompanied by policies which help an economy benefit from integration in global markets. There is a reciprocal relationship here: better health conditions and educational attainment generate economic growth which then provides additional resources to be invested in education and health.

Thus social policies are needed to increase the number of schools and clinics. Public policies are required to produce public goods (such as clean air) and to generate communal as well as individual benefits (such as immunization). Governments will have to expand basic services generally to ensure that the poor have better access to them. Governments also need to focus expenditure more efficiently on services that the private sector will not supply, such as curative health services in regions that the private sector is unlikely to serve.

Investing in people is also taken to include 'investing' in the political power of the poor: 'when poor people have political power protected by civil and political rights, they can be more effective in pressing for policies that create social and economic opportunities' (UNDP, 2003c: 69).

Guaranteeing economic assets

Ensuring that the poor benefit from economic growth requires the adoption of economic policies which enable the poor to participate in, and contribute to, growth. Rural development and urban employment have to be encouraged by sectoral and national economic policies. Increased access to land, credit and public infrastructure will increase the level of participation in growth. Public employment schemes not only create and maintain the infrastructure of roads, irrigation systems, soil conservation and forestry. They also reduce poverty in a cost-effective way by providing employment to those most in need. Improvements to the physical infrastructure, such as roads, are also important in that they remove one of the biggest obstacles standing between the poor and social service facilities such as schools and clinics, especially in rural areas.

The assets of the poor can be increased by the redistribution of land, as well as by increasing human capital. Efficiency and equity are both served again. Increasing the incomes of the poor requires public policies that increase the return to labour through higher productivity, better physical infrastructure, appropriate market incentives, new institutions, and technological innovation. To enable the poor to participate more in free markets, it is advocated that regulations governing taxation, capital requirements, licences, and tendering be simplified for small businesses which are often the major source of employment and services for the poor.

Low-income households also need to be able to participate in financial markets for credit, savings and insurance. Since government-sponsored rural credit schemes have not generally been a success, this requires the provision of micro-finance by savings groups suitable for low-income clients. However, the impact on poverty of micro-finance is hard to assess, and few lessons emerge consistently from the studies that have been made. The poorest households are not necessarily reached, and state subsidies are likely to be required (World Bank, 2001b).

When deregulation is extended to labour markets, it can have disastrous consequences for workers by reducing wages, safety standards, terms and conditions of employment, and job security. Hence support for a policy of adherence to the 'core labour standards' set out in the ILO's Declaration on the Fundamental Principles and Rights at Work, adopted in 1998. However, it is by no means clear how removing restrictions on job creation can be made consistent with the enforcement of protective labour standards, including rights to collective bargaining, the elimination of forced and child labour, and the ending of many types of discrimination. The World Bank has already ruled that minimum-wage legislation is inappropriate in some circumstances, that health and safety legislation would have to respond to market principles, that basic rights for workers should not be enforced by trade sanctions, and that the role of trade unions would have to be limited to providing social services for their members (Cammack, 2002).

Protecting the vulnerable

The World Bank and other agencies have also turned their attention to policies which protect the most vulnerable members of society from the effects of structural adjustment ('adjustment with a human face'), and which are intended to empower poor people, in both markets and politics.

It is accepted that some groups, such as those in remote regions, the old, the disabled and those acutely vulnerable to adversity, will require a comprehensive approach to poverty reduction involving transfers and safety-nets. Assistance (for the unemployed and disabled) and pensions are feasible in many urban areas as the wage and salary-earning population grows. A range of public policies for food pricing and distribution, public employment, and social security are needed to support households and communities in times of insecurity, and to ensure minimum levels of provision for those unable to gain from economic growth.

Policies to provide safety-nets are needed when spending cuts, as part of macroeconomic 'adjustment', harm the poor. Expenditure within the social budget targeted on the poor is liable to be disproportionately reduced, while spending on the non-poor tends to be protected. There is thus a need for targeted expenditure aimed at the poorest groups when public spending is being reined in, either as a public policy objective or because of financial crisis (as in Mexico in 1994–5). Such expenditure may take the form of job creation schemes (used effectively in Argentina and Maharashtra, India), subsidized credit, or food subsidies. However, since such safety-nets entail public spending, the targeting they require could equally form part of public expenditure under 'normal' conditions. Under budgetary constraints safety-nets need to be funded by reduced allocations to other services such as defence (Ravallion, 2002).

Safety-nets of different kinds are especially important during economic crises, to which transitional countries are especially prone. Crises deepen poverty and worsen income inequality by increasing unemployment, lowering wages, raising the cost of food, and reducing expenditure on social services. This is born out by a cross-national analysis of financial crises in developing countries between 1960 and 1998. Cuts in government spending on education, health care and social security are especially associated with falling incomes for the poorest groups. Protecting the poor requires governments to contain inflation and safeguard well-targeted social spending aimed at the most vulnerable groups (for example, an employment programme for young people when households headed by their youngest members experience worsening poverty: Baldacci *et al.*, 2005).

The poor need social and political organizations to obtain information on entitlement to subsidies, rations and vouchers, to ensure governmental regulations are enforced, and to demand increased incomes so that private markets are accessible. Such organizations should help society ensure there is real competition between suppliers so that monopolistic profits are not earned. They would also disseminate information on user charges and the alternative services that can be purchased so that consumers become more rational and discriminating. Efforts to develop stock markets, assist small investors, and spread ownership more widely have also been recommended.

There are clearly formidable problems to overcome if the poor and other disadvantaged groups are to be empowered. A number of strategies are currently advocated by the international development community to overcome the obstacles which the poor encounter when attempting empowerment, and stimulate pro-poor political action and policy-making. Some of these relate to the mobilization of the poor in political associations as part of a pluralistic state, as we saw in Chapter 6.

Improvements in governance

The beneficial effect on economic growth of improvements in education and health care can be undermined by bad governance, especially corruption, so public policy must include the reforms to the system of governance already examined in earlier chapters. A study of 120 developing countries from 1975 to 2000 found that poor governance reduces growth to a level which is 1.6 percentage points lower per year than it would otherwise be. Ratios of investment to GDP are 2 percentage points lower. Reducing corruption also reduces child mortality, increases school enrolment and raises growth of GDP (Baldacci *et al.*, 2005).

Politically, government policies can help the consolidation of democracy. Social policies which protect basic incomes during periods of economic transition help overcome political opposition to reform, and encourage political forces to process their demands and conflicts through democratic institutions. However, progress in human development will not necessarily protect a political system against instability if deep divisions based on ethnicity exist, as the case of Sri Lanka shows.

Nor should it be assumed that governance reforms will automatically benefit the poor. The extent to which they do will depend on whether organizations representing the poor have any influence over the reformed institutions. For example, strengthening a legislature in relation to the executive will not benefit the poor if, as in Pakistan, parliament is dominated by feudalistic landowners. Reducing corruption will be more significant for the middle class if the rural poor have no access to the public services which have been cleaned up. Civil service reform may be of greater benefit to civil servants than the poor. And so on (Grindle, 2004).

Assessment of poverty-reduction efforts

It may be too early to assess the effect of pro-poor development policy as instituted by aid donors, but a number of considerations are needed to inform continuing efforts in this area.

One is that countries emerging from authoritarianism are not just attempting to marketize their economies. They are also trying to consolidate democracy at a time when economic reform is incurring heavy social costs for some sections of society, such as falling consumption and rising unemployment. It follows that the policy-making process through which economic reforms are stipulated must be inclusive of those who inevitably experience deterioration in their material circumstances and so oppose reform. This implies a policy style built on consultation, negotiation, discussion, representation and competition. Opposition groups must be given incentives to participate in democratic politics in the form of social policies funded by progressive taxation. The dilemma for new democracies is how to create such incentives when material conditions are very likely to decline (Pereira *et al.*, 1993: 5).

Then there is the question of what is happening to poverty in different regions of the world. Of the world's population, 1 in 5 (more than 1 billion people) still survive on less than the equivalent of US$1 a day (the definition of extreme income poverty), and another 1.5 billion have less than US$2 per day. While global poverty declined between 1990 and 2005, no progress was made in Latin America and the Middle East. There were 100 million *more* in extreme poverty in Africa in 2001 than there were in 1990. The post-communist states of Eastern and Central Europe and the former USSR saw a dramatic increase in poverty, with the number living on less than US$2 a day rising from 23 million in 1990 to 93 million in 2001 (from 5 per cent of the total population of the region to 20 per cent).

While the total number of people in the world living on less than US $1 a day almost halved between 1981 and 2001, most of this was accounted for by China, and occurred in the early 1980s. When China is excluded, the number of poor people in developing countries actually rose slightly (see Table 11.1). Furthermore, the number surviving on less than $2 a day increased from 2.4 billion to 2.7 billion, with a 'bunching' just above the $1 mark. If trends established during 1981–2001 continue, the MDG for poverty reduction would, according to the World Bank and IMF, be reached globally by 2015, but only because of strong economic growth in the world's most populous countries, China and India, leaving other regions to fall short of the target. For example, in sub-Saharan Africa the

Table 11.1 *Trends in income poverty, 1981–2001 – number and percentage of people living on less than US$1 a day (million) (percentage in brackets)*

Region	1981	1984	1987	1990	1993	1996	1999	2001
East Asia and	795.6	562.2	425.6	472.2	415.4	286.7	281.7	271.3
Pacific	(57.7)	(38.9)	(28.0)	(29.6)	(24.9)	(16.6)	(15.7)	(14.9)
of which China	633.7	425.0	308.4	374.8	334.2	211.6	222.8	211.6
	(63.8)	(41.0)	(28.5)	(33.0)	(28.4)	(17.4)	(17.8)	(16.6)
excluding China	(42.0)	(33.5)	(27.0)	(21.1)	(16.7)	(14.7)	(11.0)	(10.8)
Eastern Europe	3.1	2.4	1.7	2.3	17.5	20.1	30.1	17.0
and Central Asia	(0.7)	(0.5)	(0.4)	(0.5)	(3.7)	(4.3)	(6.3)	(3.6)
Latin America	35.6	46.0	45.1	49.3	52.0	52.2	53.6	49.8
and Caribbean	(9.7)	(11.8)	(10.9)	(11.3)	(11.3)	(10.7)	(10.5)	(9.5)
Middle East and	9.1	7.6	6.9	5.5	4.0	5.5	7.7	7.1
North Africa	(5.1)	(3.8)	(3.2)	(2.3)	(1.6)	(2.0)	(2.6)	(2.4)
South Asia	474.8	460.3	473.3	462.3	476.2	461.3	428.5	431.1
	(51.5)	(46.8)	(45.0)	(41.3)	(40.1)	(36.6)	(32.2)	(31.3)
of which India	382.4	373.5	369.8	357.4	380.0	399.5	352.4	358.6
	(54.4)	(49.8)	(46.2)	(42.1)	(42.3)	(42.2)	(22.9)	(21.0)
excluding India	(42.2)	(37.0)	(41.0)	(38.7)	(33.1)	(19.7)	(22.9)	(21.0)
Sub-Saharan	163.6	198.3	218.6	226.8	242.3	271.4	294.3	312.7
Africa	(41.6)	(46.3)	(46.8)	(44.6)	(44.1)	(45.6)	(45.7)	(46.4)
World	1481.8	1276.8	1171.0	1218.5	1207.5	1097.2	1095.7	1089.0
	(40.4)	(32.8)	(28.4)	(27.9)	(26.3)	(22.8)	(21.8)	(21.1)
excluding China	(31.7)	(29.8)	(28.4)	(26.1)	(25.6)	(24.6)	(23.1)	(22.5)

SOURCE: data from Chen and Ravallion (2004), Tables 3 and 4.

goal of halving poverty is unlikely to be reached before 2147. It should also be remembered that the 390 million who rose above the $1 a day level between 1981 and 2001 are still poor by the standards of rich and even middle-income countries (Chen and Ravaillion, 2004).

Even more disturbing is the fact that, overall, progress has slowed down since the major change in donor policy. Since the mid 1990s one-dollar-a-day poverty has fallen at one-fifth of the rate recorded between 1980 and 1996. This is despite increases in economic growth, as in China. This has serious consequences for the international community's goal of halving world poverty between 1990 and 2015: 'The gap between the MDG target for halving poverty and projected outcomes is equivalent to an additional 380 million people in developing countries living on less than $1 a day by 2015' (UNDP, 2005: 18).

One of the problems here is that jobless growth can occur, as is currently being experienced in East Asia. When growth is obtained by a shift in manufacturing from low-tech, labour-intensive industries, such as garments, to high-tech and capital-intensive production, such as electronics, levels of unemployment can increase dramatically, especially among the young and women. Income inequality also worsens, even when overall poverty is reduced.

On present trends, most developing countries are unlikely to achieve most of the Millennium Development Goals. No region is likely to reduce child mortality by two-thirds, and few countries are likely to reach other human development targets, especially those for maternal mortality, HIV/AIDS and access to clean water and sanitation. (Broughton and Quereshi, 2004). In sub-Saharan Africa the 2015 goals for education and child mortality will not be reached until 2129 and 2165 respectively. The number of chronically undernourished people in the world has actually increased since 1996 by 25 million to 850 million in 2006, owing largely to trade liberalization, industrialized agriculture, genetic engineering and spending on the military. Clean water and good sanitation would contribute hugely to improvements in health and thereby to human and economic development. But UNDP has found that 1.1 billion people do not have safe water, and 2.6 billion suffer from inadequate sewerage. Half the population in developing countries is at any one time suffering from diseases caused by bad water and sanitation, and 5000 children are estimated to die every day because they drink dirty water. This is despite some of the poorest people in the world paying more for water than people in the UK or USA (UNDP, 2006).

These facts point to the importance of recognizing that not all policies are equally effective, suggesting that a wide range of anti-poverty policies is preferable to a concentration on one or two, especially if the chronic poverty associated with old age, illness, discrimination and remote rural settlements is to be dealt with effectively. It is also important to maintain a broader definition of poverty than one based on income if policies are to be devised which address deprivation in its different forms – education, health, security, political freedom and so on (Mosley and Booth, 2003).

The administrative context which would help a government to formulate pro-poor policies is still too often weak. An IMF review of loan recipients under its Poverty Reduction and Growth Facility, a scheme which covered over 40 countries in 2002 and made US$2 billion in concessionary loans available, found that a growing proportion of government budgets were being devoted to pro-poor services, especially primary education and basic health care. Improvements in the management of public expenditure (a condition of IMF assistance), such as anti-corruption measures, stronger audit, and curbs on excess spending), were also observed. However, much remains to be done to improve economic policy analysis, tax administration and public awareness of the relationship between IMF loans and poverty reduction.

Finally, it has to be acknowledged that commitment to poverty reduction has not been strong in most transitional regimes, either because governments have represented the wealthy or because they have been more concerned to pillage resources for their own private ends than to address poverty seriously. This is why a country like Equatorial Guinea, Africa's third-largest oil producer with US $3 billion a year in oil revenues, has statistically the second highest per capita income in the world (£26,000), while in practice the majority of the population live on less than a dollar a day.

However, the election of leftist governments in a few countries such as Venezuela, Bolivia, Brazil and Nicaragua has led to an expansion of pro-poor political action. In Venezuela 41 per cent of total expenditure (£9.4 billion) has been earmarked for social programmes in the 2006 budget, including housing, social security and education, making it the biggest and most comprehensive social budget in Latin America, according to UNICEF and the Inter-American Development Bank. Bolivia's Movement Towards Socialism government redistributed illegally owned land to the poor under legislation passed in 2006. In Brazil, public spending on social programmes has reduced income inequality, especially through policies for child allowances, rural pensions (which have brought the incidence of poverty among the elderly down to below the average for the population as a whole) and primary education, and despite regressive policies such as public funding for private hospitals (OECD, 2005). In Nicaragua the Sandanista president elected in 2006 has promised renewal of the effort to pull the country out of poverty.

Experience in parts of India, as well as Latin America, suggests strongly that the opportunity to elect pro-poor parties to office makes a significant difference to the strength of public policies designed to alleviate poverty, especially if the parties are unified rather than fragmented, and with a coherent ideology and programme (Moore and Putzel, 1999: 9–11).

Interventions to reduce levels of poverty and inequality need to be backed up by a new discourse on poverty and stronger legal protection of political and civil rights. Such a discourse is rarely initiated or endorsed by the state in transitional countries. Generally the preference is for a more populist rhetoric, which may refer to poverty alleviation as a policy objective but without encouraging reinterpretations of poverty's causes.

Protection of the legal rights of poor people should be more effective now that 121 of the world's 192 governments are electoral democracies. However, some of these still have poor human rights records. Over 35 per cent of the world's population (2.17 billion people) live in 48 countries classified as 'not free', where 'basic political rights are absent and civil liberties are widely and systematically denied'. Another 24 per cent (1.46 billion) live in 59 'partly free' countries, where there is 'limited respect for political rights and civil liberties' and where the rule of law is weak (Freedom House, 2002). The vast majority of countries lacking full freedoms and the rule of law are in the Third World. This draws attention to the difficulties to be faced when putting forward empowerment as a poverty-reducing strategy.

Conclusion

There has been a considerable shift in the approach taken to good policy by the major international actors involved in designing public policies for development – basically from an almost exclusive concern with reducing the role of the state in favour of the free market, to recognizing the importance of the state particularly in the campaign against poverty.

Centralized development planning by the state was favoured in most post-independence developing countries. Eventually it became clear such centralized planning was failing. Economic liberalization became a condition of further development assistance from the international aid community. Following recognition of the adverse effects of some of these measures on low-income groups, 'good policy' now refers to investment in people (mainly through education and health care), and protection of the vulnerable (especially the poor) through governmental interventions. The World Bank and other agencies have turned their attention to policies which protect the most vulnerable members of society from the effects of structural adjustment ('adjustment with a human face'), are intended to empower poor people in both markets and politics, and provide safety-nets. The consensus is that governments need to focus public expenditure more efficiently on services that the private sector will not supply.

Reducing state economic subsidies is intended to release funds for social services such as education, or reduce the price of services to the public. It is recognized that social expenditure contributes to economic growth by improving educational and health levels and thus productivity; and by producing a more equal distribution of income. Social policies to protect basic incomes during periods of economic transition also help overcome political opposition to reform, and encourage political forces to process their demands and conflicts through democratic institutions. Investment in people, through expenditure on health and education, is regarded as a priority of 'good governance'. Investment in health, especially through the provision of clean water, sanitation, and education, is particularly beneficial for the poor.

12
Conclusion

Political conditionalities and support for good governance have attracted scepticism from some quarters, leading people to question whether political reform is something that can be, or even should be, induced by external pressures. Others have tried to identify the conditions that need to be present before support for good governance is likely to be effective.

This chapter first examines the origins of this scepticism: in doubts about the relationship between democracy and development presumed by advocates of good governance; the ease with which demands for good governance are relaxed as soon as the economic or political interests of donors are at stake; and the appearance of cultural imperialism found by some in the attempts to export what are claimed to be essentially Western political concepts, institutions and modes of political behaviour. Following this a more positive and supportive critique is examined, deriving from assessments of the effectiveness of aid for governance reform which have generated advice on how to improve the delivery of financial and technical assistance designed to bring about political change.

Democracy and development

In many respects 'good governance' is just another way of describing liberal democracy, with its normative and positive prescriptions about political rights, the rule of law, accountability and state capacity. The assumption of the intergovernmental donor community is that this type of democracy will give a boost to development, both human and economic. Critics of this interpretation of the relationship between democracy and development point to the number of countries in which impressive economic growth and, more rarely, social development have been achieved under regimes more noted for their authoritarianism than their democratic credentials: Brazil, Indonesia, Thailand and the original 'Asian Tigers' – Singapore, South Korea and Taiwan (Leftwich, 1993). Democracy may even impede economic growth by empowering groups with a vested interest in redistribution and consumption rather than accumulation and investment.

However, while some authoritarian regimes have achieved remarkable economic progress, many other have been disastrous, especially in Africa. Conversely, democracy has not prevented India from achieving, albeit belatedly, remarkable rates of economic growth – 8.2 per cent in 2003, making it the second-fastest-growing economy after China. Furthermore, the view that authoritarianism helped some new states to achieve economic success, particularly in Asia, has been somewhat undermined by the crisis of 1997–8 which was not averted by strict labour laws, controlled elections, restrictions on the political opposition (in Indonesia), dictatorship (in Burma), restrictions on freedom of speech (Singapore), state control of the media (Malaysia), and other restrictions on human rights (Thompson, 2001).

More significantly, the conditions required for economic success – high levels of domestic savings, profitable small and medium-sized enterprises, investment in physical capital, the effective use of technology and labour, and a developmental state – are not put at risk by democracy. The grounds for believing that curtailing democracy is a cost worth bearing for the sake of economic benefits are in fact quite shaky.

First, the well-off do not necessarily have less of a propensity to consume than the poor, engaging as they do in non-productive consumption or capital flight to tax havens. On the other hand, consumption by the poor is an investment in human capital. Consequently it is false to believe that the economic and political rights which under good governance shift resources to the poor will inevitably reduce savings, investment, capital accumulation and, therefore, economic growth.

Second, population pressure, a threat to economic growth, can be reduced by meeting basic needs and providing women with roles outside the home, both of which lower incentives to have large families. Third, since autocrats cause economic distortions by manipulating the economy to obtain political support, there are no grounds for believing that political rights must be curbed to eliminate the economic distortions associated with regular, free elections.

The allocation of public resources, under pressure from political interests exercising their rights, actually produces outcomes close to the social optimum. The argument that the exercise of political rights within democracies diverts resources from their most productive use – the 'pork barrel' effect – is also false. The exercise of democratic rights does not jeopardize economic objectives but is supportive of them, since the democratic process reveals where remedial action is needed and applies pressure on governments to respond.

It is sometimes argued further that union agitation can harm economic growth, thus justifying withholding the right to freedom of association. However, improving pay and conditions for workers is a better long-term solution than curtailing rights. Furthermore, the uncertainties facing people under authoritarian regimes are likely to be more damaging to the economy than the costs of crime which are frequently used to justify suspending civil liberties and human rights.

Finally, since autocracies are rarely more stable in terms of public policy than democracies, there are no grounds for fearing that foreign investment will be deterred by the potential instability of regimes based on the exercise of political rights, especially when authoritarianism is supported by anti-Western rhetoric, as in Malaysia on occasions. In all, 'there is little reason to suppose that repressive regimes lead to more rapid growth or stronger economies more generally', especially if, in addition to discounting the costs of democracy, one factors in the costs of repression (Goodin, 1979; Sen, 1999; Thompson, 2001).

Democracy is also more likely to protect property rights and stimulate educational development, other prerequisites of economic growth. This is because democracy presupposes the rule of law, an independent judiciary, effective courts, freedom under the law, and the transfer of power between political leaders according to the law. Consequently, 'long-lasting democracies generally provide better property and contract rights than either transient democracies or autocracies' (Clague *et al.*, 1996: 271). Support from the international community to sustain and consolidate democracy in transitional polities should thus contribute to both the strengthening of the rule of law and economic progress.

There is also evidence that democracies are better at achieving social development than autocracies. Statistical correlations between democracy and human development for 19 Latin American states between 1970 and 2002 show that 'democracies contribute greatly to human development' (Acuna-Alfaro, 2005). Democracy in low-income countries has done better than authoritarianism in improving life expectancy, literacy, the availability of clean water, and infant mortality – and without creating larger fiscal deficits. Democracies are no less stable, do better at managing conflict in ethnically plural societies, and are less likely to experience humanitarian crises. They are more peaceful in their international relations, and harbour extremists less: 'terrorist networks ... are virtually all based in politically closed societies' (Halperin *et al.*, 2004: 12).

The success cases in Asia and elsewhere show that if any state is to achieve economic and social development it must take a 'developmental' form which fosters with appropriate public policies the expansion of manufacturing for export, develops legal institutions to resolve disputes over property rights and contracts, makes government accountable, and creates a professional bureaucracy. Particularly important is a unified and competent bureaucracy, based on merit recruitment and offering stable and rewarding careers relatively free from political interference by sectional interests. In developmental states bureaucratic cultures have been oriented towards development rather than embourgeoisement from corruption, fraud and nepotism, as in so many Third World countries (Halperin *et al.*, 2004).

Political and bureaucratic elites in developmental states have been able to impose nationalistic aims on civil society by improving living standards, reducing inequality and raising levels of educational achievement and health. The developmental state orchestrates the activities of economic bodies, offering sources of capital and other inducements in return for cooperation in the implementation of economic policies. To do this it has to 'transcend' the interests of classes and other social forces when necessary (Evans, 1995; Leftwich, 2000).

Some cross-national analysis has admittedly found it difficult to establish a clear relationship between type of regime and economic performance. But if it is the case that 'while some democratic states perform well, others perform badly, and exactly the same applies to authoritarian states' (Minogue, 2002: 127) then development is no less likely under democracy than dictatorship. So a society might as well enjoy the political rights and freedoms that democracy brings, while putting in place the policies and institutions required for economic progress. After all, democracy is an important component of *human* development, and a precondition for others, such as the spread of education. So the international community is right to promote democracy since it can be made to serve all forms of development, including economic.

The enforcement of conditionality

Unfortunately, the credibility of the quest for good governance is periodically undermined when Western governments choose to ignore violations in recipient states in order to pursue their own diplomatic or economic objectives (Stokke, 1995). Recipient states are important actors in other international relationships which may inhibit donors in their efforts to secure democratization. For example, Russia's lack of democratic credentials is regularly overlooked by Western powers seeking economic opportunities and diplomatic support. In 2003 the British government allowed the sale of arms and security equipment to countries which it had itself accused of human rights abuses, including Indonesia, Nepal and Saudi Arabia. Imports from Burma to the UK more than tripled between 1997 and 2003, despite the imposition of other sanctions in response to human rights violations.

In 2005 the Organization for Security and Co-operation in Europe found serious violations by the government of the electoral process in Azerbaijan's parliamentary elections. The West's response was muted because of the billions of dollars of investment by Western companies in oil pipelines. Similarly in Uzbekistan, where opposition parties cannot take part in elections, the media is shackled, peaceful protest is met with armed repression, and torture is rife, the USA gave over US $500 million in aid in 2002. It has economic and strategic interests in pipelines bringing oil and gas from central Asia to the Arabian Sea. Aid to Palestine has also had more to do with securing the foreign policy objectives of the West than with punishing bad governance by the Palestinian Authority.

Elsewhere the growth of international terrorism has altered priorities. Thus after 11 September 2001 the USA promised Pakistan US $1 billion in debt rescheduling, and the EU made trade concessions worth £950 million, despite the existence of a military regime, corruption, 25 per cent of its budget going to the military compared with 4 per cent on primary education, and a bad record of poverty reduction. Western powers needed Pakistan's support in the war against terrorism. In 2005 the United States ended its military embargo against Indonesia as a reward for that country's support in pursuing Islamic militants, despite the Indonesian military's corruption and lack of accountability, and undermining, according to the East Timor and Indonesian Action Network, democratic reform efforts. Consequently, aid has not ceased to flow to authoritarian regimes.

There are other reasons why aid patterns often do not match aid rhetoric. A study of British aid to Africa (Cumming, 1996) found that 'political conditionality' was more an excuse to cut the aid budget than a way of promoting serious reform of governance. Donors have not always treated like cases of bad governance alike. Nor have sanctions necessarily varied according to level of human rights violations or authoritarianism, as illustrated most graphically by the weak responses to human rights violations in China, especially in 1989, or the military dictatorship in Nigeria in 1993.

Conversely, aid has rarely been used specifically to reward countries with good governance. Because American aid has always been closely linked to security concerns and economic interests, democratic and democratizing states have not received a greater share (Hook, 1998). Bilateral aid has been given more readily to political allies and former colonies than to states selected for their democratic credentials. In the 1990s non-democratic former colonies attracted twice as much aid as democracies that were not former colonies.

Suspending or terminating aid rarely produces changes in the way countries are governed. A study of aid sanctions deployed by the EU, Sweden, the UK and the USA in the 1990s in response to human rights violations, corruption, or lack of progress in democratization, found that in the majority of cases (62 per cent) sanctions failed to secure the desired political changes (Crawford, 1997). Consequently, doubts have been expressed about whether 'conditionality' in the political realm can be made to work, unless there is joint action by donors (Robinson, 1993). For example, confrontation by concerted action on the part of aid donors was effective in bringing about reforms in Kenya in 1991 when all major donors, including the World Bank, agreed to suspend some aid until a multi-party system, reduced corruption, and economic reforms had been put in place. However, even here the level of Kenya's dependence on aid, and the potential for social unrest following any withdrawal, also played a part (Stokke, 1995). And from 1992 to 1997 donors endorsed bad governance by suppressing evidence of electoral fraud and undermining efforts to strengthen democracy further. Political order was preferred to reforms so that the economic changes sponsored by Western donors could proceed (Brown, 2001).

Unfortunately, unity of purpose on the part of donors is not easy to arrange. Donors have been reluctant to unite in confronting recalcitrant regimes. There are constraints on coordinated international support for democratization. Rivalries or ideological differences between the countries taking the lead can be inhibiting. Or donor governments may fear that disorder will be provoked (such as ethnic or religious conflict, criminality, or a refugee crisis: Whitehead, 1996).

For aid sanctions to be effective, particular strategies need to be used: directing sanctions at specific abuses such as corruption, with aid to be resumed only when the problem has been dealt with; tipping the balance of power towards those supporting reform; producing the political will within the donor government to enforce sanctions rigorously; and coordinating donor sanctions (Crawford, 1997). The problem is that applying such strategies is complicated by the time taken to achieve the results required from different reforms.

Local circumstances contribute to the outcome of sanctions, such as the relevance of aid to current crises, the level of need for aid as perceived by the recipient government, or the severity of need as perceived by donors. A cross-national study of debt relief (a form of aid) which examined whether good governance was rewarded with debt 'forgiveness' found that the major determinant of whether creditors reduced the level of debt owing to them by poor countries was the need for debt relief. Some governance indicators had a small effect on the allocation of debt relief – respect for political rights and civil liberties, public participation in the choice of policy-makers, the independence of the media, and the accountability of the government – but others had no influence, including the rule of law, corruption and administrative capacity. Overall, 'in the past debt forgiveness has not been used much to reward countries with good governance' (Neumayer, 2002: 930).

New imperialism

The West's good governance agenda is seen by critics in transitional states as partly protecting Western interests and partly exporting Western concepts of government to other cultures. It can be presented as a new kind of imperialism. For example, the Indonesian government portrayed the suspension of aid by some bilateral donors such as Denmark and the Netherlands, following the army's massacre of over 90 unarmed demonstrators in East Timor in 1991, as imperialist intervention (Stokke, 1995).

A factor which feeds an interpretation of political conditionality as imperialism is the failure of some Western states to live up to the standards expected of new democracies. Exhortations to reform need to come from credible sources. There are far too many deviations from good governance among Western donors, especially Britain and the United States, which make it easy for recipient governments or their domestic opponents to treat political conditionalities with scepticism. Donors have been accused of double standards when recipient states saw discrepancies between the governance practised by donors and the governance they advocated overseas (Robinson, 1999).

The credibility of a donor's moral stance will obviously be undermined by floutings of the rule of law (for example, holding suspects without trial at Guantanamo Bay), electoral fraud (in the presidential election of 2000 in the USA), and weak regulation of bribery (in the UK, strongly criticized by the OECD in 2001). The USA's threat in 2002 to block an international convention against torture, drawn up by the UN's Economic and Social Council, further undermined its stance on human rights abroad. Governments in both the UK and USA have been criticized for human rights violations in the so-called 'war on terrorism', the former for suspending art. 5 of the European Convention on Human Rights, the latter by Human Rights Watch which claimed in January 2005 that America's disregard for human rights has encouraged Egypt, Malaysia and Russia to follow suit. The anti-poverty stance of the international development community also sits uneasily alongside the scale of poverty in the UK and USA, where inequality in 1999 was worse than in India, Slovakia or Sri Lanka.

The violation of international law in the invasion of Iraq by Britain and America, with its attendant human and economic costs, is another poor example to set countries that are being urged to respect international treaties in, for example, their respect for human rights. The situation is not helped by the emergence of evidence that the United States military routinely and systematically uses torture in its 'war on terrorism'. The UK endorses the use of torture by using the 'intelligence' derived from it.

Nevertheless, the principles embodied in good governance are not compromised by the fact that they are advocated by agencies in countries which sometimes fall below the standards being urged on others. It has also to be recognized that characterizing political conditionalities as 'imperialism' usually lacks a specification of what should be defined in universal terms and what in localized, culturally specific terms. Failure to do this risks adopting a culturally and ethically relativist position which means everything, no matter how repugnant, has to be accepted because it is part of local culture and therefore immune to assessment from a non-local standpoint. This becomes particularly important when discussing understandings of human rights (see Chapter 3).

The multilateral organizations are less likely than bilateral aid agencies to be perceived as imperialistic, though the Bretton Woods institutions – the IMF and the World Bank – are widely regarded as being effectively owned by the most powerful Western states. Even the UN, which is much more responsive to Third World understandings of the need for aid, takes its lead from the World Bank when it comes to modes of economic analysis and the policy prescriptions that flow from them.

Making conditionality work

Since aid conditionalities in the form of sanctions seem not to work, it is unlikely that aid can force a government to become more democratic. However, once a regime is in transition from authoritarianism, there is much that can be done with technical assistance to strengthen institutions and organizations that will consolidate democracy. But there are conditions within recipient countries that have to be understood if good governance initiatives are to be successful.

Political contexts

First, technical assistance must be informed by an awareness of local political cultures and processes. It is a mistake to assume institutions can be made to work like those in the donor country when the constitutional and political contexts are very different. For example, American aid has been criticized for failing to understand that countries may have cabinet rather than presidential executives, corporate rather than bilateral models of labour relations, public rather than private ownership of some mass media, public rather than private funding of advocacy groups, religious rather than secular political parties, and legal systems without a common law base. In giving assistance, German has stressed social markets, the Netherlands the multi-party system, and the UK the Westminster model (Carothers, 1997). Aid to governance can also overlook the distribution of power between economic and political forces that explains why institutions fail to operate democratically, seeing reform as a technical rather than a political matter. This can be especially bad for the effectiveness of aid in regions where democracy has stagnated or gone into reverse (for example, parts of sub-Saharan Africa or the former USSR).

Awareness of local political conditions is particularly important in the protection of internationally recognized human rights, which is much more likely to result from domestic rather than international politics. Treaties have greater impact on domestic governance when they are incorporated into law as a result of domestic political pressures rather than international enforcement mechanisms. Consequently international support for this dimension of good governance should cultivate the local economic and social conditions supportive of human rights, and the 'domestic constituencies' (the media, NGOs, bureaucrats, academics and the judiciary) that can work to ensure that treaties are 'internalized' in, and enforced by, domestic legal and cultural institutions. Support can also be given to the establishment of national human rights institutions, such as the national human rights commissions in India, Nigeria and Sri Lanka, so that their achievements, likely to be modest, outweigh their failures.

Aid donors also need to take advantage of positive national events, such as commitments to reform human rights within national action plans (as in South Africa), periods of legal reform during which human rights can be internalized in domestic law (as in Estonia and Romania), international contracts into which governance clauses can be introduced, and the membership requirements of powerful trading blocs (such as the EU). Assistance can also be given with the development of case law based on a treaty. In the aftermath of authoritarianism, as shown by the case of Chile, an additional requirement is the reform of those coercive institutions which make violations of rights possible, particularly the military and the judiciary (Donnelly, 1993; Heyns and Viljoen, 2001). Small but significant progress can be made by identifying a set of criteria with which to assess how far governance standards are being applied in practice by government agencies, especially those involved in development programmes and projects.

Sensitivity to local conditions is also important when trying to support political pluralism. Development assistance aimed at 'civil society' can obviously do much good. But it is not without its risks. Organizations which become involved in the political process, whether parties, pressure groups, or NGOs, may be regarded as lacking legitimacy when funded from abroad by foreign governments or multilateral agencies. This is because the accountability of such groups may appear to be focused more on donor agencies and 'Northern' NGOs than on local constituencies or the beneficiaries of their advocacy or service. Much funding from the USA, for example, to support groups working for stronger democracy and human rights has proceeded regardless of levels of local support and mobilization. These 'trustee organizations' acting on behalf of 'silent constituencies' rarely consult the people 'represented'. Decision-making tends to be top-down. Hence the feeling that aid should be directed at associations that reflect members' needs, raise their own funds and recruit local volunteers (Ottaway and Chung, 1999).

Assistance to political parties (on election campaigning, the drafting of new electoral laws or coalition-building), such as that provided through links between parties in Western Europe and North America and their Eastern European counterparts, may be perceived as unwarranted foreign interference in domestic politics, as happened in Bulgaria in 1996. It then becomes easier for governments to restrict opposition campaigns, advocacy and lobbying on the grounds that they are inspired by foreign interference. Since support for what inevitably becomes political activity not only runs counter to agency traditions and even mandates, but also encounters the hostility of recipient governments if seen as interference, 'expectations of dramatic reform should be tempered' (Pridham, 1996; Stiles, 1998: 214).

In the case of political pluralism, confidence in an aid relationship between donors and political associations can be damaged if the beneficiaries are thought to be part of 'uncivil' society. Some of the civil associations which become involved in politics are distinctly *un*civil, reactionary, authoritarian and in other ways uninterested in, or opposed to, democracy (White, 1996a). They include organized crime, vigilante gangs, terrorists, secret societies, private militias, warlords and religious chauvinists. In Africa civil society is 'male dominated and gerontocratic', and includes ethnic and fundamentalist religious associations unlikely to sponsor democratization (Kasfir, 1998: 136). In parts of post-communist Europe new social groups have emerged which see collective action and social solidarity within pluralist democracy as obstacles to their economic or political interests in nationalist chauvinism, economic liberalism and an unregulated free market. Some group solidarities are achieved only through hostility towards and rejection of those defined as inferior, as with racist and fascist political organisations. In newly democratizing countries political associations also include groups that openly and freely cooperated with the previous authoritarian regime (White, 1996a).

Thus support for civil society has to be discriminating if it is to further the aims of political pluralism. If aid disbursements flow to anti-democratic bodies, such as those NGOs in Pakistan and Bangladesh known to be fronts for Islamic fundamentalists, public trust in the aid system, in both donor and recipient countries, will be undermined (Fowler, 2000: 592).

Support for good governance is by no means always culturally unaware. For example, the UN recognizes that systems of governance may vary according to values about political participation, political order and authority in different cultures. But while it is important to understand that not all reforms to politics and public administration will necessarily be workable everywhere, it is important not to become too relativistic about what is and is not possible.

Sustainable reforms

Second, reforms need to be sustainable after the overseas assistance has come to an end. For example, reforms to strengthen the rule of law, once legislated for, need to become self-sustaining, with resources and political commitment to ensure that new laws and procedures are effectively deployed. However, this condition is far from being universally satisfied. The World Bank has tended to concentrate on drafting new laws rather than seeing whether they achieved their objectives. Projects have also experienced rapid change in the political context of transitional states, with uncertain and fluctuating government commitments, high rates of turnover of officials, and a lack of enforcement of new laws. Assessments have consequently found that 'Bank objectives for legal reform stated in loan documents were not met' (Gupta *et al.*, 2002: 8).

Recipient governments do not always provide funds to sustain reforms. For example, in Georgia agencies supplied with equipment under technical assistance to judicial reform were given no resources to finance repairs and upkeep. One of two USAID-funded training centres in Ukraine has not been maintained at full capacity, and the other has been dissolved. In parts of the former Soviet Union new legal texts have not been reprinted, new training curricula have been abandoned, and NGOs seeking to improve access to the justice system for the poor receive no local funding, remaining dependent on donor support. In Russia a lack of funding has prevented the extension of jury trials beyond the nine initial regions to the other 89.

In the case of many US-supported training projects in Russia rarely has there been any follow-up 'to help ensure that the concepts taught were being institutionalized or having long-term impact after the US trainers left the country'. Projects have suffered from the lack of systematic monitoring and evaluation of their impact and sustainability. This requires the development of performance indicators of impact, rather than inputs such as the number of training courses held, publications produced, or computers installed (USGAO, 2001).

There is also the question of whether organizations given assistance under support for civil society will be self-sustaining when foreign funding ends. Sustainability here includes probity in financial management, put at risk by the rapid growth of funds resulting from overseas assistance. Technical support for party organization in the form of training seminars and conferences has often recommended practices that are too expensive to sustain (such as appointing full-time professional organizers), when it would have been better to have emphasized the role of volunteers and the adoption of feasible campaign methods (Edwards and Hulme, 1996; Ottaway and Chung, 1999).

By focusing on organizations and groups that follow the donor's political agendas, foreign support may inadvertently 'crowd out' more spontaneous associations, with detrimental consequences for political pluralism. Donor support has had the effect of encouraging associations which represent interests and demands 'in a lopsided way that favours groups with the capacity to organize and to access resources, even if their ideas are not widely held' (Ottaway, 2005: 129). Ironically, donor bias towards professional and bureaucratic organizations in urban areas with access to political decision-makers has meant that groups representing disadvantaged people, such as the rural poor, ethnic minorities and indigenous communities, have received less support.

Donor support can also stimulate rivalry and conflict between groups. For example, in Bangladesh adversarial relationships have developed between NGOs and other parts of civil society such as the business community, the labour movement and religious bodies. These groups have close party-political affiliations and view independent, externally funded bodies with great suspicion (Stiles, 2002). Such rivalry need not be counter-productive if it promotes a genuine plurality of views on public policies. What is damaging for pluralism is if some views are automatically excluded for partisan advantage.

Project design

Third, reforms need to be well designed. Poorly designed aid projects have weakened reform efforts, including those designed to strengthen the rule of law. Case-studies of Bulgaria, Cambodia, Guatemala and South Africa found that aid to the justice sector from different donors has been ad hoc and uncoordinated, leading to duplication of effort and waste of resources. Clear policy objectives have not been established, needs have not been thoroughly assessed, and beneficiaries have not always been consulted. For example, one of South Africa's reforms was drawn up without the participation of those employed in the system who consequently felt little commitment to it (ICHRP, 2000).

Problems of design arise in part from the fact that reviews of conditions in recipient countries have not always been carried out early enough by donors. This has been found in the case of law reform, when local practices for resolving disputes have not always been adequately understood, and when knowledge of which disputes need to go to court and which could better be dealt with less formally would have been more useful than new equipment or training courses. National budgets do not always provide adequate data on judicial expenditure, which again affects project planning.

Foreign aid to the rule of law has generally been based on inadequate understandings of the relationship between law and social change, and therefore of the likely effects of particular interventions. The content of reforms has been decided by foreign consultants rather than local judicial elites. Little attention has been paid to the informal and customary rules that in less developed countries play such an important part in structuring economic and social life (Faundez, 1997).

Co-ordinated assistance

Fourth, there is a need for donor assistance to be better coordinated. This is particularly so with administrative reforms. When there can be as many as seven different donors working on civil service reform and related institutional development in a single country (as was the case, for example, in Malawi in 1996), coordination of their efforts becomes imperative, as does ensuring adequate understanding of donor procurement and disbursement procedures, without which implementation can be delayed. The coordination of IMF and World Bank initiatives in particular needs to be stronger (Gupta *et al.*, 2002). The UN has also been criticized for poor coordination, with too much fragmentation and duplication of agencies and programmes, reducing efficiency in the use of resources and causing failures in poverty reduction activities.

Other requirements of an effective 'good government aid programme' (Burnell, 1994) include clarity of aims and objectives in the minds of both donors and recipients, so donors know whether aid is working and recipients know what reforms they are expected to make and by when. It also helps, among other things, to know whether the reforms being urged are within the capability of a country's leaders to deliver. For example, it is relatively easy to write a formal constitution, but very hard to depoliticize a bureaucracy.

There also needs to be transparency in the donor's purpose: is it promoting good governance for its own sake, trying to promote economic and social progress via governmental reform, or seeking to overcome opposition to aid in the donor country? A strategic grasp of the particular complexities within the recipient country is also valuable, including the strengths or weaknesses of the government responsible for pushing reforms along, and the likelihood that economic crisis will undermine the reform effort.

The governance of aid

Finally, there needs to be good government on the part of donors in their aid dealings, including equality of treatment of aid recipients and account-ability for aid arrangements (even though confidentiality in relations between donors and recipients may be regarded by both parties as essential). It has also been shown that the policies of donors, rather than the governance of recipient states, have resulted in poor economic performances. In the case of Africa, for example, making aid conditional upon achieving externally imposed targets for inflation, fiscal deficits, privatization, and trade liberalization has undermined its beneficial effect on economic growth and poverty reduction. Cancelling out the benefits of debt relief by reducing development assistance has not provided additional funds for poverty programmes, and instability in aid flows has created problems of fiscal management (Weeks, 2006). But above all, there is a need for a greater volume of overseas development assistance (ODA) from rich countries. However, it seems unlikely that ODA will rise from the US $18.6 billion per annum pledged by donors from 2006, to the US $50 billion which will be needed to achieve the United Nations Millennium Development Goals.

Bibliography

Abed, G. T. and Davoodi, H. R. (2002) 'Corruption, structural reforms and economic performance in the transition economies', in G. T. Abed and S. Gupta (eds), *Governance, Corruption and Economic Performance*, Washington, DC: International Monetary Fund.

Abed, G. T. and Gupta, S. (2002) 'The economics of corruption: an overview', in G. T. Abed and S. Gupta (eds), *Governance, Corruption and Economic Performance*, Washington, DC: International Monetary Fund.

Acuna-Alfaro, J. (2005) 'Democratic governance and human development: governance attributes' contribution to development', paper to the 11th EADI General Conference on Insecurity and Development, Bonn, 21–24 September.

Ades, A. and Di Tella (1997) 'The new economics of corruption: a survey and some new results', *Political Studies*, vol. 45, no. 3, 496–515.

Agh, A. (1995) 'Partial consolidation of the East-Central European parties. The case of the Hungarian Socialist Party', *Party Politics*, vol. 1, no. 4, 491–514.

Agh, A. (1996) 'From nomenclature to clientura. The emergence of political elites in east-central Europe', in G. Pridham and P. G. Lewis (eds), *Stabilising Fragile Democracies. Comparing New Party Systems in Southern and Eastern Europe*, London: Routledge.

Agh, A. (2000) 'Change and continuity among the members of parliaments: low incumbent retention rates in the new East Central Europe Parliaments', in L. D. Longley, A. Agh and D. Zajc (eds), *Working Papers on Comparative Legislative Studies IV. Parliamentary Members and Leaders: The Delicate Balance*, Brussels: International Political Science Association.

Ahmed, N. (1997) 'Parliamentary opposition in Bangladesh. A study of its role in the fifth parliament', *Party Politics*, vol. 3, no. 2, 147–68.

Ahmed, N. (1998) 'In search of institutionalization: parliament in Bangladesh', *Journal of Legislative Studies*, vol. 4, no. 4, 34–65.

Akire, S. (2002) 'Dimensions of human development', *World Development*, vol. 30, no. 2, 181–205.

Alam, M. S. (1991) 'Some economic costs of corruption in less developed countries', *Journal of Development Studies*, vol. 27, no. 1, 89–97.

Allen, T. R. S. (1985) 'Legislative supremacy and the rule of law: democracy and constitutionalism', *Cambridge Law Journal*, vol. 44, no. 1, 111–43.

Alonso, A. and Costa, V. (2004) 'The dynamics of public hearings for environmental licensing: the case of the Sao Paulo ring road', *IDS Bulletin*, vol. 35, no. 2, 49–57.

Alston, P. (ed.) (1992) *The United Nations and Human Rights. A Critical Appraisal*, Oxford: Clarendon Press.

Ames, B., Bhatt, G. and Plant, M. (2002) 'Taking stock of poverty reduction efforts', *Finance and Development*, vol. 39, no. 2, 9–12.

Amstutz, M. A. (1999) *International Ethics. Concepts, Theories and Cases in Global Politics*, Lanham MD: Rowan & Littlefied.

Anaya, S. J. (1995) 'The capacity of international law to advance ethnic or nationality rights claims', in W. Kymlicka (ed.), *The Rights of Minority Cultures*, Oxford University Press.

Anderson, J. and van Crowder, L. (2000) 'The present and future of public sector extension in Africa: contracting out or contracting in?', *Public Administration and Development*, vol. 20, no. 5, 373–84.

Anderson, M. R. (2003) *Access to Justice and Legal Process: Making Legal Institutions Responsive to Poor People in Less Developed Countries*, IDS Working Paper 178, Brighton: Institute of Development Studies.

Andrews, M. and Schroeder, L. (2003) 'Sectoral decentralization and intergovernmental arrangements in Africa', *Public Administration and Development*, vol. 23, no. 1, 29–40.

Apampa, S. (2005) 'The case of corruption in Nigeria', in J. G. Lambsdorff, M. Taube and M. Schramm (eds), *The New Institutional Economics of Corruption*, London: Routledge.

Aron, L. (2002) 'Russia reinvents the rule of law', *AEI Russian Outlook*, Spring.

Ashoff, G. (1999) 'The coherence of policies towards developing countries: the case of Germany', in J. Forster and O. Stokke (eds), *Policy Coherence in Development Cooperation*, London, Cass.

Asian Development Bank (2001) *Legal Empowerment: Advancing Good Governance and Poverty Reduction*, Manila: ADB.

Aworti, N. (2004) 'Getting the fundamentals wrong: woes of public-private partnerships in solid waste collection in three Ghanaian cities', *Public Administration and Development*, vol. 24, no. 3, 213–24.

Ayeni, V. O. (1997) 'Evolution of and proposals for the ombudsman in Southern Africa', *International Review of Administrative Science*, vol. 63, no. 4, 543–63.

Aziz, A. and Arnold, D. D. (1996) 'Introduction', in A. Aziz and D. D. Arnold (eds), *Decentralised Governance in Asian Countries*, New Delhi: Sage.

Baehr, P. R. (1999) *Human Rights. Universality in Practice*, Basingstoke: Macmillan.

Bailey, S. J. (1999) *Local Government Economics. Principles and Practice*, London: Macmillan.

Baldacci, E., Clements, B., Cui, Q and Gupta, S. (2005) 'What does it take to help the poor?', *Finance and Development*, vol. 42, no. 2, 20–3.

Bamberger, M. (1987) *Readings in Community Participation*, Washington DC: World Bank.

Bamberger, M. (1991) 'The importance of community participation', *Public Administration and Development*, vol. 11, no. 3, 281–4.

Baniser, D. (2003) *Freedom of Information and Access to Government Records Around the World*, Privacy International, www.freedomofinfo.org/survey.

Bardham, P. (1997) 'Corruption and development: a review of the issues', *Journal of Economic Literature*, vol. 35, no. 3, 320–47.

Bardill, J. E. (2000) 'Towards and culture of good governance: the Presidential Review Commission and public service reform in South Africa', *Public Administration and Development*, vol. 20, no. 2, 103–18.

Barr, N. (2004) *The Economics of the Welfare State*, 4th edn, Oxford University Press.

Barry, B. (2000) 'Is there a right to development?', in T. Coates (ed.), *International Justice*, Aldershot: Ashgate.

Batley, R. (1999) 'The New Public Management in developing countries: implications for policy and organizational reform', *Journal of International Development*, vol. 11, no. 5, 761–5.

Bauer, J. R. and Bell, D. A. (1999) 'Introduction', in J. R. Bauer and D. A. Bell (eds), *The East Asian Challenge for Human Rights*, Cambridge University Press.

Beblavy, M. (2002) 'Understanding the waves of agencification and the governance problems they have raised in Central and Eastern European countries', *OECD Journal on Budgeting*, vol. 2, no. 1, 121–38.

Beetham, D. (1995) 'Human rights and the study of politics', *Political Studies*, vol. 43, special issue on Politics and Human Rights, 41–60.

Belshaw, D. (2000) 'Decentralized governance and poverty reduction: relevant experience in Africa and Asia', in P. Collins (ed.), *Applying Public Administration in Development. Guideposts to the Future*, Chichester: Wiley.

Bennett, R. J. (1994) 'An overview of developments in decentralization', in R. J. Bennett (ed.), *Local Government and Market Decentralization: Experience in Industrialized, Developing and Former Eastern Bloc Countries*, Tokyo: United Nations University Press.

Bennett, S. and Mills, A. (1998) 'Government capacity to contracts: health sector experience and lessons', *Public Administration and Development*, vol. 18, no. 4, 307–26.

Biebesheimer, C. and Payne, J. M. (2001) *IDB Experience in Justice Reform: Lessons Learned and Elements for Policy Formation*, Washington, DC: Inter-American Development Bank.

Birch, A. H. (1993) *The Concepts and Theories of Modern Democracy*, London: Routledge.

Birch, S. (2003) *Electoral Systems and Political Transformation in Post-Communist Europe*, Basingstoke: Palgrave Macmillan.

Birch, S., Millard, F., Popescu, M. and Williams, K. (2002) *Embodying Democracy. Electoral System Design in Post-Communist Europe*, Basingstoke: Palgrave Macmillan.

Bird, R. and Rodriguez, E.R. (1999) 'Decentralisation and poverty alleviation. International experience and the case of the Philippines', *Public Administration and Development*, vol. 19, no. 3, 299–319.

Bird, R., Ebell, R. D. and Wallich, C. J., (eds) (1995) *Decentralisation of the Socialist State: Intergovernmental Finance in Transitional Economies*, Washington, DC: World Bank.

Bird, R., Freund, C. and Wallich, C. J. (1994) 'Decentralisation of intergovernmental finance in transitional economies', *Comparative Economic Studies*, vol. 36, no. 4, 149–60.

Bird, R. M. (1990) 'Intergovernmental finance and local taxation in developing countries: some basic considerations for reformers', *Public Administration and Development*, vol. 10, no. 3, 277–88.

Bird, R. M. and Vaillancourt, F. (1998) 'Fiscal decentralization in developing countries: an overview', in R. M. Bird and F. Vaillancourt (eds), *Fiscal Decentralization in Developing Countries*, Cambridge University Press.

Blackburn, J. (1998) *Who Changes? Institutionalising Participation in Development*, London: Intermediate Technology Publications.

Blackman, D. (1995) 'The European Parliament's aid initiatives in support of democratic development in Central and Eastern Europe', *Journal of Legislative Studies*, vol. 1, no. 2, 301–14.

Blair, H. (2000) 'Participation and accountability at the periphery: democratic local governance in six countries', *World Development*, vol. 28, no. 1, 21–39.

Blunt, P. (1995) 'Cultural relativism: "good" governance and sustainable human development', *Public Administration and Development*, vol. 15, no. 1, 1–10.

Boex, J. (2003) 'The incidence of local government allocations in Tanzania', *Public Administration and Development*, vol. 23, no. 5, 381–91.

Booth, D. (1999) 'Three tyrannies', in T. Dunne and N. Wheeler (eds), *Human Rights in Global Politics*, Cambridge University Press.

Boukhalov, O. and Ivannikov, S. (1995) 'Ukranian local politics after independence', in H. Teune (ed.), *Local Governance Around the World*, special issue of the Annals of the American Academy of Political and Social Science, vol. 540, July, 126–36.

Bowden, P. (1990) 'NGOs in Asia: issues in development', *Public Administration and Development*, vol. 10, no. 2, 141–52.

Bowornwathana, B. (2006) 'Autonomisation of the Thai state: some observations', *Public Administration and Development*, vol. 26, no. 1, 27–34.

Braye, S. and Preston-Shoot, M. (1995) *Empowering Practice in Social Care*, Buckingham: Open University Press.

Brillantes, A. B. (1994) 'Redemocratisation and decentralisation in the Philippines', *International Review of Administrative Sciences*, vol. 60, no. 4, 1994, 575–86.

Brinkerhoff, D. W. (2000) 'Assessing political will for anti-corruption efforts: an analytical framework', *Public Administration and Development*, vol. 20, no. 3, 239–52.

Brinkerhoff, D. W. (2002) 'Government–nonprofit partnerships: a defining framework', *Public Administration and Development*, vol. 22, no. 1, 19–30.

Broughton, J. M. and Quereshi, Z. (2004) 'From vision to action: how to put some oomph into the Millennium Development Goals', *Finance and Development*, vol. 41, no. 3, 42–4.

Brown, C. (1999) 'Universal human rights: a critique', in T. Dunne and N. J. Wheeler (eds), *Human Rights in Global Politics*, Cambridge University Press.

Brown, S. (2001) 'Authoritarian leaders and multi-party elections in Africa: how foreign donors help to keep Kenya's Daniel arap Moi in power', *Third World Quarterly*, vol. 22, no. 5, 725–739.

Brunetti, A., Kisunko, G. and Weder, B. (1998) 'Credibility of rules and economic growth: evidence from a worldwide survey of the private sector', *World Bank Economic Review*, vol. 12, no. 3, 353–84.

Brzezinski, Z. (1997) 'The new challenges to human rights', *Journal of Democracy*, vol. 8, no. 2, 3–7.

Buchanan, A. (1995) 'The morality of secession', in W. Kymlicka (ed.), *The Rights of Minority Cultures*, Oxford University Press.

Bull, M. J. and Newell, J. L. (2003) 'Conclusion: political corruption in contemporary democracies', in M. J. Bull and J. L. Newell (eds), *Corruption in Contemporary Politics*, Basingstoke: Palgrave Macmillan.

Burnell, P. (1994) 'Good government and democratization: a sideways look at aid and conditionality', *Democratization*, vol. 1, no. 3, 485–503.

Burnell, P. (ed.) (2000) *Democracy Assistance. International Co-operation for Democratization*, London: Cass.

Cammack, P. (2002) 'Neoliberalism, the World Bank, and the new politics of development', in U. Kothari and M. Minogue (eds), *Development Theory and Practice. Critical Perspectives*, Basingstoke: Palgrave.

Campbell, A. (1995a) 'Local government in Romania', in A.Coulson (ed.), *Local Government in Eastern Europe. Establishing Democracy at the Grassroots*, Aldershot: Elgar.

Campbell, A. (1995b) 'Regional and local government in Ukraine', in A.Coulson (ed.), *Local Government in Eastern Europe. Establishing Democracy at the Grassroots*, Aldershot: Elgar.

Campbell, A. (1995c) 'Regional power in the Russian federation', in in A.Coulson (ed.), *Local Government in Eastern Europe. Establishing Dmocracy at the Grassroots*, Aldershot: Elgar.

Campos, J., Lien, D. and Pradhan, S. (1999) 'The impact of corruption on investment: predictability matters', *World Development*, vol. 27, no. 6, 1059–67.

Carothers, T. (1997) 'Democracy assistance: the question of strategy', *Democratization*, vol. 4, no. 3, 109–132.

Carothers, T. (1998) 'The rule of law revival', *Foreign Affairs*, vol. 77, no. 2, 95–106.

Carothers, T. (2002) 'The end of the transition paradigm', *Journal of Democracy*, vol. 13, no. 1, 5–21.

Caulfield, J. (2002) 'Executive agencies in Tanzania: liberalization and Third World debt', *Public Administration and Development*, vol. 22, no. 3, 209–20.

Caulfield, J. (2006) 'The politics of bureau reform in sub-Saharan Africa', *Public Administration and Development*, vol. 26, no. 1, 15–26.

Cavarozzi, M. and Palermo, V. (1995) 'State, civil society and popular neighbourhood organisations in Buenos Aires: key players in Argentina's transition to democracy', in C. A. Reilly (ed.), *New Paths to Democratic Development in Latin America. The Rise of NGO-Municipal Collaboration*, London: Rienner.

Centre for the Study of Democracy (2001) 'System of governance and parliamentary accountability in Bulgaria', Budapest.

Chambers, R. (1995) 'Paradigm shifts and the practice of participatory research and development', in N. Nelson and S. Wright (eds), *Power and Participatory Development. Theory and Practice*, London: Intermediate Technology Publications.

Chan, J. (1997) 'Hong Kong, Singapore and "Asian Values". An alternative view', *Journal of Democracy*, vol. 8, no. 2, 35–48.

Chan, J. (1999) 'A Confucian perspective on human rights for contemporary China', in J. R. Bauer and D. A. Bell (eds), *The East Asian Challenge for Human Rights*, Cambridge University Press.

Chandler, D. (2002) 'Introduction: rethinking human rights', in D. Chandler (ed.), *Rethinking Human Rights. Critical Approaches to International Politics*, Basingstoke: Palgrave Macmillan.

Chang, H.-J. (2005) *Why Developing Countries Need Tariffs. How WTO NAMA Negotiations Could Deny Developing Countries' Right to a Future*, Geneva: South Centre.

Charlick, R. B. (2001) 'Popular participation and local government reform', *Public Administration and Development*, vol. 21, no. 2, 149–58.

Chen, S. and Ravallion, M. (2004) 'How have the world's poorest fared since the early 1980s?', *World Bank Policy Research Working Paper* no. 3341, Washington.

Chiu, N. K. (1997) 'Service targets and methods of redress: the impact of accountability in Malaysia', *Public Administration and Development*, vol. 17, no. 1, 175–80.

Chong, A. and Calderon, C. (2000) 'Causality and feedback between institutional measures and economic growth', *Economics and Politics*, vol. 12, no. 1, 69–81.

Christie, K. (1995) 'Regime security and human rights in Southeast Asia', *Political Studies*, vol. 43, special issue, 204–18.

Clague, C., Keefer, P., Knack, S. and Olson, M. (1996), 'Property and contract rights under autocracies and democracies', *Journal of Economic Growth*, vol. 1, no. 2, 243–76.

Clague, C., Keefer, P., Knack, S. and Olson, M. (1999) 'Contract-intensive money: contract enforcement, property rights and economic performance', *Journal of Economic Growth*, vol. 4, no. 2, 185–211.

Clarke, G. (1998) 'Non-governmental organizations and politics in the developing world', *Political Studies*, vol. 46, no. 1, 36–52.

Clarke, R. (2002) 'Introduction', in C. Kirkpatrick, R. Clarke and C. Polidano (eds), *Handbook on Development Policy and Management*, Cheltenham: Elgar.

Cleaver, F. (1999) 'Paradoxes of participation: questioning participatory approaches to development', *Journal of International Development*, vol. 11, no. 4, 597–612.

Cohen, J. (1993) 'The importance of public service reform', *Journal of Modern African Studies*, vol. 37, no. 1, 1–23.

Collins, P. (1993) 'Civil service reform and training in transitional economies: strategic issues and options', *Public Administration and Development*, vol. 13, no. 4, 323–44.

Conyers, D. (2003) 'Decentralization in Zimbabwe: a local perspective', *Public Administration and Development*, vol. 23, no. 1, 115–24.

Cornwall, A. (2002) *Making Spaces, Changing Places: Situating Participation in Development*, IDS Working Paper no. 170, Brighton: Institute of Development Studies.

Cotta, M. (1996) 'Structuring the new party systems after the dictatorship: coalitions, alliances, fusions and splits during the transition and post-transition stages', in G. Pridham and P. G. Lewis (eds), *Stabilising Fragile Democracies. Comparing New Party Systems in Southern and Eastern Europe*, London: Routledge.

Cranston, M. (1967) 'Human rights, real and supposed', in D. D. Raphael, *Political Theory and the Rights of Man*, London: Macmillan.

Cranston, R. (1997) 'Access to justice in South and South-east Asia', in J. Faundez (ed.), *Good Government and Law. Legal and Institutional Reform in Developing Countries*, Basingstoke: Macmillan.

Crawford, G. (1997) 'Foreign aid and political conditionality: issues of effectiveness and consistency, *Democratization*, vol. 4, no. 3, 69–108.

Crook, R. C. (2003) 'Decentralization and poverty reduction in Africa: the politics of local-central relations', *Public Administration and Development*, vol. 23, no. 1, 77–88.

Crook, R. C. and Manor, J. (1998) *Democracy and Decentralization in South Asia and West Africa. Participation, Accountability and Performance*, Cambridge University Press.

Crook, R. C. and Sverrisson, A. S. (2001) *Decentralisation and Poverty-Alleviation in Developing Countries: A Comparative Analysis or Is West Bengal Unique?*, Institute of Development Studies Working Paper no. 130, Brighton.

Cumming, G. D. (1996) 'British aid to Africa: a changing agenda?', *Third World Quarterly*, vol. 17, no. 3, 487–501.

Davey, K. (1995a) 'Local government in Hungary', in A. Coulson, (ed.), *Local Government in Eastern Europe. Establishing Dmocracy at the Grassroots*, Aldershot: Elgar.

Davey, K. (1995b) 'The Czech and Slovak Republics', in A. Coulson, (ed.), *Local Government in Eastern Europe. Establishing Dmocracy at the Grassroots*, Aldershot: Elgar.

de Maria, W. (2005) 'Whistleblower protection: is Africa ready?', *Public Administration and Development*, vol. 25, no. 2, 217–226.

de Valk, P. (1990) 'An analysis of planning policy with reference to Zimbabwe', in P. de Valk and K. H. Wekwete (eds), *Decentralization for Participatory Planning*, Aldershot: Gower.

della Porta, D. and Vannucci, A. (1997) 'The perverse effects" of political corruption', *Political Studies*, vol. 45, no. 3, 516–38.

Devas, N. and Grant, U. (2003) 'Local government decision-making, citizen participation and local accountability: some evidence from Kenya and Uganda', *Public Administration and Development*, vol. 23, no. 4, 307–16.

Devas, N., Amis, P. and Beal, J. (2001) *Urban Governance and Poverty. Lessons from a Study of Ten Cities in the South*, University of Birmingham School of Public Policy.

DFID (1995) *Technical Note on Enhancing Stakeholder Participation in Aid Activities*, London: Department for International Development.

DFID (2000) *Eliminating World Poverty: Making Globalisation Work for the Poor*, White Paper on International Development, Cm. 5006, London: HMSO.

DFID (2001) *Poverty: Bridging the Gap*, London: Department for International Development.

Diamond, L. (1988) 'Nigeria: pluralism, statism and the struggle for democracy', in L. Diamond, J. J. Linz and S. M. Lipset (eds), *Democracy in Developing Countries, vol. 2, Africa*, London: Adamantine.

Diamond, L. (1992) 'Economic development and democracy reconsidered', in G. Marks and L. Diamond (eds), *Re-examining Democracy. Essays in Honour of Seymour Martin Lipset*. London: Sage.

Diamond, L. (1997) *Civil Society and the Development of Democracy*, Working Paper 1997/101, Madrid: Juan March Institute.

Diamond, L. and Gunther, R. (2001) *Political Parties and Democracy*, Baltimore, MD: Johns Hopkins University Press.

Diamond, L., Linz, J. J. and Lipset, S. M. (1995) 'Introduction: what makes for democracy?', in Diamond, Linz and Lipset (eds), *Politics in Developing Countries. Comparing Experiences with Democracy*, 2nd edn, London: Rienner.

Dix, R. H. (1992) 'Democratization and the institutionalization of Latin American political parties', *Comparative Political Studies*, vol. 24, no. 4, 488–511.

Dodoo, R. (1997) 'Performance standards and measuring performance in Ghana', *Public Administration and Development*, vol. 17, no. 1, 115–22.

Doig, A. (1995) 'Good government and sustainable anti-corruption strategies: a role for independent anti-corruption agencies?', *Public Administration and Development*, vol. 15, no. 2, 151–66.

Doig, A. and McIvor, S. (1999) 'Corruption and its control in the developmental context', *Third World Quarterly*, vol. 20, no. 3, 657–76.

Doig, A. and Riley, S. (1998) 'Corruption and anti-corruption strategies: issues and case studies from developing countries', United Nations Development Programme/OECD Development Centre, *Corruption and Integrity Improvement Initiatives in Developing Countries*, New York: United Nations Development Programme.

Domingo, P. (1999) 'Judicial independence and judicial reform in Latin America', in A. Schedler, L. Diamond and M. C. Plattner (eds), *The Self-restraining State. Power and Accountability in New Democracies*, London: Rienner.

Donnelly, J. (1989) *The Concept of Human Rights*, London: Croom Helm.

Donnelly, J. (1993) *International Human Rights*, Boulder CO: Westview.

Donnelly, J. (1999) 'The social construction of international human rights', in T. Dunne and N. J. Wheeler (eds), *Human Rights in Global Politics*, Cambridge University Press.

Doornbos, M. (2001) '"Good governance": the rise and decline of a policy metaphor?', *Journal of Development Studies*, vol. 37, no. 6, 93–108.

Downs, K. (1987) 'Regionalization, administrative reform and democratization: Nicaragua 1979–84', *Public Administration and Development*, vol. 7, no. 4, 363–82.

Dunn, J. (1999) 'Situating democratic political accountability', in A. Przeworski, S. C. Stokes and B. Manin (eds), *Democracy, Accountability and Representation*, Cambridge University Press.

Dunne, T. and Wheeler, N. J. (1999) 'Introduction: human rights and the fifty years' crisis', in T. Dunne and N. J. Wheeler (eds), *Human Rights in Global Politics*, Cambridge University Press.

Echeverri-Gent, J. (1992) 'Public participation and poverty alleviation: the experience of reform communists in India's West Bengal', *World Development*, vol. 20, no. 10, 1410–22.

Edwards, M. and Hulme, D. (1996) 'Too close for comfort? The impact of official aid on NGOs', *World Development*, vol. 24, no. 6, 961–73.

Edwards, M. and Sen, G. (2000) 'NGOs, social change and the transformation of human relationships', *Third World Quarterly*, vol. 21, no. 4, 605–16.

Edwards, M., Hulme, D. and Wallace, T. (1999) 'NGOs in a global future: marrying local delivery to worldwide leverage', *Public Administration and Development*, vol. 19, no. 2, 117–36.

Eigen, P. (1996) 'Combatting corruption around the world', *Journal of Democracy*, vol. 7, no. 1, 158–68.

Elander, I. (1997) 'Between centralism and localism: on the development of local self-government in postsocialist Europe', *Environment and Planning C: Government and Policy*, vol. 15, no. 2, 143–59.

Elcock, H. (1998) 'The changing problem of accountability in modern government: an analytical agenda for reformers', *Public Policy and Administration*, vol. 13, no. 3, 23–37.

Elklit, J. and Svensson, P. (1997)'What makes elections free and fair?', *Journal of Democracy*, vol. 8, no. 3, 32–46.

Elster, J., Offer, C. and Preuss, U.K. (1998) *Institutional Design in Post-Communist Societies. Rebuilding the Ship at Sea*, Cambridge University Press.

Emmett, B. (2006) *In the Public Interest. Health, Education, and Water and Sanitation for All*, Oxford: Oxfam International and Water Aid.

Engberg-Pedersen, L. and Webster, N. (2002) 'Introduction to political space', in N.

Webster and L. Engberg-Pedersen (eds), *In the Name of the Poor. Contesting Political Space for Poverty Reduction*, London: Zed.

Esman, M. J. and Uphoff, N. T. (1984) *Local Organizations. Intermediaries in Rural Development*, Ithaca, NY: Cornell University Press.

Esman, M.R. (1988) 'The maturing of development administration', *Public Administration and Development*, vol. 8, no. 2, 125–34.

Estrin, S. (1994) *Privatization in Central and Eastern Europe*, London: Longman.

Evans, P. (1995) *Embedded Autonomy. States and Industrial Transformation*, Princeton University Press.

Evans, T. (1997) 'Democratization and human rights', in A. McGrew (ed.), *The Transformation of Democracy? Globalization and Territorial Democracy*, Cambridge: Polity.

Evans, T. (2001) 'If democracy, then human rights?, *Third World Quarterly*, vol. 22, no. 4, 623–42.

Evans, T. (2002) 'A human right to health?', *Third World Quarterly*, vol. 23, no. 2, 197–215.

Eyben, R. and Ladbury, S. (1995) 'Popular participation in aid-assisted projects: why more in theory than practice?', in N. Nelson and S. Wright (eds), *Power and Participatory Development. Theory and Practice*, London: Intermediate Technology Publications.

Fafchamps, M. (1996) 'The enforcement of commercial contracts in Ghana', *World Development*, vol. 24, no. 3, 427–48.

Farrell, D. M. (2001) *Electoral Systems. A Comparative Introduction*, Basingstoke: Palgrave.

Farrington, J and Lewis, D. J. (eds) (1993) *Non-Governmental Organisations and the State in Asia. Rethinking Roles in sustainable Agricultural Development*, London: Routledge.

Faundez, J. (1997) 'Legal technical assistance', in J. Faundez (ed.), *Good Government and Law. Legal and Institutional Reform in Developing Countries*, London: Macmillan.

Fearon, J. D. (1999) 'Electoral accountability and the control of politicians: selecting good types versus sanctioning poor performance', in A. Przeworski, S. C. Stokes and B. Manin (eds), *Democracy, Accountability and Representation*, Cambridge University Press.

Feld, L. P. and Voight, S. (2003) 'Economic growth and judicial independence: cross country evidence using a new set of indicators', CESifo Working Paper no. 906.

Ferreira, F. H. G. and Walton, M. (2005) 'The inequality trap. Why equity must be central to development', *Finance and Development*, vol. 42, no. 4, 34–7.

Finsterbusch, K. and Van Wicklin, W. A. (1987) 'The contribution of beneficiary participation to development project effectiveness', *Public Administration and Development*, vol. 7, no. 1, 1–23.

Fiss, O. M. (1993) 'The right degree of independence', in I. P. Stotzky (ed.), *Transitions to Democracy in Latin America: The Role of the Judiciary*, Boulder, CO: Westview.

Fjeldstad, O. (2003) 'Fighting fiscal corruption: lessons from the Tanzania Revenue Authority', *Public Administration and Development*, vol. 23, no. 2, 165–75.

Foley, M. W. and Edwards, B. (1996) 'The paradox of civil society', *Journal of Democracy*, vol. 7, no. 3, 38–53.

Foot, R. (1997) 'Human rights, democracy and development: the debate in East Asia', *Democratization*, vol. 4, no. 2, 139–53.

Forster, J. and Stokke, O. (1999) 'Coherence of policies towards developing countries: approaching the problematique', in J. Forster and O. Stokke (eds), *Policy Coherence in Development Co-operation*, London, Cass.

Forsythe, D. P. (2000) *Human Rights in International Relations*, Cambridge University Press.

Fowler, A. (1996) 'Strengthening civil society in transition economies – from concept to strategy' in A. Clayton (ed), *NGOs, Civil Society and the State: Building Democracy in Transition Societies*, Oxford: INTRAC.

Fowler, A. (2000) 'Beyond partnership: getting real about NGO relations in the aid system, *IDS Bulletin*, vol. 31, no. 3, 1–8.

Frankel, M. E. (1993) 'Concerning the role the judiciary may serve in the proper functioning of a democracy', in I. P. Stotzky (ed.), *Transition to Democracy in Latin America: The Role of the Judiciary*, Boulder, CO: Westview.

Franklin, M. N. (1996) 'Electoral participation', in L. LeDuc, R. G. Niemi and P. Norris (eds), *Comparing Democracies. Elections and Voting in Global Perspective*, London: Sage.

Freedom House (2002) *Freedom in the World. The Annual Survey of Political Rights and Civil Liberties*, New York: Freedom House.

Freedom House (2004) *Freedom of the Press 2004*, New York: Freedom House.

Freeman, M. (1995) 'Are there collective human rights?', *Political Studies*, vol. 43, special issue, 25–40.

Freeman, M. (2002) *Human Rights. An Interdisciplinary Approach*, Cambridge: Polity.

Freeman, M. (2004) 'The problem of secularism in human rights theory', *Human Rights Quarterly*, vol. 26, no. 2, 375–400.

Frischtak, L. (1997) 'Political mandate, institutional change and economic reform', in J. Faundez (ed.), *Good Government and Law. Legal and Institutional Reform in Developing Countries*, London: Macmillan.

Fukuyama, F. (2001) 'Social capital, civil society and development', *Third World Quarterly*, vol. 22, no. 1, 7–20.

Fung, A., Wright, E. O. et al. (2003) *Deepening Democracy. Institutional Innovations in Empowered Participatory Governance*, London: Verso.

Gallagher, T. (1996) 'Nationalism and the Romanian opposition', *Transitions*, vol. 2, no. 1, 30–2.

Galligan, D. J. and Smilov, D. M. (1999) *Administrative Law in Central and Eastern Europe*, Budapest: Central European University Press.

Gallup International (2004) *Governance and Democracy – the People's View. A Global Opinion Poll*, www.gallup-international.com/survey.

Ganapin, D. J. (1993) 'The Philippines Debt-for-Nature Swap programme', in Farrington, J. and Lewis, D. J. (eds), *Non-Governmental Organisations and the State in Asia. Rethinking Roles in sustainable Agricultural Development,* London: Routledge.

Garnett, H., Koenen-Grant, J. and Rielly, C. (1997) 'Managing policy formulation and implementation in Zambia's democratic transition', *Public Administration and Development*, vol. 17, no. 1, 77–92.   *Need*

Gboku, M. L. S. (1993), 'Community development in Sierra Leone', _Community Development Journal_, vol. 28, no. 2, 167–75.

Gelman, V. and Sentanova, O. (1995) 'Political reform in the Russian provinces: trends since October 1993' in J.Lovenduski and J.Stanyer (eds), *Contemporary Political Studies 1995*, vol. 1, Proceedings of the Annual Conference of the Political Studies Association, Belfast: PSA.

Ghai, D. (2000) 'Social development and public policy: some lessons from successful experiences' in D. Ghai (ed.), *Social Development and Public Policy*, Basingstoke: Macmillan.

Gill, G. J. (1998) 'Using PRA for agricultural policy analysis in Nepal: the Tarai Research Network food-grain study'; in Holland, J. and Blackburn, J. (eds) (1998) *Whose Voice? Participatory Research and Policy Change*, London: Intermediate Technology Publications.

Gillespie, K. and Okruhlik, G. (1991) 'The political dimensions of corruption cleanups. A framework for analysis', *Comparative Politics*, vol. 24, no. 1, 77–95.

Goetz, A. M. and Jenkins, R. (2005) *Reinventing Accountability. Making Democracy Work for Human Development*, Basingstoke: Palgrave Macmillan.

Golooba-Mutebi, F. (2003) 'Devolution and outsourcing of municipal services in Kampala

City, Uganda: an early assessment', *Public Administration and Development*, vol. 23, no. 5, 405–18.

Golooba-Mutebi, F. (2004) 'Reassessing popular participation in Uganda', *Public Administration and Development*, vol. 24, no. 4, 289–304.

Golub, S. (1993) 'Evaluation of Asia Foundation Legal Service/Human Rights programming in Bangladesh', mimeo, Washington, DC: the Asia Foundation.

Goodin, R. E. (1979) 'The development-rights tradeoff: some unwarranted economic and political assumptions', *Human Rights Quarterly*, vol. 1, no. 1, 31–42.

Gombay, C. and O'Manique, C. (1996) 'Uganda', in P. McCarney (ed.), *The Changing Nature of Local Government in Developing Countries*, University of Toronto Centre for Urban and Community Studies and Federation of Canadian Municipalities.

Gordillo, G. and Andersson, K. (2004) 'From policy lessons to policy action: motivation to take evaluation seriously', *Public Administration and Development*, vol. 24, no. 4, 305–20.

Graham, B. D. (1993) *Representation and Party Politics. A Comparative Perspective*, Oxford: Blackwell.

Green, M. (2002) 'Social development: issues and approaches', in U. Kothari and M. Minogue (eds), *Development Theory and Practice. Critical Perspectives*, Basingstoke: Palgrave.

Grindle, M. S. (2004) 'Good enough governance: poverty reduction and reform in developing countries', *Governance*, vol. 17, no. 4, 525–48.

Gronow, J. (1995) 'Shifting power, sharing power: issues from user-group forestry in Nepal', in N. Nelson and S. Wright (eds), *Power and Participatory Development*.

Gunatilleke, G. (2000) 'Sri Lanka's social achievements and challenges', in D. Ghai (ed.), *Social Development and Public Policy. A Study of Some Successful Experiences*, Basingstoke: Macmillan.

Gunther, R. and Diamond, L. (2003) Types and functions of parties' in L. Diamond and R. Gunther (eds.) *Political Parties and Democracy*, Baltimore MD: Johns Hopkins University Press.

Gupta, S., Plant, M. and Dorsey, T. (2002) 'Is the PRGF living up to expectations?', *Finance and Development*, vol. 39, no. 2.

Gupta, S., de Mello, L. and Sharan, R. (2002) 'Corruption and military spending', in G. T. Abed and S. Gupta (eds), *Governance, Corruption and Economic Performance*, Washington, DC: International Monetary Fund.

Hagmann, J., Chuma, E., Connolly, M. and Murwira, K. (1998) 'Scaling up participatory approaches through institutionalisation in government services: the case of agricultural extension in Masvingo Province, Zimbabwe' in J. Blackburn and J. Holland (eds), *Who Changes? Institutionalising Participation in Development*, London: IT Publications.

Halliday, F. (1995) 'Relativism and universalism in human rights: the case of the Islamic Middle East', *Political Studies*, vol. 43, no. 1, 152–67

Halperin, M. H., Siegle, J. T. and Weinstein, M. M. (2004) *The Democracy Advantage. How Democracies Promote Prosperity and Peace*, New York: Routledge.

Hammergren, L. (1998) *Political Will, Constituency Building and Public Support in Rule of Law Programmes*, Washington, DC: United States Agency for International Development.

Hardgrave, R. L. and Kochanek, S. A. (1993) *India. Government and Politics of a Developing Nation*, Fort Worth, TX: Harcourt Brace.

Harper, C. (1996) 'Strengthening civil society in transitional East Asia', in A. Clayton (ed.), *NGOs, Civil Society and the State. Building Democracy in Transitional Societies*, Oxford: INTRAC Publications.

Harrigan, J. (1995) 'Jamaica: mature democracy but questionable accountability', in J. Healey and W. Tordoff (eds), *Votes and Budgets. Comparative Studies in Accountable Governance in the South*, London: Macmillan.

Harrigan, J. (1998) 'Effects of the IMF and World Bank on public expenditure accountability on Jamaica', *Public Administration and Development*, vol. 18, no. 1, 5–22.

Harrison, G. (1999) 'Corruption as "boundary politics": the state, democratization and Mozambique's unstable liberalisation', *Third World Quarterly*, vol. 20, no. 3, 537–50.

Harriss-White, B. and White, G. (1996) 'Corruption, liberalization and democracy', *IDS Bulletin*, vol. 27, no. 2, 1–5.

Harrop, M. and Miller, W. L. (1987), *Elections and Voters. A Comparative Introduction*, London: Macmillan.

Hartney, M. (1995) 'Some confusions concerning collective rights', in W. Kymlicka (ed.), *The Rights of Minority Cultures*, Oxford University Press.

Hausermann, J. (1998), *A Human Rights Approach to Development*, London: Department for International Development.

Hawthorne, (1993) 'How to ask for good government', *IDS Bulletin*, vol. 24, no. 1, 24–30.

Hay, R. A., Koehn, P. H. and Koehn, E. F. (1990) 'Community development in Nigeria: prevailing orientations among local government officials', *Community Development Jourbnal*, vol. 25, no. 2, 147–60.

Haynes, J. (1997) *Democracy and Civil Society in the Third World. Politics and New Political Movements*, Cambridge: Polity.

Healey, J. (1995a) 'Botswana: a study in political accountability', in J. Healey and W. Tordoff (eds), *Votes and Budgets. Comparative Studies in Accountable Governance in the South*, London: Macmillan.

Healey, J. (1995b) 'Multi-party electoral politics: comparative experience and conclusions', in J. Healey and W. Tordoff (eds), *Votes and Budgets. Comparative Studies in Accountable Governance in the South*, London: Macmillan.

Hearn, J. (2000) 'Aiding democracy? Donors and civil society in South Africa', *Third World Quarterly*, vol. 21, no. 5, 815–30.

Hecht, R., Batson, A. and Brenzel, L. (2004) 'Making health care accountable', *Finance and Development*, vol. 41, no. 1, 16–19.

Heidenheimer, A. J. and Moroff, H. (2002) 'Controlling business payoffs to foreign officials: the 1998 OECD anti-bribery convention', in A. J. Heidenheimer and M. Johnston (eds), *Political Corruption: Concepts and Contexts*, New Brunswick, NJ: Transaction.

Heilbrunn, J. R. (1999) 'Corruption, democracy and reform in Benin', in A. Schedler, L. Diamond and M. C. Plattner (eds), *The Self-Restraining State. Power and Accountability in New Democracies*, London: Rienner.

Helmsing, A. H. J. (2003) 'Local economic development: new generations of actors, policies and instruments for Africa', *Public Administration and Development*, vol. 23, no. 1, 67–76.

Henisz, W. J. (2000) 'The institutional environment for economic growth', *Economics and Politics*, vol. 12, no. 1, 1–13.

Hernandez, L. and Fox, J. (1995) 'Mexico's difficult democracy: grassroots movements, NGOs and local government', in C. A. Reilly (ed.), *New Paths to Democratic Development in Latin America. The Rise of NGO–Municipal Collaboration*, London: Rienner.

Heyns, C. and Viljoen, F. (2001) 'The impact of the United Nations human rights treaties on the domestic level', *Human Rights Quarterly*, vol. 23, no. 3, 483–535.

Heywood, P. (1997) 'Political corruption: problems and perspectives', *Political Studies*, vol. 45, no. 3 (special issue on 'Political Corruption'), 417–35.

Hicks, J. F. and Kaminski, B. (1995) 'Local government reform and transition from communism', *Journal of Developing Societies*, vol. 11, no. 1, 1–20.

Hoebink, P. (1999) 'Coherence and development policy in the Netherlands', in J. Forster and O. Stokke (eds), *Policy Coherence in Development Co-operation*, London, Cass.

Holbrook, J. (2002) 'Humanitarian intervention and the recasting of international law', in D. Chandler (ed.), *Rethinking Human Rights. Critical Approaches to International Politics*, Basingstoke: Palgrave Macmillan.

Holland, J. and Blackburn, J. (eds) (1998) *Whose Voice? Participatory Research and Policy Change*, London: Intermediate Technology Publications.

Holm, J. D. (1988) 'Botswana: a paternalistic democracy', in L.Diamond, J. J. Linz and S. M. Lipset (eds), *Democracy in Developing Countries, vol. 2, Africa*, London: Adamantine.

Holmes, L. (2003) 'Political corruption in Central and Eastern Europe', in M. J. Bull and J. L. Newell (eds), *Corruption in Contemporary Politics*, Basingstoke: Palgrave Macmillan.

Holmes, S. (1990) 'Liberal constraints on private power?: reflections on the origins and rationale of access regulation', in J. Lichtenberg (ed.), *Democracy and the Mass Media*, Cambridge University Press.

Hook, S. W. (1998) 'Building democracy through foreign aid: the limitations of United States political conditionalities, 1992–1996', *Democratization*, vol. 5, no. 3, 156–80.

Howell, J. (1996) 'Drops in the ocean: NGOs in China', in A. Clayton (ed.), *NGOs, Civil Society and the State. Building Democracy in Transitional Societies*, Oxford: INTRAC Publications.

Huang, M. (2001) 'Carving out a new Estonia', *Central Europe Review*, vol. 3, no. 2, January, 1–5.

Hubbard, R. (1997) 'People: hearts and minds towards rebirth of the public service ethic', *Public Administration and Development*, vol. 17, no. 1, 109–14.

Hughes, O. E. (1998) *Public Management and Administration. An Introduction*, Basingstoke: Macmillan.

Hulme, D. and Edwards, M. (1997) 'NGOs, states and donors: an overview', in D. Hulme and M. Edwards (eds), *NGOs, States and Donors: Too Close for Comfort?*, Basingstoke: Macmillan.

Hurrell, A. (1999) 'Power, principles and prudence: protecting human rights in a deeply divided world', in T. Dunne and N. J. Wheeler (eds), *Human Rights in Global Politics*, Cambridge University Press.

Hutchcroft, P. D. (1997) 'The politics of privilege: assessing the impact of rents, corruption and clientelism on Third World development', *Political Studies*, vol. 45, no. 3, 639–58.

ICHRP (2000) *Local Perspectives: Foreign Aid to the Justice Sector*, Geneva: International Council on Human Rights Policy.

Ihonubere, J. O. (1998) 'Where is the third wave? A critical evaluation of Africa's non-transition to democray', in J. M. Mbaku and J. O. Ihonoubere (eds), *Multiparty Democracy and Political Change: Constraints to Democratization in Africa*, Aldershot: Ashgate.

IMF (2002) *The IMF's Approach to Promoting Good Governance and Combating Corruption — A Guide* , www.imf.org/external/np/gov/guide/eng/index.htm.

International Union of Local Authorities (IULA) (2000) *Poverty Eradication Policy Paper* adopted by the IULA World Executive Committee, 13 April 2000.

Ishayama, J. (2001) 'Sickles into roses: the successor parties and democratic consolidation in post-communist politics', in P. G. Lewis (ed.), *Party Development and Democratic Change in Post-Communist Europe*, London: Cass.

Jabbra, J. G. and Dwivedi, O. P. (1988) *Public Service Accountability: A Comparative Perspective*, West Hartford, CT: Kumarian.

Jain, R. B. (1988) 'Public service accountability in India', in J. G. Jabbra and O. P. Dwivedi (eds), *Public Service Accountability. A Comparative Perspective*, West Hartford, CT: Kumarian.

James, S. (1996) 'The political and administrative consequences of judicial review', *Public Administration*, vol. 74, no. 4, 613–38.

Jenkins, R. and Goetz, A. (1999) 'Accounts and accountability: theoretical implications of the right-to-information movement in India', *Third World Quarterly*, vol. 20, no. 3, 603–22.

Jimenez, E. (2000) 'Equity and the decentralization of social services', in S. J. Burki (ed.),

Annual World Bank Conference on Development in Latin America and the Caribbean 1999, New York, Oxford University Press.

Johnston, D. M. (1995) 'Native rights as collective rights: a question of group self-preservation', in W. Kymlicka (ed.), *The Rights of Minority Cultures*, Oxford University Press.

Johnston, M. (1999) 'A brief history of anti-corruption agencies', in A. Schedler, L. Diamond and M. C. Plattner (eds), *The Self-restraining State. Power and Accountability in New Democracies*, London: Rienner.

Johnston, M. (2002) 'Party systems, competition and political checks against corruption', in A. J. Heidenheimer and M. Johnston (eds), *Political Corruption: Concepts and Contexts*, New Brunswick, NJ: Transaction.

Joshi, A. and Moore, M. (2004) 'Institutionalised co-production: unorthodox public service delivery in challenging environments', *Journal of Development Studies*, vol. 40, no. 4, 31–49.

Jutting, J. and Kauffmann, C. (2004) *Decentralization and Poverty in Developing Countries: Exploring the Impact*, OECD Development Centre Working Paper 236, Paris.

Kar, K. and Phillips, S. (1998) 'Scaling up or scaling down? The experience of institutionalizing PRA in the slum improvement projects in India', in J. Blackburn and J. Holland (eds), *Who Changes? Institutionalizing Participation in Development*, London: Intermediate Technology Publications.

Karasimeonov, G. (1996) 'The legislature in post-communist Bulgaria', in D. M. Olson and P. Norton (eds), *The New Parliaments of Central and Eastern Europe*, London: Cass.

Kasfir, N. (1998) 'The conventional notion of civil society: a critique', *Journal of Commonwealth and Comparative Politics*, vol. 36, no. 2, 1–20.

Kasongo Project Team (1984) 'Primary health care for less than a dollar a year', *World Health Forum*, vol. 5, no. 2, 211–15.

Kaufmann, D. (1998) 'Revisiting anti-corruption strategies: tilt towards incentive-driven approaches?', in United Nations Development Programme/OECD Development Centre, *Corruption and Integrity Improvement Initiatives in Developing Countries*, New York: United Nations Development Programme.

Kaul, M. (1996) 'Civil service reforms: learning from Commonwealth experience', *Public Administration and Development*, vol. 16, no. 2, 131–50.

Kaul, M. (1997) 'The new public administration: management innovations in government', *Public Administration and Development*, vol. 17, no. 1, 13–26.

Khan, M., Lewis, D. J., Sabri, A. A. and Shahabuddin, M. (1993) 'Proshika's livestock and social forestry programmes', in Farrington, J. and Lewis, D. J. (eds), *Non-Governmental Organisations and the State in Asia. Rethinking Roles in sustainable Agricultural Development,* London: Routledge.

Khan, M. S. and Knight, M. D. (1986) 'Do fund-supported adjustment programmes retard growth?', *Finance and Development*, vol. 23,no. 1, 7–10.

Kiggundu, M. N. (1998) 'Civil service reforms: limping into the twenty-first century', in M. Minogue, C. Polidano and D. Hulme (eds), *Beyond the New Public Management. Changing Ideas and Practices in Governance*, Cheltenham: Elgar.

Kitschelt, H. (1995) 'Formation of party cleavages in post-communist democracies: theoretical propositions', *Party Politics*, vol. 1, no. 4, 447–72.

Klitgaard, R. (1997) 'Cleaning up and invigorating the civil service', *Public Administration and Development*, vol. 17, no. 5, 487–510.

Klitgaard, R. (2000) 'Subverting corruption', *Finance and Development*, vol. 37, no. 2, 2–5.

Knack, S. (2000) *Aid Dependence and the Quality of Governance: A Cross-Country Empirical Analysis*, Policy Research Working Paper No. 2396, Washington, DC: World Bank.

Knack, S. and Keefer, P. (1995) 'Institutions and economic performance: cross-country tests using alternative institutional measures', *Economics and Politics*, vol. 7, no. 3, 207–27.

Kombo, M. (2001) 'Parliamentary accountability and governance – the Kenyan experience', in The Parliamentary Centre, *Parliamentary Accountability and Good Governance*, Washington DC: World Bank Institute.

Kopecky, P. (1995) 'Developing party organizations in East–Central Europe. What type of party is likely to emerge?', *Party Politics*, vol. 1, no. 4, 515–34.

Kpundeh, S. J. (1998) 'Political will in fighting corruption', in United Nations Development Programme and OECD Development Centre, *Corruption and Integrity Improvement Initiatives in Developing Countries,* New York: United Nations Development Programme.

Kpundeh, S. J. (2002) 'The institutional framework for corruption control in Uganda', in A. J. Heidenheimer and M. Johnston (eds), *Political Corruption: Concepts and Contexts*, New Brunswick, NJ: Transaction.

Krishnan, G. (2001) 'Increasing information access to improve political accountability and participation. Mapping future actions in Asia Pacific', discussion paper to the Asia Pacific Regional Workshop, International Anti-Corruption Conference, Prague, October 7–11.

Kuenzi, M. and Lambright, G. (2001) 'Party system institutionalisation in 30 African countries', *Party Politics*, vol. 7, no. 4, 437–68.

Kurer, O. (1997) *The Political Foundations of Development Policies*, Lanham, MD: University Press of America.

Kurer, O. (2005) 'Corruption: an alternative approach to its definition and measurement', *Political Studies*, vol. 53, no. 1, 222–39.

Lancaster, C. (1993) 'Governance and development: the views from Washington', *IDS Bulletin*, vol. 24, no. 1, 9–15.

Larbi, G. A. (1998) 'Management decentralization in practice: a comparison of public health and water services in Ghana', in M. Minogue, C. Polidano and D. Hulme (eds), *Beyond the New Public Management. Changing Ideas and Practices in Governance*, Cheltenham: Elgar.

Larkins, C. M. (1996) 'Judicial independence and democratization: a theoretical and conceptual analysis', *American Journal of Comparative Law*, vol. 44, no. 4, 605–26.

Larson, A. M. (2003) 'Decentralization and forest manamgement in Latin America: towards a working model', *Public Administration and Development*, vol. 23, no. 3, 211–26.

Laughland, J. (2002) 'Human rights and the rule of law: achieving universal justice?', in D. Chandler (ed.), *Rethinking Human Rights. Critical Approaches to International Politics*, Basingstoke: Palgrave Macmillan.

Lee, J. M. (1995) 'British aid to parliaments overseas', *Journal of Legislative Studies*, vol. 1, no. 1, 115–35.

Leff, N. (1989) 'Economic development through corruption', in A. Heidenheimer, M. Johnston, and V. LeVine (eds), *Political Corruption: A Handbook*, New Brunswick, NJ: Transaction.

Leftwich, A. (1993) 'Governance, democracy and development in the Third World', *Third World Quarterly*, vol. 14, no. 3, 605–23.

Leftwich, A. (2000) *States of Development. On the Primacy of Politics in Development*, Cambridge: Polity.

Leite, C. and Weidmann, J. (2002) 'Does Mother Nature corrupt? Natural resources, corruption and economic growth', in G. T. Abed and S. Gupta (eds), *Governance, Corruption and Economic Performance*, Washington, DC: International Monetary Fund.

Lember, V. (2004) 'Limiting aspects of contracting out in transitional countries: the case of Estonian prisons', *Public Administration and Development*, vol. 24, no. 5, 425–35.

Lewis, B. D. (2003) 'Property tax in Indonesia: measuring and explaining administrative (under-) performance', *Public Administration and Development*, vol. 23, no. 3, 227–39.

Lewis, D. J. (1993) 'NGO–government interaction in Bangladesh: overview', in Farrington,

J. and Lewis, D. J. (eds), *Non-Governmental Organisations and the State in Asia. Rethinking Roles in Sustainable Agricultural Development,* London: Routledge.

Lewis, P. G. (1995) 'Poland's new parties in the post-communist political system', in G. Whiteman (ed.), *Party Formation in East-Central Europe: Post-Communist Politics in Czechoslovakia, Hungary, Poland and Bulgaria,* Aldershot: Elgar.

Lewis, P. G. (ed.) (1996) *Party Structure and Organization in East-Central Europe,* Cheltenham: Edward Elgar.

Lewis, P. G. (1997) 'Political participation in post-communist democracies', in D. Potter, D. Goldblatt, M. Kiloh and P. Lewis (eds), *Democratisation,* Cambridge: Polity.

Lewis, P. G. (2000) *Political Parties in Post-Communist Eastern Europe,* London: Routledge.

Lewis, P. G. (2001a) 'Conclusion: party development and democratization in Eastern Europe', in P. Lewis (ed.), *Party Development and Democratic Change,* London: Cass

Lewis, P. G. (2001b) 'The "third wave" of democracy in Eastern Europe. Comparative perspectives on party roles and political development', *Party Politics,* vol. 7, no. 5, 543–65.

Lomax, B. (1995) 'Impediments to democratization in post-communist East-Central Europe', in G. Whiteman (ed.), *Party Formation in East-Central Europe: Post-Communist Politics in Czechoslovakia, Hungary, Poland and Bulgaria,* Aldershot: Elgar.

Lomax, B. (1996) 'The structure and organization of Hungary's political parties' in P. G. Lewis (ed.), *Party Structure and Organization in East-Central Europe,* Cheltenham: Edward Elgar.

Long, C. M. (2001) *Participation of the Poor in Development Initiatives. Taking Their Rightful Place,* London: Earthscan.

Luan, T. D. (1996) 'Vietnam', in P. McCarney (ed.), *The Changing Nature of Local Government in Developing Countries,* Toronto: Centre for Urban and Community Studies, University of Toronto; and International Office, Federation of Canadian Municipalities.

Luckham, R. and White, G. (1996) 'Introduction: democratizing the South', in Luckham and White (eds), *Democratization in the South. The Jagged Wave,* Manchester University Press.

Mahmud, S. (2004) 'Citizen participation in the health sector in rural Bangladesh: perceptions and reality', *IDS Bulletin,* vol. 35, no. 2, 11–18.

Mainwaring, S. (1989) 'Grassroots popular movements and the struggle for democracy: Nova Iguacu', in A.Stepan (ed.), *Democratizing Brazil: Problems of Transition and Consolidation,* New York: Oxford University Press.

Mainwaring, S. (1998) 'Party systems in the third wave', *Journal of Democracy,* vol. 9, no. 3, July, 67–81.

Mainwaring, S. and Scully, T. R. (1995) 'Introduction: party systems in Latin America', in Mainwaring and Scully (eds), *Building Democratic Institutions. Party Systems in Latin America,* Stanford University Press.

Malova, D. and Sivakova, D. (1996) 'The National Council of the Slovak Republic: between democratic transition and national state-building', in Olson and Norton (eds), *The New Parliaments of Central and Eastern Europe,* London: Cass.

Manin, B., Przeworski, A. and Stokes, S. C. (1999) 'Elections and representation', in A. Przeworski, S. C. Stokes and B. Manin (eds), *Democracy, Accountability and Representation,* Cambridge University Press.

Maro, P. S. (1990) 'The impact of decentralization on spatial equity and rural development in Tanzania', in P. de Valk and K. H. Wekwete (eds), *Decentralizing for Participatory Planning? Comparing the Experiences of Zimbabwe, and Other Anglophone Countries in Eastern and Southern Africa,* Aldershot: Avebury.

Marzouk, M. (1997) 'The associative phenomenon in the Arab world: engine of democratisation or witness to the crisis?', in D. Hulme and M. Edwards (eds), *NGOs, States and Donors: Too Close for Comfort?*, Basingstoke: Macmillan.

Massolo, A. (1996) 'Mexico', in P. McCarney, (ed.), *The Changing Nature of Local Government in Developing Countries*, Toronto: University of Toronto Centre for Urban and Community Studies and Federation of Canadian Municipalities.

Masuko, L. (1996) 'Zimbabwe', in P. McCarney (ed.), *The Changing Nature of Local Government in Developing Countries*, Toronto: University of Toronto Centre for Urban and Community Studies and Federation of Canadian Municipalities.

Mauro, P. (1995) 'Corruption and growth', *Quarterly Journal of Economics*, vol. 60, no. 3, 681–712.

Mauro, P. (1997a) 'The effects of corruption on growth, investment and government expenditure', in K. A. Elliot (ed.), *Corruption and the Global Economy*, Washington, DC: Institute of International Economics.

Mauro, P. (1997b) 'Why worry about corruption?', *Economic Issues*, no. 6, Washington, DC: International Monetary Fund.

Mauro, P. (2002) Corruption and the composition of government expenditure', in G. T. Abed and S. Gupta (eds), *Governance, Corruption and Economic Performance*, Washington, DC: International Monetary Fund.

Mendus, S. (1995) 'Human rights in political theory', *Political Studies*, vol. 43, special issue, 10–24.

Merat, J. (2004) 'Taxation and local government accountability in a clientelist context: Colombia', *Public Administration and Development*, vol. 24, no. 3, 247–54.

Messick, R. E. (1999) 'Judicial reform and economic development: a survey of the issues', *World Bank Research Observer*, vol. 14, no. 1, 117–36.

Messick, R. E. (2000) 'International support for civil justice reform in developing and transition countries: an overview and evaluation', paper to the Conference on Judicial Reform and Economic Growth, Madrid.

Midgley, M. (1999) 'Towards an ethic of global responsibility', in T. Dunne and N. J. Wheeler (eds), *Human Rights in Global Politics*, Cambridge University Press.

Minogue, M. (1998) 'Changing the state: concepts and practice in the reform of the public sector', in M. Minogue, C. Polidano and D. Hulme (eds), *Beyond the New Public Management. Changing Ideas and Practices in Governance*, Cheltenham: Elgar.

Minogue, M. (2002) 'Power to the people? Good governance and the reshaping of the state', in U. Kothari and M. Minogue (eds), *Development Theory and Practice. Critical Perspectives*, Basingstoke: Palgrave.

Mitchison, R. (2003) 'Devolution in Uganda: an experiment in local service delivery' *Public Administration and Development*, vol. 23, no. 3, 241–8.

Mohanty, R. (2004) 'Institutional dynamics and participatory spaces: the making and unmaking of participation in local forest management in India', *IDS Bulletin*, vol. 35, no. 2, 26–32.

Montgomery, J. D. (1999) 'Administration of human rights', *Public Administration and Development*, vol. 19, no. 4, 323–37.

Moore, M. (1993) 'Good government? Introduction', *IDS Bulletin*, vol. 24, no. 1, 1–6.

Moore, M. and Putzel, J. (1999) *Politics and Poverty*, Background Paper for the World Development Report 2000/1, Washington, DC: World Bank.

Moran, J. (1999) 'Patterns of corruption and development in East Asia', *Third World Quarterly*, vol. 20, no. 3, 569–87.

Morris, S. D. (1999) 'Corruption and the Mexican political system: continuity and change', *Third World Quarterly*, vol. 20, no. 3, 623–43.

Moser, C. and Holland, J. (1998) 'Can policy-focused research be participatory? Research on violence and poverty in Jamaica using PRA methods', in Holland, J. and Blackburn, J. (eds) (1998) *Whose Voice? Participatory Research and Policy Change*, London: Intermediate Technology Publications.

Mosley, P. and Booth, A. (2003) 'Introduction and context', in A. Booth and P. Mosley (eds), *The New Poverty Strategies. What Have They Achieved? What Have We Learned?*, Basingstoke: Macmillan.

Mosse, D. (1995) 'Local institutions and power: the history and practice of community management of tank irrigation systems in south India', in N. Nelson and S. Wright (eds), *Power and Participatory Development. Theory and Practice*, London: Intermediate Technology Publications.

Mukandala, R. S. (1992) 'Bureaucracy and agricultural policy: the experience of Tanzania', in H. K. Asmerom, R. Hoppe and R. B. Jain (eds), *Bureaucracy and Development Policies in the Third World*, Amsterdam: VU University Press.

Mukherjee, R. and Manning, N. (2001) *New Lending for Civil Service Reform in Fiscal Years 1999 and 2000*, Washington, DC: World Bank.

Mustafa, S., Rahman, S. and Sattar, G. (1993) 'Bangladesh Rural Advancement Committee (BRAC). Backyard poultry and landless irrigation programmes', in Farrington, J. and Lewis, D. J. (eds), *Non-Governmental Organisations and the State in Asia. Rethinking Roles in Sustainable Agricultural Development,* London: Routledge.

Naim, M. (1995) 'New competitive tigers or old populist nationalisms?', in J. S. Tulchin and B. Romero (eds), *The Consolidation of Democracy in Latin America*, London: Rienner.

Ncholo, P. (2000) 'Reforming the public services in South Africa: a policy framework', *Public Administration and Development*, vol. 20, no. 2, 87–102.

Neumayer, E. (2002) 'Is good governance rewarded? A Cross-national analysis of debt forgiveness, *World Development*, vol. 30, no. 6, 913–30.

Ng, M. (1997) 'Why Asia needs democracy', *Journal of Democracy*, vol. 8, no. 2, 10–23.

Nickson, R. A. (1995) *Local Government in Latin ameirca*, Boulder, CO: Rienner.

Norris, M. (1983) 'Sudan: administrative versus political priorities', in P. Mawhood (ed.) *Local Government in the Third World. The Experience of Tropical Africa*, Chichester: Wiley.

Nye, J. S. (2002) 'Corruption and political development: a cost-benefit analysis', in A. J. Heidenheimer and M. Johnston (eds), *Political Corruption: Concepts and Contexts*, New Brunswick, NJ: Transaction.

Obimpeh, S. (2001) 'Parliament and the budget cycle – the Ghanaian experience', in The Parliamentary Centre, *Parliamentary Accountability and Good Governance*, Washington DC: World Bank Institute.

O'Donnell, G. O. (1994) 'Delegative democracy', *Journal of Democracy*, vol. 5, no. 1, 55–69.

OECD (1997) *Final Report of the DAC Ad Hoc Working Group on Participatory Development and Good Governance*, Paris: Organisation for Economic Co-operation and Development.

OECD (2001) *The DAC Guidelines. Poverty Reduction*, Paris: Organisation for Economic Co-operation and Development.

OECD (2003), 'Development Cooperation 2002 Report. Efforts and Policies of the Members of the DAC', *The DAC Journal*, vol. 4, no. 1, 12–15.

OECD (2004) *Lessons Learned on Donor Support to Decentralization and Local Governance*, DAC Evaluation Series, Paris: Organisation for Economic Co-operation and Development.

OECD (2005) *Economic Survey of Braqzil 2005*, Paris: Organisation for Economic Co-operation and Development.

Olowu, D. (1999) 'Redesigning African civil service reforms', *Journal of Modern African Studies*, vol. 37, no. 1, 1–23.

Olowu, D. (2003) 'Local institutional and political structures and processes: recent experience in Africa', *Public Administration and Development*, vol. 23, no. 1, 41–52.

Olson, D. M. (1998) 'Party formation and party system consolidation in the new democracies of central Europe', *Political Studies*, vol. 46, no. 3, 432–64.

Olson, D. M. and Norton, P. (1996) 'Legislatures in democratic transition', in Olson and Norton (eds), *The New Parliaments of Central and Eastern Europe*, London: Cass.

Osmani, S. R. (2001) 'Participatory governance and poverty reduction', in A. Grinspun (ed.), *Choices for the Poor: Lessons from National Poverty Strategies*, New York: United Nations Development Programme.

Othman, N. (1999) 'Grounding human rights arguments in non-western culture: Shari'a and the citizenship rights of women in a modern Islamic state', in J. R. Bauer and D. A. Bell (eds), *The East Asian Challenge for Human Rights*, Cambridge University Press.

Ottaway, M. (2005) 'Civil society', in P. Burnell and V. Randall (eds), *Politics in the Developing World*, Oxford University Press.

Ottaway, M. and Chung, T. (1999) 'Debating democracy assistance: toward a new paradigm', *Journal of Democracy*, vol. 10, no. 4, 99–113.

Ouma, S. O. A. (1991) 'Corruption in public policy and its impact on development: the case of Uganda since 1979', *Public Administration and Development*, vol. 11, no. 5, 473–90.

Owusu, F. (2005) 'Livelihood strategies and performance of Ghana's health and education sectors: explaining the connections', *Public Administration and Development*, vol. 25, no. 2, 157–74.

Oyugi, W. O. (1992) 'Bureaucracy and the management of health services in Kenya', in H. K. Asmerom, R. Hoppe and R. B. Jain (eds), *Bureaucracy and Development Policies in the Third World*, Amsterdam: VU University Press.

Parekh, B. (1999) 'Non-ethnocentric universalism', in T. Dunne and N. J. Wheeler (eds), *Human Rights in Global Politics*, Cambridge University Press.

Park, C. W. (1998) 'The National Assembly in the Republic of Korea', *Journal of Legislative Studies*, vol. 4, no. 4, 66–82.

Paul, S. (1987) *Community Participation in Development Projects*, World Bank Discussion Paper No. 6, Washington DC: The World Bank.

Pauly, M. V. (1973) 'Income redistribution as a local public good', *Journal of Public Economics*, vol. 2, no. 1, 35–58.

Pearce, J. (1997) 'Between co-option and irrelevance? Latin American NGOs in the 1990s', in D. Hulme and M. Edwards (eds), *NGOs, States and Donors: Too Close for Comfort?*, Basingstoke: Macmillan.

Pender, J. (2001) 'From "structural adjustment" to "comprehensive development framework": conditionality transformed?', *Third World Quarterly*, vol. 22, no. 3, 397–411.

Pereira, L. C. B., Maravall, J. M. and Przeworski, A. (1993) *Economic Reforms in New Democracies. A Social-Democratic Approach*, Cambridge University Press.

Perera, M. (1987) 'Sri Lanka', in M. Maetz and M. G. Quieti (eds), *Training For Decentralized Planning. Lessons From Experience*, Rome: Food and Agriculture Organization.

Peterson, G. E. (1997) *Decentralization in Latin America. Learning Through Experience*, Washington, DC: World Bank.

Philp, M. (1997) 'Defining political corruption', *Political Studies*, vol. 45, no. 3, 436–62.

Pietrzyk, D. I. (2003) 'Democracy or civil society?', *Politics*, vol. 23, no. 1, 38–45.

Pinto-Duschinsky, M. (1991) 'Foreign political aid: the German political foundations and their US counterparts', *International Affairs*, vol. 67, no. 1, 33–63.

Pistor, K. and Wellons, P. (1999) *The Role of Law and Legal Institutions in Asian Economic Development*, Hong Kong: Oxford University Press.

Plamenatz, J. P. (1968) *Consent, Freedom and Political Obligation*, 2nd edn, Oxford University Press.

Polidano, C. (2001) 'Administrative reform in core civil services: application and applicability of the new public management', in W. McCourt and M. Minogue (eds), *The Internationalization of Public Management. Reinventing the Third World State*, Cheltenham: Elgar.

Pope, J. and Vogl, F. (2000) 'Making anti-corruption agencies more effective', *Finance and Development*, vol. 37, no. 2, 6–9.

Power, T. J. and Gasiorowski, M. J. (1997) 'Institutional design and democratic consolidation in the Third World', *Comparative Political Studies*, vol. 30, no. 2, 123–55.

Pridham, G. (2001) 'Patterns of Europeanization and transnational party co-operation: party development in central and eastern Europe', in P. Lewis (ed.), *Party Development and Democratic Change*, London: Cass.

Pridham, G. and Lewis, P. (1996) 'Introduction: stabilizing fragile democracies and party system development', in G. Pridham and P. G. Lewis (eds), *Stabilizing Fragile Democracies. Comparing New Party Systems in Southern and Eastern Europe*, London: Routledge.

Prud'homme, R. (2003) 'Fiscal decentralization in Africa: a framework for considering reform', *Public Administration and Development*, vol. 23, no. 1.

Przeworski, A. (1995) *Sustainable Democracy*, Cambridge University Press.

Quah, J. S. T. (1995) 'Controlling corruption in city states: a comparative study of Hong Kong and Singapore', *Crime, Law and Social Change*, vol. 22, no. 3, 391–414.

Quah, J. S. T. (1999) 'Combating corruption in South Korea and Thailand', in A. Schedler, L. Diamond and M. C. Plattner (eds), *The Self-restraining State. Power and Accountability in New Democracies*, London: Rienner.

Quah, J. S. T. (2002) 'Responses to corruption in Asian societies', in A. J. Heidenheimer and M. Johnston (eds), *Political Corruption: Concepts and Contexts*, New Brunswick, NJ: Transaction.

Rakodi, C. (1990) 'Policies and preoccupations in rural and regional development planning in Tanzania, Zambia and Zimbabwe', in D. Simon (ed.), *Third World Regional Development. A Reappraisal*, London: Chapman .

Ramamurti, R. (1999) 'Why haven't developed countries privatized deeper and faster?', *World Development*, vol. 27, no. 1, 137–55.

Ramseyer, J. M. (1994) 'The puzzling (in)dependence of courts: a comparative approach', *Journal of Legal Studies*, vol. 23, no. 2, 721–47.

Randall, V. (1988) *Political Parties in the Third World*, London: Sage.

Randall, V. and Svasand, L. (2002) 'Party institutionalization in new democracies', *Party Politics*, vol. 8, no. 1, 5–29.

Raphael, D. D. (1967) 'Human rights, old and new', in D. D. Raphael, *Political Theory and the Rights of Man*, London: Macmillan.

Ravallion, M. (2002) 'An automatic safety net?', *Finance and Development*, vol. 39, no. 2, 21–3.

Rawls, J. (1972) *A Theory of Justice*, Oxford University Press.

Regulska, J. (1997) 'Decentralisation or (re)centralisation: struggle for political power in Poland', *Environment and Planning C: Government and Policy,* vol. 15, no. 2, 187–207.

Reilly, B. (2002) 'Electoral systems for divided societies', *Journal of Democracy*, vol. 13, no. 2, 156–70.

Reilly, C. A. (1995) 'Public policy and citizenship', in C. A. Reilly (ed.), *New Paths to Democratic Development in Latin America. The Rise of NGO–Municipal Collaboration*, London: Rienner.

Rishmawi, M. (ed.) (2000) *Attacks on Justice. The Harassment and Persecution of Judges and Lawyers*, Geneva: Centre for the Independence of Judges and Lawyers.

Riskin, C. (2000) 'Social development and China's changing development strategy', in D. Ghai (ed.), *Social Development and Public Policy. A Study of Some Successful Experiences*, Basingstoke: Macmillan.

Robertson-Snape, F. (1999) 'Corruption, collusion and nepotism in Indonesia', *Third World Quarterly*, vol. 20, no. 3, 589–602.

Robinson, M. (1993) 'Will political conditionality work?', *IDS Bulletin*, vol. 24, no. 1, 58–66.

Robinson, M. (1995) 'Political conditionality: strategic implications for NGOs', in O. Stokke (ed.), *Aid and Political Conditionality*, London: Cass.

Robinson, M. (1996) 'The role of aid donors in strengthening civil society', in A. Clayton (ed.), *NGOs, Civil Society and the State. Building Democracy in Transitional Societies*, Oxford: INTRAC Publications.

Robinson, M. (1997) 'Privatising the voluntary sector: NGOs as public service contractors', in D. Hulme and M. Edwards (eds), *NGOs, States and Donors: Too Close for Comfort?*, Basingstoke: Macmillan.

Robinson, M. (1999) 'Governance and coherence in development co-operation', in J. Forster and O. Stokke (eds), *Policy Coherence in Development Co-operation*, London, Cass.

Robinson, M. and White, G. (1998) 'Civil society and social provision: the role of civic organizations', in M. Minogue, C. Polidano and D. Hulme (eds), *Beyond the New Public Management. Changing Ideas and Practices in Governance*, Cheltenham: Elgar.

Robinson, M., Farrington, J. and Satish, S. (1993) 'NGO-government interaction in India: overview', in J. Farrington and D. J. Lewis (eds), *Non-Governmental Organisations and the State in Asia. Rethinking Roles in sustainable Agricultural Development*, London: Routledge.

Rodriguez, P. S. (1995) 'Local government, decentralisation and democracy in Colombia', in C. A. Reilly (ed.), *New Paths to Democratic Development in Latin America. The Rise of NGO–Municipal Collaboration*, London: Rienner.

Rojas, M. V., Rodriguez-Acosta, C. and Rosenbaum, A. (1998) 'Decentralising the health service delivery system in an emerging democracy: a case study of organisational change, citizen participation and local institution-building in Paraguay', paper to the 24th International Congress of Administrative Sciences, Paris, 7–11 September 1998.

Rose-Ackerman, S. (1996) 'Democracy and "grand" corruption', *International Social Science Journal*, vol. 48, no. 3, 365–80.

Rose-Ackerman, S. (1998) 'Corruption and the global economy', in United Nations Development Programme/OECD Development Centre, *Corruption and Integrity Improvement Initiatives in Developing Countries*, New York: United Nations Development Programme.

Rose-Ackerman, S. (1999) *Corruption and Government. Causes, Consequences and Reform*, Cambridge University Press.

Rubinoff, A. G. (1998) 'The decline of India's Parliament', *Journal of Legislative Studies*, vol. 4, no. 4, 13–33.

Ruland, J. (1984) 'Political change, urban services and social movements: political participation and grassroots politics in Metro Manila', *Public Administration and Development*, vol. 4, no. 4, 325–33.

Ryan, C. R. (1998) 'Elections and parliamentary democratization in Jordan', *Democratization*, vol. 5, no. 4, 176–96.

Salzberger, E. M. (1993) 'A positive analysis of the doctrine of separation of powers, or: why do we have an independent judiciary?', *International Review of Law and Economics*, vol. 13, no. 4, 349–79.

Samaranayake, M. (1998) 'Introducing participatory learning approaches in the Self-Help Support Programme, Sri Lanka', in J. Blackburn and J. Holland (eds), *Who Changes? Institutionalizing Participation in Development*, London: Intermediate Technology Publications.

Santin del Rio, L. (2004) 'Decentralization and civil society in Mexico', in P. Oxhorn, J. S. Tulchin and A. D. Selee (eds), *Decentralization, Democratic Governance and Civil Society in Comparative Perspective. Africa, Asia and Latin America*, Washington, DC: Woodrow Wilson Centre Press.

Sarris, A. H. (1987) *Agricultural Stabilization and Structural Adjustment Policies in Developing Countries*, Economic and Social Development Paper no. 65, FAO, Rome.

Schedler, A. (2002) 'The means of manipulation', *Journal of Democracy*, vol. 13, no. 2, 36–50.

Schick, A. (1998) 'Why most developing countries should not try New Zealand reforms', *The World Bank Research Observer*, vol. 13, no. 1, 123–31.

Schmitter, P. (1992) 'Interest systems and the consolidation of democracy', in G. Marks and L. Diamond (eds), *Re-examining Democracy. Essays in Honour of Seymour Martin Lipset*. London: Sage.

Schwartz, R. and Sharkansky, I. (2000) 'Collaboration with the "Third Sector" – issues of accountability: mapping Israeli versions of this problematic', *Public Policy and Administration*, vol. 15, no. 3, 92–106.

Segall, S. (2005) 'Political participation as an engine of social solidarity: a skeptical view', *Political Studies*, vol. 53, no. 2, 362–78.

Selee, A. D. and Tulchin, J. S. (2004) 'Decentralization and democratic governance: lessons and challenges', in P. Oxhorn, J. S. Tulchin and A. D. Selee (eds), *Decentralization, Democratic Governance and Civil Society in Comparative Perspective. Africa, Asia and Latin America*, Washington, DC: Woodrow Wilson Centre Press.

Sen, A. (1999) *Development as Freedom*, New York: Anchor Books.

Sen, A. (2000) 'What is the role of legal and judicial reform in the development process?', paper to the World Bank Legal Conference, Washington, June.

Sengupta, A. (2002), 'On the theory and practice of the right to development', *Human Rights Quarterly*, vol. 24, no. 4, 837–89

Seroka, J. (1996) 'Enhancing public management competence on the local level in post-socialist East-Central Europe' in S. Nagel, W. Crotty and J. Scarritt (eds), *Political Reform and Developing Nations*, Greenwich, Conn: JAI Press.

Shah, A. and Schacter, M. (2004) 'Combating corruption: look before you leap', *Finance and Development*, vol. 41, no. 4, 40–3.

Shetreet, S. (1985) 'Judicial independence: new conceptual dimensions and contemporary challenges', in S. Shetreet and J. Deschenes (eds), *Judicial Independence: The Contemporary Debate*, Dordrecht: Nijhoff.

Shklar, J. N. (1998) *Political Thought and Political Thinkers*, University of Chicago Press.

Shue, H. (1996) *Basic Rights: Subsistence, Affluence and US Foreign Policy*, Princeton University Press.

Simon, M. D. (1996) 'Institutional development of Poland's post-communist Sejm: a comparative analysis', in D. M. Olson and P. Norton (eds), *The New Parliaments of Central and Eastern Europe*, London: Cass.

Sindzingre, A. (2002) 'A comparative analysis of African and East Asian corruption, in A. J. Heidenheimer and M. Johnston (eds), *Political Corruption. Concepts and Contexts*, New Brunswick NJ: Transaction.

Singh, G. (1997) 'Understanding political corruption in contemporary Indian politics', *Political Studies*, vol. 45, no. 3, 626–38.

Skidmore, M. J. (1996) 'Promise and peril in combating corruption: Hong Kong's ICAC', *Annals of the American Academy of Political Science*, no. 547, 118–30.

Slater, D. (1995) 'Democracy, decentralisation and state power: on the politics of the regional in Chile and Bolivia', in D. J. Robinson (ed.), *Yearbook of the Conference of Latin American Geographers*, vol. 21, Austin, TX: Conference of Latin Americanist Geographers.

Smith, B. C. (1998) 'Participation without power: subterfuge or development?', *Community Development Journal*, vol. 33, no. 3, 197–204.

Smith, B. C. (2003) *Understanding Third World Politics. Theories of Political Change and Development*, 2nd edn, Basingstoke: Palgrave Macmillan.

Solum, L. B. (1994) 'Equality and the rule of law', in I. Shapiro (ed.), *The Rule of Law*, New York: New York University Press.

Souza, C. (1994) 'Political and financial decentralisation in democratic Brazil', *Local Government Studies*, vol. 20, no. 4, 588–609.

Stephenson, M. C. (2003) ' "When the devil turns…": the political foundations of indepen- dent judicial review', *Journal of Legal Studies*, vol. 32, no. 1, 59–89.

Stiles, K. (2002) 'International support for NGOs in Bangladesh: some unintended conse- quences', *World Development*, vol. 30, no. 5, 835–46.

Stiles, K. W. (1998) 'Civil society empowerment and multilateral donors: international insti- tutions and new international norms', *Global Governance*, vol. 4, no. 2, 199–216.

Stockton, H. (2001) 'Political parties, party systems and democracy in East Asia', *Comparative Political Studies*, vol. 34, no. 1, February, 94–119.

Stokke, O. (1995) 'Aid and political conditionality: core issues and state of the art', in O. Stokke (ed.), *Aid and Political Conditionality*, London: Cass.

Storey, H. (1995) 'Human rights and the new Europe: experience and experiments', in D. Beetham (ed.), *Politics and Human Rights*, Oxford University Press.

Stotzky, I. P. and Nino, C. S. (1993) 'The difficulties of the transition process', in I. P. Stotzky (ed.), *Transition to Democracy in Latin America: The Role of the Judiciary*, Boulder, CO: Westview.

Struyk, R. J. (2002) 'Non-profit organizations as contracted local social service providers in Eastern Europe and the CIS', *Public Administration and Development*, vol. 22, no. 5, 429–37.

Subedi, S. P. (1998) 'The journey from an oligarchy to a parliamentary democracy: a case study of parliament in Nepal', *Journal of Legislative Studies*, vol. 4, no. 4, 163–82.

Taagepera, R. (1998) 'How electoral systems matter for democratization', *Democratization*, vol. 5, no. 3, 68–91.

Tan, K. Y. L. (1999) 'Economic development, legal reform and rights in Singapore and Taiwan', in J. R. Bauer and D. A. Bell (eds), *The East Asian Challenge for Human Rights*, Cambridge University Press.

Tangri, R. (1995) 'The politics of Africa's public and private enterprise', *Journal of Commonwealth and Comparative Politics*, vol. 33, no. 2, 169–84.

Tanzi, V. (1998) 'Corruption around the world. Causes, consequences, scope and cures', *IMF Staff Papers*, vol. 45, no. 4, 559–94.

Tanzi, V. and Davoodi, H. R. (2002) 'Corruption, growth, and public finances', in G. T. Abed and S. Gupta (eds), *Governance, Corruption and Economic Performance*, Washington, DC: International Monetary Fund.

Taras, W. (1993) 'Changes in Polish public administration 1989–1992', *Public Administration*, vol. 71, nos. 1 and 2, 13–32.

Tatsuo, I. (1999) 'Liberal democracy and Asian orientalism', in J. R. Bauer and D. A. Bell (eds), *The East Asian Challenge for Human Rights*, Cambridge University Press.

Tavits, M. and Annus, T. (2006) 'Agencification in Estonia', *Public Administration and Development*, vol. 26, no. 1, 3–14.

Taylor, M. (1996) 'Between public and private: accountability and voluntary organisations', *Policy and Politics*, vol. 24, no. 1, 57–72.

Tendler, J. (1997) *Good Government in the Tropics*, Baltimore MD: Johns Hopkins University Press.

Ter-Minassian, T. (1997) 'Decentralizing government', *Finance and Development*, vol. 34, no. 3, 36–9.

Therkildsen, O. (2000) 'Public sector reform in a poor, aid-dependent country, Tanzania', *Public Administration and Development*, vol. 20, no. 1, 61–71.

Thimmaiah G. (1987) 'India', in M. Maetz and M. G. Quieti (eds), *Training For Decentralized Planning. Lessons From Experience*, Rome: Food and Agriculture Organization.

Thompson, J. (1995) 'Participatory approaches in government bureaucracies: facilitating institutional change', *World Development*, vol. 23, no. 9, 1521–54.

Thompson, M. R. (2001) 'Whatever happened to "Asian Values"?', *Journal of Democracy*, vol. 12, no. 4, 154–65.

Toka, G. (1996) 'Parties and electoral choices in east-central Europe', in G. Pridham and P. G. Lewis (eds), *Stabilising Fragile Democracies. Comparing New Party Systems in Southern and Eastern Europe*, London: Routledge.

Tomasevski, K. (1993) *Development Aid and Human Rights Revisited*, London: Pinter.

Tordoff, W. and Young, R. A. (1994) 'Decentralisation and public sector reform in Zambia', *Journal of Southern African Studies*, vol. 20, no. 2.

Toye, J. (1987) *Dilemmas in Development*, London: Blackwell.

Transparency International (2002) *Corruption Perceptions Index 2002*, Berlin.

Turner, M. (1999a) 'Conclusion: learning from the case-studies' in M. Turner (ed.), *Central–Local Relations in Asia-Pacific. Convergence or Divergence?*, Basingstoke: Macmillan.

Turner, M. (1999b) 'Local government reform and community-driven development: Asia-Pacific experiences', paper to the *Public Administration and Development* Jubilee Conference, Oxford, 12–14 September 1999.

Turner, M. and Hulme, D. (1997) *Governance, Administration and Development. Making the state Work*, Basingstoke: Macmillan.

UNDP (1995) *UNDP and Civil Society Organizations: A Policy of Engagement*, New York: United Nations Development Programme.

UNDP (1997a) *Corruption and Good Governance*, Discussion Paper no. 3, New York: United Nations Development Programme.

UNDP (1997b) *Reconceptualising Governance*, Discussion Paper no. 2, New York: United Nations Development Programme.

UNDP (1998) *Integrating Human Rights with Sustainable Human Development*, UNDP Policy Document, New York York: United Nations Development Programme.

UNDP (1999) *Fighting Corruption to Improve Governance*, New York: United Nations Development Programme.

UNDP (2000a) *Human Development Report 2000. Human Rights and Human Development*, New York: United Nations Development Programme.

UNDP (2000b) *Overcoming Human Poverty*. UNDP Poverty Report 2000, New York: United Nations Development Programme.

UNDP (2003a) 'Human Development Indicators 2003', ww.undp.org/hdr2003/indicator.

UNDP (2003b) 'What Is human development?', www.undp.org/hd.

UNDP (2003c) *Human Development Report 2003. Millennium Development Goals: A Compact Among Nations to End Human Poverty*, New York: Oxford University Press.

UNDP (2004) 'Promoting democracy through justice sector reform', www.undp.org/governance/justice.

UNDP (2005) *Human Development Report, 2005. International Co-operation at the Crossroads: Aid, Trade and Security in an Unequal World*, New York: United Nations Development Programme.

UNDP (2006a), *Human Development Report 2006. Power, Poverty and the Global Water Crisis*, New York: United Nations Development Programme.

UNDP (2006b) *Supporting Efficient, Responsive and Transparent Public Services*, www.undp.org/governance/sl-par.

USAID (1999) *The Role of Media in Democracy: A Strategic Approach*, Centre for Democracy and Governance, Washington, DC: United States Agency for International Development.

USAID (2000) *USAID's Experience in Decentralization and Democratic Local Governance*, Centre for Democracy and Governance, Washington, DC: US Agency for International Development.

USAID (2003) *Foreign Aid in the National Interest*, ch.1, www.usaid.gov/assisting_governance.

USAID (2005) *Office of Democracy and Governance: Civil Society*, www.usaid.gov/our_work/democracy_and_governance/technical_areas.

Useem, M., Setti, L. and Kachanabucha, K. (1988) 'Predictors of success in a particpatory village development project in Thailand, *Public Administration and Development*, vol. 8, no. 3, 289–303.

USGAO (2001) *Former Soviet Union. US Rule of Law Assistance Has Had Limited Impact and Sustainability*, Testimony from the General Accounting Office to the House Committee on Government Reform.

Van Biezen, I. (2000) 'On the internal balance of party power: party organizations in new democracies, *Party Politics*, vol. 6, no. 4, 395–417.

Van Dyke, V. (1995) 'The individual, the state, and ethnic communities in political theory' in W. Kymlicka (ed), *The Rights of Minority Cultures*, Oxford: Oxford University Press.

Van Rijckeghem, C. and Weder, B. (2002) 'Bureaucratic corruption and the rate of temptation: how much do wages in the civil service affect corruption?', *Journal of Development Economics*, vol. 65, no. 2, 307–31.

Varese, F. (1997) 'The transition to the market and corruption in post-socialist Russia', *Political Studies*, vol. 45, Special Issue, 579–96.

Vidlakova, O. (1993) 'Options for administrative reform in the Czech Republic', *Public Administration*, vol. 71, nos. 1–2, 65–74.

von Benda-Beckmann, F. (2001) 'Legal pluralism and social justice in economic and political development', *IDS Bulletin*, vol. 32, no. 1, 46–56.

von Braun, J. and Grote, U. (2002) 'Does decentralization serve the poor?', in IMF (ed.), *Fiscal Decentralization*, Washington, DC: Routledge Economics.

Vyas, Y. (1992) 'The independence of the judiciary: a Third World perspective', *Third World Legal Studies*, 127–77.

Waller, M. (1995) 'Adaptation of the former communist parties of East-Central Europe', *Party Politics*, vol. 1, no. 4, 473–90.

Waller, P. (1995) 'Aid and conditionality: the case of Germany, with particular reference to Kenya', in O. Stokke (ed.), *Aid and Political Conditionality*, London: Cass.

Waltzer, M. (1995) 'Pluralism: a political perspective', in W. Kymlicka (ed.), *The Rights of Minority Cultures*, Oxford University Press.

Ware, A. (1996) *Political Parties and Party Systems*, Oxford University Press.

Weber, B. (1995) 'Legal systems and economic performance: the empirical evidence', in M. Rowat, W. H. Malik and M. Dakolias (eds), *Judicial Reform in Latin America and the Caribbean*, World Bank Technical Paper No. 280, Washington, DC: World Bank.

Webster, N. (2002) 'Local organisations and political space in the forests of West Bengal', in N. Webster and L. Engberg-Pedersen (eds), *In the Name of the Poor. Contesting Political Space for Poverty Reduction*, London: Zed.

Wedeman, A. (1997) 'Looters, rent-scrapers and dividend collectors: corruption and growth in Zaire, South Korea and the Philippines', *Journal of Developing Areas*, vol. 31, no. 4, 457–78.

Weeks, J. (2006) 'Forty years of ODA and conditionality in Africa', paper to Centre for Development Studies seminar, Bath University, 17 November 2006.

Weimer, B. and Fandrych, S. (1999) 'Mozambique: administrative reform – a contributor to peace and democracy', in P. S. Reddy (ed.) *Local Government Democratization and Decentralization. A Review. of the Southern African Experience,* Kenwyn: Juta.

Weiss, T. G. (2000), 'Governance, good governance and global governance: conceptual and actual challenges', *Third World Quarterly*, vol. 21, no. 5, 795–814.

Wesolowski, W. (1996) 'The formation of political parties in post-communist Poland', in G. Pridham and P. G. Lewis (eds), *Stabilizing Fragile Democracies. Comparing New Party Systems in Southern and Eastern Europe*, London: Routledge.

White, G. (1996a) 'Civil society, democratization and development', in R. Luckham and G. White (eds), *Democratization in the South. The Jagged Wave*, Manchester University Press.

White, G. (1996b) 'Corruption and market reform in China', *IDS Bulletin*, vol. 27, no. 2, 40–7.

White, G. and Robinson, M. (1998) 'Towards synergy in social provision: civic organizations and the state', in M. Minogue, C. Polidano and D. Hulme (eds), *Beyond the New Public Management. Changing Ideas and Practices in Governance*, Cheltenham: Elgar.

Whitehead, L. (1996) 'Concerning international support for democracy in the South' in R. Luckham and G. White (eds), *Democratization in the South: the Jagged Wave*, Manchester: Manchester University Press.

Whitehead, L. (2002) 'High level political corruption in Latin America: a "transitional" phenomenon?', in A. J. Heidenheimer and M. Johnston (eds), *Political Corruption: Concepts and Contexts*, New Brunswick, NJ: Transaction.

Widner, J. (1999) 'Building judicial independence in common law Africa', in A. Schedler, L. Diamond and M. C. Plattner (eds), *The Self-Restraining State. Power and Accountability in New Democracies*, London: Rienner.

Wightman, G. (1995) 'Conclusion', in G. Whiteman (ed.) *Party Formation in East-Central Europe*, Cheltenham: Elgar.

Williams, D. and Young, T. (1994) 'Governance, the World Bank and liberal theory', *Political Studies*, vol. 42, no. 1, 84–100.

Wordofa, D. (1998) 'Internalizing and diffusing the PRA approach: the case of Ethiopia', in J. Blackburn and J. Holland (eds), *Who Changes? Institutionalizing Participation in Development*, London: Intermediate Technology Publications.

World Bank (1990) *World Development Report, 1990*, New York: OxfordUniversity Press.

World Bank (1992) *Governance and Development*, Washington, DC.

World Bank (1994) *Better Health in Africa. Experience and Lessons Learned*, Washington DC.

World Bank (1996) *The World Bank Participation Sourcebook*, Washington, DC.

World Bank (1997) *World Development Report 1997. The State in a Changing World*, New York: Oxford University Press.

World Bank (1998) *Development and Human Rights: the Role of the World Bank*, Washington DC: The World Bank.

World Bank (2000a) *Anti-corruption in Transition. A Contribution to the Policy Debate*, Washington, DC.

World Bank (2000b) *World Development Report 1999/2000. Entering the 21st. Century*, New York: Oxford University Press.

World Bank (2001a) *World Development Indicators*, Washington, DC.

World Bank (2001b) *World Development Report 2000/2001. Attacking Poverty*, New York: Oxford University Press.

World Bank (2001c) *Anticorruption*, www1.worldbank.org/publicsector/anticorruption/index.

World Bank (2001d) 'Civic Engagement in Public Expenditure Management Case Studies: Uganda – Tracking Public Expenditures (PETS)', unpublished, Washington, DC: World Bank. www.worldbank.org/participation/web/webfiles/cepemcase5.htm

World Bank (2002) 'Country Groups by Income', www.worldbank.org/data/countryclass/classgroups.htm; Transparency International.

World Bank (2004) *World Development Report 2004. Making Services Work for Poor People*, New York: Oxford University Press.

World Health Organisation (1993) *Evaluation of Recent Changes in the Financing of Health services*, Technical Report no 829, Geneva, WHO.

Wunsch, J. (2001) 'Decentralization, local governance, and "recentralization" in Africa', *Public Administration and Development*, vol. 21, no. 4, 277–88.

Yanai, N. (1999) 'Why do political parties survive? An analytical discussion', *Party Politics*, vol. 5, no. 1, 5–17.

Zsamboki, K. and Bell, M. (1997) 'Local self-government in Central and Eastern Europe: decentralization or deconcentration?', *Environment and Planning C: Government and Policy*, vol. 15, no. 2, 177–86

Index